Systems of Care for
Children's Mental Health
Series Editors:
Beth A. Stroul, M.Ed.
Robert M. Friedman, Ph.D.

From Case Management
to Service Coordination for Children
with Emotional, Behavioral,
or Mental Disorders

This book is printed on recycled paper.

From Case Management to Service Coordination for Children with Emotional, Behavioral, or Mental Disorders

Building on Family Strengths

Edited by

Barbara J. Friesen, Ph.D.
Director, Research and Training Center on
    Family Support and Children's Mental Health
Professor, Graduate School of Social Work
Portland State University
Portland, Oregon

and

John Poertner, D.S.W.
Professor
School of Social Welfare
University of Kansas
Lawrence, Kansas

·P·A·U·L·H·
BROOKES
PUBLISHING CO.

Baltimore · London · Toronto · Sydney

Paul H. Brookes Publishing Co.
Post Office Box 10624
Baltimore, Maryland 21285-0624

Typeset by Maple-Vail Composition Services, Binghamton, New York.
Manufactured in the United States of America by
The Maple Press Company, York, Pennsylvania.

Library of Congress Cataloging-in-Publication Data

From case management to service coordination for children
  with emotional, behavioral, or mental disorders : building on family
  strengths / [edited by] Barbara J. Friesen, John Poertner.
      p.   cm.—(Systems of care for children's mental health)
  Includes bibliographical references and index.
  ISBN 1-55766-204-5
  1. Child mental health services.   2. Continuum of care.
  I. Friesen, Barbara J.   II. Poertner, John.   III. Series.
  [DNLM: 1. Mental Disorders—in infancy & childhood.   2. Mental
  Disorders—rehabilitation.   3. Mental Health Services—organization &
  administration.   4. Patient Care Planning.   5. Family.   WS 350.2
  B867   1995
  RJ499.F793   1995
  362.2'083—dc20
  DNLM/DLC
  for Library of Congress   94-36994
                                                                               CIP

British Library Cataloguing-in-Publication data are available from the
British Library.

Contents

SECTION I

Challenges for an Emerging Field: Overview
and Principles of Mental Health
Service Coordination for Children and Families

SECTION II

SECTION III
Promoting Effectiveness:
Implementation and Accountability Issues

SECTION IV
Training and Supervising Service Coordinators

SECTION V
State-of-the-Art Programs: Examples from the Field

Series Preface

In 1982, Knitzer's seminal study, *Unclaimed Children*, was published by the Children's Defense Fund. At that time, the field of children's mental health was characterized by a lack of federal or state leadership, few community-based services, little collaboration among child-serving systems, negligible parent involvement, and little or no advocacy on behalf of youngsters with emotional disorders. Since that time, substantial gains have been realized in both the conceptualization and the implementation of comprehensive, community-based systems of care for children and adolescents with severe emotional disorders and their families.

A vast amount of information has emanated from the system-building experiences of states and communities and from research and technical assistance efforts. Many of the trends and philosophies emerging in recent years have now become widely accepted as the "state of the art" for conceptualizing and providing services to youngsters with emotional disorders and their families. There is now broad agreement surrounding the need to create community-based systems of care throughout the United States for children and their families, and the development of these systems has become a national goal. Such systems of care are based on the premises of providing services in the most normative environments, creating effective interagency relationships among the key child-serving systems, involving families in all phases of the planning and delivery of services, and creating service systems that are designed to respond to the needs of culturally diverse populations.

A major need is to incorporate these concepts and trends into the published literature. This need stems from the critical shortage of staff who are appropriately trained to serve youngsters in community-based systems of care, with new philosophies and new service delivery approaches. Of utmost importance is the need to provide state-of-the-art information to institutions of higher education for use in the preservice education of professionals across disciplines, including the social work, counseling, psychology, and psychiatry fields. Similarly, there is an equally vital need for resources for the in-service training of staff in mental health, child welfare, education, health, and juvenile justice agencies to assist the staff in working more effectively with youngsters with emotional disorders and their families.

This book series, *Systems of Care for Children's Mental Health*, is designed to fulfill these needs by addressing current trends in children's mental health service delivery. The series has several broad goals:

- To increase awareness of the system-of-care concept and philosophy among current and future mental health professionals who will be providing services to children, adolescents, and their families

- To broaden the mental health field's understanding of treatment and service delivery beyond traditional approaches to include innovative, state-of-the-art approaches
- To provide practical information that will assist the mental health field to implement and apply the philosophy, services, and approaches embodied in the system-of-care concept

Each volume in this continuing series addresses a major issue or topic related to the development of systems of care. The books contain information useful to planners, program managers, policy makers, practitioners, parents, teachers, researchers, and others who are interested and involved in improving systems of care for children with emotional disorders and their families. As the series editors, it is our goal for the series to provide an ongoing vehicle and forum for exploring critical aspects of systems of care as they continue to evolve.

REFERENCES

Knitzer, J. (1982). *Unclaimed children.* Washington, DC: Children's Defense Fund.

Editorial Advisory Board

Series Editors

Foreword

In the late 1980s, while the adult mental health community was busy creating a new case management *profession* to serve a well-defined need in the care of adults with serious and persistent mental illness, those who worked with child mental health were concerned about the development of the case management *concept*. This less structured approach better fits the needs of children and adolescents with severe emotional disorders and their families. Child and family services require a multifaceted case management process that mirrors the multiagency needs of their affected children and adolescents. The range of need defined by these children cannot be addressed adequately by a single professional case management job description; rather, we must view case management as a function that can be actualized in numerous ways.

To do this, the concept of case management must be normalized and seen as an extension of the child management function that parents and other guardians perform every day. Almost all parents are directly involved in the management of and service coordination for their children. This care includes regular family functions such as taking a child to the family doctor or health clinic, escorting a child to school and/or talking with the teacher, and involving a child in a recreation league. When a child has problems that generate the need for more intensive or complicated care, most parents require assistance in managing and organizing that care. In families in which a child or adolescent has a severe emotional disorder, this need arises when the problems are so complex that a specialized service coordination approach is needed or when the child's needs exceed the family's capacity to organize an integrated multiagency plan of care. When viewed in this way, professional case management becomes a process in which the child's family is aided in performing its usual, customary functions. The case management role will necessarily be defined differently for each family, being determined by the parents' strengths and the specific needs of the child.

This volume is the result of the 10-year developmental process of defining case management for this population of children with emotional, behavioral, or mental disorders. It represents a decade of exciting exploration in program development, training, financing and program support, research, and policy development by those individuals who have been most prominently involved on both national and local levels. As such, it presents a treasure trove of vital practical information that family members, human services professionals, and policy makers will find useful in developing, implementing, sustaining, and participating in the case management and service coordination functions in which they are involved.

However, to take full advantage of this text, the reader should look for subtle, and often not so subtle, messages that define the most appropriate understanding of children's case management. For example, the first impression that the reader receives is from the title, which expands the concept of case management beyond its prior narrow definition to include a range of function—*from case management to service coordination.* This sets the tone and indicates that case management is not a *thing* but a *process.* In the first section, as we are introduced to the full extent of the field, we are reminded that the function of case management is to help a family meet *its* needs as it struggles with a difficult-to-care-for child. This point is driven home by the family focus of all the chapters. In addition, the presentation of a "family as case manager" concept truly demonstrates the continuum between the role that all parents play as case managers for their children and the formal professional case management function. The reader will discover other major themes presented by the editors as they weave a multidimensional picture of what case management is, and should be, for children and adolescents with severe emotional disorders and their families.

Until now, the case management literature has offered little on the conceptual, practice, and research issues in child mental health. Although there is still much to be done, this book represents an important step toward addressing this gap.

Ira S. Lourie, M.D.
Human Service Collaborative
Washington, D.C.

Contributors

Caren Abate, M.S.
Children and Families Specialist
New York State Office of Mental
    Health
Hudson River Regional Office
Branch B, 373 North Road
Poughkeepsie, NY 12601

Lisa K. Armstrong, L.C.S.W.
Northside Mental Health Center
12512 Bruce B. Downs Boulevard
Tampa, FL 33612

Lenore B. Behar, Ph.D.
Head
Child and Family Services Branch
Division of MH/DD/SAS
325 North Salisbury Street
Raleigh, NC 27603

Nancy Birkett, M.A.
Northeast Kingdom Mental Health
    Services
Newport, VT 05855

G. Kay Bishop
Department of Psychiatry and
    Behavioral Sciences
Duke University Medical Center
Box 3454
Durham, NC 27710

Lydia Brennan, M.A.
Post Office Box 319
RD 1
Mansfield, PA 16933

Harold E. Briggs, Ph.D.
Research and Training Center on
    Family Support and Children's
    Mental Health
Portland State University
P.O. Box 751
Portland, OR 97207-0751

Eric Bruns
Department of Psychology
University of Vermont
John Dewey Hall
Burlington, VT 05405-0134

Anthony Broskowski, Ph.D.
Director
Health Care Information
    Management
The Prudential Insurance Company
200 Wood Avenue, South
Iselin, NJ 08830

John D. Burchard, Ph.D.
Department of Psychology
University of Vermont
John Dewey Hall
Burlington, VT 05405-0134

Barbara J. Burns, Ph.D.
Department of Psychiatry and
    Behavioral Sciences
Duke University Medical Center
Box 3454
Durham, NC 27710

Michelle Carro
Department of Psychology
University of Vermont
John Dewey Hall
Burlington, VT 05405-0134

Robert F. Cole, Ph.D.
Deputy Director
Mental Health Services Program for
    Youth
Washington Business Group on
    Health
777 North Capitol Street, N.E.
Suite 800
Washington, DC 20002

Barbara Conrad
P.O. Box 453
Wayland, NY 14572

Beth Dague, M.A.
Stark County Family Council
800 Market Avenue, North
Suite 1600
Canton, OH 44702

S. Rachel Dedmon, Ph.D.
School of Social Work
University of North Carolina
CB 3550
Chapel Hill, NC 27599-3550

Connie Dellmuth, M.S.W.
Georgetown University
Child Development Center
National Technical
    Assistance Center
For Children's
    Mental Health Policy
3307 M Street, N.W.
Washington, DC 20007–3935

Richard Donner, M.S.W., Ph.D.
4125 Southwest Gage Center Drive
Number 201
Topeka, KS 66604

Jana Duncan
1812 Pembroke Lane
Topeka, KS 66604

Theresa J. Early, M.S.W., Ph.D.
Psychiatric Association
Lifeskills, Inc.
641 East Main
Bowling Green, KY 42101

Harriette B. Fox, M.S.S.
President
Fox Health Policy Consultants
1747 Pennsylvania Avenue, N.W.
Suite 1200
Washington, DC 20006

Catherine Roberts Friedman, M.S.
Clinical Case Management and
    Wraparound Program
    Coordinator
Northside Mental Health Center
12512 Bruce B. Downs Boulevard
Tampa, FL 33612

Barbara J. Friesen, Ph.D.
Director
Research and Training Center on
    Family Support and Children's
    Mental Health
Professor
Graduate School of Social Work
Portland State University
P.O. Box 751
Portland, OR 97207-0751

Mary Gentry
3237 Northwest Brickyard Road
Topeka, KS 66618

Robert Goerge, Ph.D.
Chapin Hall Center for Children
University of Chicago
1155 East 60th Street
Chicago, IL 60637

Elizabeth Anne Gwaltney, M.A.
Department of Psychiatry and
    Behavioral Sciences
Duke University Medical Center
Box 3454
Durham, NC 27710

Marilyn Henry
Parents Involved Network
4133 Davison Avenue
Erie, PA 16504

Mary Lou Hicks, M.A.
Chief
Bureau of Child and Adolescent
    Services
Department of Mental Health and
    Developmental Disabilities
400 Stratton Office Building
Springfield, IL 62765

Betsy Hinden
Department of Psychology
University of Vermont
John Dewey Hall
Burlington, VT 05405-0134

Barbara Huff
Executive Director
Federation of Families for
    Children's Mental Health
1021 Prince Street
Alexandria, VA 22314-2971

Susan Ignelzi, M.A.
Office of the Governor
77 South High Street
Columbus, OH 43215

Deborah Franks Jacobs, M.S.W.,
Ph.D.
Assistant Professor
Department of Social Work
Shippensburg University
220 Horton Hall
Shippensburg, PA 17257

Nancy McGrath, L.P.N.
Northeast Kingdom Mental Health
Services
Newport, VT 05855

Deborah McKinney
419 Taylor
Topeka, KS 66603

Ruth Osuch, M.S.W., M.P.H.
Evaluation Coordinator
LaGrange Area Department of
Special Education
1301 West Cossitt
LaGrange, IL 60525

Nancy Pandina, M.S.
Department of Psychology
University of Vermont
John Dewey Hall
Burlington, VT 05405-0134

John Poertner, D.S.W.
Professor
School of Social Welfare
University of Kansas
Twente Hall
Lawrence, KS 66045

Norma Radol Raiff, Ph.D.
Intense Case Management Program
Western Psychiatric Institute and
Clinic
University of Pittsburgh Medical
Center
Pittsburgh, PA 15213

John Ronnau, Ph.D., A.C.S.W.,
L.I.S.W.
Associate Professor
Department of Social Work
New Mexico State University
Box 30001, Department 3SW
Las Cruces, NM 88003-0001

Suzanne Santarcangelo, Ph.D.
Director
Child, Adolescent and Family
Program
Clara Martin Center
Post Office Box G
Randolph, VT 05060-0167

Mark Schaefer, Ph.D.
Yale Child Study Center
230 South Frontage Road
New Haven, CT 06510-8009

Patty Silver
6106 Balboa #22
Merriam, KS 66202

Beth A. Stroul, M.Ed.
Vice President
Management and Training
Innovations
6725 Curran Street
McLean, VA 22101'

Sharon Thompson
809 Sheridan Circle
Olathe, KS 66061

Kenley Wade, M.A.
Director's Office of Management
Development
Illinois Department of Mental
Health and Developmental
Disabilities
401 South Spring Street
Room 401
Springfield, IL 62765

Marie Overby Weil, D.S.W.
University of North Carolina
223 East Franklin Street CB 3550
Chapel Hill, NC 27599-3550

Lori B. Wicks, J.D.
Senior Research Associate
Fox Health Policy Consultants
1747 Pennsylvania Avenue, N.W.
Suite 1200
Washington, DC 20006

Irene Nathan Zipper, M.S.W.
School of Social Work
University of North Carolina
223 East Franklin Street
Chapel Hill, NC 27599-3550

Acknowledgments

Our work in this important area of case management has received financial and conceptual support from two federal agencies and their program staff. Judith Katz-Leavy of the Services and System Development Section, Center for Mental Health Services, Substance Abuse and Mental Health Services Administration, Division of Demonstration Programs, Child, Adolescent and Family Branch, U.S. Department of Health and Human Services, recognized the urgent need for information about service coordination for children with emotional, behavioral, and mental disorders and their families and encouraged us to accelerate our work in this area. Roseann Rafferty, our project officer at the National Institute on Disability and Rehabilitation Research (NIDRR), U.S. Department of Education, also gave her support and allowed us important flexibility throughout the project. Both federal agencies provided partial financial support for this work, in particular for the conference titled *Building on Family Strengths: Case Management for Children with Emotional, Behavioral, and Mental Disorders and Their Families*, which was organized around the content of this book. These funds were provided through the NIDRR, U.S. Department of Education, and the Substance Abuse and Mental Health Services Administration, U.S. Department of Health and Human Services (NIDRR Grant No. 133B90007-93). The content of this publication, however, does not necessarily reflect the views or policies of the funding agencies.

Many individuals helped to make this book possible, from the initial concept to the last copyedited page. First, we would like to thank Naomi Karp, who encouraged us to produce a book about children's mental health for students, practitioners, and family members. Chapter authors gave their primary, invaluable contributions as they translated their ideas, experience, and wisdom into written documents so that others can benefit from their knowledge. We particularly want to thank all the family members who participated in writing chapters. The energy required to care for a child with a severe emotional disorder and to struggle with the system leaves little time or energy for efforts that may seem more academic. However, the input of family members is essential and we are thankful for their efforts. On a more practical note, the chapter authors also showed good humor and patience throughout the many stages of this project. They accepted and responded to feedback from conference participants, editorial suggestions, and the imposition of multiple deadlines. In addition, the comments of conference participants and external reviewers helped to refine this work and make it more responsive to the information needs of a broad audience. Thanks to all who helped in this way.

Many staff members of the Research and Training Center on Family Support and Children's Mental Health at Portland State University and the

University of Kansas contributed to this book by responding to the overall concept and to individual chapters. Five individuals, however, deserve special recognition. Stephanie Limoncelli collected, abstracted, and organized the extensive bibliography on case management and service coordination that served as an important resource for many chapter authors and for the editors. We greatly appreciate her thoughtful and meticulous approach to this task.

Marilyn McManus applied her excellent editing skills to early chapter drafts. Her most important contribution, however, was her adaptation of the monograph *Financing Care Coordination Services for Children and Adolescents with Severe Emotional Disorders under Medicaid,* by Harriette B. Fox and Lori B. Wicks, for inclusion as a chapter in this book. Marilyn's effort was extensive, equal to an "author's agony," and we want to publicly acknowledge her essential and much appreciated work.

Theresa Early also applied her editing skills to a set of early chapter drafts. Her journalism, social work, and case management skills were put to good use in providing feedback to authors. Several chapters are more clearly presented due to her efforts.

Shad Jessen organized and maintained the physical files containing multiple drafts of chapters, kept the word-processing files and diskettes in order, and used his outstanding word-processing skills to produce final drafts for many of the chapter authors. Along with Katie Schultze, he also managed the mountain of correspondence and other papery details associated with such an effort. Kudos, Shad.

Finally, we want to recognize Katie Schultze, whose efforts were central to all phases of this project. Katie gave feedback on the initial ideas for this book, provided support and assistance to chapter authors, edited tirelessly and with great skill, and generally helped to keep this project on course. Thanks, Katie, for your persistence and good judgment, which made all the difference.

Barbara J. Friesen
John Poertner

Introduction

Developing and providing appropriate services for children and adolescents with emotional, behavioral, or mental disorders and their families is an extremely complex task. First, the youths' disabilities require special attention to a variety of domains (e.g., emotional, social, physical, cognitive) that call for professional expertise and other resources dispersed across many community agencies and organizations. These service providers and organizations are unlikely to provide a coordinated response either for specific children and their families, or at the system level without special attention focused on that need. Service delivery is further complicated by the dynamic nature of the needs and circumstances of children and their families. In addition to the changes associated with a growing, developing child, it is often difficult to predict how emotional disabilities will be expressed, as they are sometimes cyclical in nature. Thus, the needs of children and their families may change rapidly over short time periods, as well as gradually over the entire life span. These circumstances have highlighted the need for service planning, coordination, and monitoring strategies (case management) that promote a match between the children's and families' needs and the cluster of services that they may require at any given time.

Recently, states and local communities have accelerated their efforts to develop and implement case management services for children with emotional disorders and their families. There is, however, very little published literature that provides a specific conceptual foundation for the development of practice, program, or policy. In the absence of a body of knowledge on children's mental health case management, administrators, program developers, and practitioners are fashioning case management services largely built on ideas and strategies adapted from other fields, as well as on insights gained from their immediate experience.

This book on case management is designed to address this serious gap in the sparse children's mental health literature. The chapters were specifically commissioned to include a broad range of challenges that characterize service coordination efforts in the children's mental health field. The authors presented their ideas to participants at a conference focused on case management in the field of children's mental health and then used the feedback of the conference participants to refine and finalize their written work.

Weaving the ideas presented in this book into a coherent whole has been challenging. Many of the authors who wrote chapters for this volume were breaking new ground in their respective areas, producing the first work specifically addressing these issues for children with emotional disorders and their families. Not only did the authors often lack specific literature upon which to build, but also many case management programs in children's mental health have not yet had the benefit of systematic evaluation and feedback. Hence, some of the authors had to use their own good judgment in assessing program and practice effectiveness.

The most important undertaking was to define what we meant by *case management* or *service coordination* and to map the territory to be addressed in this book. Part of this task has been to make sense of existing literature, especially to sift and choose ideas that appear to be relevant to this population. Another challenge was to select terminology that was both understandable and descriptive on the one hand and acceptable to both practitioners and family members on the other. The two challenges, clarity and acceptability, are intertwined.

The terms *case management* and *service coordination* are used frequently, and sometimes interchangeably, to describe a set of activities designed to plan, organize, connect, and monitor services for children and adults with a variety of physical, sensory, emotional, or cognitive disabilities. The terms are used to embrace a variety of purposes and activities, resulting in a confusing welter of definitional options. We include here a framework that we have found helpful in discussing the central set of activities around which this book is organized. The central ideas of this framework are presented in Figure 1.

Level at which activity occurs	Purpose of Service Coordination Efforts			
	Improving match between client needs and system response	Direct service: Initiation and maintenance of client change	System change	Cost containment
Child and Family (Case)	Primary	Possible	Possible	Possible
Systems	Secondary	No	Primary	Possible

Figure 1. Relationship between the purpose of service coordination efforts and the level at which activity occurs.

An examination of two major dimensions, the primary purpose of the service coordination activity and the level at which it occurs, can be used to organize important concepts associated with case management and service coordination. Figure 1 illustrates how these two dimensions, *purpose* and *level*, interact. Four broad categories of purpose are identified on the horizontal axis: 1) improving the match between client needs and service system response, 2) initiation and/ or maintenance of client change, 3) system change, and 4) cost containment. Two levels at which the service coordination activities primarily occur are the child and family (case) level and the systems level; these levels of activity are presented on the vertical axis of Figure 1.

Clearly, the concept of service coordination carries with it both a systems-level definition and a client-level meaning. This dual-level focus is mentioned by a number of authors and is explicitly promoted by some, but most of the focus in the literature is on the client level. The chapters in this book also reflect an emphasis on activity at the child and family level, where the primary purpose of the service is to improve the match between the needs of the child and family and the response of the service delivery system. This arena of activity is represented by "Child and Family (Case)" in Figure 1. In addition to the service linking function, those who assume responsibility for service coordination at the child and family level may also provide direct service, advocate for or initiate systems change, or be concerned with cost containment. These additional functions, however, are often seen as secondary or optional, and sometimes there is controversy about whether or not they should be carried out by the same person who is responsible for the service-linking functions.

At the system level, activity is primarily focused on system change designed to improve the coordination of services. Strategies include entering into interagency agreements designed to facilitate the movement of children and their families among agencies, joint programming aimed at maximizing the efficient use of resources and improving the integration of services, and the pooling of resources to create flexible funds to increase the individualization of services.

The issue of terminology is not simple. The term *case management* is viewed with disfavor across many fields, reflecting the well-known sentiment expressed by Nicholas Hobbs that children and families are not "cases," nor do they wish to be managed. Dislike of the term *case manager* has stimulated a variety of alternatives, with *service coordinator* leading the list, followed by labels such as *family advocate, ombudsperson, service broker,* and *resource manager*. One problem with substituting *service coordination* for *case management* is that although *case management* has been primarily used to refer to client-level intervention, *service coordination* is used to mean either a client-level focus, a systems-level focus, or both.

In the field of children's mental health, although a number of creative systems-level service coordination efforts have been undertaken, the term *case management* has mostly been reserved for service coordination efforts on behalf of individual children and their families. This usage is no doubt underlined by the provision in PL 99-660 and PL 102-321, which states that in order to qualify for block grant funds states must provide case management services for children with the "most serious mental and emotional disabilities. Similarly, because Medicaid, a major source of funding for mental health services for children, uses the term *targeted case management*, both the use of the term *case management* and its meaning as client-level service coordination currently dominate the children's mental health field, despite dissatisfaction with the term.

Given these considerations, the choice that we have made for this book is to use the term *case management* when discussing the activities of a designated person aimed at improving the circumstances of specific children and families and the term *service coordination* to describe activities and processes that have implications for a broader set of children and families or for the shape and structure of the service delivery system.

It is hoped that the care we have taken to address issues of terminology and to improve conceptual clarity will facilitate the accessibility of this book to a broad variety of readers. As planners, program developers, practitioners, and family members begin to operate from a common frame of reference, the coordination of services for children with emotional, behavioral, and mental disorders and their families should improve. Much work and careful evaluation is needed to build on this beginning foundation and to make that proposition a reality.

From Case Management to Service Coordination for Children with Emotional, Behavioral, or Mental Disorders

CHALLENGES FOR
AN EMERGING FIELD
Overview and Principles of Mental Health
Service Coordination for Children and Families

Case Management in a System of Care

Beth A. Stroul

PROGRESS IN CHILDREN'S MENTAL HEALTH

The most recent epidemiological estimates suggest that approximately 14%–20% of all children from birth to age 18 have some type of mental health disorder and that about 3%–5% of all children have a serious disorder (Brandenburg, Friedman, & Silver, 1990; Costello, Burns, Angold, & Leaf, 1993). The call for increased attention to be given to the needs of youngsters with mental health disorders and their families dates back to the research of the Joint Commission on the Mental Health of Children (1969), which found this population was typically unserved or served inappropriately in excessively restrictive settings. These findings were substantiated by numerous subsequent studies, task forces, commissions, and reports (Office of Technology Assessment, 1986; President's Commission on Mental Health, 1978).

A study published by the Children's Defense Fund documented that of the 3 million children with serious emotional disorders in the United States, two thirds were not receiving the services they needed and many more were receiving inappropriate care (Knitzer, 1982). These youngsters were characterized as "unclaimed children," essentially abandoned by the agencies that had the responsibility for helping them. All these reports concurred that coordinated systems of care providing a range of services are required in order to serve these youngsters and their families effectively and, furthermore, called for concerted action to develop systems of care throughout the United States.

Since the mid-1980s, remarkable progress has been made toward improving services for children and adolescents with emotional disorders and their families. Progress is apparent in areas such as federal and state leadership, family involvement, the definition of

3

the system of care concept, the development of systems of care, research, and advocacy. For example, federal leadership in the area of children's mental health was virtually nonexistent until 1984 when the National Institute of Mental Health (NIMH) launched the Child and Adolescent Service System Program (CASSP), now part of the Center for Mental Health Services (CMHS). CASSP has provided funding to all 50 states and a number of territories to assist them in planning for and developing systems of care and has sponsored a wide range of technical assistance activities (Day & Roberts, 1991).

Similarly, there was a serious gap in state-level leadership for children's mental health. Knitzer (1982) reported that more than one half of state mental health agencies did not have a unit, or even one person, who focused on children. Currently, every state has at least one person with this designated responsibility (Davis, Yelton, & Katz-Leavy, 1993), and all states are now required by federal legislation to have plans for the development of community-based systems of care for children with severe emotional disturbances and their families.

Dramatic progress has been achieved in the development of community-based systems of care. A number of demonstrations of these systems have been undertaken, and foundations such as the Robert Wood Johnson and Annie E. Casey Foundations have funded major initiatives to develop such systems. These communities are demonstrating promising new ways of organizing and financing service systems. State-sponsored initiatives are also resulting in noteworthy progress toward system development, and federal legislation passed in 1992 (the Comprehensive Community Mental Health Services Program for Children included in Public Law 102-321, the ADAMHA Reorganization Act, Part E: Children with Serious Emotional Disturbances) will provide resources to develop a more complete service array in selected communities. These and other advances signify that there has, in fact, been more than a decade of progress in children's mental health.

SYSTEM OF CARE CONCEPT AND PHILOSOPHY

Overview

From the time of the report of the Joint Commission on the Mental Health of Children in 1969, there was considerable discussion about the "system of care" concept, but much uncertainty about what the system should encompass, how it should be organized, what components should constitute such a system, and what principles should guide service delivery. A project devised by the CASSP program was initiated to define the system of care concept and philosophy and resulted in the monograph *A System of Care for Children and Youth with Severe Emotional Disturbances* (Stroul & Friedman, 1986). This document provides a conceptual framework for a system of care that has been widely used by states and communities to assist them in planning.

Fundamental to the system of care concept presented by Stroul and Friedman (1986) is the contention that the system of care is more than a network of service components. Rather, it represents a *philosophy* about the way in which services should be delivered to children and their families. Although the actual components and organization of systems may differ from state to state and from community to community, all systems should be guided by a set of basic values.

As shown in Table 1.1, three core values have been identified for the system of care. These values are that systems of care should be child centered and family focused, community based, and culturally competent. The first value specifies that the needs of the child and his or her family should dictate the types and mix of service provided and that services should be adapted to the child and his or her family rather than expecting them to adapt to agency and program constraints. The second value emphasizes that children should be served in community-based programs with less restrictive and more normative environments that are within or close to their home communities. Furthermore, the term *community based* implies that ownership and management of the system of care should be at the community level. The core value of cultural competence dictates that children and families be served within their own unique and specific cultural and ethnic contexts. Ten principles (see Table 1.1) delineate a set of basic beliefs about the way the system of care should operate. Case management is one of the guiding principles that is considered to be an essential underpinning of the system of care concept and philosophy. The principle holds that case management is needed to ensure that multiple services are delivered in a coordinated manner and that services are adapted to the changing needs of youngsters and their families over time.

The system of care model (Figure 1.1) is organized in a framework that consists of eight major service dimensions. Each dimension represents an area of need for children and their families. The model is not intended to specify which type of agency should fulfill any of the particular functions or needs. Many of the services in the system of care model are provided by different agencies in different communities and many are provided through multiagency collabora-

Table 1.1.   System of care values and principles

Core Values for the System of Care

1. The system of care should be child centered and family focused, with the needs of the child and family dictating the types and mix of services provided.
2. The system of care should be community based, with the locus of services as well as management and decision-making responsibility resting at the community level.
3. The system of care should be culturally competent, with agencies, programs, and services that are responsive to the cultural, racial, and ethnic differences of the population they serve.

Guiding Principles for the System of Care

1. Children with emotional disturbances should have access to a comprehensive array of services that address the child's physical, emotional, social, and educational needs.
2. Children with emotional disturbances should receive individualized services in accordance with the unique needs and potentials of each child and guided by an individualized service plan.
3. Children with emotional disturbances should receive services within the least restrictive, most normative environment that is clinically appropriate.
4. The families and surrogate families of children with emotional disturbances should be full participants in all aspects of the planning and delivery of services.
5. Children with emotional disturbances should receive services that are integrated, with linkages between child-serving agencies and programs and mechanisms for planning, developing, and coordinating services.
6. Children with emotional disturbances should be provided with case management or similar mechanisms to ensure that multiple services are delivered in a coordinated and therapeutic manner and that they can move through the system of services in accordance with their changing needs.
7. Early identification and intervention for children with emotional disturbances should be promoted by the system of care in order to enhance the likelihood of positive outcomes.
8. Children with emotional disturbances should be ensured smooth transitions to the adult service system as they reach maturity.
9. The rights of children with emotional disturbances should be protected, and effective advocacy efforts for children and youth with emotional disturbances should be promoted.
10. Children with emotional disturbances should receive services without regard to race, religion, national origin, sex, physical disability, or other characteristics, and services should be sensitive and responsive to cultural differences and special needs.

From Stroul, B., & Friedman, R. (1986). *A system of care for severely emotionally disturbed children and youth* (rev. ed.), p. 17. Washington, DC: Georgetown University, CASSP Technical Assistance Center; reprinted by permission.

tive efforts. In the system of care model, case management is considered an "operational service" because of its importance to the effective operation of the system.

The mental health dimension consists of seven nonresidential services and seven residential services (Table 1.2). Services included in other dimensions (e.g., respite services, behavioral aides, family

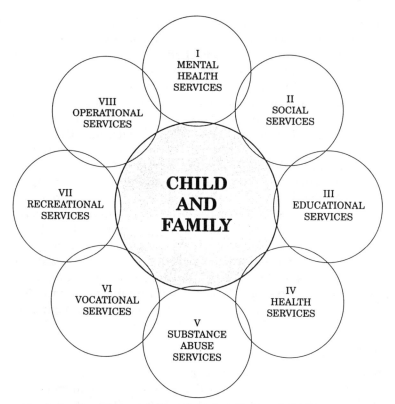

Figure 1.1. System of care framework. (From Stroul, B., & Friedman, R. [1986]. *A system of care for severely emotionally disturbed children and youth* [rev. ed.], p. 30. Washington, DC: Georgetown University, CASSP Technical Assistance Center; reprinted by permission.)

Table 1.2. Mental health dimension of the system of care

NONRESIDENTIAL SERVICES	RESIDENTIAL SERVICES
Prevention	Therapeutic foster care
Early identification & intervention	Therapeutic group care
Assessment	Therapeutic camp services
Outpatient treatment	Independent living services
Home-based services	Residential treatment services
Day treatment	Crisis residential services
Crisis services	Inpatient hospitalization

From Stroul, B., & Friedman, R. (1986). *A system of care for severely emotionally disturbed children and youth* (rev. ed.), p. 31. Washington, DC: Georgetown University, CASSP Technical Assistance Center; reprinted by permission.

support groups, and case management) also have proven to be critical components of a system of care for youngsters with emotional disorders. An important characteristic of an effective system is an appropriate balance among the components, particularly between the more restrictive and less restrictive services.

States and communities increasingly are adopting the system of care concept and philosophy and are applying these concepts in localities across the United States. The communities that have implemented such systems of care are beginning to demonstrate some important and encouraging results. A review of data (Stroul, 1993) from approximately 30 communities with well-developed systems of care found that children served within such systems were less likely to receive services in restrictive service environments, were less likely to be placed out of their homes for treatment, and showed improvements in functioning. Parents of children receiving services within such systems of care reported higher levels of satisfaction with services, and the costs of providing systems of care appeared to be less than the costs associated with traditional service delivery patterns, which rely more heavily on expensive treatment environments.

Need for System-Level and Client-Level Coordination

The notion of "coordination" is intrinsic to the system of care concept based on the recognition that children with emotional disturbances and their families have multiple needs that cut across agency and system boundaries. One system of care principle calls for "linkages between child-caring agencies and programs and mechanisms for planning, developing, and coordinating services" (Stroul & Friedman, 1986, p. 22). This principle refers to the need for structures and mechanisms to ensure *system-level* coordination. In order to best meet the needs of children and their families, integrated, multiagency networks are needed to blend the services provided by mental health, education, child welfare, health, juvenile justice, substance abuse, and other agencies. These components must be interwoven into a coherent system with provisions for joint planning, service development, problem solving, funding, and evaluation of services. Communities have designed various types of interagency entities to accomplish these system-level coordination functions (Stroul, Lourie, Goldman, & Katz-Leavy, 1992).

Another level of coordination is reflected in the principle that calls for case management in systems of care. Case management focuses on *client-level* coordination and is intended to ensure that children and their families receive the services they need, that services are coordinated, and that services are appropriate to their changing needs over time. The importance of case management in a system of care is evidenced by the way it has been described in the literature. Case management has been characterized as the "backbone of the system of care," the "glue that holds the system together," and essential to the success of the service system (Stroul & Friedman, 1986, p. 109). Case management also has been portrayed as the most essential unifying factor in service delivery (Behar, 1985) and as the key to systemic success in a complex system of services (Behar, 1991).

Lourie and Katz-Leavy (1986) asserted that it is nearly impossible to ensure adequate services for a youngster without a primary service person being responsible for coordination of the treatment plan and service delivery. Case management appears to play an especially critical role in individualized service approaches in which the case manager is responsible for facilitating the planning and implementation of an individualized plan of care, including "wraparound" services, for each youngster and his or her family (Katz-Leavy, Lourie, Stroul, & Zeigler-Dendy, 1992). (Wraparound services include both traditional and nontraditional services and supports that are specifically designed for individual youngsters and/or families to enable them to achieve the goals specified in a customized service plan.) Thus, in all systems of care, some form of case management or care coordination plays a critical role in planning, orchestrating, monitoring, coordinating, and adjusting services.

CASE MANAGEMENT IN A SYSTEM OF CARE

A review of the literature is likely to leave the reader confused by the endless variety of terms used to describe the set of functions typically associated with case management. Terms including care coordination, service coordination, therapeutic case management, clinical case management, therapeutic case advocacy, and others abound, and few clear, consistent distinctions have been drawn to clarify their usages. Many of these terms are used interchangeably. It has been suggested that the term *case management* is gradually being replaced, most notably by the term *service coordination* (Doel, 1991). This shift may be associated with the negative, depersonalizing connotation sometimes attached to the term *case management*. Preference for the term *service coordination* was expressed by Illback and Neill (1995) based on two biases—that individuals do not like to be referred to as cases to be managed and that case management cannot occur outside the service system context.

In addition to the diversity of terms, confusion is created by the plethora of implicit and explicit definitions of case management that are found in the literature and in the field. In fact, the disparate definitions of case management led Schwartz, Goldman, and Churgin (1982) to suggest that the concept represents a Rorschach test on which one can project any image one wishes. Despite the multiplicity of both terms and associated definitions, there appears to be growing consensus as to the basic definition and purposes of case management.

In its broadest sense, case management refers to a set of functions designed to mobilize resources to meet client needs (Doel, 1991). Rubin (1992) defined case management as an approach that attempts to ensure that individuals receive all the services that they need in a timely, appropriate, and coordinated fashion. Solomon (1992) similarly stated that case management is a coordinated strategy on behalf of clients to obtain the services that they need, when they need them, and for as long as they need them. Weil and Karls (1985) portrayed case management as a set of logical steps and a process of interaction within a service network which assure that a client receives an array of services in a supportive, effective, efficient, and cost-effective manner. These and other commonly used definitions are based on the premise that case management is a "boundary-spanning approach" through which case managers link clients to the multiple providers, agencies, services, and resources and assume responsibility for ensuring that the service delivery system is responsive to clients' needs (Rubin, 1992). Most definitions share two major features, specifying that case management is: 1) a set of functions, and 2) intended to mobilize, coordinate, and maintain an array of services and resources to meet the needs of individuals over time.

Historical Perspective

The origins of case management have been traced to the 1960s, a period during which a wide range of human services programs underwent extraordinarily rapid growth (Rose, 1992). Many specialized programs, which often served a narrowly defined target population or responded to a narrowly defined problem, began to emerge during this time. The resulting network of services was increasingly perceived as highly complex, fragmented, duplicative, and uncoordinated (Intagliata, 1982; Rubin, 1987). Particularly for individuals with multiple and complex needs and disabilities, the challenges inherent in navigating the maze of agencies, service providers, and services became overwhelming. By the early 1970s, case management approaches began to emerge in order to assist clients in gaining access to and coordinating services and to assist them in "managing" their involvement with the service delivery system (Rose, 1992). The role of case managers as "systems agents" or brokers of services received increasing attention and was increasingly seen as a critical aspect of service systems; this led to a large number of federally funded demonstration projects experimenting with various approaches (Raiff & Shore, 1993). These approaches generally involved holding one worker accountable for the overall care of a client and for the responsiveness of the entire service delivery system. This designation of a case manager as a strategy for overcoming the neglect and fragmentation of the service system was characterized by Rubin (1987) as an "attempt to ensure that there is somebody who is accountable and who is helping the client hold the service delivery system accountable, someone who cannot pass the buck to another agency or individual when and if services are not delivered quickly and appropriately" (p. 212).

The use of case management rapidly spread, with such techniques applied to a range of populations including individuals who are elderly, who have developmental disabilities, who have chronic health conditions, or who are involved with the child welfare system. In the field of mental health, the deinstitutionalization movement contributed to the growth of case management. Although the primary locus of care was moved from institutions to the community, individuals with serious, persistent mental illnesses needed a wide range of services and supports that often were unavailable, inaccessible, or restricted by complex and confusing eligibility requirements, policies, or procedures. It became increasingly apparent that these individuals were not receiving the needed services and supports and that they often were unable to negotiate complex and unresponsive service delivery systems (General Accounting Office, 1977; Rose, 1992). Case management in the mental health arena has evolved in response to these systemic problems and has been conceptualized as an essential component of a comprehensive community support system for adults with serious, persistent mental illnesses (Chamberlain & Rapp, 1991; Stroul, 1989). Despite the fact that case management became firmly established in adult mental health services, little attention was given to the need for case management for youngsters with emotional disturbances until the 1980s. As the system of care concept and philosophy were defined (Stroul & Friedman, 1986) and experimentation with the development of such systems proceeded, the role and importance of case management for children and their families gained prominence.

The U.S. government has played a crucial role in the growth of case management through federally funded demonstrations and legislative mandates for case management services for a variety of target populations. In mental health, the critical role of case management in service delivery systems has been recognized in several recent federal laws. For example, the Omnibus Health Act (PL 99-660, amended by the ADAMHA Reorganization Act, PL 102-321) requires states to create plans to develop and deliver community-based services for individuals (both adults and children) with serious mental illnesses. The legislation mandates the provision of case management services to individuals receiving substantial amounts of publicly funded services. Public Law 99-457 (the Education of the Handicapped Act Amendments of 1986) is intended to improve services (including mental health services) for infants and toddlers with disabilities and their families. Individualized family service plans (IFSPs) are required, as are case managers who are responsible for implementation of the plan and service coordination.

Public Law 102-321 authorized the new Child Mental Health Services Initiative, which is being implemented by the CMHS. The program provides grants to develop a broad array of community-based services for children with serious emotional disorders as part of coordinated local systems of care. The legislation identifies case management as a critical function and requires case management services for all youngsters who are offered access to the system of care. In addition, Medicaid waivers and provisions for targeted case management have enabled states to use Medicaid as a source of financing for case management services for individuals with mental illnesses.

In this context, case management has proliferated with great diversity in emphasis, approach, philosophy, intensity, and so forth. Recent applications of case management have emphasized its potential role in system management and cost containment. Raiff and Shore (1993) discuss "the new case management" in which case managers have great authority to "drive the service package" and are viewed as powerful forces for systems change. Similarly, case management is increasingly seen as a tool for cost containment in mental health service delivery, with case managers responsible for ensuring cost-effective services and for minimizing the current rampant overutilization and inappropriate utilization of the most expensive treatment environments. These variations, which add a "system-focused" dimension to case management along with the more traditional "client-focused" stance, contribute to the intriguing varieties and blends of case management approaches that are evolving in the 1990s.

Case Management Functions

The functions associated with case management have roots in the social work and public health nursing fields. In fact, there has been considerable debate as to whether case management functions represent something new or are simply rediscovered interventions that are part of the long-standing history of the social work profession (Raiff & Shore, 1993; Rose, 1992). Despite this discussion, there appears to be considerable consensus that case management comprises a core set of functions including assessment, service planning, service implementation, service coordination, monitoring, and advocacy.

This set of functions can be carried out in a variety of ways and by various individuals within a system of care. Rose (1992) noted that not every person who is called a case manager performs all these core functions and that, conversely, not every person who performs some or all of these functions is called a case manager. Some agencies and programs assign these functions to other service providers and clinicians, while agencies with specialized case managers may expand upon these core functions and assign additional roles and functions to their case management staff. Often, the parents of youngsters with emotional disorders perform case management functions. Currently, recognizing the variability inherent in the field, these core elements of case management are widely accepted as essential functions to be performed on behalf of and in collaboration with youngsters who have emotional disorders and their families (Katz-Leavy et al., 1992; Raiff & Shore, 1993; Rose, 1992; Stroul & Friedman, 1986). These functions are as follows:

1. *Assessment*   The assessment function involves determining the comprehensive needs of children and their families as well as current and potential strengths that can be built upon through the helping process. Assessment often involves convening and facilitating a multidisciplinary or multiagency team (which includes the parents and, often, the youngsters) to complete a broad-based, ecological assessment of strengths and needs.

2. *Service planning*   The planning function involves coordinating the development of an individualized service plan to address identified needs. This process is accomplished in close partnership with the child and his or her family. Case managers are responsible for assisting families in becoming involved in the service planning process. The development of the service plan or plan of care is often accomplished within the context of a multiagency team, which is facilitated by the case manager.

3. *Service implementation* The service implementation function involves ensuring that the individualized service plan is executed as intended in a timely, appropriate manner. Implementing the service plan entails referring and linking the child and his or her family to appropriate agencies and service providers, as well as arranging for, procuring, and brokering needed services and resources. Service implementation extends beyond accessing formal services to include informal and nontraditional supports. In some instances, case managers become "resource developers" who must creatively locate or design the services and supports needed by a child and his or her family. On many occasions, this function also involves troubleshooting in order to overcome obstacles to the utilization of services and resources.

4. *Service coordination* The coordination function involves linking the various agencies, systems, and individuals who may be involved with the care of the youngster including the family, school, mental health providers, child welfare or juvenile justice workers, health care providers, and any other involved individuals or programs. For older adolescents, establishing linkages with the adult service system in order to facilitate transition becomes a critical aspect of this activity. Effective service coordination requires ongoing contact with the child and his or her family and with other providers to ensure that services are implemented in a logical manner and that multiple services and interventions are consistent and directed toward the same goals. The case manager often serves as the hub of all service-related interaction among involved providers.

5. *Monitoring and evaluation* This function involves monitoring the adequacy and appropriateness of services over time. Monitoring is directed toward ensuring the continuity of service provision as well as the continuing appropriateness of the services being delivered in view of changes in the youngster's functioning at home, in school, and in the community. Continuous evaluation of the effectiveness of services and progress toward treatment objectives also is an integral part of the case manager's role, resulting in necessary adjustments in service plans and interventions.

6. *Advocacy* This function involves serving as an advocate for the child and his or her family to ensure that they receive needed services, resources, and entitlements. The case manager works to address and overcome barriers and deficiencies that clients encounter when interacting with the service delivery system. An integral part of this function involves helping to empower families with the skills and knowledge to serve more effectively as their own advo-

cates. Moving beyond case advocacy for individual youngsters and their families, case managers often become involved in "class advocacy" or promoting changes in the service delivery system that will benefit all children and families.

These functions are not discrete, but should be seen instead as a process with sequential and often overlapping tasks (Raiff & Shore, 1993). All these functions are performed within a context of a warm, supportive, caring, and collaborative relationship with the child and his or her family. In fact, the case manager–client relationship represents the core of the case management process, ensuring that case management services are not mechanistic but rather a highly personal form of helping (Modrcin, Rapp, & Chamberlain, 1985; Stroul & Friedman, 1986). In addition to considering the quality of the relationship between the case manager and the child and his or her family, Raiff and Shore (1993) advocate the use of a set of quality standards by which to assess the caliber of the case management services, including such standards as the degree of cultural competence, the level of consumer empowerment, and the quality of the family–professional partnership.

Two newer roles are increasingly ascribed to case managers—clinical services and financial management. Clinical services, such as training in daily living skills, crisis intervention, medication management, supportive counseling, and individual and family therapy, are functions that case managers fulfill in some systems of care. Financial management of services and interventions also is an expanding role for some case managers, involving functions such as developing and managing a budget for the care of individual youngsters and their families, overseeing the expenditure of flexible funds for service delivery, gatekeeping for the most expensive services and settings, and cost containment (Applebaum & Austin, 1990). These aspects of case management are some of the most significant variables among case management services in the field.

MAJOR CASE MANAGEMENT VARIABLES

Although most case management services share similar goals and a set of core functions, such services differ significantly in many respects. The following discussion reviews the major variables accounting for these differences in the implementation and delivery of case management services for children with emotional disturbances and their families.

Clinical Services

The debate as to whether clinical services per se should be part of the case management role or remain separate is long standing, and the inclusion of clinical services in the role of case managers varies widely. Some programs emphasize the clinical nature of their activities and refer to their services as "clinical case management" or "therapeutic case management" (Roberts, Mayo, Alberts, & Broskowski, 1986). These programs tend to view case management itself as a therapeutic intervention. The opposite point of view has been argued, specifically that the requirements of case management are extensive and most likely beyond the capabilities of clinicians who are providing direct treatment at the same time. Furthermore, it has been argued that case managers who are not the primary treatment agent are in a position to review clients' progress more objectively and independently and to advocate more effectively.

It has become increasingly apparent over time that it is difficult, if not impossible, to separate clinical functions entirely from case management. Supportive counseling, crisis intervention, parent education, and medication management are functions of a clinical nature that are closely bound with the core case management functions. However, vast differences still exist as to the degree to which clinical services are included and encouraged and as to the acceptance of the case manager as the primary treatment provider or therapist. Those with a clinical case management perspective see case management as a treatment in its own right, with the case manager viewed as an "outreach therapist"; others see case managers as brokers and enablers rather than agents of personal growth and therapeutic change (Bachrach, 1989).

Financial Management

One of the most significant variables affecting the delivery of case management services is whether a financial management function is included among the other core functions. This financial management function has been described as a "system-oriented fiduciary focus," generally directed at the goal of cost containment (Raiff & Shore, 1993). It often is associated with insurance companies and other health care organizations that are attempting to manage the care provided to consumers in order to promote more efficient service delivery and contain costs. A rapidly increasing array of both public and private sector systems of services are adding a financial management role to the other responsibilities of case managers in order to respond to the escalating costs of service delivery. According to Raiff and Shore, the addition of this function is considered by some to be the "advance guard of future case management programming," while others express profound concern about the seductive promise of being able both to contain costs *and* to ensure the delivery of needed services.

The addition of the financial management function may create a tension among the various goals of case management, specifically in terms of the relative emphasis on improved access to services versus resource allocation and gatekeeping (Austin, 1983; Loomis, 1988). Is the case manager to be primarily an advocate for the client or a resource manager acting in the interests of the larger society? Case management with a financial management, or managed care, focus has been characterized as "client unfriendly" and as reflecting the interests of payors rather than of consumers. However, positive aspects of this function have also been identified, including enhancing collaboration with service providers, forcing the service system to provide alternatives to costly (and often inappropriate) care in restrictive service environments, and adding provisions for ensuring appropriate and high-quality service delivery (Raiff & Shore, 1993). Although concerns about the effect of the financial management function on access to services and quality of care persist, examples in the field have shown that financial management functions can coexist with other, more traditional, case management functions.

Intensity

Case management services vary according to intensity, generally referring to the amount of time and resources devoted to serving each youngster and his or her family. As case management services increase in intensity, they generally are characterized by more frequent contact with clients, more time spent with each client and family, smaller caseloads,[1] more *in vivo* approaches, an expanded range of roles and functions, and expanded services and supports to family members and significant others.

A trend noted by Raiff and Shore (1993) is the targeting of high levels of case management services to the most high-risk populations—persons with more severe and persistent disorders, persons with complex and multiple needs, persons who are the most difficult to serve, and persons who are high utilizers of services and, therefore, costly to serve. The term *intensive case management* refers to the

---

[1] Use of the term *caseload* raises the same issues discussed earlier with respect to the term *case management*. While the term may depersonalize children and families, it is currently widely recognized and used by researchers and practitioners. It is used in this chapter to refer to the number of children and families served by each worker.

many examples of such services that have recently emerged to serve these individuals. The individualized service approach, typically used for youngsters with more severe disorders, centers around an intensive form of case management performed by highly skilled case managers and based on the challenges presented by the youngsters served and the complexity and uniqueness of their intervention plans (Katz-Leavy et al., 1992).

Caseload Size

The number of clients assigned to each case manager is highly variable, ranging from as few as 4 to as many as 75 or more. The dangers of having too many clients have been emphasized in the literature. For example, Rose (1992) stated that having too many clients may impair the quality and effectiveness of services by reducing case managers' contact with clients, diminishing opportunities to build close relationships, and predisposing case managers to respond to crises rather than anticipate problems. Stroul and Friedman (1986) warned that although it may appear cost effective to have many clients, it is important to keep caseloads small when serving a population of children with serious emotional disturbances due to their multiple needs, the severity and complexity of their problems, the frequency with which crises develop, and the high cost of failure. Case management for individualized services, in particular, requires small caseloads because of the complexity of the functions that case managers must perform and the fact that they are serving the most needy target population.

Suggested optimal caseload sizes range from 5 to 15 youngsters (Katz-Leavy et al., 1992; Raiff & Shore, 1993; Santarcangelo, 1989). Caseload size may depend on the intensity of the needs of the youngsters to be served. For example, youngsters and their families in the initial stages of service provision require more time and effort, while those in maintenance or transition phases need lower levels of services and support. Some regions in Kentucky have developed a weighting system for limiting caseload size, with weights assigned to each case based on the level of intensity of the services required (Illback & Neill, 1995).

Philosophy

The philosophy guiding case management services varies across programs. Two convictions appear to be emerging as essential philosophical underpinnings of effective case management services—the belief in a family-centered approach and the belief in a strengths-based approach. Presently, the degree to which these precepts have been accepted and incorporated into service delivery differentiates case management programs.

The adoption of a family-centered philosophy of care is based on the recognition that the family is the most important resource for a child and that it is the family that plays the primary role in the care of youngsters with emotional disorders, a very difficult and demanding task. A family-centered approach to case management is built around seeing families (or surrogate caregivers) as full partners in all aspects of the planning and delivery of services. In addition, an array of services and supports (e.g., parent education, counseling, respite care, and home aid services) are offered to families to support and enhance their ability to care for their children effectively.

The strengths-based approach involves careful analysis of the skills, resources, and other strengths that the child and his or her family have and the building of intervention plans around these strengths. This philosophy of care emphasizes existing strengths and resources rather than focusing solely on deficits, problems, and needs—an approach that has typified past service delivery. The strengths-based approach is considered to be less stigmatizing and demoralizing and recognizes that even the most troubled youngsters and families have assets that can be enlisted and utilized in the helping process.

Specialization

Another variable affecting case management services is whether the services are provided by specialized case managers or whether they are provided by staff who have other treatment or service delivery responsibilities in addition to fulfilling case management functions. Some systems utilize specialized case managers who are hired and trained for this role and who serve as full-time case management specialists. A number of advantages to using such specialized case managers have been identified. For example, they can provide case management services without competing priorities resulting from other responsibilities; they become experienced in working with youngsters with difficult and complex problems and skilled at managing individual intervention plans; and they develop an intimate knowledge of the resources available in the community for children and their families and become adept at assisting families to gain access to these resources (Stroul et al., 1992).

Although there are clear advantages to using specialized case managers, many systems of care do not have sufficient resources to provide specialized case managers to all youngsters who need case management services. Thus, the assignment of case management responsibilities to a staff person in a service provider agency is an often-used approach. This approach is described as using a "lead case manager" from the most logical agency, the agency with the longest relationship with the child and his or her family or the one with the primary, or greatest level of, service responsibility. Most often, systems of care use some combination of these approaches to meet the need for case management services.

Staff Qualifications

The level of education of case managers is another significant variable, with the educational background of staff ranging from high school diplomas to doctoral degrees. This variability reflects differences in the perception of case management. Some perceive it as a type of intervention that requires well-educated and highly skilled and experienced staff; others see case management as a transitioning profession that is amenable to more alternative hiring approaches (Raiff & Shore, 1993). Rose (1992) discussed the dilemma related to case managers' educational backgrounds. He noted that most programs require bachelor's degrees, but that questions have been raised regarding the sufficiency of this level of training in view of the range and complexity of the required activities, the need to work independently, and the need to establish credibility with other professionals and administrators who may regard them as "paraprofessionals." However, more highly educated professionals may be less willing and enthusiastic about performing case management functions, particularly those that involve more mundane tasks, such as accompanying and transporting clients. Prior experience is also considered in hiring decisions made by case management programs, but there is little current consensus as to the relative importance of professional training and experience. This lack of consensus is reflected in the variability with respect to staff qualifications across programs. Many assert that preservice education, at whatever professional level, has not adequately prepared staff for case management roles. Educational programs and curricula focusing specifically on the skills and knowledge needed for case management are a fairly recent phenomenon and are not yet widely used. As a result, the need for on-the-job and in-service training for case managers is especially critical, and there has been an increasing emphasis on case management training.

Another recent trend is the employment of consumers and parents as case managers. Raiff and Shore (1993) state that this practice is built on the acknowledgment that persons with extensive experience as users of services bring a unique level of understanding and skill to the delivery of case management services to others. Their first-hand experience with the system of care contributes a pragmatic perspective to the process, and they may be better able to establish rapport and serve as role models for clients. Thus, while some systems are raising professional requirements for case managers, others are becoming more open to innovations such as the hiring of parents and consumers for case management roles.

Use of Teams

Some case management services involve using teams in various ways to help plan and coordinate service delivery for youngsters and their families. There is wide variability in the types of teams that are used and in the general purposes that such teams serve. One approach involves the use of a "case management team," which comprises a group of case managers who share responsibility for a caseload of youngsters. There are many possible variations in the size of the team, the extensiveness of client sharing, and the level of mutual backup provided. Raiff and Shore (1993) cited a number of practical considerations that favor the use of such case management teams, including enhancing continuity of care, facilitating 24-hour on-call availability and coverage during sick leave and vacation, allowing for flexible management of crises, accommodating staff turnover more efficiently, and facilitating mutual support and consultation among staff. A review of research indicates that both the team and individual approaches to case management are equally effective (Rothman, 1992).

Another use of teams as part of case management services involves the use of multidisciplinary or multiagency teams to assist in planning and overseeing services to individual youngsters and their families. These teams typically are organized by the case manager and are composed of the persons who are the most involved and influential in the child's life. These persons include the parents and child themselves and all professionals who are serving the child or who will potentially serve the child. With the case manager playing a facilitative leadership role, the team meets and works together over time to develop and implement a comprehensive, individualized service plan for the youngster and his or her family that addresses all the child's life domains. At the instigation of the case manager, the team continues to meet as needed to monitor progress and to reconfigure the service plan and approaches based on the child's changing needs (Katz-Leavy et al., 1992). These types of service planning teams are increasingly being used as an integral part of the case management process.

Organizational Context

Case management programs and services are offered under a wide variety of organizational auspices and locations. Such services may be part of a freestanding agency or program, may be housed within a particular provider agency, or may be provided under the auspices of an interagency team. Examples of these organizational arrangements and others can be found in systems of services for children with emotional disorders and their families. Problems and challenges have been noted with respect to all types of organizations. For example, Illback and Neill (1995) stated that case managers do not fit neatly into traditional niches within mental health organizations and as a result, they experience such problems as turf battles, questions of competence, regulatory gridlock, and a general devaluation of their role. Case managers in freestanding agencies may be too far removed or isolated from other service providers to establish effective working relationships and secure needed resources.

The placement of case managers within an organization is also an important factor affecting their ability to influence decisions and secure resources within their own agency and from other agencies. Stroul and Friedman (1986) emphasized the importance of placing case managers in a position that accords them considerable influence within the overall system. Without such placement, the ability of case managers to effectively advocate for clients, to coordinate and broker services, and to monitor intervention plans becomes limited.

Authority

The amount of authority and autonomy given to case managers in planning and implementing the intervention plan for a youngster and his or her family varies tremendously. In some systems, case managers have considerable authority to make decisions, to gain access to both traditional and nontraditional services and supports, and to influence agencies and providers. In fact, the authority of case managers in some systems has been extended in such a way that they can control funds used to purchase services for youngsters and their families. In some program examples, case managers control a capitated budget, which is used to purchase all needed services; in other examples, case managers have access to flexible funds for use on an individual case basis to purchase specialized services or supports.

The extent of the authority of case managers may be a crucial factor in determining the effectiveness of case management services

(Rose, 1992). Strategies for enhancing the authority of case managers include clarifying and codifying the authority of case managers in interagency agreements, giving case managers greater discretion over funds used to purchase services, and enhancing the credibility of case managers through informal working relationships with administrators and service providers.

CONCLUSION

The implementation of case management services, with many variations, continues to progress at a rapid pace. Individuals who administer systems of care for children and adolescents with emotional disorders and their families are reporting that case management is vital to their service delivery approach. Illback and Neill (1995) conclude that case management "remains compelling as an essential mechanism to ensure comprehensive, high-quality, and integrated services for this population" (p. 26). Despite these reports, some skepticism remains as to whether case management can overcome the serious deficiencies in service delivery systems for persons with disabilities. Rose (1992) argues that service integration strategies alone will not ameliorate these deficiencies and that much greater expenditures of resources to enhance services are needed. He calls for research to determine whether case management is a viable strategy or whether scarce funds might be better spent by directly filling service gaps rather than by creating boundary-spanning mechanisms.

Continued research is needed to firmly establish the value and effect of case management, recognizing that the wide variations in definitions and functions of case management make it difficult to isolate the effects of the core case management functions and case management approaches that incorporate additional functions, particularly clinical services. However, the value of case management services cannot be established outside the context of a system of care. This context includes all the essential elements—an array of service options, mechanisms for system-level coordination, and mechanisms for client-level coordination (i.e., case management). In the context of the system of care, case management does play a vital role in ensuring the continuous, effective, and efficient delivery of services to children with emotional disabilities and their families.

REFERENCES

ADAMHA Reorganization Act, Part E: Children with Serious Emotional Disturbances, PL 102-321. (July 10, 1992). Title 42, U.S.C. 201 et seq: *U.S. Statutes at Large, 106,* 349–358.

Applebaum, R., & Austin, C.D. (1990). *Long-term case management: Design and evaluation.* New York: Springer-Verlag.

Austin, C. (1983). Case management in long-term care: Options and opportunities. *Health and Social Work, 8*(2), 16–30.

Bachrach, L. (1989). Case management: Toward a shared definition. *Hospital and Community Psychiatry, 40*(9), 883–884.

Behar, L. (1985). Changing patterns of state responsibility: A case study of North Carolina. *Journal of Clinical Psychology, 14,* 188–195.

Behar, L. (1991). Fort Bragg demonstration project: Implementation of the continuum of care. *Close to home: Community-based mental health for children.* Raleigh: North Carolina Division of Mental Health, Mental Retardation, and Substance Abuse Services.

Brandenburg, N., Friedman, R., & Silver, S. (1990). The epidemiology of childhood psychiatric disorders: Prevalence findings from recent studies. *Journal of the American Academy of Child and Adolescent Psychiatry, 29,* 76–83.

Chamberlain, R., & Rapp, C. (1991). A decade of case management: A methodological review of outcome research. *Community Mental Health Journal, 27,* 171–188.

Costello, E., Burns, B., Angold, A., & Leaf, P. (1993). How can epidemiology improve mental health services for children and adolescents? *Journal of the American Academy of Child and Adolescent Psychiatry, 32*(6), 1106–1117.

Davis, M., Yelton, S., & Katz-Leavy, J. (1993, March). *Unclaimed children revisited: The status of state children's mental health services.* Paper presented at the sixth annual research conference (A System of Care for Children's Mental Health: Expanding the Research Base) Tampa, FL.

Day, C., & Roberts, M. (1991). Activities of the child and adolescent service system program for improving mental health services for children and families. *Journal of Clinical Child Psychology, 20*(4), 340–350.

Doel, M. (1991). *Early intervention systems change: A review of models.* Portland, OR: Association of Retarded Citizens.

Education of the Handicapped Act Amendments of 1986, PL 99-457. (October 8, 1986). Title 20, U.S.C. 1400 et seq. *U.S. Statutes at Large, 100,* 1145-1177.

General Accounting Office. (1977). *Returning the mentally disabled to the community: Government needs to do more.* Washington, DC: Author.

Illback, R., & Neill, T.K. (1995). Service coordination in mental health systems for children, youth, and families: Progress, problems, prospects. *Journal of Mental Health Administration, 22 (1),* 17-28.

Intagliata, J. (1982). Improving the quality of community care for the chronically mentally disabled: The role of case management. *Schizophrenia Bulletin, 8*(4), 655–674.

Joint Commission on the Mental Health of Children. (1969). *Crisis in child mental health.* New York: Harper & Row.

Katz-Leavy, J., Lourie, I., Stroul, B., & Zeigler-Dendy, C. (1992). *Individualized services in a system of care.* Washington, DC: Georgetown University, CASSP Technical Assistance Center.

Knitzer, J. (1982). *Unclaimed children.* Washington, DC: Children's Defense Fund.

Loomis, J. (1988). Case management in health care. *Health and Social Work, 13*(3), 219–225.

Lourie, I., & Katz-Leavy, J. (1986). Severely emotionally disturbed children and adolescents. In W. Menninger (Ed.), *The chronically mentally ill* (pp. 159–185). Washington, DC: American Psychiatric Association.

Modrcin, M., Rapp, C., & Chamberlain, R. (1985). *Case management with psychiatrically disabled individuals: Curriculum and training program*. Lawrence: University of Kansas, School of Social Welfare.

Office of Technology Assessment. (1986). *Children's mental health: Problems and services—A background paper*. Washington, DC: U.S. Government Printing Office.

Omnibus Health Act, PL 99-660. (November 14, 1986) Title 42, U.S.C. 300 et seq: *U.S.C. Statutes at Large, 100*, 3794-3797.

President's Commission on Mental Health. (1978). *Report of the sub-task panel on infants, children, and adolescents*. Washington, DC: U.S. Government Printing Office.

Raiff, N., & Shore, B. (1993). *Advanced case management: New strategies for the nineties*. Newbury Park, CA: Sage Publications.

Roberts, C., Mayo, J., Alberts, F., & Broskowski, A. (1986). *Child case management for severely disturbed children and adolescents*. Unpublished manuscript, Northside Center, Tampa, FL.

Rose, S. (1992). *Case management and social work practice*. New York: Longman.

Rothman, J. (1992). *Guidelines for case management: Putting research to professional use*. Itasca, IL: F.E. Peacock.

Rubin, A. (1987). Case management. In A. Minahan (Ed.), *Encyclopedia of social work* (pp. 212-222). Silver Spring, MD: National Association of Social Workers.

Rubin, A. (1992). Is case management effective for people with serious mental illness? A research review. *Health and Social Work, 17*(2), 138–150.

Santarcangelo, S. (1989). *Case management for children and adolescents with a severe emotional disturbance and their families*. Waterbury: Vermont Department of Mental Health and Mental Retardation, Child and Adolescent Service System Programs.

Schwartz, S., Goldman, H., & Churgin, S. (1982). Case management for the chronically mentally ill: Models and dimensions. *Hospital and Community Psychiatry, 33*, 1006–1009.

Solomon, P. (1992). The efficacy of case management services for severely mentally disabled adults. *Community Mental Health Journal, 28*, 163–180.

Stroul, B. (1989). Community support systems for persons with long-term mental illness: A conceptual framework. *Psychosocial Rehabilitation Journal, 12*(3), 9–26.

Stroul, B. (1993). *Systems of care for children and adolescents with severe emotional disturbances: What are the results?* Washington, DC: Georgetown University, CASSP Technical Assistance Center.

Stroul, B., & Friedman, R. (1986). *A system of care for children and youth with severe emotional disturbances* (rev. ed.). Washington, DC: Georgetown University, CASSP Technical Assistance Center.

Stroul, B., Lourie, I., Goldman, S., & Katz-Leavy, J. (1992). *Profiles of local systems of care for children and adolescents with severe emotional disturbances* (rev. ed.). Washington, DC: Georgetown University, CASSP Technical Assistance Center.

Weil, M., & Karls, J. (Eds.). (1985). *Case management in human service practice*. San Francisco: Jossey-Bass.

Expectations
of Case Management
for Children
with Emotional Problems
A Parent Perspective

Richard Donner, Barbara Huff, Mary Gentry,
Deborah McKinney, Jana Duncan,
Sharon Thompson, and Patty Silver

This chapter represents a unique opportunity for parents to share their perspectives on one of the most critical services needed by their children with emotional problems—case management. Here, parents who have children with serious emotional problems express their expectations without regard to what is currently occurring. In this way, the chapter serves as an ideal to which agencies and programs can respond. Fulfilling parental expectations is not easy, but in terms of working with parents to meet the needs of youth who have serious emotional disorders, it is worth the effort.

Historically, family members of children with serious emotional problems have not been involved in determining what the children need (Knitzer, 1982). Parents have not fared well in a system that is confusing and gives them little or no assistance. Too often, families have gone through a tragic chronology of events in trying to get help for their children that includes repeated evaluations, blame, and harassment. This is unfortunate because parents are usually the first to identify their child's difficulties, know their child from first-hand experience, and see their child as a whole person.

Most often services have been designed "for" families, not "with" families. In order to receive services, families have had to meet certain eligibility criteria or they did not receive services. Parents are rarely asked what they think their child needs nor are they asked to participate in defining the services needed or the competencies that service providers should have to be responsive to families.

Due in part to the efforts of statewide parent organizations, as well as the efforts of national organizations of parents who have children with serious emotional disorders such as the Federation of Families for Children's Mental health (FFCMH) and the National Alliance for the Mentally Ill's Child and Adolescent Network (NAMI-CAN), parent involvement at all levels of decision making regarding services for their children is expanding.

PROCESS

To gather parents' perspectives on case management in a systematic fashion, a method designed to involve consumers in the decision-making process of human services was employed. This method, the Consumer Report Method, was developed by Bushell (personal communication, September 15, 1985) and Fawcett, Seekins, Whang, Muiu, and Suarez de Balcazar (1982) and is similar to the process of focus groups (Stewart & Shmdasani, 1990). It includes four steps: 1) identifying participants, 2) meeting to respond to the questions being addressed, 3) identifying the issues and perspectives that arise from the meeting, and 4) having the participants validate the identified responses.

Identification of parents who have children with emotional problems was facilitated by a statewide parent-driven organization called Keys for Networking, Inc., of Kansas. Keys for Networking was established in 1988 to provide information, support, training, and parent assistance to families of children with emotional problems. The organization has touched the lives of many Kansas families and is also recognized as being a leader in parent support efforts across the country.

By way of Keys for Networking contacts with families across Kansas, staff members identified six parents interested in participating in the meeting. These parents were either recipients of case management services or were in contact with a number of other parents through support groups. Three of the participants had worked with a case manager; three had not. The participants were all parents whose children have a serious emotional problem, often including behavioral problems as well. These parents have experienced all the problems and frustration, both with their children's behavior and with the formal systems, that are now so widely reported in the literature (Friesen, 1989).

This group of parents met to discuss their views and ideas regarding case management using a focus-group format. The 3-hour audiotaped meeting was held in Topeka, Kansas. The meeting addressed the following topics:

1. What do parents expect from case management services?
2. How would parents know if the case manager was responsive and effective?
3. What training and standards are necessary for effective case management?
4. What should a parent's role be in case management?
5. What components do parents want to see included in case management models?

The questions were not discussed in any specific order, but rather the discussion was free-flowing and open. After the meeting, the audiotapes were reviewed and separated into categories using a categorization method similar to that suggested by Spradley (1979), which included domain analysis, taxonomic analysis, componential analysis, and theme analysis. This list was sent to the participants, who gave feedback regarding the accuracy of the information and the domains identified. The changes and clarifications provided by the participants are incorporated into this chapter.

The information shared by the parents regarding their expectations of case management and the case manager is grouped into five areas. These areas are: 1) attitudes parents seek in case managers, 2) commitment to establishing a relationship with families, 3) assistance with the service system, 4) creation of a support network of informal resources, and 5) organizational variables that support parents and case managers. Selected quotes from the parents are used to illustrate the ideas that were expressed.

Attitudes Parents Seek in Case Managers

The attitudes of case managers are the foundation for developing a working relationship with parents. Specifically, parents want case managers to have supportive attitudes toward families. That is, they want case managers to have attitudes that give parents hope and help them to dream about the possibilities for their child's future.

> I think that case managers have a responsibility to give a family some hope, a dare to dream.

In addition, case managers need to see families in a positive, nonblaming way and know that, regardless of what happens, parents are invested in their children. Therefore, parents want case managers to be invested and committed to their children and their families.

Most important, parents expect case managers to have the attitude that youngsters should be with their families and that their families are the experts on their needs. Parents want case managers to be able to look at the world from the family's perspective and set priorities based on what the family wants. This requires case managers to be nonjudgmental regarding parents' lifestyles. They need to be sensitive to cultural, environmental, racial, religious, and sexual orientation differences.

Commitment to Establishing a Relationship with Families

To be able to accomplish the tasks of case management, parents indicated that the case manager needs to have the right attitude as well as the skills to establish positive, ongoing, trusting relationships with parents, their children, and agencies.

> The ultimate success of case management depends on the relationship between the case manager and his or her ability to work with the parent and the child.

This relationship is built by asking parents what they need and by having the skills to locate the resources and supports that will help parents meet their needs. This includes the ability to translate family concerns into resources and services.

> They've got to be able to take the words of the parent and put those words into services.

For example, if parents say that they need to take a break from being with their child, the case manager translates this into a service or resource, such as respite care. It is important, however, for the case manager to recognize that family needs do change and to have the skills to be responsive when such change occurs.

Parents stated that it is important for them to believe that they are contributing to their child's progress. That is, it is imperative for families to feel as if they are part of the "team" of people working with their child. What a particular parent wants and can do depends on the parent's own unique abilities and desires. For example, a parent who is a special education teacher may want to negotiate an individualized education program (IEP) for the child since he or she knows that system. In contrast, a parent may want the case manager to help with an IEP if he or she teaches within the same school, as being a powerful advocate might jeopardize the parent's position.

At times, parents will want the case manager to be very involved in what is going on with the family and may even want the case manager to resolve a situation, while at other times, parents will not want any involvement with the case manager. Case managers need to have the skill to grow with families as their concerns change and to be comfortable with moving in and out of the lives of families as demands dictate. The essential point is that parents need to be listened to and involved in all decisions regarding their child.

Parents expect case managers to have the competence to highlight family strengths, to build on these strengths, and to see the value of each family member. Because all people have capabilities and strengths, the case manager needs to see families as being capable and as doing the best that they can. Even when parents are at their worst, they still need the case manager to support them as a family.

> Someone's been talking about strengths and I think one thing that case managers can do is to start reframing how the families have stayed together even among some incredible odds. That's a real strength, and sometimes parents need some feedback such as, "Gee you've really done a good job with what you've had to deal with."

In fact, how the case managers do their work is important in developing relationships with parents. Case managers should exhibit flexibility, ease, and a personal touch. Flexibility in the case manager–caregiver relationship is demonstrated, for example, when case managers reach out to parents but do not always expect families to respond. Parents want the case manager to be a participant in the successes that occur for their children. Parents want the case manager to be comfortable, for example, to be willing to cry with them when things are not going well. Although it may seem trivial, it was also important to parents that the case manager dress in a manner that coincides with what the case manager is doing at a particular time. That is, if he or she is going to take a child to a ball game, then he or she should not dress for a night of dancing.

> Well, they have to meet the family where the family is. It's real intimidating for us when they are all dressed up and go into a home like that.

Case management relationships are not one-sided. To have an effective relationship, parents also need to know the case manager on a somewhat personal basis. Case managers need to be comfortable with being informal and sharing information about themselves in order to build a mutual relationship with parents. If the relationship is mutual, a positive working relationship is more likely.

Parents want the case manager to be like an extended family member who gets paid. They want the case manager to be interested, involved, available, supportive, and know when it is time to leave. At the same time, case managers must know their own limits and how to take care of themselves. It is important for case managers to develop ways to support each other.

Assistance with the Service System

Parents expect the case manager to understand that they are responsible to families even though they are being paid by an agency. Parents want the case manager to make things happen for them and not against them. In dealing with the formalized, fragmented services available to their child, parents expect the case manager to be in touch with all the other persons involved in working with them and their child. This requires case managers to know of community resources and how to obtain access to them. Case managers also need to be aware of the regulations and eligibility criteria for other formalized services. For example, if a child is eligible for Medicaid services, parents expect the case manager to know what Medicaid will pay for and assist them in securing the services. This requires the case manager to know enough about Medicaid to be sure that services such as attendant care can pay for a volunteer to accompany a child to various activities.

Parents expect case managers to develop relationships with other service providers so that they have the "pull" to get things done and the skill to know whom to contact and when. Parents want the case manager to have the capacity and the authority to make decisions with them regarding their child. This is especially critical in a crisis when families need to have assistance in getting emergency services.

> I know what people to contact, but I don't have the pull. They have the pull. And if they don't have the pull, then they should get it.

Parents want the case manager to act as a liaison with programs in which the child is involved. One of the most important systems with which the case manager needs to work closely is the child's school system. Because many children with emotional disorders are in special education services, the case manager needs to be involved with the IEP and work closely with the child's teacher and the special services staff.

Creating a Supportive Network of Informal Resources

Parents want their child to be involved in normal, age-appropriate activities. They want their child to have the opportunity to be involved in recreational programs such as swimming, skating, or Little League; social events such as school dances, church groups, or scouts; and community activities such as movies, the YMCA, or summer camps. Therefore, parents expect the case manager to assist them in gaining access to informal supports for their child. Parents need the case manager to be a skilled advocate for these informal services just as they are with formal services. For example, if their child would benefit from going to a summer camp, parents want the case manager to help find scholarships to pay for it, deal with the director to be sure their child is allowed to participate, and find an attendant to assist their child if one is needed.

Parents expect case managers to help create resources when they do not exist. For example, parents want the case manager to assist them in finding transportation to appointments and activities. They want the case manager to recruit volunteers and support the volunteers' work with their child. For example, if a child is interested in Scouts, the case manager could find a person who could be a buddy and attend scouting events with the child. The case manager should be available to the volunteer to help him or her understand the child so that both the child and the volunteer gain from the experience.

Because so many parents are isolated from other parents, they want the case manager to introduce them to other families who have children with emotional problems. They see the case manager as being able to serve as a bridge between families experiencing similar stresses. Parents also want the case manager to set up opportunities to network with support groups and local, state, and national organizations that advocate on behalf of children with emotional or behavioral problems.

Organizational Variables that Support Parents and Case Managers

When agencies design case management programs, they must be focused on the family and not just the child; they need to be responsive to families, and they need to be flexible. Flexibility refers to program features such as having a small number of clients so that case managers have time to spend with families. Case managers need a flexible schedule so that they can meet families and children at times when it is convenient for all involved. They must be allowed to be available to the family and provide transportation when needed.

Families think it is critical for the case manager to have regular daily contact with them and their child. If the case manager cannot provide face-to-face contact, parents believe that the case manager should at least telephone on a regular basis to check in.

> Keep in contact with me almost daily and give me a list of community activities that my child could be involved in, and perhaps arrange transportation to these activities.

Case management services need to be set up so that there is always someone available to respond to a parent's needs when a particular case manager is not available. It may be necessary to have different levels of case management to meet the diverse needs of families. Until case management is available for all families who want it, agencies need to be sure to provide support to families who are waiting for the service. This could take the form of support groups or referral to other resources.

Parents expect the service to match their needs and abilities rather than their having to match the services. For example, it is important to families that the case manager have money available to purchase some of the resources that their child needs. For example, if a child's strength is a musical talent, there may need to be money available to assist in paying for music lessons. In addition, the case manager should have access to money so that the case manager or a volunteer can take a child for a soft drink or to a movie. The case manager needs to have funds to pay for the things that the child needs and allow the child to participate in community activities.

Families want the case management service to have family-centered policies. For example, agencies have used confidentiality as an excuse for not communicating with each other regarding children. Parents also have to get through a lot of "red tape" to get services. Case management services need to be designed to allow for acquiring resources creatively. To do this, the case manager will have to be creative, flexible, and even sneaky at times.

> They need to get so creative in their thinking that they can utilize everything.

Parents should be involved in the development of case management services, the policies that affect the services, and the implementation of the services. Parents should be integrally involved in all levels of case management and not just token representatives on committees or respondents to agency satisfaction surveys. Similarly, parents strongly believe that they should be involved in the training of case managers. Parents want to offer their unique perspective on what it is like to have a child with emotional problems. Many parents have been doing case management for years, and they can share their experiences and insights with trainees. In addition to being trainers, parents also want to be encouraged and allowed to attend the training.

CONCLUSION

The expectations that caregivers have of case managers (Table 2.1) may easily seem overwhelming to individual case managers and supervisors. From a parent's point of view, all these expectations are essential and it is the task of individual case managers and supervisors to determine how this ideal is to be brought about. Essentially, parents are saying that case managers are accountable first to parents and then to agencies, policies, communities, or the myriad of other possible constituents.

This position may seem unrealistic or unreasonable. However, these expectations can be the beginning of a dialog between parents and service providers, considered as an ideal, and agencies can work

Table 2.1. Caregivers' expectations of case managers

Attitudes parents seek in case managers
  Give caregivers hope and a vision of the future.
  Believe that children should be with families.
  Believe that families are the experts on their caregiving needs.
  Be nonjudgmental and value-free regarding parents' lifestyles.

Commitment to establishing a relationship with families
  Ask parents what they need to care for their child.
  Translate family concerns into resources and services.
  Permit families to determine what tasks they will do and what tasks they want the
    case manager to do.
  Identify and build on family strengths.
  Be comfortable moving in and out of families' lives.
  Reach out to parents.
  Participate in the successful things that happen in families.
  Be comfortable in being informal and sharing information about themselves.
  Know their own limits.

Assistance with the service system
  Be in touch with all people involved with the family and the child.
  Know community resources and have the ability to acquire and influence them.
  Have the capacity and authority to make decisions.
  Act as a liaison with programs.

Creating a supportive network of informal resources
  Assist and advocate for the youth to be involved in normal age-appropriate activities.
  Create resources when they do not exist.
  Have flexible funds available to acquire informal resources.
  Introduce caregivers to other families and support and advocacy groups.

Organizational variables that support parents and case managers
  Small number of clients.
  Flexible work schedules.
  Regular daily contact with the caregivers and their child.
  Someone always available.
  Parent-centered policies.
  Parents should be involved in the development and implementation of case manage-
    ment services, policies, and training.

to bring policies, practices, skills, and abilities up to this level. Case managers can use the list of expectations as a checklist to assess their behavior or program. Supervisors and program developers can use this list to assess their policies. Supervisors can also examine this list for guidance on issues such as number of clientele, flexibility of time, funds, policies, and so forth.

If case management is family sensitive and implemented in a comprehensive and integrative way, it can be the backbone of a system of care for children with emotional disorders. When successful, case management can ensure that families receive the services and supports that they need to keep their children at home.

REFERENCES

Fawcett, S., Seekins, T., Whang, P. L., Muir, C., & Suarez de Balcazar, Y. (1982). Involving consumers in decision-making. *Social Policy, 13*(2), 36–41.

Friesen, B. (1989). National study of parents whose children have serious emotional disorders. In A. Algarin, R. Friedman, A. Duchnowski, K. Kutashr, S. Silver, & M. Johnson (Eds.), *Children's mental health services and policy: Building a research base* (Second annual conference proceedings) (pp. 36-52). Tampa: Florida Mental Health Institute.

Knitzer, J. (1982). *Unclaimed children.* Washington, DC: Children's Defense Fund.

Spradley, J. (1979). *The ethnographic interview.* New York: Holt, Rinehart and Winston.

Stewart, D., & Shmdasani, P. (1990). *Focus groups: Theory and practice.* Newbury Park, CA: Sage Publications.

Examining Current Approaches to Case Management for Families with Children Who Have Serious Emotional Disorders

Theresa J. Early and John Poertner

Case management for children and adolescents with emotional and behavioral disorders and their families is a new, still developing, and rapidly expanding service. The roots of children's mental health case management lie in mental health services for adults with severe and persistent mental illness, in particular the Community Support Program of the late 1970s and its emphasis on case management. Case management also has been a component of services for other populations, such as individuals with physical or developmental disabilities, and is being developed for newly identified service populations, such as people infected with human immunodeficiency virus (HIV) and people who are homeless. The development of case management for these various populations is driven by three common concerns: 1) a need for integrated services to overcome the fragmentation of service delivery systems and to ensure care for the whole person, 2) a need for continuity of care as needs change, and 3) a need for individualized treatment to meet individuals' different constellations of need. Recent federal legislation also has provided impetus for states to develop mental health case management services for children and adolescents; the mental health plans submitted to the National Institute of Mental Health (NIMH) under the Omnibus Health Act (PL 99-660) require states to describe their case management services. In fact, since 1991, state plans must specifically address such services for both children and adolescents.

The purpose of this chapter is to describe and evaluate children's mental health case management at the practice level. In order to accomplish this purpose, case management of children with emotional disorders is examined from several perspectives, including: 1) the empirical literature, to determine what is known about the effectiveness of various approaches; 2) current practice, to determine how case management services are operationalized; and 3) the perspectives of a group of parents who have children with serious emotional disorders. First, it is necessary to define what is meant by the term *case management*.

DEFINITION OF CASE MANAGEMENT

In 1987, the newsletter *Update*, published by the Florida Research and Training Center for Children's Mental Health, reported on the developing case management services for children with emotional disorders and their families, characterizing the status of such services at that time as comparable to the weather: "something that everybody talks about, but not much is done about" (Florida Mental Health Institute, 1987, p. 11). Although this is no longer true, *case management* today is a term that everyone defines differently.

Other terms, such as *service coordination* and *therapeutic case advocacy*, have been used to denote the service or activity that the authors of this chapter call "case management" (Knitzer, 1982; Regional Research Institute for Human Services, 1986). Case management has been described as a method of services coordination and accountability (Weil & Karls, 1985) and as a set of functions (Harrod, 1986). These brief descriptions are for the most part accurate. More specifically, there seems to be agreement that the functions of case management are:

1. *Assessment*—the process of determining needs or problems
2. *Planning*—the identification of specific goals and the selection of activities and services needed to achieve them
3. *Linking*—the referral, transfer, or other connection of clients to appropriate services
4. *Monitoring*—ongoing assurance that services are being delivered and remain appropriate, and the evaluation of client progress
5. *Advocacy*—intervention on behalf of the client to secure services and entitlements (Cutler, Blume, & Shore, 1981)

What seems to be lacking from both the descriptions and the list of functions is reference to a goal or expected outcome of the service. Therefore, for the purpose of this chapter, the goal of case management for children with emotional disorders and their families is for the children to live in the most family-like environment possible (preferably with their own family) within the community.

Thus, *children's mental health case management* is a set of services consisting of assessment, planning, linking, monitoring, and advocacy to keep the child in the family setting. Later, in the review of current case management practice, different approaches to case management are discussed, which place relatively more emphasis on some elements of the services and less on others.

CASE MANAGEMENT LITERATURE

Research is conducted to attempt to determine through scientific means what a particular population needs and the best way to meet those needs. Ideally, human services interventions are based on this research. The "best way" may be the least expensive, the fastest, or the longest lasting way, depending on the interests of the body responsible for planning and implementing the human services intervention. Case management is one such human services intervention that already is being provided in many areas. Funders, professionals, families, and others concerned with children who have emotional disorders have decided that case management is a service that children with emotional disorders need. The next step is to determine the specific features of case management that best meet the needs of children with emotional disorders and their families.

In a search for specific features of case management that best meet the needs of children with emotional disorders and their families, the authors conducted a search for research literature relevant to children's mental health case management. That literature includes empirical literature on case management involving children with emotional disorders and their families, on case management for children with other disabilities or health care needs, and on case management with adults who have mental illness.

As case management has been developed for a variety of populations, a body of literature has accumulated that primarily describes it. The literature on case management for families with children who have serious emotional disorders reflects the recent interest in children's mental health issues, that is, the literature is sparse and primarily descriptive. A few articles describe state or local programs (e.g., Behar, 1985; Santarcangelo, 1989; Stoep & Blanchard, 1992). Another writing, the program update section of the Florida Research and Training Center's newsletter, *Update*, highlighted case management services for children and adolescents with serious emotional disorders by describing several model programs and applying concepts from literature on case management with adults who have mental illness (Florida Mental Health Institute, 1987). At the two most recent research conferences on children's mental health sponsored by the Florida Research and Training Center for Children's Mental Health, seven papers were presented on case management, four in 1992 and three in 1993. This conference represents the state of the art in children's mental health services research. The seven papers were representative of the literature on children's mental health case management: two were single-program evaluation studies (Jacobs, 1993; Joyner, 1992); one was an analysis of statewide utilization patterns (Lemoine et al., 1993); one described introduction of the service to a new client population (Stoep & Blanchard, 1992); one was a preliminary report of a national study of state-level implementation of case management (Jacobs, 1992); one discussed measurement issues (Marquart, Pollak, & Bickman, 1992); and one discussed the use of a statistical technique in monitoring case management services (Poertner & Early, 1993).

The evaluation or outcome studies that have been completed typically examine the clientele of a single agency or geographic area. Although such studies are able to show positive changes for clients, it is not possible to determine whether the changes are the result of the case management intervention or something else. Studies using more rigorous designs and control groups are necessary to be able to accurately attribute changes to the intervention. No controlled outcome studies of children's mental health case management were located in the review of literature. However, some should be forthcoming soon because of recent research initiatives in the area of children with serious emotional disorders by the NIMH (1989), projects such as the Fort Bragg Evaluation Project, being conducted by the Mental Health Policy Institute at Vanderbilt University (Breda et al., 1993), and evaluation of the Robert Wood Johnson Foundation Mental Health Services Program for Youth (Gardner, Saxe, Lovas, & Glass, 1993). Likewise, there were no controlled outcome studies of case management involving children with other disabilities or health care needs.

Obviously, although there is considerable literature that describes children's mental health case management and its place in a system of care for children with emotional problems, as of yet, there is no model, approach, setting, or set of functions that has demonstrated effectiveness in terms of enabling children and youth to live successfully in family environments within the community. Nor is there any literature on what does not work.

Another body of literature relevant to children's mental health case management is that concerning case management with adults who have severe mental illness. A recent review of this literature identified six outcome studies during the 1980s that evaluated case management as an intervention, focused on results from clients as the outcome, and used either an experimental or quasi-experimental design (Chamberlain & Rapp, 1991). In general terms, all but one study demonstrated some positive results. In terms of hospitalizations (measured differently across studies), two of the projects found significant positive differences (Bond, Miller, Krumwied, & Ward, 1988; Borland, McRae, & Lycan, 1989), one found significant differences in favor of the control group (Franklin, Solovitz, Mason, Clemens, & Miller, 1987), and two studies found no differences (Goering, Farkas, Wasylenki, Lancee, & Ballantyne, 1988; Goering, Wasylenki, Farkas, Lancee, & Ballantyne, 1988; Modrcin, Rapp, & Poertner, 1988). Along the dimensions of functional assessments and quality of life, five of the six studies found positive results in such areas as occupational functioning, social isolation, and independent living. These differences were most evident after relatively long-term interventions. From these studies, it appears that the results of case management are mixed in terms of achieving the goal of community tenure and that modest changes over time in some intermediate outcomes (e.g., functioning, social isolation) can be expected.

From these studies, it is not clear which aspects of case management produced what results. The six studies used four different types of case management: a generalist approach, a rehabilitation approach, a strengths approach, and an assertive community treatment approach. Another recent study empirically evaluated the extent to which particular models of case management—minimal, coordination, and comprehensive (Ross, 1980)—were implemented with adults with severe mental illness (Korr & Cloninger, 1991). Analysis of data from three agencies validated the three models that vary primarily in number and types of services provided, but did not evaluate the efficacy of any of the models. Therefore, because case management for adults with serious mental illness has been the focus of attention for some time, we know that there are different approaches to the intervention, we have a moderate amount of information about outcomes for participants, and we know relatively little about how case management works.

Applying the results of research on case management with adults who have severe mental illness to families of children with serious emotional disorders is difficult. Although the interventions may be similar, the needs of the two populations are somewhat different. In general, working with children and their families is more complex because there are more systems and more people directly involved—both the children with emotional disorders and their parents or caregivers. If the results apply at all, they suggest that it may be possible to reduce hospitalizations of children and youth and that it is possible to assist youth to acquire certain skills necessary to live within the community. There are no parallel results for family caregivers.

To summarize, there is little empirical literature to direct case management practice with children who have emotional problems and their families. Thus, in analyzing practice or designing programs, we must turn to other sources for direction. However, before an analysis of children's mental health case management is undertaken, current practice must be more clearly described.

DOMINANT CASE MANAGEMENT APPROACHES

As case management with adults who have severe and persistent mental illness has evolved, two different typologies of models have been described in the literature (Robinson & Toff-Bergman, 1989; Ross, 1980). One typology comprises three models, the minimal, the coordinated, and the comprehensive (Ross, 1980). Differentiation among these models is based on number and type of services, ranging from the minimal model offering only the basic services of outreach, assessment, case planning, and referral to service providers, to the comprehensive model offering basic services along with client advocacy, direct casework, developing natural support systems, reassessment, advocacy for resource development, monitoring quality, public education, and crisis intervention. The other typology identified four models of case management: broker, personal strengths, rehabilitation, and full support. Differentiation among these models is based on 16 operational features including philosophy/focus, assessment, staff structure, range of responsibilities, target population, outcomes, staff ratio, and staff credentials (Robinson & Toff-Bergman, 1989).

These typologies arose in the development of case management for this population as descriptions of "what is" rather than what works or what should be. Since research in the field of children's mental health case management is not yet able to tell us what works, the authors of this chapter followed the lead of writers in adult case management. They identified four dominant practice approaches employed at this time in the evolution of case management services with families of children who have serious emotional disorders.

These four approaches are not differentiated into categories. Two of the approaches are differentiated based on the case manager playing multiple roles (e.g., therapist or interdisciplinary team member). The other two approaches are differentiated by the way particular functions are emphasized. We identified these approaches through contact with model programs, reviewing descriptive studies and state program descriptions, and through technical assistance contacts. The four approaches to case management with children who have emotional disorders and their families are commonly called outpatient therapy/case management, brokerage, interdisciplinary or interagency team, and strengths. Each of these approaches is described as follows in terms of the case management functions of assessment, planning, linking, advocacy, and monitoring. A brief comparison of these approaches by function is depicted in Table 3.1.

Outpatient Therapy/Case Management

As mental health centers and systems have struggled to implement case management with few resources, many agencies have responded to this challenge by adding the case management functions to existing outpatient therapy programs. In some cases outpatient therapists, upon hearing about the case management functions, respond that this is nothing more than good clinical practice (Lamb, 1980). Because this approach is so widespread, it is described in this section.

Assessment in this approach is first driven by the need to obtain a *Diagnostic and Statistical Manual of Mental Disorders (third edition– revised; DSM-III-R)* (American Psychiatric Association, 1987) diagnosis, both for reimbursement purposes and clinical purposes of the therapist. Beyond diagnosis, additional clinical assessment is determined by the particular therapeutic model used by the therapist/ case manager. The assessment process then turns into a planning process, with the therapist/case manager being involved with the child and various family members in a mutual process of problem definition. The history of the family and the present situation are seen as important elements in understanding the problem, which is commonly defined in terms of needed behavior or psychological change. For example, behavior change could be controlling angry outbursts or responding to a curfew, and psychological change could include increasing impulse control and decreasing suicidal thoughts.

The plan of care follows the format indicated by the mental health center and its funding agencies. The plan usually involves a series of actions, identified by the therapist/case manager for the child and/or parent to accomplish in the next week or two, that are

Table 3.1. Case management with children who have emotional disorders—types and functions

Functions	Outpatient therapy/case management	Broker	Team	Strengths
Assessment	Based on *DSM-III-R* diagnosis	Case manager determines service needs based on functional assessment	Case manager completes or arranges for comprehensive, clinical assessment	Case manager engages child and family in strengths assessment
Planning	Mental health center treatment plan or plan of care	Case manager identifies and arranges for services	Team plans and arranges for services	Case manager sets goals with youth and caregiver based on what caregiver needs to provide care and on what youth needs to remain in the community
Advocacy	Advocacy efforts focused on family to acquire other services deemed necessary for child or family	Advocacy efforts directed at other service providers to obtain flexibility of eligibility criteria or payment arrangements; may include creation of needed services	Advocacy efforts unnecessary because all agencies/disciplines have agreed to provide services	Advocacy efforts on behalf of individual children and families to obtain needed services; also directed at informal resources in the community in the form of education on what it would take for child to participate in normal activities. Efforts are also directed at agency/system change by individual case managers and by supervisors identifying common barriers as targets for change.

Monitoring	Plan evaluated through client feedback	Plan revised when crisis occurs (i.e., child runs away or is terminated from service)	Team evaluates plan at regular intervals	Ongoing evaluation of goals with youth and with caregiver
Linking	Linking to other agencies, services as need arises for additional services, usually a passive referral to existing community agencies	Varies from merely making family aware of services specified in plan of care to active referral including securing payment	Varies from one person responsible for linking child and/or family to services specified in plan of care to parent having full responsibility for obtaining indicated service	Linking to services and resources is specified in plan of care. Responsibility for linking may rest with the case manager, the parent, the child, or with some combination of individuals. Identifying or creating informal resources often is included.

DSM-III-R, Diagnostic and Statistical Manual of Mental Disorders (third edition–revised) (American Psychiatric Association, 1987).

thought to lead to resolution or improvement of the problem. The specific contents of the plan of care depend to a large degree on the clinical model used by the therapist/case manager.

As the therapist/case manager and the child and/or parent see the need for additional services, they begin to link to other services and agencies. For example, the therapist/case manager might suggest day treatment for the child and financial counseling and the services of a behavioral therapist for the family caregiver. Given the limitations of being office based and having a schedule of clinical hours, such linking is often restricted to passive referral to existing community agencies. Some therapists/case managers could have considerable telephone contact with collaterals for referral and monitoring, but since such telephone contact does not generate billable hours, it usually is limited.

Restrictions on the therapist/case manager's time and access to the community also impose limits on their advocacy efforts. In some instances, therapists/case managers are well known in the community, and their opinions are valued and sought by other service providers. Therefore, when these case managers advocate for a service for a child or family member, they may be successful in spite of limits. However, for the therapist who does not have relationships with other service providers, the necessity of staying in the office and limited availability by telephone may lead to less successful advocacy efforts. Therapists/case managers sometimes call other service providers together for case conferences and may hold in-home sessions, although 50-minute office-based sessions are the norm, based in part on efficient use of time.

Monitoring and evaluation in this approach focuses on the work done by the child and/or parent between sessions. The child and/or parent reports on their efforts since the last session. For example, what did the child do to control his or her outbursts? Did it work? What additional strategies could he or she try next week? The results of these efforts are then used to determine the next steps. In some cases, the established plan of care is simply reinforced. If the plan is not working, the therapist/case manager may discuss feelings to try to determine why the plan failed. In other situations, the plan is modified in an effort to be more successful in the future. In still other cases, the entire plan of care is changed because the therapist/ case manager and the child and/or the caregiver agree that the problem definition has changed.

One of the factors that may affect the way a therapist/case manager accomplishes the case management functions is the therapist/ case manager's professional training. For instance, the case management functions are more in line with the training and traditions of social workers than psychologists. Agency policies also affect this approach to case management, especially in regard to in-home services, case conferences, and time for collateral contact.

Brokerage

Although brokerage is the linking function of case management and, therefore, some persons would argue that it is not a separate approach, practice patterns do exist that emphasize this dimension of the work to the exclusion of other dimensions. In the brokerage approach, the main responsibility of a case manager is to make arrangements for clients to receive services. The notion is that the service delivery system is not well coordinated or flexible. In order for children with emotional disorders to receive the full range of services that they need, someone must be available who knows what services there are, knows how to gain access to them, and plays the role of broker on behalf of clients. By definition, a *broker* is one who acts as an agent to procure something for someone who employs the broker. It is the stockbroker's job, for example, to know which commodities are for sale at what prices and to make arrangements for purchase at the best price. In case management, it is the broker/case manager's job to know what services are available to meet the client's needs and to make whatever arrangements are necessary for the client to receive the services.

The broker/case manager is responsible for assessing the need for services based on both information gathered from agencies and individuals who have provided services to the child and his or her family and information obtained directly from the child and his or her family. As with the therapist/case manager, assessment sometimes extends to determining a *DSM-III-R* diagnosis for funding purposes or determining program eligibility. Broker/case managers may obtain this diagnosis through their own clinical assessment or may make arrangements for appropriate clinical assessment.

Once needs are determined, planning for the family and the child consists of the broker/case manager identifying services to meet their needs. For example, the case manager may identify the need for respite care for the mother, a special education advocate to assist with the development of an individualized education program (IEP), and an afterschool program for the child.

Linking, or establishing the means by which the child or his or her family acquires the services, is an element of this approach that varies widely and is influenced by how the brokers view their job, agency auspice, number of clients, agency mandates, and agency philosophy. In some cases, the case manager simply makes the child and his or her family aware of services. In others, the case manager makes phone calls to establish appointments. In still others, the case manager is active on behalf of the child and his or her family to ensure that space is found in the program, a means of paying for the service is located, and the specific needs of the child or his or her family are clearly communicated to the service provider.

Monitoring, or evaluation, is the process of determining whether the current mix of services is meeting the needs defined in the plan of care and whether different or additional services are required. As with linking, this function varies widely. In some cases, the plan is revised only when a crisis signals a clear need for additional or different services. In others, the plan is periodically evaluated by the case manager with the child and/or family to determine whether the current services are meeting their needs and whether different or additional services are needed. In some situations, the case manager obtains the evaluation of the other service providers. Some case managers do this in conjunction with the child and/or his or her parents, while others simply seek an independent evaluation.

In some senses, advocacy is seldom seen as the broker/case manager's role. If there is a need for educational advocacy, for example, then the service of a protection and advocacy agency is indicated. Advocacy in terms of assisting children and/or parents to obtain needed services is sometimes done in the more comprehensive instances of this approach. However, many brokers/case managers see themselves as being limited to the services available within the community and the current service system and its capacity.

Interdisciplinary or Interagency Team

Two similar yet distinct approaches to case management use teams. The *interdisciplinary team* is often used for children with multiple medical needs, such as those with a variety of developmental delays, medical problems, and emotional disorders. The team consists of a group of specialists, often from the same agency or organization. This approach often is used as an early intervention service. The *interagency team*, however, is primarily a coordinating mechanism, used when the child is currently involved in several service systems such as the court, special education, child welfare, and mental health. This team is composed of a group of service providers from different agencies. The extent to which family members are included on either type of team varies widely.

Assessment is conducted by the various team members. Each team member has a specialty and assesses the child and/or family from a particular perspective using the normal procedures of his or her profession or agency. In the interdisciplinary team, for example, the psychologist conducts assessment using various psychological tests and measures, the audiologist conducts assessment using audiology devices, and the social worker conducts assessment of the child, family, and environment using genograms, ecomaps, or other evaluation tools. After each individual assessment, the team meets to develop an overall perspective through the sharing of their individual points of view. Planning also is a team effort, developed through the combination of professional perspectives, and normally results in a group of specialized services to be provided by the specialties represented on the team. For example, it may be determined that the child needs individual therapy and that the parent or caregiver needs respite care and training in behavior management. In the interagency team, the plan would detail specific services to be provided by each agency and funding arrangements between agencies.

Linking is performed in a variety of ways. In some cases, there is a person designated as the lead case manager who is responsible for linking the child and/or family member to the services. In others, each team member is seen as a case manager and, therefore, is the agent linking the "client" to the agency or specialized service. Sometimes, the plan of care is simply given to the family or caregivers and they are expected to obtain the indicated services. The family may be able to designate one team member as the primary case manager, as provided for in early intervention legislation.

Monitoring or evaluation is often seen as the responsibility of the individual service providers or clinical experts. Since they are providing professional, specialized services, their normal method of evaluating services is seen as sufficient. The team may meet to discuss the child's situation only when a service provider or a family member requests such a meeting, or the team may meet to discuss the child's progress on a regular basis. The latter is most often true of interagency teams involving representatives of community child-serving agencies.

In team approaches, advocacy is often not an important function because the gatekeepers to the services are represented on the team, take part in the decision making, and can assist the "client" to obtain the indicated services. In other approaches, where a case manager is designated, he or she may assume the role of advocate.

In this instance, the case manager may have the team members assist him or her in obtaining the needed services.

Strengths

Strengths approaches are emerging from a variety of ideas that have to do with people achieving their goals by building upon their resources or strengths (Saleebey, 1992). These approaches are emerging in many areas, such as in adults with long-term mental illness (Rapp & Chamberlain, 1985), in work with older women (Rathbone-McCuan, 1992), in work with public assistance recipients (Bricker-Jenkins, 1992) and in individual and family therapy (de Shazer, 1991; de Shazer, Berg, & Lipchik, 1986). Some view a strengths approach as a philosophical position that any case manager who recognizes client strengths can assume. However, in the developing strengths-based practice field, the emphasis is on an entire approach or model for which each task or function is different from ordinary practice. The strengths approach to case management with children and their families is more than the philosophy of identifying child and family strengths; it is a particular way to carry out the functions of case management.

Assessment in this approach consists of the identification of personal abilities and family resources, denoted as "strengths." Those things that the child and/or family caregiver does well are strengths upon which plans of care can be built. Family history, structure, relationships, and functioning are explored in the assessment process—not to identify problems but to identify strengths. For example, the child may have a keen interest in science and the family caregiver may have a strong commitment to caring for the child, with close friends and neighbors as resources. All these are strengths. These strengths are the foundation for the plan of care. This differs from approaches that are based on identification of problems. In each of the approaches described so far, although there may be some attention to strengths, the focus of the intervention is on problem identification and solution.

Planning for care in the strengths approach is child and caregiver directed and consists not of problem solving but of prospective goal setting. Goals set with the child recognize the desires of the child in terms of living a normal life and learning life skills. The central feature of goal setting with youth is asking them what they need to succeed in school, the family setting, and the other life domains. The desires of the youth determine the goals on which the youth and case manager will work. The strengths of the youth are a key to this plan. Areas in which the youth does well or that he or she likes become the basis for the plan of care.

Goals set with caregivers are directed at assisting the caregiver in providing care to the child within the family. The primary question for caregivers is, "What do you need to provide care to this child in your home and community?" The goal is for the caregivers to acquire the needed resources to provide care, whether they be services, informal resources, and/or information. The caregiver's strengths become an integral part of working toward the goal. For example, a caregiver's background in nursing can become a key ingredient in obtaining needed information from a doctor.

Plans of care are developed with the child and caregiver by identifying specific steps or tasks necessary to acquire a needed resource or learn a specific skill. For each task, a joint determination is made as to who will do the task and by when the task will be done. The emphasis is on shared responsibility and development of parent and youth abilities so that the case manager is no longer needed.

Linking the child and/or family to resources is dictated by the mutually defined plan of care. The tasks clearly identify who will do what in the linking process. In this way, linking is not a sole function of the case manager. The intent is for the parent and youth to learn to become effective consumers of services rather than to always rely on a case manager. When formal resources do not exist, the case manager's job is to identify and to use or create informal resources. Strengths are an important part of this creation of resources. For example, a neighborhood friend (i.e., a strength or resource) may be enlisted to assist with the afterschool supervision of a child. If the friend also is able to teach the youth something he or she is interested in, such as auto mechanics or dog training, more than one purpose is served.

Monitoring and evaluation are ongoing processes dictated by the plan of care. Each task in the plan is the responsibility of a specified person (e.g., youth, caregiver, or case manager) and has a mutually agreed upon date by which it is to be accomplished. Evaluation consists of reviewing the plan of care and the tasks according to the specified timetable with the child and/or caregiver. Evaluation may result in celebrating with the child and/or family for what has been accomplished, identifying additional tasks needed to accomplish the plan, and/or writing a new plan.

Advocacy takes several forms, from assisting the child and/or caregiver to learning the steps necessary for acquiring a resource; to going with the child and/or family to negotiate with a service provider; and to educating agencies, professionals, and individuals about making reasonable accommodations for families and children with emotional disorders. The focus is not on the case manager advocating for the youth or family caregiver but on advocacy being integrated into the goal-setting process. The child, family, and professional mutually determine the tasks required, participants in a particular task, and individuals responsible for task accomplishment.

EVALUATING DIFFERENT APPROACHES TO CASE MANAGEMENT

In the preceding review of literature, the authors conclude that the empirical literature relevant to case management with children who have emotional disorders and their families provides an insufficient base for evaluation of case management approaches. As noted earlier, human services interventions are "ideally" based on scientific information about what is needed by a population and what works to meet those needs. Because empirical practice principles are unavailable, case management services must be evaluated against another set of principles, such as values. The views of parents are sources that have been underutilized for determining the needs of children with emotional disorders. Because the authors believe that this perspective contains valuable information that has not yet received systematic attention, they turned to parents to determine a set of principles to use in evaluating current case management practices.

Obtaining Parents' Views

Chapter 2, written by a group of parents, was used as an initial source of principles. Approximately 17 principles were extracted from an early version of the chapter and, using a modified Delphi approach, mailed to a variety of parents who attended a national case management conference or who were state leaders of parent organizations. These caregivers were asked to select the six principles that were most important to them; they could also add principles. Results were tallied and those principles receiving the most votes were selected as a basis for examining current case management practice. Five principles were generated based on frequency of rating. These five principles are as follows:

1. Parents should have a major role in determining the extent and degree of their participation as case manager.

2. Case managers should have frequent contact with the child, family, and other key individuals in the child's life.
3. A single case manager should be responsible for helping families to gain access to needed resources.
4. Both parents and the child should be involved in decision making.
5. Case manager roles and functions should support and strengthen family functioning.

COMPARING PRACTICE WITH CAREGIVERS' DESIRES

Therapist/Case Manager

The constraints placed on the therapist/case manager make it difficult for the best-intentioned professional using this approach to meet the stated desires of the panel of caregivers. As noted, the therapist/case manager is constrained by being office bound and having a schedule consisting of 50-minute blocks of time. Therefore, although the therapist/case manager may wish to have the parent determine the extent and degree of his or her participation, the reality is that the parent needs to go to the office to be involved and must fit the visits into 50-minute hours or into the 10-minute window available each hour for phone contact. Frequent contact with the child, parent, and other key individuals is similarly constrained.

Helping parents to gain access to needed resources is dependent on the therapist/case manager's contacts and reputation. A well-known therapist/case manager might be able to influence other programs and services. However, if acquiring services requires active advocacy in the office of the other service provider, the therapist/case manager is constrained by his or her inability to leave the office.

Whether the therapist/case manager's practice is in concert with the principles of parent and child involvement in decision making and support and strengthening of family functioning depends more on the therapist/case manager's philosophical outlook and clinical approach than on other features of this approach. Therefore, a therapist/case manager could well satisfy these two principles.

It is unlikely that the therapist/case manager would be the single case manager across systems; therefore, this approach does not satisfy that principle. Overall, the office-based constraints placed on this case manager limits the degree to which the parent-derived principles can be fulfilled. However, for the parent who wishes and is able to be an active participant in advocacy and linking, the therapist/case manager approach would fulfill more of the principles.

Broker/Case Manager

Brokerage/case management has the potential of satisfying more of the parent-derived principles than therapy/case management. Frequently, parents determine their level of participation and decision making by doing as much as they wish. The parent may do most of the work, or may allow the case manager to do all or most of the work. Contact with the child and his or her family in this approach is dictated more by the caseload of the broker/case manager than by the basic approach. The broker/case manager with 6 cases is more likely to have frequent contact with parents and other key actors than the broker/case manager with 30 cases. The extent to which family functioning is supported or strengthened is determined to a greater degree by the case manager's attitudes and beliefs than by the specific services brokered. For example, day treatment services obtained to provide afterschool care may support the caregiver's ability to continue to provide care or may replace the caregiver's inadequate supervision of the child. In the first instance, family functioning is supported and, in the second instance, a family function is replaced by a service.

Team Approach

For those team approaches that identify a single case manager to implement the plan of care, if this case manager views the role as strengthening family functioning and as having frequent contact, three of the five parent-derived principles are satisfied. This approach has the greatest potential to satisfy the principle of a single case manager providing access to needed services, especially in the interagency team approach.

When parents have a role in decision making and in determining the extent of their involvement, the team approach may be more problematic. It is frequently difficult for a parental caregiver to be a full partner in decision making with a group of professionals. The parent is less likely to be comfortable with the technical language used in a meeting of professionals, is less likely to know the team members, and is less likely to ask questions or volunteer information and opinions. An assertive case manager may successfully advocate for a parent in this situation. However, it takes extraordinary skills on the part of both the parent and the case manager to realize these two principles.

Strengths Approach

A first impression may suggest that the strengths approach naturally satisfies all the parent-derived principles and that this chapter has been set up so that the other approaches serve as "straw men," making the strengths approach appear to be the only reasonable alternative. The truth is that the strengths approach has been developed in conjunction with parental caregivers and, therefore, may be unique. Certainly, the goal-setting process is a mechanism that allows parents to have a major role in decision making and in determining the extent of their involvement.

Given the task focus of this approach, the frequency of contact is an explicitly negotiated element of service. Therefore, frequency of contact will be based on the goals set in each case and on the extent of support that both parents and youth need in task accomplishment. Frequency of contact may also be affected by agency constraints such as large clientele numbers or rural, far-flung settings. Similarly, the focus on shared responsibility to gain access to resources may give the case manager less responsibility than the family member desires. Finally, the degree to which the case manager supports and strengthens family functioning is limited by the goal-setting focus. The focus on assisting caregivers to acquire what they need to care for a child necessarily limits the scope and degree of family functioning strengthened. However, it is the job of the case manager to support functioning in any area the parent identifies as related to caring for the child.

IMPLICATIONS FOR DEVELOPMENT
OF CASE MANAGEMENT SERVICES

Given the status of case management for children who have serious emotional disturbances and their families, there are implications for development of a variety of areas of this important service. In the area of research, it is clear that we do not know enough and must begin to develop an empirical base upon which to build case management services. There is important research being conducted that is beginning to focus on case management; it is the beginning of a long, costly process. Much of the literature cited in this chapter is based on case management research with adults who have severe and persistent mental illness. The experience of this literature tells us that it takes many years of well-constructed studies to begin to learn what is needed to design effective services. The adult case management literature has taken about 10 years to develop and now is providing insights into some effects of case management services for adults. Yet, it still has not linked specific approaches or functions to outcomes. In addition, while it is tempting to use the research on case management for another population in order to develop lessons for developing case management for children who have serious emotional disorders and their families, it may be more important to research case management specific to this population. We simply do not know the ways in which adults and children are similar or different. Our experience does suggest, however, that there are some important ways in which children and youth are different. The facts that children have families who are responsible for their care, children are required to be in schools, and schools are required to accommodate children are just a few of these differences.

Another important area of implication concerns the expectations of case management from multiple perspectives. The authors have chosen to examine current case management approaches in light of a set of expectations generated by a relatively small group of parents. Parents' perspectives have not been systematically sought, and exploring the expectations of a large, representative group of caregivers would add to the knowledge. In addition, there are others who are important to the case management process, and it would be helpful for the development of case management services to obtain their expectations and begin the process of blending multiple sets of expectations. These other perspectives might include youth, key individuals in the community (e.g., school personnel), and representative members of the community.

Certainly, training of case managers is an important area to consider when examining the implications of this review. Chapter 10 examines these issues in relation to training. From the case managers' perspective, most people newly assuming this role want to know what works. The difficulty is that it is not possible to tell case managers what is effective across cases or programs. It is possible to give case managers an image of what is possible through individual child and family success stories, and it is possible to train case managers to respond to the expectations of the multiple constituents that are involved in a case. Furthermore, it certainly is a priority to train case managers to develop working relationships with parents, youth, and the multitude of other persons involved with the family due to the child's disorder. It is also possible to establish boundaries for this working relationship through structured goal setting with the multiple parties. One can easily continue with what training can and ought to include, and this is a worthwhile endeavor. At the same time, case managers need to understand the limits of their role and functions.

Another area of implication for development of case management services from current practice is the supervision, management, and design of case management services. Chapters 12 and 4 of this book address these aspects of case management. Chapter 12, the chapter on supervision, shares insights from two individuals who supervise case management units. Chapter 4, the chapter on organizational arrangements, shares ideas and experiences on various ways of organizing case management services. These chapters are important for several reasons. For example, as this chapter illustrates, what case managers are able to do somewhat depends on the program in which they operate. This includes the supervisory supports that exist, as well as any organizational constraints that result from the placement of the case management services in a larger organizational and community context. In many ways it is the program designer, manager, or supervisor who helps case managers respond to multiple, sometimes conflicting, and sometimes unclear expectations.

CONCLUSION

Aspirations for case management are high, yet our knowledge is just developing. This challenges us—parents, researchers, practitioners, and policy makers—to work together to identify the tasks, structures, and methods that produce desired results, including normalization of children with serious emotional disorders, satisfaction of the norms established by parents, and assurance in the safety of both children and family or caregivers. From this point of view, it is less important who performs case management or what it is called; it is more important to focus on the approaches that will produce the desired results.

REFERENCES

American Psychiatric Association. (1987). *Diagnostic and Statistical Manual of Mental Disorders (third edition–revised)*. Washington, DC: Author.

Behar, L. (1985). Changing patterns of state responsibility: A case study of North Carolina. *Journal of Clinical Child Psychology, 14*, 188–195.

Bond, G.R., Miller, L., Krumwied, R., & Ward, R. (1988). Assertive case management in three CMHCs: A controlled study. *Hospital and Community Psychiatry, 39*(4), 411–418.

Borland, A., McRae, J., & Lycan, C. (1989). Outcomes of continuous intensive case management. *Hospital and Community Psychiatry, 40*(4), 369–376.

Breda, C., Davis, K., Heflinger, C., Brannan, A., Weiss, B., Lambert, W., Bickman, L., & Hodges, V. (1993, March 1–3). *Patterns of children's mental health status and service utilization: Preliminary findings from the Fort Bragg*

Evaluation Project. Symposium presented at A System of Care for Children's Mental Health: Expanding the Research Base, Tampa, FL.

Bricker-Jenkins, M. (1992). Building a strengths model of practice in the public social services. In D. Saleebey (Ed.), *The strengths perspective in social work practice* (pp. 122–135). New York: Longman.

Chamberlain, R., & Rapp, C.A. (1991). A decade of case management: A methodological review of outcome literature. *Community Mental Health, 27*(3), 171–188.

Cutler, D., Blume, J., & Shore, J. (1981). Training psychiatrists to work with community support systems for chronically mentally ill persons. *American Journal of Psychiatry, 138*(1), 98–101.

de Shazer, S. (1991). *Putting difference to work.* New York: W.W. Norton.

de Shazer, S., Berg, I.K., & Lipchik, E. (1986). Brief therapy: Focused solution development. *Family Process, 25,* 207–221.

Florida Mental Health Institute. (1987). *Update.* Tampa, FL: Research and Training Center for Children's Mental Health.

Franklin, J., Solovitz, B., Mason, M., Clemons, J., & Miller, G. (1987). An evaluation of case management. *American Journal of Public Health, 77*(6), 674–678.

Gardner, J., Saxe, L., Lovas, G., & Glass, A. (1993, March 1–3). *Evaluation of the Robert Wood Johnson Foundation Mental Health Services Program for Youth at mid-project.* Symposium presented at A System of Care for Children's Mental Health: Expanding the Research Base, Tampa, FL.

Goering, P., Farkas, M., Wasylenki, D., Lancee, W., & Ballantyne, R. (1988). Improved functioning for case management clients. *Psychosocial Rehabilitation Journal, 12*(1), 3–17.

Goering, P., Wasylenki, D., Farkas, M., Lancee, W., & Ballantyne, R. (1988). What difference does case management make? *Hospital and Community Psychiatry, 39*(3), 272–276.

Harrod, J.B. (1986). Defining case management in community support systems. *Psychosocial Rehabilitation Journal, 9*(3), 56–61.

Jacobs, D.F. (1992). Children's case management state level survey. In K. Kutash, C. Liberton, A. Algarin, & R. Friedman (Eds.), *A system of care for children's mental health, expanding the research base, Fifth Annual Research Conference Proceedings* (pp. 315–322). Tampa, FL: Research and Training Center for Children's Mental Health.

Jacobs, D.F. (1993, March 1–3). *Peeking inside the black box of case management/ service coordination for children and youth with SED: Findings from an evaluation of Mecklenburg County, North Carolina local CASSP program.* Paper presented at A System of Care for Children's Mental Health: Expanding the Research Base, Tampa, Florida.

Joyner, J.I. (1992). A method to assess client progress in a case management agency. In K. Kutash, C. Liberton, A. Algarin, & R. Friedman (Eds.), *A system of care for children's mental health, expanding the research base, Fifth Annual Research Conference Proceedings* (pp. 315–322). Tampa, FL: Research and Training Center for Children's Mental Health.

Knitzer, J. (1982). *Unclaimed children.* Washington, DC: Children's Defense Fund.

Korr, W.S., & Cloninger, L. (1991). Assessing models of case management: An empirical approach. *Journal of Social Service Research, 14*(1/2), 129–146.

Lamb, H.R. (1980). Therapist case managers: More than brokers of services. *Hospital and Community Psychiatry, 38,* 762–764.

Lemoine, R., Speier, T., Ellzey, S., Balson, P., Dumas, T., & Sherrington, W. (1993, March 1–3). *Case management services for children and adolescents with severe emotional disturbances: A statewide analysis of service utilization patterns and outcomes.* Paper presented at A System of Care for Children's Mental Health: Expanding the Research Base, Tampa, FL.

Marquart, J., Pollak, L., & Bickman, L. (1992). Quality in intake assessment and case management: Perspectives of administrators, clinicians and consumers. In K. Kutash, C. Liberton, A. Algarin, & R. Friedman (Eds.), *A system of care for children's mental health, expanding the research base, Fifth Annual Research Conference Proceedings* (pp. 347–356). Tampa, FL: Research and Training Center for Children's Mental Health.

Modrcin, M., Rapp, C., & Poertner, J. (1988). The evaluation of case management services with the chronically mentally ill. *Evaluation and Program Planning, 11,* 307–314.

National Institute of Mental Health (NIMH). (1989, November). *Currently funded research grants research on mental health services for children and adolescents.* Washington, DC: Author.

Omnibus Health Act, PL 99-660. (November 14, 1986). Title 42, U.S.C. 300 et. seq: *U.S.C. Statutes at Large, 100,* 3794-3797.

Poertner, J., & Early, T. (1933,March 1–3). *Using analysis to monitor case management with children.* Paper presented at A System of Care for Children's Mental Health: Expanding the Research Base, Tampa, Florida.

Rapp, C., & Chamberlain, R. (1985). Case management services for the chronically mentally ill. *Social Work, 30,* 417–422.

Rathbone-McCuan, E. (1992). Aged adult protection services clients: People of unrecognized potential. In D. Saleebey (Ed.), *The strengths perspective in social work practice* (pp. 98–110). New York: Longman.

Regional Research Institute for Human Services. (1986). *Focal point.* Portland, OR: Research and Training Center on Family Support and Children's Mental Health.

Robinson, G.K., & Toff-Bergman, G. (1989). *Choices in case management: Current knowledge and practice for mental health programs.* Washington, DC: Mental Health Policy Resource Center.

Ross, H. (1980). *Proceedings of the Conference on the Evaluation of Case Management Programs.* Los Angeles: Volunteers for Services to Older Persons.

Saleebey, D. (Ed.). (1992). *The strengths perspective in social work practice.* New York: Longman.

Santarcangelo, S. (1989). *Case management for children and adolescents with a severe emotional disturbance and their families.* Waterbury: Vermont Department of Mental Health and Mental Retardation, Child and Adolescent Service System Programs.

Stoep, A.V., & Blanchard, T. (1992). Introduction of mental health case management to homeless youth in King County, Washington. In K. Kutash, C. Liberton, A. Algarin, & R. Friedman (Eds.), *A system of care for children's mental health, expanding the research base, Fifth Annual Research Conference Proceedings* (pp. 315–322). Tampa, FL: Research and Training Center for Children's Mental Health.

Weil, M., & Karls, J. (1985). *Case management in the human services.* San Francisco: Jossey-Bass.

SUSTAINING PROGRAMS
Organization and Funding

The Organization and Structure of Service Coordination Mechanisms

Barbara J. Friesen and Harold E. Briggs

Although many experts on management and organizational behavior recognize the influence of organizational structure and location on service delivery (Gitterman & Miller, 1989; Kettner, Daley, & Nichols, 1985; Norman, 1985), most of the case management literature is silent about this issue. A preponderance of this literature, including the sparse literature addressing children's mental health case management, focuses on issues such as the appropriate roles and functions of individual case managers and the impact of case management services on clients or children and their families. Research conducted from this perspective conceptualizes case management as an "independent variable," examining the extent to which things such as the purpose, role, intensity, and duration of case management services affect outcomes such as changes in client functioning, community adjustment, cost, and other client-related variables (Anthony & Blanch, 1989; Chamberlain & Rapp, 1991; Rubin, 1992). This perspective of case management does not take into account what Bailey (1989) calls the "ecological circumstances" in which case management services are delivered.

In this chapter, the case management/service coordination function is viewed as a dependent variable (i.e., the authors emphasize the influence of the organizational and interorganizational context on the way that case management services are or can be delivered). Although little attention has been paid to structural and organizational issues related to case management thus far in the children's mental health field, there is empirical support for the proposition that they may be powerful forces that influence, for better or worse, the nature and effectiveness of services. For example, variables such as organizational size (Rotegard, Hill, & Bruininks, 1983), staffing

63

levels (Spector & Takada, 1991), centralization (Hall, 1991), and formalization (Glisson & Martin, 1980) have all been shown to affect organizational processes or the outcomes of services. Furthermore, these structural and organizational dimensions constitute not just a way of understanding why services turn out the way they do; they may also be viewed as legitimate objects of intervention.

In the following pages, the authors identify a number of key issues related to the organization of case management or services coordination and then present eight structural options that exemplify some ways that case management in children's mental health is currently organized, or could be organized. For each of these options, the authors suggest possible advantages and limitations and address four key dimensions related to service coordination: 1) continuity, 2) accountability, 3) authority, and 4) autonomy. This analysis is intended to provide planners, policy makers, administrators, service providers, and family members with tools not only to understand how services are affected by the organizational context, but also to make informed choices about how services should be organized in order to attain desired results at both the system and organizational levels and, ultimately, for children and their families.

IMPORTANCE OF STRUCTURE
IN SERVICE COORDINATION EFFORTS

The use of organizational arrangements to promote service coordination in the United States dates back to the late 19th century, when concern about the coordination of resources for the poor was central to the development of the Charity Organization Societies (Trattner, 1979). The creation of the Charity Organization Societies, which served as clearinghouses for all the charitable bodies in a community, reflected a dual concern with increasing efficiency and reducing duplicate payments to poor families and improving service quality and access. These contrasting philosophies (i.e., concern about cost containment and fraud vs. a focus on client needs and preferences) still characterize many service coordination efforts to this day (Baker & Vischi, 1989; Kane, 1988).

A number of policy initiatives since the 1960s have been directed toward the goal of coordinated services. Both the Mental Retardation Facilities and Community Mental Health Centers Construction Act of 1963 (PL 88-164) and the Economic Opportunity Act (EOA) passed in 1964 (PL 88-452) were concerned with service coordination at both the client and systems levels. The Community Mental Health Centers Act required that applicants demonstrate linkages among required service components and work to develop services to address gaps in the continuum of care (Dinerman, 1992). Emphasis on service integration in the EOA's community action programs and later in federally sponsored services integration initiatives in the 1970s led to a variety of approaches designed to increase client access and promote interagency communication and coordination. These efforts include system-level initiatives such as client-tracking systems, information and referral mechanisms, interagency planning, and formal service agreements (Intagliata, 1982; Rubin, 1987). Another approach to reducing service fragmentation was the development of one-stop "multiservice centers" that brought together a variety of public services under one roof. These programs also often included a "system agent" to coordinate resources for clients and link them to appropriate services (Rubin, 1987).

PL 99-457, the Education of the Handicapped Act Amendments of 1986, includes the mandate that case-level service coordination, or case management, be available to all families with young children who have disabilities if they need and want such services. This major policy statement also institutionalized system-level service coordination concepts such as single portal of entry (Doel, 1991) and interagency planning. The implementation of PL 99-457 has resulted in important changes in the organization of service coordination strategies, according to Anderson, Place, Gallagher, and Eckland (1991). They conclude that prior to 1986, service coordination approaches in early intervention were mostly implemented within single agencies, while much emphasis on developing structures for interagency coordination has been part of PL 99-457 implementation efforts.

There is, as of yet, no published research about child and family service coordination in children's mental health, although a small number of studies are currently underway (Armstrong & Evans, 1992; see Chapter 19). With the exception of the work of Glisson and James (1992), which examines environmental as well as case-level influences on service coordination, the current studies conceptualize case management as an independent variable designed to promote desired outcomes for children and do not address the organizational and interorganizational context of the case management activities.

Beyond children's mental health, a small number of authors discuss the importance of the organizational and system context within which case management is conducted. This is especially the case in the areas of adult mental health and long-term care of the elderly. A few authors more directly address organizational or systems influences on the content or process of case-level service coordination.

For example, in an early article addressing the development of case management services for adults with psychiatric disabilities, Lourie (1978) suggested that effective case management was almost impossible given the structural circumstances that prevailed at the time. He identified lack of services and service fragmentation as two system characteristics that impeded effective case management and suggested that responsibility for case management should be assigned to one agency at the local level.

Norman (1985) suggests that the clinical background of most service coordinators contributes to their tendency to overlook the impact of organizational structure on services. Similarly, Hage (1986) asserted that mental health services would be more effective when properly structured, and this sentiment was echoed by Mechanic and Aiken (1987). They stated that "if case management is to be effective, it must be embedded in an organizational strategy that clearly defines who is responsible for care, that has in place the necessary service elements to provide the full spectrum of needed services, and that can control a range of resources so that balanced decisions can be made" (Mechanic & Aiken, 1987, p. 1635). These authors identify authority, control over financing, and intraorganizational relations as key issues to be resolved. They define the entire system of care as an "organization"; therefore, many of their recommendations address interorganizational issues as well. Authority, funding options, and the organizational location of services are also highlighted by Beatrice (1981) as program design issues in long-term care management.

A few authors identify or propose specific structural options in their respective fields. Intagliata (1982) recommends that special coordinating power and authority be given to a specified agency at the local level and emphasizes the importance of developing formal contracts and interagency agreements among agencies. Steinberg and Carter (1983) state that case management organizations for the elderly are principally influenced by their primary mission, organizational setting, authority base, professional reference groups, and target populations. In a chapter on organizational influences on case management, these authors identify seven types of organizational settings from which case management services for elderly persons are delivered, and they discuss some advantages and disadvantages of each.

Hurth (1992) identifies a number of structural options used by states to improve coordination in the field of early intervention. Her focus tends to be on the organizational position of the case management function in relation to specific early intervention programs.

Hurth's options include: 1) service coordination provided by full-time case managers in settings independent of the early intervention program (e.g., another state agency, private program or agency, or parent or advocacy group); 2) service coordination provided by early intervention programs through a variety of arrangements; 3) interagency teams identify who will function as the service coordinator based on the needs of individual families; or 4) statewide service coordination systems may identify service coordination responsibilities at state, regional, and local levels (can be a mix of options described in the first two items). Also in the field of early intervention, Garland, Woodrudd, and Buck (1988) discuss a variety of team approaches to case management, such as the transdisciplinary team that operates within one agency and a variety of transagency teams, including an arrangement whereby a group of agencies pools funds to hire case managers who provide services to clients from all the agencies in the group.

CONCEPTUAL APPROACHES
TO THE ORGANIZATION OF SERVICE COORDINATION

Two major conceptual approaches are pertinent to thinking about the organization of case management services. The first is concerned with the goals and content of service coordination and addresses such questions as the following: What are the goals of service coordination, what are its core functions, and what are the service coordination tasks that need to be accomplished? Key concepts within this perspective are *continuity* and *accountability*. A second important way of thinking about service coordination focuses on structure and process issues concerned with how service coordination will be carried out. Central issues include the structure and distribution of service coordination roles and tasks, and how and by whom decisions will be made. Key concepts to be examined from this perspective are *authority* and *autonomy*.

Goals and Content of Service Coordination

Definitions of case management often address the goals and purposes of case management. An example is Rubin's (1987) assertion that the general goal of case management is "to ensure that clients with complex, multiple problems and disabilities receive all the services they need in a timely and appropriate fashion" (p. 212). The definition provided by the Virginia Department of Mental Health, Mental Retardation and Substance Abuse Services (1991) also embodies the purpose of case management: "Case management is an intervention which assures that service systems and community supports are maximally responsive to the specific, multiple, and changing needs of individual clients and families" (p. 2). Statements about the purposes of case management services also often contain implicit principles, such as those in Intagliata's (1982) discussion of the purposes of case management: 1) to ensure continuity of care (continuity), 2) to ensure that services will be responsible to the person's full range of needs as they change over time (comprehensiveness and flexibility), 3) to help individuals overcome obstacles and gain access to services (accessibility), and 4) to ensure that services match clients' needs (appropriateness).

Most authors take as given the need for a formal service coordination role, or case management, and approach the definition of that role from a descriptive/normative perspective, discussing either "what is" or "what should be" in terms of the roles and functions of case managers. One common approach is to describe a set of core functions such as assessment, planning, linking, monitoring, and evaluating (Kane, 1988; Rubin, 1987). This approach may also include attempts to distinguish case management from functions such as advocacy or roles such as ombudspersons (Blazyk, Crawford, & Wimberley, 1987).

Another topic that has received considerable attention in the literature concerns the breadth, or comprehensiveness, of service coordination responsibilities. This includes questions such as whether the service coordination function is limited to maintaining liaison with other agencies with whom the client/family is involved or whether the service coordination function should be viewed much more comprehensively, including tasks such as resource development (i.e., locating or creating community resources needed by the family, but not currently available) and advocacy (i.e., helping clients gain access to entitlements and ensuring that their rights are protected). In addition to these client-oriented issues, a few authors also discuss case management as having the potential to bring about system change (Austin, 1990), as well as demonstrate a concern for the effect of case management on clients' lives.

A great deal of the literature in the case management field has been oriented to these concerns. An exclusive focus on the goals and content of case management, however, appears to reflect the assumption that the case management role can be described relatively independently of the characteristics of the service delivery systems, the circumstances of children and their families, and/or the organizational context in which services are delivered.

Another approach to defining what service coordination tasks need to be undertaken is rooted in the concepts of individualized, family-centered services that are increasingly being adopted in the children's mental health field (Burchard & Clarke, 1990; Friesen & Koroloff, 1990; Stroul & Friedman, 1988). This approach uses a contingency framework for developing roles and functions related to service coordination. From this perspective, service coordination roles depend on the needs and preferences of the children and their families and the characteristics of the service delivery system with which they must interact. Within this perspective, service coordination functions are defined as "whatever it takes" (Rubin, 1987) to ensure that children and their families receive the services that they need in a timely fashion. Services are identified and organized on a child-by-child, family-by-family basis and must be flexible to accommodate the dynamic circumstances of children and their families. Thus, the characteristics of the service delivery system and the needs and circumstances of families interact to influence the amount of formal case management service that is necessary, as well as the tasks that need to completed at any given time.

This contingency perspective is not at odds with the normative approach to defining case management (i.e., identifying general functions such as assessing, planning, and linking), but its emphasis is quite different. Here, the focus is shifted from identifying and categorizing case management roles to concerns such as ensuring full and effective family participation in service planning, meeting a wide range of needs that may be identified, and gathering sufficient authority and flexibility to address changing needs over time.

Continuity The concept of continuity is central to the service coordination function. Ideally, well-coordinated services should constitute what some have called a seamless web (i.e., smooth transitions from one service to the next). In this chapter the term *continuity* embodies three aspects that are summarized in Table 4.1. First, within specific programs, continuity refers to the ability to provide uninterrupted service over time. Issues such as scheduling and deployment of staff, program stability, and staff turnover all affect continuity within programs. A second aspect of continuity is related to cross-program and interagency phenomena and addresses coordination of actions and resources (keeping disruption to a minimum) across programs and organizations as the child and his or her family use a variety of formal and informal services. The third aspect of continuity is child specific and refers to the easing of transitions across developmental stages or statuses (e.g., beginning school, entering puberty, or entering or leaving formal services) (Koroloff,

Table 4.1. Key concepts in service coordination

Concept	Description of related activity	Terms	Level/focus
Continuity	Providing uninterrupted service over time	Interagency continuity	Intra-agency
	Minimizing disruption as children and families use formal and informal services across agencies and programs	Interorganizational continuity	Interorganizational
	Easing transitions across developmental stages or statuses	Child-specific continuity	Child/family
Accountability	Responding to needs and preferences of the people who receive services	Child and family accountability	Child/family
	Providing evidence to stakeholders of conformity to program, legal, and fiscal requirements	Organizational accountability	Program/ organization
	Sharing responsibility for joint action	Verbal/social contract	Group engaged in joint endeavor
Formal authority	Making decisions about issues by virtue of power and perogative vested in an organizational position or legal status	Authority	Organizational/ formal or legal
Interpersonal influence	Affecting or altering the behaviors of another based on sources of power such as personal characteristics, expertise, and opportunity	Influence	Interpersonal, informal
Autonomy	Having sufficient freedom and flexibility to provide responsive services	Case-level autonomy	Child/family
	Maintaining freedom to act independently of other organizations	Organizational autonomy	Program or agency

1990). Because of their nature, services such as foster care or residential treatment, which involve changes in the young person's living situation, require more effort to minimize disjunctive experiences (i.e., to maximize continuity).

Accountability With respect to service coordination, the concept of accountability is both a value and a goal and involves three main ideas (see Table 4.1). The first aspect of accountability, that of the responsibility to answer to the needs and preferences of the people who receive services, or "clients," is identified by Gates (1980) as "the dominant ethic of the social service professions" (p. 84). This chapter uses the term *child and family accountability* to refer to this concern.

The second aspect of accountability, tied to formal organizational and fiscal requirements, involves what Gates (1980) calls "legitimate sources of authority and influence" (p. 65) and includes organizations, programs, and individuals as all having the capacity of being accountable. Gates suggests that responsiveness to legitimate authority constitutes accountability and that lack of responsiveness to legitimate authority is unaccountable behavior. When no legitimate source of authority either exists or chooses to exercise influence, behavior is discretionary, according to Gates. This emphasis on formal, legitimate authority is also implicit in Rossi and Freeman's (1989) concept of accountability as the responsibility of program staff to provide evidence to stakeholders and sponsors about conformity to program coverage, treatment, and legal and fiscal requirements. This chapter uses the term *formal accountability* to describe this second aspect of accountability.

Taber (1988) takes quite a different view when he proposes that "accountability is where all key actors are accountable to all others in terms of their joint action, where information required by actors is available to them in time, and where each person responsible for the joint outcome has appropriate power to intervene" (p. 116). From this perspective, accountability can be established by mutual consent and may or may not involve formal mechanisms such as written agreements. Because much of the joint planning that occurs for the purpose of coordinating services at the case level is of this type, resting on the coordination and goodwill of representatives of a variety of agencies, this third aspect of accountability, the "verbal/social contract," is especially important.

Structure and Process of Service Coordination

Although the need for system-level coordination is almost universally acknowledged by authors writing in the case management field, there is considerable controversy about the need for either separate programs or for separate roles to accomplish the service coordination function at the case level. One position in this debate is articulated by Lamb (1980) and Ashley (1988), among others, who argue that for adults with long-term psychiatric disabilities the service coordination function must be joined with the therapeutic function in the primary therapist. Advocates of this position address the issue of structure at least implicitly when they argue for the service coordination function to be diffused throughout service delivery agencies, attached to lead, or primary, therapists. Others (e.g., Kanter, 1989) appear to accept as given a separately constituted case management program, but argue strongly that the role of case managers must include a clinical function.

Lourie (1978) was among the first to argue for a systems response that clarified which organizations were responsible for case management. Addressing service coordination for adults with long-term psychiatric disabilities, he maintained that service would be disjointed if each categorical service provider attempted to perform comprehensive service rather than carrying out their more specialized functions, especially when cases belong to other systems. Over the last 15 years, this perspective has been further developed and supported within the adult mental health field (i.e., formal assignment of case management responsibility for specific clients to clearly identified community systems) (Brekke & Test, 1992). Two sets of concepts important to achieving effective service coordination are the ability to get things done (authority and influence) and the degree to which individuals and organizations can act independently or are likely to be interdependent and work together (autonomy). We assert that these conditions are often a function of how service delivery is organized. This proposition is discussed in the following sections and illustrated through the various organizational options that are presented.

Authority and Influence   These terms refer to power, or the ability of the case manager to "make things happen" on behalf of children and their families. Bacharach and Lawler (1981) identify four sources of power: 1) structural or position, 2) personal characteristics, 3) expertise (specialized information), and 4) opportunity. They suggest that the term *authority* should be reserved for formal organizational or interorganizational relationships. Authority refers to the situation in which a person has the right to make the final decision about a given issue because the power to make that decision has been vested in the position occupied by the decision maker. In other words, it is possible to identify the range of decision-making power associated with each position in an organization; that power constitutes the authority associated with each role (e.g., supervisor, case worker, executive director). Authority is clearly tied to organizational structure and formal (probably written) arrangements. As Bacharach and Lawler characterize it, authority is "zero sum"; a person either has the right to make a decision or he or she does not. Authority is not relative. The concept of authority also includes legal rights, such as the ability of parents to give permission for medical procedures or to sign individualized education programs (IEPs).

In contrast to the zero sum and absolute nature of authority, the term *influence* is relative and refers to the ability of one person to affect or alter the behavior of another. Influence is not based on organizational position but rather relies on the other sources of power identified by Bacharach and Lawler (1981)—personal characteristics, expertise, and opportunity. Wimpfheimer, Bloom, and Kramer (1990) suggest that authority is an organizational term, while influence involves interpersonal skills at persuasion. Structural position and opportunity are the two sources of power that are mostly clearly tied to (and are dependent on) the organizational configuration, or structure of services, while influence related to personal characteristics and expertise is relatively independent of position and the structure of the organization.

Autonomy   Both at the case and organizational level, the term *autonomy* refers to the degree of control that a person or organization has over its environment; that is, it refers to the ability to make decisions (Rogers & Whetten, 1982). Autonomy carries two very different meanings, however, depending on the level of concern. At the case level, the person carrying out the service coordination functions must have sufficient freedom to act on behalf of children and their families, especially when operating within a flexible, "whatever it takes" service philosophy. Thus, greater autonomy for individual workers is desirable and is likely to be linked to greater service effectiveness. Rogers and Whetten (1982) comment on the need for service coordinators to have autonomy in their discussion of potential tensions and conflict associated with interagency coordination:

> Personal role tension and stress can develop for "boundary spanners," individuals whose roles require that they frequently cross the boundaries of their organizations to plan and act jointly with representatives of other organizations. Boundary spanners may experience tension and stress when their roles are ambiguous, when they are subject to conflicting demands, and when their autonomy is too limited. (p. 135)

Although autonomy is a desirable condition for the individual case manager, at the organizational level, the concept of service coordination and organizational autonomy are likely to be at odds.

Rogers and Whetten (1982) point out that organizations commonly attempt to maintain their power with respect to other organizations and adopt interorganizational strategies that least affect their autonomy. These authors also hypothesize that service coordination strategies such as joint ventures that involve more permanent, higher-ranking persons are more likely to pose threats to organizational autonomy than less formal, temporary arrangements among lower-ranking personnel. This suggests that attempts to develop written interagency agreements to address issues such as the flow of clients or allocation of funds are more likely to be seen as potential threats to organizational autonomy than strategies such as interagency case conferences about specific children and their families.

STRUCTURAL OPTIONS FOR SERVICE COORDINATION

In the following section, organizational options are presented to illustrate the general proposition that service coordination tasks are affected by the organizational arrangements in which they are imbedded. The authors describe eight structural options and discuss some apparent advantages and limitations of each. These options are derived both from a review of the literature and from an analysis of currently operating programs; thus, they represent both actual and potential organizational arrangements. No single option is identified as the most desirable; each has advantages and limitations. Preferences for one option over another are likely to be affected by philosophical and theoretical considerations, as well as by practical issues such as the options that already exist in a given community, their history, and perceived effectiveness.

Two important issues that affect all service coordination options are the importance of family participation and the extent to which the lack of services interferes with appropriate service coordination. The participation of the family (and child, when possible) in service planning and decision making will maximize the extent to which the services planned are appropriate and acceptable to the child and his or her family, thus increasing child and family accountability. Although ensuring family participation increases the complexity of service planning, communication, and practical issues, such as the scheduling of meetings, full family participation is a principle that should be implemented across all structural options. The lack of needed services for any given child and his or her family, as well as the general resource circumstances of each community, clearly interact with and shape the role of the service coordinator and influence the resources needed to maximize effective service delivery. When needed services do not exist, more time and energy of the service coordinator will be spent developing resources than in a relatively service-rich environment and access to a pool of flexible funds, so critical to individualizing services, becomes even more important.

The following eight options range from a circumstance where no formal service system resources are invested in the case management function (family as case manager) to a separate organization developed solely for the purpose of providing service planning and coordination to children and their families who are receiving services from a variety of community agencies and from informal sources. The description of each option is supported by a diagrammatic illustration of the approach to organizing service represented by the option.

Option I: Family as Case Manager

Under this option, service coordination is provided by families of children with serious emotional disorders (Figure 4.1). Family members usually assume service coordination responsibilities under one of two major conditions. Either the family chooses service coordina-

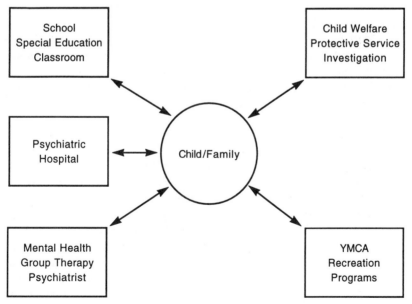

Figure 4.1. Family as case manager.

tion responsibility, their expertise is acknowledged and they either have resources of their own or are provided adequate resources, or (more likely) the family has service coordination responsibility because no other assistance is available. This chapter's discussion of this option assumes that families have chosen to assume the service coordination responsibility for their own children, but that they are not being compensated for this activity. A discussion about parents or other family members acting as paid service coordinators is provided by Ignelzi and Dague (Chapter 17).

Advantages Family members have expertise about the child's history, behavior, strengths, and interests that is invaluable in building an appropriate service plan. Given their relationship to the child and the likelihood that they will be available as the child experiences transitions across developmental stages, the family's commitment promotes continuity of concern about the child's developmental, emotional, and behavioral needs. This option probably provides more long-term attention to the easing of the child through various developmental stages than any of the other service coordination options examined in this chapter.

Accountability of service coordination at the child and family level is likely to be assured because families will most likely pursue services and programs based on their self-interests. This option focuses responsibility for coordinating the array of service efforts and programs used by the family with the family.

Within this option, families have the authority to make decisions about which services are appropriate and they may act as autonomously as needed on behalf of their child. They act without constraint because they can elect to use services or decide not to use them, depending on their child's particular needs and circumstances.

Limitations Although family members are in a good position to provide a long-term view and to attend to the issue of continuity as it relates to the child's development, continuity of services may be difficult to arrange, especially when several service providers are involved. Family members are the primary institution for ensuring and promoting mental health; however, they do not control the "seamless web" of services their child needs. The degree of child and family accountability on the part of formal service providers is dependent on mutual agreement between them and the family about specific goals and objectives. Family members may not always have the support of service providers to address their children's particular needs based on the family's definition and choice. Because most organizations' funding and other resources do not directly depend on how well they achieve consumer or family satisfaction, very little formal accountability exists within this option unless it is established through formal written agreements.

Another possible limitation of using families as case managers is related to the demands of service coordination tasks. The additional time, expenses, and resources needed to perform service planning and coordination tasks may be excessive for many family members, especially those who are employed full time.

For the most part, family members do not have formal authority within the service delivery system. One exception is mandated family participation in individualized education programming in special education (through PL 94-142 [Education for All Handicapped Children Act of 1975] and PL 101-476 [Individuals with Disabilities Education Act of 1990]), whereby family members must approve and sign the IEP and have access to legal remedies when disagreements about the appropriate plans and programs for their children cannot be resolved. When family members have no formal authority, they must rely on interpersonal influence strategies with service providers. When attempts at interpersonal influence fail, the child and his or her family may have to accept a set of services that may not meet their expectations and needs.

Although families have a great deal of autonomy, the nature of service coordination requires interdependence. Thus, the exercise of a great deal of autonomy by family members may decrease their ability to work with others. Service providers also vary according to how they operate and with regard to the value they place on family participation in service delivery. Some service providers may not view family members as part of the solution and may be reluctant to relate to them in a service provision role. Conflicts may arise especially when the family service coordinator and formal service providers differ in their preferences and beliefs about appropriate services. Training for family members assuming service coordination responsibilities and for the service providers with whom they work should ease misunderstandings and clarify roles.

Summary   The advantages of Option I are as follows:

- Family has expertise about the child's history, behavior, strengths, and preferences.
- Family has a long-term commitment; family members are likely to carry major responsibility for advocacy over time.
- Family members are able to make decisions and sign off on a service plan.
- Family can act without organizational constraint.

- Family has experience in dealing with child's transitions across developmental stages and significant life events.

Limitations include the following:

- Family cannot make system accountable to them.
- Family has no authority over service organizations and cannot act on behalf of the organization/system.
- Family depends on the action of others; if service providers do not act, service coordination efforts are stymied.
- Family has no way to ensure continuity within and between programs and services.

Option II: Intra-agency, Decentralized

Under this option, service coordination functions are performed by the child's and family's primary therapist or service provider as an additional and often secondary responsibility (Figure 4.2). The rationale often given by proponents of this option is that there is no need for specialized or additional service coordination because the child's and family's needs can be addressed by the person(s) who works most closely with them. In fact, separate case management functions impose an unnecessary layer of bureaucracy. The organization is generally not paid a separate fee for service coordination and performs this function until the child and his or her family are no longer eligible for therapy or other primary service.

Advantages   Continuity of service is a function of the relationship among the child, family, and therapist. Service coordination is accomplished by having one person perform both therapy or other direct services and service coordination activities. This single point of service coordination assigns responsibility for the identification

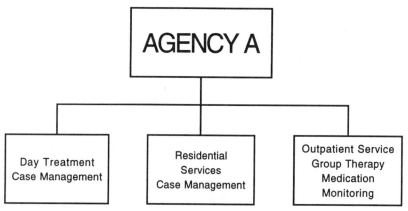

Figure 4.2.   Intra-agency, decentralized.

of problems, goals, objectives, services, and outcomes of service delivery to a key person; accountability is focused in one service provider. Within a single agency, formal organizational and fiscal accountability is high. When the family and service provider develop a mutually agreed-upon plan, child and family accountability is also enhanced. This option allows for the centralization of decision making and decreases the need for communication between the child and his or her family and other staff. The degree of authority to act on behalf of the child and his or her family is also high when family members agree with the plan of action. The autonomy of manager is a function of the structure and policies of each agency. Staff are more likely to be able to act with relatively few constraints within their own organizations compared to interagency settings.

Limitations   Continuity of service coordination is usually interrupted when agency services are terminated. Clearly, this poses a problem to the child and his or her family who may no longer need a particular service but need ongoing service coordination. Service coordination is often seen as secondary to the main activity of providing treatment, and persons trained as educators or therapists may not necessarily have training in case management. When the child and his or her family need service from more than one agency, the increase in the number of people, their agendas, and competing program policies and decisions may reduce continuity. The same holds true for accountability when several organizations are involved. The lack of a formally designated person to coordinate the host of services and programs among service providers may decrease the likelihood that service coordination activities are performed optimally. This problem is at least partially addressed when there is a specific interagency agreement about who should take the lead with respect to service coordination.

In the absence of a formal agreement, the therapist assigned to this role will not have formal authority across organizations and agencies and must rely on interpersonal influence to get things done. To the degree that planning serves to reduce the autonomy of the agencies involved (appropriately constraining and channeling the behavior of multiple players on behalf of the child and his or her family), conflict among representatives of various agencies or resistance to joint action may be an issue.

Summary   The advantages of Option II include the following:

- One person is responsible for service coordination.
- The therapist/service coordinator sees the child and/or his or her family on a regular basis.

- Service coordination is provided as long as the child is eligible for service.

Limitations are as follows:

- Service coordination is a secondary activity; time and reimbursement are issues.
- The service coordinator may experience accountability dilemmas when the child needs more than one service within the same agency or from other service providers.
- The service coordinator does not have formal authority with respect to other agencies.
- The high autonomy of the service coordinator could threaten collaboration within and among service providers.
- Continuity of service coordination is disrupted when the child no longer requires services from a primary therapist.

Option III: Intra-agency, Specialized Unit (Internally Oriented)

The rationale for this option is that service coordination is best handled by people who have the time, training, and commitment to specialize in this function (Figure 4.3). Under this option, a specialized unit within an agency provides service coordination for children and their families across that agency's programs. Compared with Option II, this option places more emphasis on the service coordination function.

Advantages Service coordination is a central (and possibly billable) service. Responsibility for service coordination is assigned to staff members as a primary function; service coordination tasks are not subordinated to other service delivery tasks. As long as the child and his or her family are eligible for services from the agency, *continuity* is preserved. Staff accountability to the child and his or her family is high, because the responsibility is focused. At the organization level, formal accountability may be enhanced when the service coordination unit has intra-agency department service plans that link services in an integrated and planful way. Service coordinators are likely to have formal authority and administrative support for their roles within their organizations. They may also have considerable influence within their own organization as a function of their access to resources and information.

Limitations Continuity of services to the child and his or her family may be interrupted if service coordination is tied to the need for other services of the agency (i.e., if the child and family lose eligibility for service coordination when other services are terminated). Compared with the therapist/service coordinator option, a

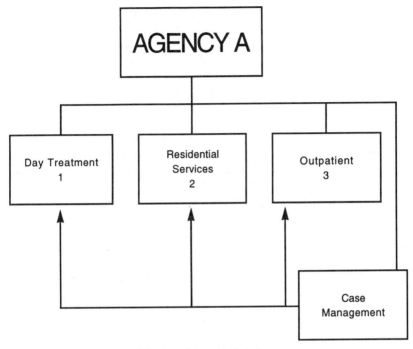

Figure 4.3. Intra-agency, specialized unit (internally oriented).

separate service coordination function is likely to increase the complexity of communication within the organization. This option adds another "player" that the child and his or her family deals with, if not another "layer" of bureaucracy. When the child and his or her family requires services outside the organization, program accountability becomes complicated as the number of involved agencies increases. As in Option II, the service coordinator has no formal authority with respect to other organizations, and accountability is created through interagency plans and agreements for each family, as well as through verbal contracts with others.

Summary   Option III advantages include the following:

- Service coordination is seen as central (and possibly billable) service.
- Responsibility for service coordination is vested with a designated person, thus promoting accountability.

Limitations are as follows:

- The continuity of service coordination activity may be disrupted when the child no longer requires services from the agency.

- There is an increased complexity of intra-agency communication when other layers and players are added.
- When service coordination between agencies is needed, the service coordinator lacks formal authority vis-à-vis other agencies.
- Attempts to develop formal agreement among agencies (limit autonomy and promote coordination) may create conflict and resistance.

Option IV: Intra-agency, Specialized Unit (Externally Oriented)

The expansion of service coordination as a funded service presents opportunities for agencies to diversify and expand their service delivery capabilities (Figure 4.4). Under this option, an agency is paid to provide case management services to children and their families who are not necessarily enrolled in its other services. The eligible service population may be based on a geographic service area or may consist of clients of other designated service organizations. This option is generally developed when the funding source (e.g., the state mental health authority) believes that existing agencies have the capability and willingness to provide service coordination.

Advantages The inclusion of service coordination activities

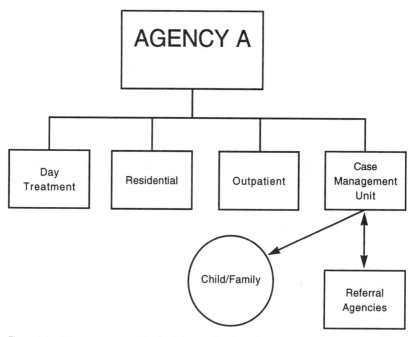

Figure 4.4.   Intra-agency, specialized unit (externally oriented).

provides an additional revenue base for the agency and expands the agency's service capacity. Service coordination is a central (and billable) service; service coordination needs are not subordinated to other service delivery tasks. The child and his or her family can receive these services as long as they are eligible for the case management services. Thus, continuity is not tied to the services of a single agency. Compared with Options II and III, service coordination is more likely to be long term. Because the funding source is likely to give authority for service coordination through a contracting process and to promote interagency agreements, accountability of service providers to the child and his or her family is enhanced. Under this option, much of the responsibility for dealing with agencies' responses to threats to autonomy is shifted from the individual service coordinator to the funding source (contractor).

Limitations   Conflict of interest may be a problem if the needs of the lead agency are at odds with the needs of children in families (e.g., if the lead agency wants its services to be given preference). In this case, the lead agency may attempt to limit the autonomy of the service coordination unit or individual case managers. When the funding source does not act to formalize relationships among agencies, service coordinators lack formal authority, and their influence vis-à-vis other organizations is based on goodwill and mutual consent.

Summary   Option IV advantages include the following:

- Service coordination is a central (and billable) service.
- Service coordination is vested in one person or team.
- The service coordination contract enhances agency capacity and provides additional revenue base for the agency.
- Accountability and authority are usually supported by formal agreements.
- Continuity of service coordination is preserved as long as the child and his or her family are eligible for service coordination.

Limitations are as follows:

- The potential exists for conflict of interest between the lead agency and its service coordination unit.
- In the absence of formal agreements among agencies, accountability and authority are weakened.

Option V: Interagency Team, Ad Hoc

Under this option, representatives from multiple agencies with whom the family is involved, family members, and the child (when possible) meet to develop service plans and service coordination options (Figure 4.5). Each agency representative may be the "primary therapist," or lead service provider, within his or her own agency. A coordinated response from all involved reduces duplication, confusion, and unintended stress for the family and reduces duplication and overlap of services.

Advantages Continuity of service provision is variable but higher than single agency Options II and III, assuming that the interagency committee continues to meet over time. Child and family accountability is enhanced by having family participation and agreement across agencies about the most appropriate services and distribution of responsibility. Written interagency service plans formalize this mutual consent and facilitate service monitoring. Formal authority for service coordination does not exist under this option. If all member agencies and the family reach consensus about the service plan and agree to do what they indicate in the service plan, then accountability is enhanced through a social contract assumed by group members.

Limitations Continuity may be affected by staff changes or if the child and his or her family no longer meet eligibility requirements for multiple agencies. The service coordination function is often seen as secondary because agency representatives have other primary (therapeutic, educational) responsibilities. Accountability across programs and services is low without formal agreement. Des-

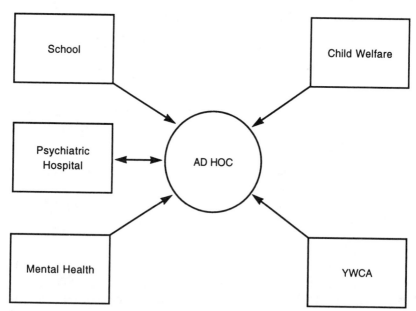

Figure 4.5.   Interagency team, ad hoc.

ignation of a "lead" case manager in this model is usually added to other service provision tasks (as in the intra-agency decentralized model). Interdependence of the interagency committee is necessary to orchestrate the array of services used by the child and his or her family and the development of written agreements among interagency representatives and their agencies. The interagency team may be subject to interagency politics and agendas.

Authority for ensuring that the service plan is followed is derived from the goodwill and intentions of agency personnel. Development of a formal service plan partially addresses this problem and enhances accountability. However, service coordination may be impeded when players lack sufficient authority to make decisions or commit resources on behalf of their respective agencies. Holding ad hoc meetings around each child and his or her family is also very time consuming, and this option may not be feasible if service providers have a large number of clients and many complex cases.

Summary   The advantages of Option V include the following:

- Good working relationships and clear communication are facilitated among agency representatives and between the family and the service system.
- Service plans developed by multiple agencies are more likely to be comprehensive than plans developed by single agencies.
- Accountability is enhanced through a formal service plan.
- Continuity is higher than other single agency service coordination options because many service providers work together on behalf of the child and his or her family and service coordination efforts do not end when any single service is terminated.

Limitations are as follows:

- The designation of a "lead case manager role" is usually added to other responsibilities.
- Team members are subject to the agendas of their own agencies.
- The continuity of service coordination may be impaired by staff or agency changes.
- Usually, there is no formal authority; enforcement of agreements is based on goodwill.
- Ad hoc meetings are time consuming.
- It is not feasible with a large number of clients and many complex cases.

Option VI: Interagency Team, Standing Coordinating Committee

This service coordination arrangement often exists around a specific set of issues or decisions (e.g., whether a child should be admitted to the state hospital, placed out of the home, or receive access to flexible funds) (Figure 4.6). A standing committee is often used to plan and authorize services for children with very complex needs that have not been successfully addressed by other means. This type of group, therefore, often has a gate-keeping and/or resource distribution function. Responsibility for service coordination may be assigned to a lead member, but often actual service coordination responsibility is not carried out by committee members.

Advantages Stability of the group is enhanced by permanent membership. Team members may collect information and perspectives on community needs that can lead to system or policy changes. When the focus is on the organization and system level, accountability is high because the purpose of the team is to make decisions regarding expenditures, distribution, and allocation of resources. Child and family accountability is enhanced as long as the group membership maintains a family-centered perspective. Formal authority and accountability of the group to develop sound policies and programs are enhanced through formal agreement and permanent membership.

Limitations Continuity of services for specific children and their families may not be affected by the work of the committee when attention is focused on system needs. Team dynamics may reflect or be affected by interagency relationships. When the focus is on the

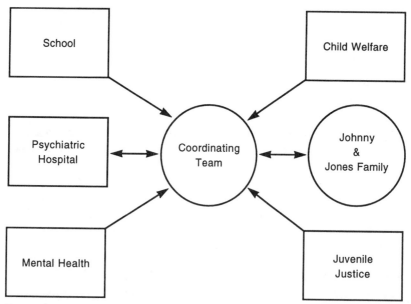

Figure 4.6. Interagency team, standing coordinating committee.

child and his or her family, the degree of child and family accountability is variable because this option's focus is often on the system as the unit of attention. Responsibility for service coordination is often designated to staff from participating agencies. Overall, accountability is dependent on the goodwill of each agency, the existence of written agreements, and the stability of membership.

Although no one agency has the authority to make decisions about how another organization will distribute resources, some interagency bodies address this issue through formal agreements, including the pooling of funds. The committee may or may not monitor decisions made with regard to individual children and their families.

Summary The advantages of Option VI include the following:

- Committee accountability is enhanced when there are formal agreements and the focus is on the organization and system.
- Team members have a responsibility for making decisions about expenditures and resource allocation.
- Team members may collect information and perspectives on community needs that can lead to system or policy changes.

Limitations are as follows:

- The focus is often not on the child and his or her family but on system needs.
- The team may not have enforcement responsibility for the service plan.

Option VII: Semi-autonomous Case Management Unit

The rationale for this option is that service coordination is best handled by people who have the time, training, and commitment to specialize in this function and that the service coordination unit will have appropriate autonomy and perhaps provide services in an equitable manner if it is not physically or administratively tied to any specific agency (Figure 4.7). This arrangement is designed to increase the autonomy of the service coordination function and to reduce problems associated with Options V and VI. Under this option, participating agencies come together to create a separate case management unit, either by donating personnel or by pooling funds to hire service coordinators. Service coordination is provided to children and their families from all participating agencies. Such arrangements are often governed by a board or coordinating committee consisting of representatives from participating agencies.

Advantages Because eligibility is not dependent on a single agency, continuity of service is enhanced. Service coordination is a

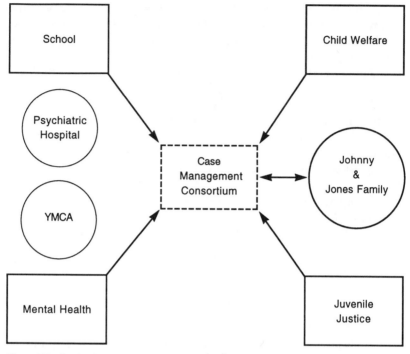

Figure 4.7. Semi-autonomous case management unit.

central (and perhaps billable) service; service coordination needs are not subordinated to other service delivery tasks. Child and family accountability is enhanced because the primary focus is on the child and his or her family, although as always, this is dependent on the extent to which the child and his or her family are included in decision making. Accountability across organizations is enhanced to the extent that the arrangement includes a commitment on the part of the participating agencies to abide by the service plan. Conflicts among agencies or between service coordinators and agencies can be resolved by appeal to the board or coordinating committee. Formal authority is often derived from the interagency agreement that creates this entity.

Limitations The existence of the service coordination unit is dependent on resources from the participating agencies. Formal authority is "borrowed," in that it is derived from agencies that create it, and if workers are donated (salaries paid by each participating agency), conflict of interest may exist when workers need to monitor and enforce service plans with respect to their own agencies. Autonomy of the service coordination unit will vary according to the inter-agency agreement that created it. The service coordination unit may be subject to political pressures, or if it gains too much power or asserts its influence too strongly, it may be abolished by its creators. In addition, under conditions of scarce resources, specialized service coordination units are often cut to preserve "core" services.

Summary   The advantages of Option VII are summarized as follows:

- Service coordination is seen as a central (and perhaps billable) service.
- Competing demands and agendas felt by individual service coordinators from their own agencies may be reduced by formal agreement.
- Authority is often derived from an interagency agreement that creates an entity.
- Accountability is enhanced because member agencies buy into the need for a service plan and agree to monitor the service plan.
- The coordinating committee is available to settle disputes.
- Continuity is enhanced compared to single agency options.

Limitations include the following:

- The existence of a service coordination unit depends on resources from participating agencies.
- Authority is "borrowed."
- The service coordination function may be subject to political pressures.
- Funding of the service coordination unit is vulnerable to cuts and is likely to be of lesser priority than primary services of participating agencies.

Option VIII: Autonomous Case Management Agency

The rationale for this option is that case managers must have sufficient autonomy, authority, and resources to do their jobs, and these conditions are best met through a separate, autonomous agency whose sole function is to provide case management services (Figure 4.8). Creation of a separate service coordination agency creates the necessary autonomy and may or may not address the authority and resources question, depending on the funding source and legal mandates. Many autonomous case management agencies have flexible funds and are also charged with resource development.

Advantages   Service coordination is a central (and billable) service. Service coordination functions are not subordinated to other service delivery tasks. The existence of this type of agency reflects

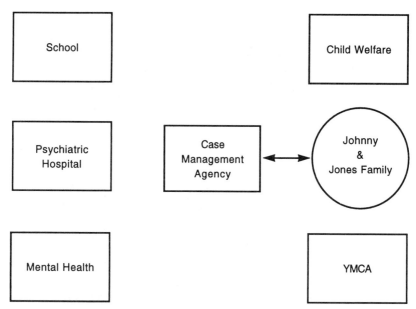

Figure 4.8.   Autonomous case management agency.

the commitment of the funding agency (e.g., state mental health or child welfare agency) to service coordination as a central function. Continuity, accountability, authority, and autonomy are enhanced as long as the child and his or her family are eligible for services and the agency has control of funds and is sanctioned as a regulatory agent. Continuity of services within and between agencies is also preserved. The child and his or her family and formal accountability issues are addressed if this agency also has control of service dollars and/or has regulatory authority. Service coordinators are not directly affected by multiple agency agendas, although they must build relationships across a number of agencies from the "outside." This option eliminates the conflict of interest problems associated with Options VI and VII. Staff are specialized and trained.

Limitations   In conditions of scarce resources, specialized service coordination funds are often cut to preserve "core" services. This option includes an additional service delivery layer and creates a new organization that, although designed to promote coordination and flexibility, may become institutionalized, bureaucratized, and inflexible.

Summary   The advantages of Option VIII include the following:

- Service coordination is a central (and billable) service.
- The existence of this agency reflects the commitment of the funding agency to service coordination.

- Accountability, authority, autonomy, and continuity are enhanced.

Limitations include the following:

- The service coordination agency is subject to funding cuts.
- It is an additional layer of bureaucracy.

CONCLUSION

This chapter postulates that the organizational and interorganizational context of service coordination activities can have a profound effect on the way these services are delivered. To illustrate this argument, eight possible ways are proposed that service coordination activities are, or could be, organized. Each of these ways is examined in terms of how the key concepts of continuity, accountability, authority, and autonomy may be enhanced or inhibited by the organizational arrangements in question. The ideas presented in this chapter should be considered as beginning steps toward the application of organizational and interorganizational knowledge to service coordination in children's mental health. This chapter's analysis of the structural options and the possible advantages and limitations of each option are supported in some cases by existing research, but in many cases they represent the authors' best judgment about the likely effects of the various structural relationships. They should, therefore, be considered propositions that require further study, and the authors look forward to systematic examination and refinement of their work.

Clearly, the options this chapter presents do not include one "perfect" structure that would be appropriate for every community situation. In addition, options that work well during one era may be less appropriate as new issues emerge in the service delivery system and the interorganizational environment. It is hoped that the conceptual tools presented will stimulate the examination of existing approaches to service coordination, as well as the thoughtful design and testing of new strategies to promote effective, coordinated responses to the needs of children with emotional, behavioral, and mental disorders and their families.

REFERENCES

Anderson, K., Place, P., Gallagher, J., & Eckland, J. (1991). *Status of states' policies that affect families: Case management.* Chapel Hill: University of North Carolina at Chapel Hill, Carolina Policy Studies Program.

Anthony, W.A., & Blanch, A. (1989). Research on community support services: What have we learned? *Psychosocial Rehabilitation Journal, 12*(3), 55–81.

Armstrong, M.I., & Evans, M.E. (1992). Three intensive community-based programs for children and youth with serious emotional disturbance and their families. *Journal of Child and Family Studies, 1*(1), 61–74.

Ashley, A. (1988). Case management: The need to define goals. *Hospital and Community Psychiatry, 39*(5), 499–500.

Austin, C.D. (1990). Case management: Myths and realities. *Families in Society: The Journal of Contemporary Human Services, 71*(7), 398–407.

Bacharach, S.B., & Lawler, E.J. (1981). *Power and politics in organizations.* San Francisco: Jossey-Bass.

Bailey, D.B. (1989). Case management in early intervention. *Journal of Early Intervention, 13*(2), 120–134.

Baker, F., & Vischi, T. (1989). Continuity of care and the control of costs: Can case management assure both? *Journal of Public Health, 10*(2), 204–213.

Beatrice, D.F. (1981). Case management: A policy option for long-term care. In J. J. Callahan & Wallack S. S. (Eds.), *Reforming the long-term-care system: Financial and organizational options* (pp. 121–161). Lexington, MA: Lexington Books.

Blazyk, S., Crawford, C., & Wimberley, T. (1987). The ombudsman and the case manager. *Social Work, 32*(5), 451–453.

Brekke, J.S., & Test, M.A. (1992). A model for measuring the implementation of community support programs: Results from three sites. *Community Mental Health Journal, 28*(3), 227–247.

Burchard, J.D., & Clarke, R.T. (1990). The role of individualized care in a service delivery system for children and adolescents with severely maladjusted behavior. *Journal of Mental Health Administration, 17*(1), 48–60.

Chamberlain, R., & Rapp, C. (1991). A decade of case management: A methodological review of outcome research. *Community Mental Health Journal, 27*(3), 171–188.

Dinerman, M. (1992). Managing the maze: Case management and service delivery. *Administration in Social Work, 16*(1), 1–9.

Doel, M. (1991). *Early intervention systems change: A review of models.* Portland, OR: Systems Change Project, Association of Retarded Citizens.

Economic Opportunity Act, PL 88-452. (August 20, 1964). Title 42, U.S.C. 2701 et seq: *U.S. Statutes at Large, 78,* 508–534.

Education for All Handicapped Children Act of 1975, PL 94-142. (August 23, 1977). Title 20, U.S.C. 1400 et seq: *U.S. Statutes at Large, 89,* 773–796.

Education of the Handicapped Act Amendments of 1986, PL 99-457. (October 8, 1986). Title 20, U.S.C. 1400 et seq: *U.S. Statutes at Large, 100,* 1145–1177.

Friesen, B.J., & Koroloff, N.M. (1990). Family-centered services: Implications for mental health administration and research. *Journal of Mental Health Administration, 17,* 13–25.

Garland, C., Woodrudd, G., & Buck, D.M. (1988). *Case management: Division for Early Childhood white paper.* Washington, DC: Division for Early Childhood, Council for Exceptional Children.

Gates, B.L. (1980). *Social program administration: The implementation of social policy.* Englewood Cliffs, NJ: Prentice Hall.

Gitterman, A., & Miller, I. (1989). The influence of the organization on clinical practice. *Clinical Social Work Journal, 17*(2), 151–164.

Glisson, C., & James, L. (1992). The interorganizational coordination of services to children in state custody. *Administration in Social Work, 16*(3/4), 65–80.

Glisson, C., & Martin, P. (1980). Productivity and efficiency in human service organizations as related to structure, size and age. *Academy of Management Journal, 23*(1), 21–37.

Hage, J. (1986). Conceptualizing mental health delivery systems: Organizational theory applied. In W.R. Scott & B.L. Black, (Eds.), *The organization of mental health services: Societal and community systems* (pp. 53–76). Beverly Hills: Sage Publications.

Hall, R.H. (1991). *Organizations: Structure, processes and outcomes* (5th ed.). Englewood Cliffs, NJ: Prentice Hall.

Hurth, J.L. (1992). *Models of service coordination.* Chapel Hill, NC: National Early Childhood Technical Assistance System.

Individuals with Disabilities Education Act, PL 101-476. (October 30, 1990). Title 20, U.S.C. 1400 et seq: *U.S. Statutes at Large, 104* (part 2), 1103–1151.

Intagliata, J. (1982). Improving the quality of community care for the chronically mentally disabled: The role of case management. *Schizophrenia Bulletin, 8*(4), 655–674.

Kane, R.A. (1988). Crew management: Ethical pitfalls on the road to high-quality managed care. *Quality Review Bulletin, 13,* 161–166.

Kanter, J.S. (1989). Clinical case management: Definition, principles, components. *Hospital and Community Psychiatry, 40*(4), 361–368.

Kettner, P., Daley, J.M., & Nichols, A.W. (1985). *Initiating change in organizations and communities: A macro practice.* Monterey, CA: Brooks Cole.

Koroloff, N.K. (1990). Moving out: Transition policies for youth with serious emotional disabilities. *Journal of Mental Health Administration, 17*(1), 78–86.

Lamb, H.R. (1980). Therapist-case managers: More than brokers of service. *Hospital & Community Psychiatry, 31*(11), 762–765.

Lourie, N.V. (1978). Case management. In J.A. Talbott (Ed.), *The chronic mental patient* (pp. 159–164). Washington, DC: American Psychiatric Association.

Mechanic, D., & Aiken, L. (1987). Improving the care of patients with chronic mental illness. *New England Journal of Medicine, 317*(26), 1634–1638.

Mental Retardation Facilities and Community Mental Health Centers Construction Act of 1963, PL 88-164. (October 31, 1963). Title 42, U.S.C. 2670 et seq: *U.S. Statutes at Large, 77,* 282–298.

Norman, A.J. (1985). Applying theory to practice: The impact of organizational structure on programs and providers. In M. Weil, J.M. Karls, & Associates (Eds.), *Case management in human service practice* (pp. 72–93). San Francisco: Jossey-Bass.

Rogers, D.L., & Whetten, D.A. (1982). *Interorganizational coordination: Theory, research, and implementation.* Ames: Iowa University Press.

Rossi, P.H., & Freeman, H.E. (1989). *Evaluation: A systematic approach.* Newbury Park, CA: Sage Publications.

Rotegard, L., Hill, B., & Bruninks, R. (1983). Environmental characteristics of residential facilities for mentally retarded persons in the United States. *American Journal of Mental Deficiency, 88*(1), 49–56.

Rubin, A. (1987). Case management. In A. Minahan (Ed.), *Encyclopedia of social work* (pp. 212–222). Silver Spring, MD: National Association of Social Workers.

Rubin, A. (1992). Is case management effective for people with serious mental illness? A research review. *Health and Social Work, 17*(2), 138–150.

Spector, W., & Takada, H. (1991). Characteristics of nursing homes that affect resident outcomes. *Journal of Aging and Health, 4*(3), 427–454.

Steinberg, R.M., & Carter, G.W. (1983). *Case management and the elderly.* Lexington, MA: Lexington Books.

Stroul, B.A., & Friedman, R. (1988). Principles for a system of care. *Children Today, 17*(4), 11–15.

Taber, M.A. (1988). A theory of accountability for the human services and the implications for social program design. *Administration in Social Work, 11*(3/4), 115–126.

Trattner, W.I. (1979). *From poor law to welfare state: A history of social welfare in America* (2nd ed.). New York: The Free Press.

Virginia Department of Mental Health, Mental Retardation and Substance Abuse Services. (1991). *Guidelines for case management service delivery.* Richmond: Commonwealth of Virginia, Department of Mental Health, Mental Retardation and Substance Abuse Services.

Wimpfheimer, R., Bloom, M., & Kramer, M. (1990). Inter-agency collaboration: Some working principles. *Administration in Social Work, 14*(4), 89–103.

Financing Care Coordination Services Under Medicaid

Harriette B. Fox and Lori B. Wicks

The Medicaid program can be used to finance a variety of care coordination approaches for the growing number of children and adolescents with emotional disorders who have Medicaid coverage. Although there are no precise data on the number of such youth, Newacheck's (1991) unpublished tabulations from the 1989 National Health Interview Survey revealed that 13.5% of children and adolescents under the age of 19 were enrolled in the Medicaid program in 1989. It can be estimated that approximately 5% of these children and adolescents, some 450,000 Medicaid-enrolled youth, would have had severe emotional problems (Knitzer, 1982). The actual percentage of Medicaid enrollees under the age of 19 with serious emotional disorders is likely to be higher since disabilities are known to be more prevalent among low-income populations.

Furthermore, the number of children and adolescents eligible for Medicaid benefits will increase substantially during the next 10 years. As a result of the 1990 Omnibus Budget Reconciliation Act (OBRA) (PL 101-508), states are now mandated to phase in Medicaid eligibility for all youth age 19 years of age and younger in families with incomes of up to 100% of the federal poverty level on an annual basis. The phase-in began with 6- and 7-year-olds in July of 1991, and will be completed in July of 2001, when all 18-year-olds are covered. This new mandate marked a major departure from previously existing policy, which limited Medicaid coverage for school-age youth primarily to those who receive Aid to Families with Dependent Children (AFDC) or Supplemental Security Income (SSI) cash assitance or to those who participate in foster care or a publicly subsidized adoption program.

In addition, it is likely that there will be more children and adolescents with severe emotional disorders eligible for Medicaid benefits over the next few years as a result of the U.S. Supreme Court

As this book goes to press in March 1995, there is a great deal of uncertainty about how Medicaid benefits will be structured in the future because of proposed Congressional action.

decision in *Sullivan v. Zebley* (1990), which liberalized the eligibility criteria for federal SSI cash assistance benefits. Receipt of SSI benefits qualifies the majority of children for Medicaid coverage in all states but New Hampshire. One state Medicaid program applies more restrictive disability and resource criteria to SSI child applicants; seven other states apply more restrictive income or resource criteria, although in some instances the differences are not very significant. (There are three additional states that apply more restrictive income or resource criteria, but they are applicable only to adult SSI applicants.)

Sullivan was a class action lawsuit on behalf of all children with disabilities who had been denied SSI. The U.S. Supreme Court affirmed a lower court's ruling that the Social Security Administration's (SSA's) regulations had imposed a more rigid disability standard on children than on adults and that the agency would have to establish new rules that permit individual assessments of children's physical and other disabilities.

This chapter demonstrates how Medicaid can be used to pay for a range of care coordination activities aimed at youth who have severe emotional disorders and their families—from basic mental health service coordination to multi-agency case management and comprehensive managed mental health care. The authors also provide information on the ways in which state Medicaid agencies are currently financing care coordination services for this population.

MEDICAID REQUIREMENTS
RELEVANT TO CARE COORDINATION

Medicaid offers a range of options for financing the coordination of services to Medicaid-enrolled children and adolescents. Discrete types of coordination activities, as well as multi-agency comprehensive case management, can be reimbursed by the Medicaid program. In addition, certain kinds of care coordination activities involving the authorization of services can be financed under both fee-for-service and prepaid, capitated arrangements.

There are, however, a number of basic federal Medicaid program requirements that each state's children's mental health program staff must keep in mind when determining the appropriate avenue for obtaining Medicaid reimbursement of the care coordination components of their proposed or operating service delivery systems. These requirements, with few exceptions, apply to all services furnished to Medicaid enrollees unless a state is able to secure a special federal waiver.

The federal Medicaid statute, the Social Security Act (PL 89-97), and accompanying regulations set forth several requirements that are relevant to coverage of care coordination services. These requirements concern *Medicaid enrollees' rights of access* to services and *service providers' rights to participate* in the Medicaid program.

Among the basic federal requirements that states ordinarily must meet to ensure Medicaid enrollees' rights of access to services are the requirements for *statewideness* and *comparability* and the requirement of *freedom of choice* by Medicaid recipients. The *"statewideness"* requirement dictates that all the benefits that a state provides under its Medicaid plan must be available to recipients in all areas of the state.

The comparability requirement provides that, with certain exceptions, all Medicaid recipients who qualify for coverage as categorically needy must have access to the same package of benefits. *Categorically needy* recipients are those who qualify for the regular Medicaid program, as distinct from a medically needy program. These recipients include: 1) persons participating in a cash assistance program, such as AFDC, SSI, or foster care and adoption assistance; 2) persons who meet at least some of the criteria for AFDC or SSI cash assistance and are covered either under a federal mandate or under a state option; and 3) children and pregnant women given "qualified" categorically needy status on the basis of low or moderate income.

Certain limited exceptions to the comparability requirement exist without federal waiver approval. Each of these exceptions is important to the financing of child and adolescent services. Under the Early and Periodic Screening, Diagnosis, and Treatment (EPSDT) program, a state is required to furnish children and adolescents, who are 21 years of age or younger, all medically necessary diagnostic and treatment services that are federally allowed under Section 1905(a) of the Medicaid statute, even if the services are not otherwise covered in the state plan. There is no comparability requirement to furnish this service to adults. Under the targeted case management benefit, a state is permitted to restrict the availability of case management services to a specific population group or geographic area. No other Medicaid service may be limited in this way. Under Section 1915(a) of the federal Medicaid statute, a state that has contracted with a health maintenance organization (HMO) or prepaid health plan (PHP) to serve enrollees in a particular geographic area on a prepaid basis may include services that are federally allowable but not otherwise reimbursable under the state plan. This opportunity is not available except where Medicaid enrollees agree to participate in a capitated arrangement on a voluntary basis.

The comparability requirement also applies to all recipients who qualify for coverage as medically needy, although services available to the medically needy cannot be more generous than those available to the categorically needy. *Medically needy* recipients are those who qualify for Medicaid benefits under a special eligibility option available to states. A state may establish a medically needy program to extend eligibility to low-income individuals who meet the categorical, but not the financial, criteria for cash-assistance–related Medicaid eligibility. States are able to set medically needy income standards at levels of up to 133⅓% of the maximum AFDC payment standard for similar-size families. Through a spend-down provision, individuals with incomes above the medically needy standard also may become eligible if their medical expenses are high enough to reduce their countable income below the medically needy maximum.

The freedom-of-choice requirement establishes that states must permit all Medicaid enrollees to receive covered services from any qualified provider of that service, including one who provides or arranges for it on a prepaid basis. There are only a few limited situations in which states are exempt from the freedom-of-choice requirement without obtaining a federal waiver under Section 1915(b) of the federal Medicaid statute. The broadest exception is for recipients who use Medicaid-covered services inappropriately. At a state's option, these recipients may be "locked in" to a single service provider, or group of service providers, for a reasonable amount of time and with certain safeguards in order to control their utilization. Another of the exceptions is that a state may enter into a contract to purchase laboratory and X-ray services and medical devices for Medicaid recipients. The state must certify, however, that adequate services or devices are available under the arrangements, that laboratory services are purchased from facilities meeting certain ownership and quality of care criteria, and that participating laboratories base no more than 75% of their charges on services to Medicaid enrollees.

Two key federal requirements that are relevant to the delivery of care coordination services govern service providers' rights to participate in the Medicaid program. One requirement pertains to the qualifications for providing services. State Medicaid agencies are free to establish service provider qualification standards for Medicaid services, but federal law requires that such standards be reasonable and objective and that they not serve to arbitrarily deny participation by any type of service provider. Once qualification standards have been established, the state must allow all service providers who meet them to participate in the program in order to ensure maximum freedom of choice for Medicaid enrollees.

The other requirement pertains to the conditions that must be met by service providers or other entities who submit claims for reimbursement. As a general rule, state Medicaid agencies are permitted to accept billings from and provide reimbursement only to the direct provider of a Medicaid service. There are a number of situations set forth in the law, however, under which a direct service provider's claim for reimbursement can be submitted by another entity. Payment for an individual practitioner service may be made to the practitioner's employer if that is a condition of employment, to the facility in which the care is furnished if this arrangement is part of the contractual agreement between the independent practitioner and the facility, or to a governmental agency if the practitioner has assigned payment to that agency. In addition, a practitioner may use a billing agency to submit claims provided that the agent's compensation is unrelated to the amount of billings and not dependent on actual collection.

OPTIONS FOR FINANCING
CARE COORDINATION SERVICES UNDER MEDICAID

The federal Medicaid statute and regulations make a number of options for financing care coordination services to children and adolescents with severe emotional disorders available. These options permit coverage of care coordination services as: 1) a state Medicaid administrative expense, 2) a direct or indirect component of a treatment services benefit, 3) a targeted case management service, 4) part of a waivered specialty physician services arrangement, and 5) part of prepaid contracting without a waiver.

Care Coordination as a State Medicaid Administrative Expense

Certain care coordination activities carried out by a public agency under a formal agreement with a state Medicaid agency can be financed as a state Medicaid program administrative expense. Federal law and guidance to the states establish the availability of federal Medicaid funds for costs related to the "proper and efficient" administration of the state Medicaid plan generally (42 C.F.R. §433.15[b][7]) and, in particular, to the provision of EPSDT administrative case management.

Administrative case management activities under EPSDT include notifying parents when it is time for a child to receive screening services, scheduling appointments for the family, assisting the family with transportation to the appointments if necessary, and following up to ensure that any needed diagnostic or treatment services are provided (Health Care Financing Administration, 1990). This means that the Medicaid agency may, for example, contract with the state or county mental health agencies to perform designated administrative services for children and adolescents with severe emotional disorders and then claim federal Medicaid funds for a portion of the costs.

Since an objective of the Medicaid program is to ensure access to health care services for eligible individuals, certain types of care coordination activities are allowable administrative expenses. These activities may be targeted to groups of Medicaid enrollees and those who are presumed to be eligible. They may include assisting with intake procedures, assembling a team to assess the need for Medicaid-covered services, scheduling appointments for Medicaid-covered services, and following up to ensure that the services were actually received. These activities cannot be therapeutic in nature, nor can they include coordination efforts involving non-Medicaid services such as subsidized housing, public assistance, or recreational programs. In addition to care coordination activities with individual clients, utilization review, data systems operation, and contract monitoring are other activities that may be financed as state Medicaid administrative expenses.

Although the federal government generally provides state Medicaid agencies with a 50% federal financial participation (FFP) rate for administrative expenses, an enhanced FFP rate of 75% exists for any state Medicaid administrative activity that, by its nature, must be performed or supervised by a skilled medical professional. Skilled medical professionals are defined in Medicaid regulations as physicians, dentists, nurses, and other specialized personnel who have professional education and training in the field of medical care or appropriate medical practice (42 C.F.R. §432.2). The enhanced rate is available for skilled medical professionals who perform duties directly related to the administration of the Medicaid program regardless of whether they are employed by the state Medicaid agency or by another state or local public agency.

For a mental health program to receive Medicaid funds for care coordination activities as a state Medicaid administrative expense, an interagency agreement delineating the program's responsibilities and the Medicaid agency's payment obligation must be in effect. The mental health agency also must maintain records identifying the costs associated with providing the care coordination services to Medicaid enrollees because Medicaid can pay only for actual expenses.

Benefits of the Administrative Expense Approach

1. The eligible population of children and adolescents with emotional problems can be defined by the state Medicaid agency in collaboration with the mental health program.
2. No amendment to the state plan is required.
3. The enhanced FFP rate of 75% should be available because the care coordination activities for children and adolescents with severe emotional disorders are likely to require the direct or supervisory involvement of skilled medical professionals.
4. Service providers do not have to submit claims for direct services to individual Medicaid enrollees in order to secure Medicaid reimbursement.

Concerns About the Administrative Expense Approach

1. This financing option must be used in conjunction with another option because not all types of care coordination services needed by children and adolescents with severe emotional disorders can be paid for as a state administrative expense.
2. If the interagency agreement specifies a cap on administrative expenses, then Medicaid funds may not be available to finance care coordination services that exceed initial projections.
3. Care coordinators have no authority to control a child's or adolescent's use of mental health services.
4. Only state or local public agency staff can furnish care coordination services.

Care Coordination as a Component of a Treatment Services Category

Some care coordination activities can be financed under one of Medicaid's treatment services benefits, such as rehabilitative services, clinic services, hospital outpatient services, or even various independent practitioner services. A Medicaid agency can *directly* reimburse a service provider under these benefit categories for a particular type of care coordination service by establishing a specific billing code for that service. It can also reimburse the provider *indirectly* for a wider range of care coordination activities by including the costs of these activities in its calculation of the service provider's overhead expenses for direct services.

Direct Billing The kind of care coordination activities that can be reimbursed *directly* as a component of a treatment services category are generally referred to as *collateral contacts*. Coordination activities billed under a collateral contact or similar code by independent practitioners, clinic staff, hospital outpatient unit staff, or providers of rehabilitative services may include discussions with parents, teachers, health care providers, and other professionals to identify ways in which a particular child's progress could be facilitated at home, in school, and in other community settings. State Medicaid agencies that permit billing for collateral contact services can, if they choose, set medical necessity criteria and practitioner qualifications specifically for these services.

Establishing a billing code for collateral contacts under an already covered treatment services category does not require a federally approved state plan amendment. The state Medicaid agency only needs to define the reimbursable unit of service and determine a reasonable payment rate. Service units for collateral contacts are typically specified increments of time, such as 15-minute intervals. Individuals billing for collateral contacts must document the amount of the service they furnish and submit claims accordingly.

Payments to state Medicaid agencies for the federal share of collateral contact reimbursements are based on the state's regular FFP matching rate for Medicaid services. This rate varies across states, depending on each state's per capita income, but is never less than 50% and never more than 80%.

Benefits of the Direct Billing Approach

1. Medicaid necessity criteria for care coordination services reimbursed under a treatment code may be broadly defined to include all children and adolescents who receive therapeutic services or they may be narrowly defined to include, for example, only those who have severe emotional disorders and require therapeutic intervention in multiple settings. Moreover, the billing code may be established only for mental health clinics or only for specific practitioners (e.g., psychologists) who furnish care coordination services to youth in clinics or other settings.
2. Medicaid funds are available to reimburse service providers for all the time spent on care coordination activities.
3. A collateral contacts billing code typically could be added to an existing covered service category without a state plan amendment.
4. Reimbursable care coordination activities are limited only to the extent that they cannot address housing, public assistance, or other needs not directly related to therapeutic treatment.

Concerns About the Direct Billing Approach

1. The delivery of care coordination services must be documented and claims must be submitted for reimbursement.
2. The care coordination service provider has no authority to control a child's or adolescent's use of mental health services.

Indirect Billing The types of care coordination activities that can be financed indirectly by Medicaid as an integral part of a reimbursable intervention provided under a treatment services category are team treatment planning, appointment scheduling, staff meetings, collateral contacts, and other activities concerned with the coordination of the treatment services for a given child or adolescent. A state using this option folds the cost of these activities into the reimbursement rate that it pays to providers of treatment services for specific interventions, such as individual therapy, group therapy, and day treatment, as part of their overhead expenses (along with rent, utilities, and other similar expenses). In this way, a portion of the cost of the service provider's care coordination activities is paid each time a therapeutic intervention is reimbursed.

Using this option to pay for care coordination activities does not require a state plan amendment. The indirect costs associated with care coordination are simply added to the existing service rate and calculated according to the same rate-setting methodology (e.g., percentage of service provider cost or percentage of service provider's usual and customary charges).

Benefits of the Indirect Billing Approach

1. Depending on the state's objectives, care coordination costs may be folded into the rates under the clinic services or other category used to serve all youth with mental health problems or under the rehabilitative services or other benefit category targeted specifically to children and adolescents with severe emotional disorders.
2. No tracking or submission of claims is required.
3. The range of care coordination activities financed indirectly by Medicaid under a treatment service category may be structured very broadly and may exclude only coordination efforts unrelated to treatment outcomes.
4. Reimbursement rates for already covered treatment services may be increased to reflect care coordination costs without a state plan amendment.

5. States using a cost-based reimbursement methodology may vary their rate increases to reflect geographic and population differences.

Concerns About the Indirect Billing Approach

1. Medicaid financing for care coordination activities would not increase if the amount of time spent on care coordination versus therapy increased, unless the indirect cost component of the therapy rate is revised.
2. Practitioners performing care coordination services have no authority to control mental health services used by Medicaid-enrolled children and adolescents.
3. Medicaid payment for care coordination activities would be made with every therapy service reimbursement, but neither the Medicaid nor the state mental health agency could easily determine whether these activities actually were being performed by mental health program practitioners.

Care Coordination as a Targeted Case Management Service

A broad array of care coordination activities may be reimbursed as a direct service under the targeted case management category. The case management benefit is defined expansively under federal Medicaid law to include all activities that assist enrollees in gaining access to needed medical, social, educational, and other services. It can include, therefore, various kinds of meetings, collateral contacts, assistance with applications, and other activities involved in the coordination not just of Medicaid services, but the coordination of any service or subsidy needed by a Medicaid-enrolled child or adolescent with a serious emotional disorder and his or her family. Only therapeutically oriented services are precluded from reimbursement under this category.

The targeted case management category is exempt from the usual statutory requirements pertaining to comparability and statewideness. States using the case management option may target these services to any high-risk population group or geographic area.

Although Medicaid's usual prohibition on restricting a recipient's freedom of choice among qualified service providers remains in effect, Congress established certain exceptions for case management services furnished to individuals with mental health, substance abuse, or developmental problems. States providing targeted case management benefits to these groups are permitted to specify the particular types of service providers that qualify as the best ones to furnish the service. A state, for example, may elect to designate community mental health centers or schools as the qualified case management agencies for children and adolescents with severe emotional disorders. Families, however, would retain their freedom of choice among service provider agencies and individual case managers. For all other types of care coordination services under the targeted case management category, the state Medicaid plan amendment may not specify a particular type of service provider, but instead, must present the standards that a service provider would have to meet in order to be allowed to participate (Health Care Financing Administration, 1988).

Other freedom-of-choice provisions apply as well. Children and their families may not be forced to accept targeted case management services and, if they choose to receive them, these services may not be used to deny them access to other services available under the state Medicaid plan (Health Care Financing Administration, 1988).

In order to use the targeted case management category as a means of financing care coordination services to children and adolescents with emotional problems, state Medicaid agencies must obtain federal approval for a state Medicaid plan amendment. The amendment request must specify the eligible population, define the service, specify individual service provider qualifications, and either designate specific service provider agencies or practitioners or identify service provider standards. Reimbursement may be made under a number of approaches—an increment of time, an activity, or according to a monthly capitated fee. The Health Care Financing Administration (HCFA) has expressed concerns, however, about the validity of a pure capitation approach since it provides no way of tracking the actual delivery of case management services. HCFA staff would prefer that states paying a prospectively based monthly payment to case management service providers conduct a fiscal reconciliation at the end of the year to adjust for actual service provision.

A state may elect not to include targeted case management for youth with emotional disorders in its state Medicaid plan and to provide this coverage instead whenever it finds the service medically necessary as the result of an EPSDT screening examination. The 1989 OBRA amended the Medicaid statute to require states to reimburse all federally allowable services needed to correct or ameliorate a problem detected through an EPSDT screening; however, in most states, reimbursing case management services as EPSDT-mandated services would be operationally cumbersome. Because decisions in most states are made on a case-by-case basis, the EPSDT approach does not ensure that all children with similar problems have access to the same services and would generally entail substantial delay in securing Medicaid authorization for coverage. Whether furnished as a regular Medicaid service or as an EPSDT-mandated service, the FFP matching rate for all targeted case management services is the usual rate paid to the state for Medicaid services.

The federally allowable services needed to correct or ameliorate a problem detected through an EPSDT screening are as follows: inpatient hospital services; inpatient psychiatric hospital services for individuals under the age of 21; intermediate nursing facility care for persons with mental retardation; outpatient hospital services; clinic services (including rural health clinics and federally qualified health centers); home health care services; hospice services; physician services; dental services; private duty nursing services; nurse midwife services; certified pediatric and family nurse practitioner services; physical therapy and related services; respiratory therapy services; medical and remedial care by other licensed practitioners; laboratory and X-ray services; prescription drugs, dentures, and prosthetic devices; eyeglasses prescribed by an ophthalmologist or optometrist; other diagnostic, screening, preventive, or rehabilitative services; any other medical or remedial care specified by the Secretary of Health and Human Services (e.g., personal care services, nursing facility services for individuals under the age of 21); and case management services (42 C.F.R. §440.10–440.170).

Benefits of the Targeted Case Management Category Approach

1. A state Medicaid agency may define the population of children and adolescents eligible to receive case management services so that, for example, it targets only those with severe emotional or behavioral problems or those in certain rural or inner-city areas.
2. A wide array of activities involved with accessing and coordinating multi-agency services for children and adolescents with emotional disorders may be reimbursed.
3. Case management service providers for children and adolescents with emotional problems may be specified by the mental health agency to include only those service providers affiliated with the state mental health program.

Concerns About the Targeted Case Management Category Approach

1. Financing care coordination under the targeted case management category requires a state plan amendment and federal approval.

2. Case management service providers must track the services they provide to specific Medicaid enrollees and submit claims for reimbursement.
3. The case manager cannot restrict access to Medicaid services and, therefore, cannot prohibit inappropriate service usage.

Care Coordination as Part of a Waivered Specialty Physician Services Arrangement

Care coordination activities may be covered as part of a specialty physician services arrangement authorized by the freedom-of-choice waiver program under Section 1915(b)(1) of the federal Medicaid statute. This section enables the U.S. Secretary of Health and Human Services to waive the usual federal Medicaid requirements for freedom of choice, comparability, and statewideness for states seeking to establish a specialty physician services arrangement. The purpose of such arrangements is to reduce costs or slow the rate of cost increases by managing the use of specialty services. Waivers are approved for a 2-year period and may be renewed for additional 2-year periods. The waiver application is, however, very complex (see Health Care Financing Administration, 1985, for more information).

Because Medicaid's comparability and statewideness requirements are waived, states can design specialty physician services arrangements to manage service delivery to any identified Medicaid group, regardless of whether states choose to make their participation in the arrangements mandatory or voluntary. Specialty physician services arrangements may be used to serve individuals who meet certain age or level-of-need criteria or who live in certain geographic areas.

Under this kind of arrangement, participating service providers agree to locate, coordinate, and monitor the use of certain designated specialty services. Since the freedom-of-choice requirement is waived, these service providers perform a care coordination function that includes *gatekeeping*, or controlling Medicaid enrollees' access to covered services. For example, a Medicaid agency may contract with community mental health centers or other mental health providers to authorize, or even furnish, all mental health services for children and adolescents with severe emotional disorders.

States implementing a specialty physician services arrangement must contract with service providers who meet the state's established standards and agree to furnish services at an acceptable rate. All service providers meeting these standards are allowed to participate unless the state also obtains a waiver under Section 1915(b)(4) of the federal Medicaid statute to contract selectively with service providers. Participating service providers may include clinics and HMOs, as well as solo or group practitioners.

Selective contracting for service providers is one of three other purposes for which a Section 1915(b) waiver may be granted. States may obtain permission to allow only service providers who meet state-established reimbursement, quality, and utilization standards to furnish Medicaid services. These waivers will be granted only if the standards used are consistent with access, quality, efficiency, and the economical provision of covered services; if they do not discriminate among classes of service providers on grounds unrelated to their demonstrated effectiveness; and if they do not apply in emergency situations. States also may obtain a waiver to allow localities to serve as central brokers in assisting recipients to select from among competing health care plans. In addition, states may be granted a waiver to share cost savings (in the form of additional services or reduced cost sharing) that result from the use of cost-effective medical care with recipients. This is to provide an inducement for recipients to participate in cost-effective arrangements.

States have several options for paying specialty physician service providers. Reimbursement for the care coordination function itself is not mandatory; however, states choosing to pay for care coordination activity may pay service providers on either a capitated or fee-for-service basis. If capitated, the specialty physician services arrangement is considered to be a prepaid health plan and certain Medicaid requirements relating to prepaid service contracts come into effect. Similarly, for the specialty services that service providers furnish directly, payment may also be on a capitated or fee-for-service basis. Although the payment amount for care coordination cannot include the cost of coordinating services outside the scope of the specialty physician services arrangement, targeted case management (usually furnished by the service provider directly) can be one of the services designated under the arrangement.

Payments to states for the federal share of specialty physician services arrangement costs are based on the state's regular FFP matching rate for services. This rate is between 50% and 80%, depending on each state's per capita income.

Benefits of the Specialty Physician Services Financing Arrangement

1. Participation in a specialty physician services arrangement may be structured to include the general population of children and adolescents with serious emotional disorders or only a subgroup with specific diagnoses or complicating problems.

2. Participation may be statewide or limited to certain geographic areas.
3. Excessive or otherwise inappropriate use of the children's mental health care system may be prevented by requiring that specialized services be obtained from designated service providers.
4. A waiver to establish a specialty physician services arrangement may be combined with a waiver to selectively contract with service providers making it easier to limit Medicaid reimbursement for children's mental health services to service providers functioning as part of a regionalized system of care.

Concerns About the Specialty Physician Services Financing Arrangement

1. The establishment of a specialty physician services arrangement requires federal approval of a complex waiver application.
2. Financing care coordination activities designed to secure access to services outside of the specialty physician services arrangement requires that the targeted case management category be used as well.
3. To ensure their continuation, specialty physician services must be demonstrably cost effective.
4. With the exception of the ability to mandate participation by children and youth with high-cost mental health problems, the benefits of using a freedom-of-choice waiver to pay for care coordination under a specialty physician services arrangement may be obtained through other Medicaid financing options that are easier to implement.

Care Coordination as Part of Prepaid Contracting Without a Waiver

A final way in which care coordination may be financed by Medicaid is as part of a prepaid, capitated service contract. Under this option, care coordination is paid for indirectly as a function integral to the management of a prepaid contracting arrangement. Because the service provider organization generally is placed at some financial risk for costs that exceed the capitated amount, there is a strong incentive to coordinate and monitor the delivery of each participant's care. Moreover, since the Medicaid enrollees who participate are required to obtain covered services only through the designated service provider organization, the goal of managed-care coordination is relatively easy to achieve.

The kind of care coordination functions performed under a prepaid services contract include assisting with intake procedures, assessing and reviewing service needs, arranging for the delivery of services through the primary service provider organization and its subcontractors, and monitoring to ensure quality and efficiency. If targeted case management is a service included in the prepaid, capitated arrangement, then care coordination also would include assisting the Medicaid enrollee in accessing social, education, and other needed services and subsidies. If targeted case management services are not included in the arrangement, they are provided only at the discretion of the prepaid service provider.

The cost of care coordination activities other than targeted case management services cannot always be included as a component of the capitated rate. Under a risk-based contract, only costs related to the delivery of direct services can be included in the rate. Care coordination and other administrative costs are covered only if the service provider is successful in furnishing the required package of services for less than the total amount of capitated payments. A risk-based contract is one under which the contractor incurs a loss whenever the cost of providing the covered services exceeds the payment amounts specified under the terms of the contract. A risk-based contract can be structured, however, so that the contractor is not at risk for extraordinary costs incurred for an individual enrollee.

Under a nonrisk contract, care coordination and other administrative costs may be included in the rate to the extent that the Medicaid agency can identify savings in its administrative costs stemming from the use of a prepaid, capitated provider. A nonrisk contract is one under which the contractor is not at financial risk for service costs that exceed the terms of the contract. Under a nonrisk contract, the state Medicaid agency may make retroactive adjustment during and at the end of the contract period so that the contractor is reimbursed for costs actually incurred, subject to Medicaid upper payment limit provisions.

Medicaid law and regulations describe two types of service providers that may enter into agreements to serve Medicaid recipients on a prepaid basis—HMOs and PHPs. HMOs are defined in Medicaid regulations in such a way as to effectively exclude service providers that furnish only mental health services. In contrast, PHPs are simply defined as any non-HMO entity that contracts to provide services on a prepaid basis. Therefore, community mental health centers or other mental health service providers may be PHPs and can be used to implement a Medicaid managed-care program for child and adolescent mental health services.

However, most organizations that can qualify as PHPs (and certainly all those that furnish only mental health services) cannot enter into a risk-based contract to provide what Medicaid terms a "comprehensive" package of services. A Medicaid service package is considered comprehensive if it includes either 1) inpatient hospital services and one of several mandatory Medicaid benefits specified in 42 C.F.R. §434.21(b) (i.e., outpatient hospital services and rural health clinic services, other laboratory and X-ray services, nursing facility services, EPSDT and family planning services, physicians' services, and home health services), or 2) three or more of the specified mandatory Medicaid benefits. Any organization contracting on a risk basis for a comprehensive service package must meet the federal criteria for an HMO or for one of the special PHP categories. The entities that may enter into contracts for comprehensive services on a risk basis are: 1) federally qualified HMOs; 2) state-certified HMOs that either were organized primarily for the purpose of providing health care services, that make the services they provide available to non-Medicaid as well as Medicaid enrollees, or that make provisions against the risk of insolvency; 3) most currently funded community health, migrant health, and Appalachian health centers; and 4) HMOs that arrange for services and operated before 1986 (42 C.F.R. §434.20[a]).

As a result of these requirements, state Medicaid agencies may contract on a nonrisk basis for a PHP to deliver any package of Medicaid services, but on a risk basis they are subject to certain restrictions. In general, risk-based capitated contracts with PHPs may specify only up to two mandatory Medicaid benefits—assuming inpatient hospital services is not one—and any number of optional benefits. Among the mandatory benefits that may be included are physician services and hospital outpatient services. The optional benefits include clinic services, rehabilitative services, prescription drugs, targeted case management, and licensed practitioner services (e.g., psychologists, social workers).

Participation by Medicaid enrollees in any prepaid service program must be voluntary if the state Medicaid agency is to avoid the need to secure a freedom-of-choice waiver. Enrollees must also be able to choose their health care providers from among those available through the primary service provider organization to the extent that it is possible and appropriate.

State Medicaid agencies may elect to contract on a prepaid, capitated basis only for services furnished to a particular population of Medicaid enrollees. As a result, participation in prepaid, capitated arrangements may be established as an option only for Medicaid enrollees meeting certain criteria (e.g., age, level of need) or residing in a certain area of the state.

Section 1915(a) of the federal Medicaid statute provides that states offering Medicaid enrollees the option to participate in prepaid, capitated contracting arrangements are granted automatic exceptions to the comparability and statewideness requirements and certain components of the freedom-of-choice requirement. This means that a state may include one or more benefits not otherwise available under the state Medicaid plan in a prepaid, capitated contract. It also means that states offering at least one additional benefit can designate the service provider with whom it will contract (e.g., only community mental health centers), whereas they otherwise must be willing to negotiate with any service provider able to meet the contract requirements.

To establish a prepaid capitated arrangement, a state Medicaid agency must have an approved state plan amendment that documents compliance with a number of federal Medicaid regulations applicable to all prepaid capitated care contracts with state Medicaid agencies. These regulations address the provisions that must be included in the contract (42 C.F.R. §436 et seq.), the responsibilities of the state Medicaid agency in prepaid contracting, and the limitations on cost-sharing obligations that may be imposed on enrollees (42 C.F.R. §447.50–447.58). The responsibilities of the state Medicaid agency in prepaid contracting include ensuring that HMOs or PHPs have the capability for appropriate, quality health care service delivery; auditing medical records; restricting other payments to contract service providers; ensuring continuity of care for enrollees terminating participation in a capitated program; computing the capitated rate; and monitoring the operation of enrollment, termination, and grievance procedures. Most of these requirements can be met relatively easily. State Medicaid agencies receive FFP at the same rate for services furnished under a prepaid capitated arrangement as they receive for other services furnished under the state plan.

Benefits of the Prepaid Contracting Financing Arrangement

1. A prepaid, capitated arrangement may be established on a pilot or statewide basis for children and adolescents with severe emotional disorders, if their enrollment is voluntary.
2. Home-based, school-based, and other federally allowable Medicaid services not otherwise included in the state Medicaid plan can be made available in states that make participation in a capitated arrangement voluntary.
3. Services may be limited to the target youth population and offered only through the Medicaid agency's selected primary service provider organization and its subcontractors.

4. Care coordination services need not be tracked nor Medicaid claims submitted for discrete units of service.
5. The care coordinator has control over utilization of mental health services by children and adolescents with severe emotional disorders.

Concerns About the Prepaid Contracting Financing Arrangement

1. Unless targeted case management is included as a capitated service, Medicaid financing for care coordination activities generally would be available to the contract service provider of child and adolescent mental health services only if it is able to achieve cost savings by reducing the use of high-cost services.
2. A governmental entity or service provider organization must be willing and able to contract with the state Medicaid agency as a PHP.
3. A state plan amendment is required.
4. At least one benefit in addition to those available under the state Medicaid plan must be provided to PHP enrollees in order to make exceptions to the comparability, statewideness, and service provider participation requirements.

CURRENT STATE MEDICAID POLICIES FOR REIMBURSING CARE COORDINATION SERVICES TO CHILDREN AND ADOLESCENTS WITH SEVERE EMOTIONAL DISORDERS

Fox Health Policy Consultants conducted a survey of Medicaid agency staff in 49 states and the District of Columbia in May of 1991 to learn about current Medicaid financing of care coordination services for children and adolescents with severe emotional disorders. Arizona was omitted from the survey because its entire Medicaid program operates under a federal waiver. The District of Columbia is referred to as a state throughout the survey discussion for the sake of readability. The survey questionnaire was designed to elicit information on whether and how the Medicaid program was paying for care coordination services to these children. The questionnaire asked about the nature of the care coordination service, the targeted population covered, service provider qualifications, and the way in which payment rates were developed. The questionnaire was pretested and administered over the telephone by two interviewers. A 100% return rate was obtained through multiple call-backs to the agencies.

The results of the survey indicate that each of the options for Medicaid financing of care coordination services previously identified in this chapter is in use in at least one state (Table 5.1). The targeted case management benefit option is the most common way that state Medicaid agencies are paying for care coordination services to youth with severe emotional disorders. The least common ways are the freedom-of-choice waiver program option and the prepaid, capitated arrangement option.

The survey also revealed that about one third of the states are using more than one option in order to reimburse different types of care coordination activities. Most of these have combined the targeted case management option with a direct billing code for collateral contacts and consultation. Targeted case management is being used to reimburse the activities of a case manager—developing a care plan, arranging and advocating for service delivery, monitoring service delivery, and revising the service plan. The billing code for collateral contacts is being used to reimburse discussions between the child's or adolescent's therapist and family members, professionals, and others whose interactions with the child or adolescent can affect the therapeutic outcome.

The survey also indicates that all states, regardless of the option used for care coordination services, have attempted to compensate service providers for related salary, fringe benefits, and overhead expenses. Most often, states found it necessary to undertake a special study to identify these costs among service providers already furnishing case management services, although only rarely did they go to the extent of providing a time-and-motion analysis. Time-and-motion studies provide the most accurate way of identifying the costs associated with a particular task when a staff person performs multiple tasks. Staff of the federal Medicaid agency like to see that time-and-motion studies have been done as part of state rate-setting work, but such studies are expensive and cumbersome to perform. Nearly as often, however, states were able to ascertain these costs by reviewing annual or quarterly cost reports prepared by service providers already furnishing case management services. States occasionally faced the challenge of estimating case management costs without the benefit of having service providers who already furnished case management services to the target population. In this situation, they usually developed a formula for setting the reimbursement rate and "plugged in" estimates of case manager salary, fringe benefits, overhead costs, and units of service per case manager. In a few instances, however, states relied on historical data on service costs to set the reimbursement rates for care coordination, but they often expressed doubt as to the adequacy of the payment.

Care Coordination as a State Medicaid Administrative Expense

Only three states pay for care coordination services furnished to youth with severe emotional disorders as a state administrative expense (Table 5.2). The breadth of the population being provided care coordination services varies across states—from all Medicaid enrollees needing assistance from the social services agency, to all enrollees receiving mental health services, to only children in need of expanded mental health benefits under the EPSDT program.

The three states using this option have taken some similar approaches. Two use the option to pay for an array of case management activities that include service needs assessment, appointment scheduling, and service delivery negotiation. All have entered into arrangements under which a county agency is paid to provide the care coordination services for which FFP is then obtained as a state administrative expense; however, two claim only the 50% FFP rate because the services are not considered to require performance by a skilled medical professional.

Care Coordination as a Component of a Treatment Services Category

Sixteen states—nearly one third of all states—have established a billing code under one or more Medicaid benefit categories to *directly* reimburse care-coordination–related services for children and adolescents with severe emotional disorders (Table 5.3). Most of the states permit the billing code to be used for services to any person with mental illness. A few of the states are more restrictive, however, and make direct reimbursement available only to those with chronic mental illnesses or those served by community mental health centers.

Although states using the direct billing option for financing care coordination show some variation, they still share certain characteristics. More than one half of the states established the billing code under the clinic services option, and two of these states established the billing code under some type of independent practitioner category as well. In addition, more than one half of the states developed the billing code in order to pay for collateral contact services (all but two of these reimburse discussions between the therapist and virtually any other individual with whom the child regularly interacts). All 16 states limit use of the billing codes to one or more types of mental service providers—most often those certified by the state mental health agency. Furthermore, slightly more than one half of

Table 5.1. State Medicaid policies for reimbursing care coordination services to children and adolescents with severe emotional disorders, May 1991

State	Care coordination reimbursement option					
	Targeted case management	Direct billing code	Indirect reimbursement	Administrative expense	1915(b) program	1915(a) plan
Alabama	X					
Alaska						
Arizona						
Arkansas		X				
California	X	X				
Colorado		X				
Connecticut						
Delaware						
District of Columbia						
Florida	X					
Georgia	X		X			
Hawaii						
Idaho						
Illinois		X				
Indiana						
Iowa						
Kansas	X	X				
Kentucky		X				
Louisiana	X					
Maine	X	X				
Maryland						
Massachusetts						
Michigan		X				
Minnesota	X			X		
Mississippi		X				
Missouri						
Montana		X				

Nebraska		X				
Nevada	X	X				
New Hampshire						
New Jersey	X		X			
New Mexico	X		X			
New York	X	X				
North Carolina	X					
North Dakota						X
Ohio	X					
Oklahoma	X					
Oregon			X	X		
Pennsylvania	X	X	X			
Rhode Island				X		
South Carolina	X					
South Dakota		X				
Tennessee						
Texas	X					
Utah	X				X	
Vermont	X					
Virginia	X		X			
Washington		X				
West Virginia	X					
Wisconsin	X	X				
Wyoming						
TOTAL	22	16	5	3	1	1

Information obtained by Fox Health Policy Consultants through telephone interviews with state Medicaid and mental health agency staff in May 1991.

Table 5.2. State coverage of care coordination for children and adolescents with severe emotional disorders as a state Medicaid administrative expense, May 1991

State	Type of state administrative expense being claimed for care coordination activities	Population receiving care coordination activities	Type of activities being claimed as state administrative expenses	Provider agency	Provider standards	FFP rate (%)	Basis for payment
Minnesota	General state plan administration	All Medicaid enrollees	Case management	County SS agency	SS agency staff	50	Percentage of staff time
Oregon	EPSDT program administration	All children needing expanded MH benefits	Case management	County MH agency	Qualified MH professional	75	Percentage of staff time
Pennsylvania	General state plan administration	All individuals with MI	Provider contract management	County MH agency	MH agency staff	50	Percentage of staff time

Information obtained by Fox Health Policy Consultants through telephone interviews with state Medicaid and mental health agency staff in May 1991.
EPSDT = Early and Periodic Screening, Diagnosis, and Treatment; FFP = federal financial participation; MI = mental illness; SS = social services; MH = mental health.

Table 5.3. State use of direct billing codes to reimburse care coordination for children and adolescents with severe emotional disorders, May 1991

State	Benefit category	Eligible children	Nature of billable service	Allowable providers	Limit on coverage	Billing unit	Reimbursement rate	Rate-setting approach
Arkansas	Rehabilitative services	All individuals with MI	Broad collateral contacts	Certified MH centers	26 hours/ year	15 minutes	Varied with provider type	Varied with provider type
California	Clinic services	All individuals with MI	Case management	Certified MH providers	None[a]	Encounter	> $75/encounter	Conducted study of case management costs
Colorado	Rehabilitative services	SED only	Case management	CMHCs	None	Encounter	Varied with provider	Conducted study of case management costs
Illinois	Clinic services	All individuals with MI	Case management	Certified MH providers	20 hours/ month	15 minutes	$25–$50/hour	Historical
Kansas	Rehabilitative services	All individuals with MI	Broad collateral contacts	CMHCs	12 hours/ year[b]	1 hour	$50–$75/hour	Reviewed provider charges for individual therapy
Kentucky	Rehabilitative services	Patients of CMCHs	Broad collateral contacts	CMHCs	None	15 minutes	Varied with provider	Reviewed provider cost reports
Maine	Clinic services	All	Broad collateral contacts	Certified MH providers	None	15 minutes	Varied with provider type	Conducted study of case management costs
Michigan	Clinic services	All individuals with MI	Case management	Certified MH providers	1/week	Encounter	$175/encounter	Conducted study of case management costs
Mississippi	Rehabilitative services	All individuals with MI	Broad collateral contacts and case management	Certified MH centers	144 hours/ year	15 minutes	< $25/hour	Conducted study of case management costs
Montana	Clinic + other licensed practitioner services	All individuals with MI	Broad collateral contacts	CMHCs + licensed psychologists/ social workers	None	15 minutes	Varied with provider type	Conducted study of case management cost

(continued)

Table 5.3. (continued)

State	Benefit category	Eligible children	Nature of billable service	Allowable providers	Limit on coverage	Billing unit	Reimbursement rate	Rate-setting approach
Nebraska	Clinic services	All individuals with MI	Broad collateral contacts	CMHCs	None	15 minutes	Varied with provider type	Reviewed provider charges for individual therapy
New York	Rehabilitative services	All individuals with MI	Family consultation + case management	Certified MH rehabilitative services providers	None[c]	Varies with code	Varied with provider type	Historical
Pennsylvania	Rehabilitative services	SED only	Interagency service planning meeting	County MH agency	None	Meeting attendee	Varied with attendee	Reviewed provider cost reports
South Dakota	Clinic services	All individuals with MI	Broad collateral contacts	CMHCs	None	15 minutes	$50–$75/hour	Conducted study of case management cost
Washington	Clinic services	All individuals with MI	Case management	Licensed MH case management providers	None	15 minutes	> $75/hour	Conducted study of case management cost
Wisconsin	Clinic + physician services	All individuals with MI	Family consultation	CMHC staff + psychiatrists	None[d]	6 minutes	Varied with provider type	Historical

Information obtained by Fox Health Policy Consultants through telephone interviews with state Medicaid and mental health agency staff in May 1991.

MI = mental illness; SED = severe emotional disorders; CMHC = community mental health center; MH = mental health.

[a] California requires special documentation of the need for services after 12 contacts/month have been provided.

[b] Kansas limits reimbursement to 6 hours/year for children not participating in Medicaid's Early and Periodic Screening, Diagnosis, and Treatment (EPSDT) program.

[c] New York requires special documentation of the need for services after certain amounts of each service have been provided.

[d] Wisconsin requires prior authorization after 15 hours or $500 of service/year have been provided to an individual.

them pay different reimbursement rates to different service providers of the billable service.

Five states have elected to reimburse the cost of care coordination services to children and adolescents with severe emotional disorders *indirectly*, by folding the costs into the rates paid for various mental health therapy services (Table 5.4). The reimbursement rates paid for the services are intended to cover the cost of case management and collateral contacts with family members, education personnel, and other health professionals in all five states, as well as staff meetings in three of these states.

In addition, three of the states using this option increased reimbursement for mental health services covered under the rehabilitative services benefit category. The other two states increased reimbursement for services under the clinic services benefit category.

Despite the assurances of the five states that a deliberate effort had been made to identify the care coordination costs and fold them into the reimbursement rates for mental health services, only one state could say what proportion of the reimbursement rates was intended to cover the costs. In this state, the proportion varied between 15% and 55% among service providers because of differences in travel time and complexity of client needs. Interestingly, one additional state that currently is paying for care coordination under a targeted case management benefit is considering replacing this approach with the indirect reimbursement approach to eliminate paperwork for the case managers.

Care Coordination as a Targeted Case Management Service

Twenty-one states provide a targeted case management benefit that can be used to reimburse care coordination services for children and adolescents with severe emotional disorders (Table 5.5). In all but two states, the benefit is limited to children determined to have severe emotional disabilities. Of the remaining two states, one makes the benefit available to at-risk children as well as those with manifest severe emotional problems; the other makes it available for children who are at risk for any level of impaired emotional development.

There are several points of commonality in the way that most states have structured their targeted case management benefit for children and adolescents with severe emotional disorders. All but a few states take advantage of the option to designate those individuals who are considered to be "qualified" case management service providers, most often specifying the state mental health agency and requiring individual case managers to have a bachelor's degree and some relevant experience. More than one half of the states require

Table 5.4. State indirect reimbursement of care coordination for children and adolescents with severe emotional disorders, May 1991

State	Reimbursed service rates that include payment for care coordination	Care coordination activities paid for indirectly	Approach to "costing out" care coordination activities
Georgia	All clinic mental health services	Case management, broad collateral contacts, + staff meetings	Reviewed provider cost reports
New Jersey	Day treatment clinic services	Case management, broad collateral contacts + staff meetings	Reviewed provider cost reports
New Mexico	All mental health rehabilitative services	Case management, broad collateral contacts, + staff meetings	Historical
Pennsylvania	Intensive in-home mental health rehabilitative services	Case management, broad collateral contacts, + travel time	Conducted study of these care coordination costs
Virginia	Intensive in-home mental health rehabilitative services	Case management + broad collateral contacts	Conducted study of these care coordination costs

Information obtained by Fox Health Policy Consultants through telephone interviews with state Medicaid and mental health agency staff in May 1991.

that targeted case management services be billed in increments of time (usually 15-minute units). Two thirds of the states do not impose any limits on the reimbursement of targeted case management services. Also, more than one half of the states pay between $25 and $50 per hour for these targeted case management services.

Several findings of interest are not evident from Table 5.5. In specifying minimum criteria for case managers, a few states set different criteria for different types of case management activities, requiring a master's degree to assess needs and develop a plan of care, but only a bachelor's degree to arrange for and monitor services delivery. Of the three states that reimburse targeted case management services on a monthly basis, all permit billing only if a specified minimum amount of contact with the recipient has occurred. One state that reimburses both private nonprofit agency staff and public agency staff for targeted case management services established different monthly reimbursement rates for each—private agencies are paid $450, and public agencies are paid $850.

Care Coordination as Part of a Waivered
Specialty Physician Services Arrangement

Only one state, according to the authors' survey, is paying for care coordination services as part of a specialty physician services arrangement under a freedom-of-choice waiver as authorized under Section 1915(b)(4) of the federal Medicaid statute (Table 5.6). The program operates on a statewide basis for all Medicaid enrollees; each enrollee selects or is assigned to a program service provider responsible for furnishing or authorizing all the mental health services covered under the state Medicaid plan.

The state limits eligible program providers to CMHCs and other entities that subcontract with CMHCs for services in order to help ensure comprehensive, coordinated service delivery. In addition, service providers applying to participate in the program must have a subcontract with a hospital to provide inpatient mental health services. To further limit program service providers to those offering the highest quality services at the lowest cost to the Medicaid program, the state has procured a selective contracting waiver as outlined under Section 1915(b)(4) of the federal Medicaid statute.

Reimbursement for all waiver program services, including case management, is in the form of a monthly capitated payment. The payment level is based on bids submitted by interested service providers and, thus, it varies. Potential service providers were asked to submit bids on the basis of the specified package of services.

Table 5.5. State use of the targeted case management category for children and adolescents with severe emotional disorders, May 1991

State	Eligible children	Designated case management provider	Minimum case manager requirements	Billing unit	Limit on coverage	Reimbursement rate[a]	Rate-setting approach
Alabama	SED only	State MH agency	Bachelor's degree if experienced	5 minutes	None	$25–$50/hour	Reviewed provider cost reports
California	SED only	State MH agency	Bachelor's degree if experienced	15 minutes	None	$50–$75/hour	Conducted study of case management cost
Florida	SED only	CMHCs	Bachelor's degree if experienced	15 minutes	8 hours/day	$25–$50/hour	Reviewed provider cost reports
Georgia	SED only	County MH agencies	Bachelor's degree if experienced	Monthly	None	$102/month	Reviewed provider cost reports
Kansas	SED only	CMHCs	Bachelor's degree if trained	Hourly	150 hours/year	$25–$50/hour	Conducted study of case management cost
Louisiana	SED only	None	Less than a bachelor's degree if experienced	15 minutes	212 hours/year	$25–$50/hour	Conducted study of case management cost
Maine	SED only	State MH agency	Bachelor's degree if experienced	Monthly	None	$350/month	Conducted study of case management cost
Minnesota	SED only	County MH agencies	Bachelor's degree if experienced	15 minutes	6 hours/month	$25–$50/hour	Applied formula
Nevada	SED only	State MH agency	Bachelor's degree if experienced	15 minutes	None	$25–$50/hour	Applied formula
New Mexico	All at risk for impaired emotional development	State MH agency	Less than a bachelor's degree if experienced	15 minutes	None	$25–$50/hour	Reviewed provider cost reports
New York	SED only	State MH agency	Bachelor's degree if experienced	Monthly	None	Varied with provider type	Reviewed provider cost reports
North Carolina	SED only	County MH agency	Bachelor's degree if experienced	Hourly	None	$50–$75/hour	Applied formula

State							
Ohio	SED only	County MH agencies	Varied across state	Hourly	None	$50–$75/hour	Applied formula
Oklahoma	SED only	State MH agency	Bachelor's degree if experienced	Half hourly	104 hours/year	$25–$50/hour	Conducted study of case management cost
Pennsylvania	SED only	County MH agencies + county governments	Less than a bachelor's degree if experienced	15 minutes	None	$25–$75/hour	Reviewed provider cost reports
South Carolina	SED only	State MH agency + special program	Bachelor's degree if trained	15 minutes	Varied with need	Not available	Applied formula
Texas	SED only	State MH agency	Varied with case management function	Each contact	None	Varied with type of contact	Conducted study of case management cost
Utah	SED only	CMHCs	Bachelor's degree if experienced	15 minutes	None	$25–$50/hour	Studied cost of TCM being done by another agency
Vermont	SED only	CMHCs	Varied with case management function	15 minutes	$200/day for all MH care	$25–$50/hour	Conducted study of case management cost
Virginia	SED and at risk of SED	Community MH agencies for SED/none for at-risk group	Less than a bachelor's degree if experienced	15 minutes	None	$50–$75/hour	Reviewed provider cost reports
West Virginia	SED only	None	Bachelor's degree	15 minutes	None	$25–$50/hour	Conducted study of case management cost
Wisconsin	SED only	County MH agencies	Varied with case management function	Half hourly	None	$25–$50/hour	Reviewed provider therapy charges

Information obtained by Fox Health Policy Consultants through telephone interviews with state Medicaid and mental health agency staff in May 1991.

SED = severe emotional disorders; MH = mental health; CMHC = community mental health center; TCM = targeted case management.

[a] The reimbursement rate falls within the range of rates listed for most states.

Table 5.6. State coverage of care coordination for children and adolescents with severe emotional disorders as part of a Section 1915(b)(1) specialty physician services arrangement, May 1991

State	Eligible children	Care coordination services included in waiver program	Qualified providers	Limits	Reimbursement rate	Rate-setting approach
Utah	All	Case management	CMHCs or entities contracting with CMHCs	None	Varied with provider	Based on bids submitted by providers

Information obtained by Fox Health Policy Consultants through telephone interviews with state Medicaid and mental health agency staff in May 1991.

CMHC = community mental health center.

Care Coordination as Part of Prepaid Contracting without a Waiver

Only one state was found to be paying for care coordination services to children and adolescents with severe emotional disorders as part of a prepaid, capitated arrangement using the state plan exceptions provision in Section 1915(a) of the federal Medicaid statute (Table 5.7). It is a small program developed specifically to serve youth with severe emotional disorders who are in, or at risk of, an out-of-home placement and who reside in a targeted area of one county. Participation in the program is voluntary.

The state Medicaid agency contracted with the county mental health board to deliver the prepaid services, which include targeted case management. Many of the services are furnished through subcontracts with various private, nonprofit service providers.

The state established a capital rate by identifying the children who were likely to be served through the program and then preparing service plans for each. This gave the state a highly accurate indicator of the total units of each service (including case management) that were likely to be needed. This approach could probably only be used for small programs, although a state might be able to negotiate a rate based on the service needs of a sample of children served by a large program.

CONCLUSION

As a result of OBRA 1990 and the U.S. Supreme Court decision in *Sullivan v. Zebley* (1990), many more children and adolescents with severe emotional disorders are or will be eligible to receive Medicaid benefits in the future. For this reason, programs furnishing care coordination will be able to obtain Medicaid financing for an increasing proportion of their total services.

Programs interested in establishing Medicaid coverage for care coordination services must ensure that their coverage approach meets certain federal requirements governing enrollees' access to services and service providers' rights to participate in the Medicaid program. States may select from five strategies for financing care coordination services to children and adolescents with severe emotional disorders under Medicaid. These include coverage as: 1) a state Medicaid administrative expense, 2) a direct or indirect component of a treatment services benefit, 3) a targeted case management service, 4) part of a waivered specialty physician services arrangement, and 5) part of prepaid contracting without a waiver.

Table 5.7. State coverage of care coordination for children and adolescents with severe emotional disorders as part of a prepaid capitated arrangement, May 1991

State	Eligible children	Care coordination services included in waiver program	Prepaid provider	Limits	Reimbursement rate	Rate-setting approach
Ohio	SED only in target area of one county	Case management	County MH board	None	$760.75/month	Applied formula

Information obtained by Fox Health Policy Consultants through telephone interviews with state Medicaid and mental health agency staff in May 1991.
SED = severe emotional disorders; MH = mental health.

Table 5.8. Key characteristics of state approaches to financing care coordination services for children and adolescents with severe emotional disorders, May 1991

Financing approach	FFP rate	Requires federal approval	Covered activities may include those directed at securing non-Medicaid services	Care coordinator can directly control service utilization	Requires claim submissions	Requires capitation methodology	Limited to public agency staff
State administrative expense	50% or 75%	No	No	No	No	No	Yes
Direct coverage	State FFP rate for services	No[a]	Yes	No	Yes	No	No
Indirect coverage	State FFP rate for services	No[b]	No	No	No	No	No
Targeted case management	State FFP rate for services	Yes	Yes	No	Yes	No	No
Section 1915(b)(1) arrangement	State FFP rate for services	Yes	No	Yes	No	No	No
Prepaid capitation arrangement	State FFP rate for services	No	No	Yes	No	Yes	No

Information obtained by Fox Health Policy Consultants, July 1991.

FFP = federal financial participation.

[a]Federal approval would not be required simply to establish a new billing code under a benefit category already included in the state Medicaid plan. If no suitable benefit category was already in use, however, federal approval of an amendment adding a benefit category to the state plan would be required.

[b]Federal approval would not be required as long as the rate-setting methodology used by the state did not change.

There are pros and cons with each of these approaches for financing care coordination, and the appropriate choice for any given state will depend on a number of factors. One is the nature of the care coordination activities to be financed. Another is who will be providing the care coordination services; that is, whether they will be furnished by public or private agency staff. A third is the level of effort that would be required to implement the strategy. For example, some approaches require a state plan amendment and HCFA approval and others require only the addition of a billing code or recalculation of a reimbursement rate. A fourth factor concerns the need to require extensive management controls. Some states, for example, may want to institute relatively onerous record keeping and billing in order to assure provider accountability while others would not find this necessary.

A recent survey of 49 states and the District of Columbia revealed that each of the five strategies is in use in at least one state (Table 5.8.) The most common way that state Medicaid programs are financing care coordination services to youth with severe emotional disorders is under the targeted case management option. The least common ways, which also are the most complicated to implement, are the waivered specialty physician services arrangement option and the prepaid contracting option.

REFERENCES

Health Care Financing Administration, Health and Human Services, Contracts, 42 C.F.R. §434.20(a), 1991.

Health Care Financing Administration, Health and Human Services, Eligibility, 42 C.F.R. §435 et seq., 1991.

Health Care Financing Administration, Health and Human Services, Payments for Services, 42 C.F.R. §447.50–447.58, 1991.

Health Care Financing Administration, Health and Human Services, Prerequisites for agreement to use public or private agencies to facilitate payment for services, 42 U.S.C. 1395(h)(b), 1991.

Health Care Financing Administration, Health and Human Services, Services: General Provisions, 42 C.F.R. §440.10–440.170, 1991.

Health Care Financing Administration, Health and Human Services, State Personnel Administration, 42 C.F.R. §432.2, 1991.

Health Care Financing Administration, Health and Human Services, State Fiscal Administration, 42 C.F.R. §433.15(b)(7), 1991.

Health Care Financing Administration, Health and Human Services, 42 C.F.R. §434.21(b), 1991.

Health Care Financing Administration, Health and Human Services, 42 C.F.R. 436 et seq., 1991.

Health Care Financing Administration. (1985, August). *State Medicaid manual*, §2105–2110, Transmittal 35.

Health Care Financing Administration. (1988, January). *State Medicaid manual*, §4302.2, Transmittal 46.

Health Care Financing Administration. (1990, April). *State Medicaid manual*, §5150, §5230, Transmittal 3.

Knitzer, J. (1982). *Unclaimed children*. Washington, DC: Children's Defense Fund.

Newacheck, P.W. (1991). [Tabulations from the 1989 National Health Interview Survey.] Unpublished data, Institute for Health Policy Studies, University of California at San Francisco.

Omnibus Budget Reconciliation Act of 1989. PL 101-239. Title 42, U.S.C. §§1396–1396[u]: *U.S. Statutes at Large, 103,* 2106–2491.

Omnibus Budget Reconciliation Act of 1990. PL 101-508. Title 42, U.S.C. §§1396–1396[u]: *U.S. Statutes at Large, 104,* 1388-1–1388-630.

Social Security Act (1900). PL 89-97. Title 42, U.S.C. §§1396–1396[u]: *U.S. Statutes at Large, 79,* 286–423.

Sullivan v. Zebley, 493 U.S. 521, 110 S.Ct. 885, 107 L.Ed2d 967 (1990).

CHAPTER 6

Financing Case Management Services Within the Insured Sector

Anthony Broskowski

Case management that includes a managed-care component can promote cost-effective services (i.e., increase quality and contain costs) for children and adolescents with serious emotional disorders. This chapter includes a review of the issues considered by private insurance companies and other managed-care organizations that assume some or all of the financial risks for the cost of services incurred by insured persons. Although the focus is on the case management of children and adolescents with serious emotional disorders, there are few, if any, financial issues that are unique to this age group when it comes to case management of insured populations. Specifically, this chapter 1) reviews some general statistics on the cost of psychiatric and substance abuse services for children and adolescents; 2) presents the general methods by which insurance companies and managed-care organizations manage the utilization, cost, and quality of this group's use of services; 3) describes the factors affecting the costs of operating the case management system; and 4) assesses the savings in treatment costs that are used to finance the cost of the case management system.

Case management for children and adolescents who have emotional disorders operates within the larger context of managed care as it is currently being expressed within all types of health care, including the broader financial factors affecting increasing health care costs. Most of the forces driving private sector payors, insurance companies, and employers toward case management of children and adolescents are the same forces promoting management of all health care and population subgroups, namely high costs (Coile, 1991; Feldstein, Wickizer, & Wheeler, 1988; Foster-Higgins, 1989). The responses of payors, including both the government and employers, to these rising health care costs have been to restrict unlimited access to care through a variety of mechanisms that have come to be called "managed care."

INCREASES IN MENTAL HEALTH COSTS FOR YOUTH

The cost of treating privately insured children and adolescents for psychiatric and substance abuse problems has risen very rapidly within the last decade, at a rate far beyond the rates of increase seen for adults or for most other types of medical conditions (Broskowski, 1991; Fox & Neuschler, 1991; Frank & Lave, 1992; Hadley, Schinnar, & Rothbard, 1992). Furthermore, these high costs are not distributed evenly across the population of children and youth that need mental health services; a relatively small percentage of youth in "high-end" services accounts for a large proportion of costs. The following example illustrates the problems faced by a self-insured employer who has three options—to continue paying an increasingly higher cost treatment bill, to pay for case management of more cost-effective care, or to drop or reduce coverage of psychiatric conditions to the extent that the law will allow (Sullivan & Miller, 1991).

In 1990, an employer with 10,000 employees, representing approximately 25,000 lives under a generous mental health benefit plan, could easily have experienced an average claim cost of more than $350 per employee/per year (EE/yr) for psychiatric and substance abuse services. In some areas of the United States, such as southern California, Texas, or New York, the costs could be as high as $650/EE/yr. These "average" costs, however, are generally due to a very small number of employees and dependents who use the mental health and substance abuse services. Typically, in a benefit plan in which the employer/insurer pays 80%–90% of the eligible charges (i.e., 80%–90% co-insurance coverage) for psychiatric or substance abuse inpatient care and 50%–80% co-insurance coverage of outpatient care, at a maximum of 50 visits per year, 70%–80% of the costs paid out by the employer/insurer are due to 1% of the covered persons who use inpatient treatment. The remaining 20%–30% of costs are incurred by 3%–5% of the insured lives who use outpatient care. Generally, 94% of employees and their family members will not have incurred any costs for the employer/insurer.

This maldistribution in the consumption of resources is exaggerated further when age and sex distributions of costs are examined. Children and adolescents who typically represent 25% of all insured lives will consume 45%–55% of the dollars spent on psychiatric and substance abuse services, of which 80%–90% can be used for inpatient treatment characterized by long lengths of stay. Consequently, the most costly episodes of care from an employer's perspective include complicated childbirths, organ transplants, and psychiatric admissions of employees' dependents (Foster-Higgins, 1989). Although insurance costs are not expected to be evenly distributed among all employees, the highly skewed distribution for mental health and the high average cost per episode of care make it stand out as suspect, begging for some controls or limitations.

Factors Contributing to High Costs

To appreciate case management as a quality promotion and cost containment tool worth paying for, the specific and general factors related to this broad formula can be examined:

$$\text{Total costs} = \text{Units used} \times \text{Price per unit}$$

Thus, the increase in health care costs can be traced to two general sets of factors—increasing prices charged for health services and increasing utilization. The National Center for Health Statistics estimates that increases in service utilization accounted for one third of the health care cost increases between 1965 and 1980, leaving two thirds driven by cost/price increases (VandenBos, 1983). Of course, these two components are not entirely independent in the sense that a low-volume use of a very expensive service can have costs equal to the high-volume use of an inexpensive service.

Utilization encompasses two quantitative factors—the number of users or episodes of care and the units consumed by each user within each episode. Furthermore, the total number of episodes can be directly related to the quality of care given to a first-time user. Poor quality care, or inappropriate care, is more likely to lead to repeated utilization and the consumption of a relatively greater number of units. Poor care can, in some cases, cause even more problems than it attempts to cure. For example, early and unnecessary hospitalization of a child may cause the child to be stigmatized or may further reduce the cohesiveness and problem-solving capacities of the family unit, leading to further reliance on hospitalization.

With respect to children and adolescents, psychiatric and substance abuse treatment utilization has risen dramatically on all counts, stimulated in large measure by the increasing availability of private sector programs that have invested heavily in marketing targeted toward privately insured families (Anderson, 1989). Although some of the increased utilization probably reflects a true rise in the incidence of serious problems among children and adolescents, many suspect that the increase in the number of children and adolescent patients using the most expensive programs, namely private psychiatric hospitals and residential treatment centers, reflects unnecessary care, or more intensive or longer care, than is medically necessary or appropriate.

However, while we have seen great increases in utilization, we have also noted large price increases. The average prices charged for the most intensive levels of care easily exceed $700 per day for the basic hospital charges before the physician's fees are included. In some parts of the United States, the cost per day will exceed $1,000–$1,500. Average lengths of stay also vary but are typically in the range of 45–60 days, sometimes extending beyond 90, or even 180, days. Therefore, the cost per episode of inpatient treatment can range from $15,000 to more than $100,000.

Efforts to Control Use

Insurance companies have historically tried to control unnecessary utilization through features of the benefit plan, which is basically a written contract. For example, requiring the eligible person to pay a share of each charge, known as co-insurance, or to pay 100% of the initial cost up to a limit, known as deductible, helps to discourage people from seeking unnecessary care (Sullivan & Miller, 1991). In addition, companies try to control the level of charges submitted by the service provider through crude "usual and customary" (U&C) fee schedules that do little more than pay the 80th percentile of the distribution of all service providers' charges. Over time, however, this does not effectively prevent service providers from increasing their average charges. Furthermore, insurance benefit plans commonly create perverse incentives for patients to use hospitals—the most expensive forms of care—because the insurance benefit plan provides higher levels of coverage for inpatient care. Also, although in most cases illegal, a hospital might not collect the balance of the bill to be paid by the hospital (i.e., the part not covered by insurance), thereby mitigating any of the patient's disincentive to overuse this expensive form of care.

Unlike other areas of economics, insured health coverage seems to follow a different law of supply and demand, that is, an increase in the supply of a medical resource tends to increase the level of demand and consumption. Fueled by the growing numbers of children and adolescents covered by insurance plans with improved mental health coverage, especially for inpatient care, the number of private child and adolescent psychiatric facilities increased, further fueling efforts at marketing and case finding designed to fill the available beds.

VARIOUS MECHANISMS
TO INFLUENCE COST, QUALITY, AND ACCESS

As general health care costs rose in the 1970s and 1980s, insurance companies and self-insured employers began following the government's lead by introducing a wide range of mechanisms designed to contain the rise in costs while trying to maintain the quality of care (Bagby & Sullivan, 1986; Goran, 1992; Herzlinger & Calkins, 1986). As costs increased, many payors began restricting unlimited access to care through benefit plan limitations, limits in the choice of service providers, or limits in the levels of utilization.

As the use of these various mechanisms has come to be called *managed care* over time, it has taken on a number of different meanings. To some, managed care means any external review of a service provider designed to limit utilization; others interpret it to mean proactive and comprehensive case management of a patient's treatment to coordinate and ensure continuity of care. To others, it means some form of prepayment to service providers who then assume the financial risk for overutilization of care among the insured group, commonly called a health maintenance organization (HMO). In fact, these are only three of the many mechanisms used in managed-care systems. Although some of these mechanisms are used in isolation, when organized in a coherent fashion, they constitute various types of managed-care systems.

Table 6.1 summarizes the mechanisms being used and the various types of service delivery organizations that have evolved by offering various combinations of these mechanisms (Curtiss, 1989). Any of the primary mechanisms in Table 6.1 may relate to some or all of the primary goals; a one-on-one relationship between mechanisms, goals, and types of service organizations is not intended.

Although many different mechanisms have been created, the primary mechanisms used to reduce utilization include: 1) pretreatment authorization (e.g., approval of services and expenditures before service begins); 2) concurrent utilization review (e.g., review and approval for ongoing service); 3) benefit plans designed to provide financial incentives to receive care from efficient service providers (e.g., requiring lower copayments for approved service providers); and 4) increasing requirements for greater employee or patient/user cost sharing (e.g., asking the employee to pay a share of the premium).

The primary mechanisms used to control price include: 1) prepayments to a set of service providers to assume the financial risks for a defined group of beneficiaries (i.e., capitation payments); 2)

Table 6.1. Managed-care mechanisms and service delivery organizations

Primary mechanisms	Primary goals	Types of service organizations
Usual and customary (U&C) fees		Health maintenance organizations (HMOs)
Negotiated discounts		Staff
Prospective pricing	↕ Price	Independent practice association
Bundled services/payments		Group practice
Capitation payment		Network
Share of premium		Preferred provider organizations (PPOs)
Referral/precertification		Insurer/payor
Utilization review (UR)	↕ Access	Provider
Peer review		Employer
Benefit (re)design		Independent
Employee cost sharing		Managed fee for service
Employee incentives		Employer
Benefit carve-outs		Insurer
Quality criteria		Third-party administrator (TPA)
Outcome measurement	↕ Quality	Derivative organizations
Health promotion		Open-ended/point of service
Risk appraisal/screening		Specialty vendors (UR/PPO)
Database integration		Hybrid risk sharing
Fraud/abuse detection		Exclusive provider organizations

Adapted from Curtiss (1989).

negotiated fee-for-service payments to preferred service providers selected for quality and efficiency; 3) prospective fixed payments for diagnostically related groups of illnesses (DRGs); 4) retrospective claims review; and 5) insurance benefit plans redesigned to cover less expensive but equally effective treatment alternatives (Foster-Higgins, 1989). The general application of these mechanisms for psychiatric disorders and their implications for mental health service organizations are further reviewed in Broskowski (1991) and Broskowski and Marks (1992).

DEFINITION OF CASE MANAGEMENT

There are probably as many definitions of case management as there are definitions of managed care. Although some consider the terms synonymous, managed systems of care encompass more than just case management of individual patients. Within the range of service delivery organizations outlined in the right column of Table 6.1, case management of psychiatric patients, including children and adolescents, can range from exclusive reliance on a telephone connection between an external reviewer/case manager and a treating service provider to frequent and face-to-face meetings between the case manager and the service provider and/or patient.

In addition to variations in how reviewers interact with service providers, there are variations in the types of administrative or contractual relationships that may exist between the case management organization and the service provider organization. For example, at one extreme, the case manager and the service provider may both be employees and colleagues working for the same staff-model HMO, with similar values, goals, and financial incentives. At the other extreme, there may be no legal or contractual arrangement between the reviewer and the service provider, other than that the latter is expected to cooperate with the former because the patient's insurance plan requires such a review, or there may be financial implications for the service provider and/or patient if there is no review. Another common arrangement is for the case manager to be employed by one firm, which has signed "preferred provider" contracts with selected service providers. The preferred service providers expect to experience an increase in referrals from the case management firm, in exchange for offering discounts on service fees, coupled with rapid payment of fees. In such an arrangement the service provider has various incentives to cooperate with the case management process.

Within the domain of private insurance, there is usually a clear distinction made between the case manager's role and that of the service provider. The service provider remains responsible for the final decisions regarding what treatments and services to provide to the patient. The case manager's role may encompass a variety of consultative and supportive activities and, at its best, includes the ability to authorize or deny payment for services rendered by the service provider. The authorization or denial process, however, is guided by a fairly strict interpretation of the insurance "contract" language, which usually calls for the payment of a service only if deemed to be "medically necessary." Although many types of services may not be inappropriate, or at worst not harmful, for a given condition (e.g., inpatient care for depression), appropriateness of care does not imply that the service is medically necessary. Usually on the basis of written criteria, the case manager may deem that the amount or level of services being planned by the service provider do not match the level of service medically necessary to help the patient. In this instance, the case manager will deny payment for unnecessary care, but almost always will authorize payment for some alternative, medically necessary treatment.

Network Management

Although initially limited to phone-based review of only hospitalized patients, the case management of patients who have a severe illness or who are difficult to manage, particularly children and adolescents, has evolved into a more proactive, comprehensive process. Now, case managers commonly work as an integral component of an organized network of service providers. Usually, the case manager's role is further reinforced by an insurance benefit plan that calls for differential levels of co-insurance or deductibles depending on whether the patient chooses to use a preferred or nonpreferred service provider. Therefore, the case manager has the ability and the resources to influence the patient's choice of service providers as well as the range of services they will consume. Of course, the costs of network development and maintenance must be included in the price charged for the service.

The case management of children and adolescents works best when the network includes a full range of commonly needed services, including effective lower-cost alternatives to traditional hospital care. Of particular interest to the insurance industry are service providers who are qualified and willing to develop in-home intervention programs, including crisis stabilization services, that would further reduce the rate of initial hospital admissions of children and adolescents. Unfortunately, it seems that service providers are more inclined to build expensive facilities than to work with the child within his or her family and community. Service providers and insurers must begin to negotiate sufficiently attractive fees for providers to establish creative, effective alternatives that can serve child and adolescent patients who are difficult to manage. The cost savings from reduced admissions and bed-days will more than offset large profit margins built into in-home programs.

There are also difficulties faced by any single insurance company in promoting the development of alternative services within a moderately populated community. Any one insurance company may have as few as 10,000 lives covered within a community. The incidence of serious psychiatric problems among children and adolescents among that size of group would be in the range of 25–75 cases. The savings on alternatives, compared with traditional care, may not be great enough to warrant the considerable investment needed to motivate service providers to develop an alternative. From the service providers' perspective, why would they develop a program requiring them to invest money that would also have the effect of reducing the volume of care in their existing and highly profitable facilities? It is not until a number of employers and their insurance carriers begin to adopt similar managed-care policies, thereby affecting a considerable majority of persons in the community, that the volume of cases becomes significant enough to provide an incentive for service providers to develop alternative programs. This same scenario is further exacerbated in smaller communities and rural areas.

Cost and Pricing of Case Management

Of course, the direct costs of the various case management mechanisms vary in direct proportion to the level of professional skills and time consumed per case and associated overhead for support staff, malpractice coverage, supplies, and equipment. Therefore, the less expensive letter or phone-based review systems generally are used for the majority of patients, while face-to-face assessments and on-site reviews are used on the small number of very difficult and potentially costly cases. However, the costs for case management are not based solely on the case manager's time and effort, but also include the costs of building and maintaining an appropriate network of service providers.

The costs of case management within the private sector are generally covered through a variety of pricing mechanisms. The earliest pricing systems for child and adolescent case management were based on a "price per case." In this approach, an employer or insurance company was charged a price by the case management company for each individual patient who was in the care of the service provider. There was usually a minimum cost per patient, with additional cost increments based on additional time or effort required. This pricing mechanism was used when the concept was fairly new and the number of patients was fairly low.

As this case management service was requested more often and the number of patients became more predictable, the basic pricing structure became a fixed fee per insured employee or insured life. In the late 1980s, for example, a case management firm might have charged as little as $3.60/EE/yr for psychiatric and substance abuse case management using a phone-based system restricted only to hospitalized patients. This price would not have included the use of a preferred service provider network with discounted charges for services being rendered in the hospital.

The next step in pricing occurred when a full range of traditional and specialized service providers had to be identified, selected, and organized into preferred provider networks, with contracts and outpatient treatment. The price then rose considerably but the case management vendors could still claim to save the employer money above and beyond what they were paying for treatment in previous years without case management. For example, a vendor of psychiatric case management services in 1990 might have charged between $25/EE/yr to $30/EE/yr to set up a specialized network and provide basic, phone-based case management services that were supplemented by limited on-site reviews. If the vendor could save the employers at least as much as the price of their fees, presumably everyone was better off if the savings were not achieved simply at the expense of denying needed services or limiting access to care.

As the buyers of such systems became more knowledgeable, they began asking for the vendor to set performance targets with respect to claims cost and, in some cases, set goals or minimum standards for access and quality of care. Furthermore, the vendors of case management were expected to assume some financial risks if their system was not able to meet such savings targets while maintaining standards of access and quality care.

For example, consider the case in which, in a previous year without case management, Company XYZ paid out an average of $300/EE/yr for psychiatric and substance abuse treatment. Based on their historical utilization pattern suggesting excessive use of long-term inpatient care, the vendor and Company XYZ agree that a reasonable target for claims costs under a managed-care system would be $240/EE/yr. In this scenario, Company XYZ would ask the vendor to accept a lower fixed fee, such as $20/EE/yr, and be paid an additional 10% of all savings realized if treatment costs are less than $240, or pay back 10% of any excess claim costs that are more than the $240 target.

In order to not give the vendor an incentive to establish savings through denial of necessary care, Company XYZ would also a set a limit on the size of the bonus, such as $5/EE, as well as establish minimum access standards such as the following: 1) the number of persons using care cannot drop, and 2) all denials or limitations are subject to appeal. Also, the company does not want the vendor to be too severely penalized if the target cannot be reached because of factors beyond the vendor's control or unknown errors in setting the initial target at $240. Therefore, the size of the penalty may also be capped at a maximum of $5/EE/yr.

Table 6.2 illustrates five possible financial outcomes for the vendor and Company XYZ that could result from the previous agreement, depending on how the actual claim costs compared with the target. The first row illustrates the circumstance in which, after 1 year of case management, the claims actually cost $300/EE/year, the same as the last year without case management, and $60 more than the target. Ten percent of the difference would result in a $6 penalty, but because the maximum penalty was set at $5, the vendor is penalized only $5/EE, resulting in a net fee of only $15/EE/ ($20 − $5) for the vendor and a total cost of $315 ($300 + $15) for the company. The second row illustrates the case in which the target is still not met, but a 10% penalty results in only a $2/EE payback and a net fee for the vendor of $18. Notice, however, that in this case the company is still realizing a net savings of $12/EE ($300 − $278) in the total dollars they spent on treatment in the prior year. The third row shows a case in which the target is met; the last two rows show circumstances where the vendor receives a bonus. Table 6.2 does

Table 6.2. Possible financial outcomes from a risk/reward agreement[a]

Annual claims costs			Vendor's results		Company's results
Target	Actual	Difference	Bonus or penalty	Net fee	Total costs for claims and vendor
$240	$300	− $60	− $5	$15	$315
$240	$260	− $20	− $2	$18	$278
$240	$240	0	0	$20	$260
$240	$220	$20	$2	$22	$242
$240	$180	$60	$5	$25	$205

[a] All figures are on a per employee basis.

not show how these results would be further adjusted if other standards were not met.

In subsequent years, the case management vendor also has to negotiate higher rates or extend bonuses to their most effective service providers in the network, thereby introducing additional costs into the system. Presumably, less effective service providers can be eliminated, reducing some costs. Over time, the company, the vendor, the preferred service providers, and the employees should reach a point of equilibrium at which there is a reasonable outlay of money for quality treatment for those who need it, with reasonable fees being paid to service providers and the case management vendor.

FINANCING CASE MANAGEMENT
THROUGH SAVINGS AND QUALITY IMPROVEMENTS

It should now be clear why and how the private sector pays for psychiatric case management. It has been demonstrated to be so effective in reducing exorbitant and unnecessary costs, without diminishing quality or access to care, that most employers whose psychiatric and substance abuse costs have been averaging more than $200/EE/yr find that they can reduce their costs to more than offset the cost of the case management services they buy. For example, an employer without managed care may have noted average costs to be greater than $200/EE/year, with only 1% of covered persons using inpatient services with average lengths of stay for adults between 20 and 30 days, and adolescents between 45 and 60 days, and 3%–5% of persons using outpatient services, averaging eight visits per episode. Instituting a managed-care system, increasing and improving the coverage in the benefit plan, coupled with case management and a preferred service provider network, will commonly lead to an increase in the number of persons who have access to mental health benefits coupled with a decrease in the total costs, including the cost of setting up and maintaining the case management system.

This paradox is easily explained when it is noted that inpatient use will often decrease by as much as 50% (.5% of persons with average lengths of stay, running 7–14 days for adults and 15–30 days for children and adolescents), while the use of outpatient modalities will increase 5%–7%. Instead of an average of eight visits per outpatient episode caused by a large number of dropouts and premature terminations from therapy coupled with a small number of patients using 25–50 sessions, case management can achieve an average of 10–12 visits per episode, resulting from most patients consuming and benefiting from planned brief treatment.

To fully appreciate the potential savings, it may help to compare the relative differences in costs of treatment for children and adolescents under two scenarios—one without case management and one with case management. The difference in costs between these two scenarios produces the funds necessary: 1) to pay for case management, 2) to offer an expanded plan of benefits, 3) to offer an enhanced network of alternatives, and 4) to increase the number of children and adolescents who gain access to treatment.

Table 6.3 illustrates these two scenarios. The following assumptions were used. For an employer with 10,000 employees, we would expect to have 25,000 covered lives. Of this number, approximately 6,250 (25%) would be children or adolescents. We would expect about 1.6% of these persons to have some type of serious emotional problem within a given year. If the employer purchased a case management system, including alternative services, for an annual fee of $33/EE/year, at least 25% of that amount (or almost $82,000) could be justified as the cost of managing any care needed among the 6,250 children and adolescents. However, assuming that case management for children and adolescents is even more difficult than for most adults, let us estimate that the case management vendor allocates $164,000 to the task of child and adolescent case management.

Scenario 1 represents how 100 insured children and adolescents typically may be served or not served in a community that emphasizes inpatient and residential treatment because of advertising or the general lack of sophistication among typical professionals when it comes to working with families. These 100 children and adolescents are distributed among six possible services and a category of "No Treatment," which is often the case due to minimal outreach or orientation to appropriate, specialized services among insured families in traditional, nonmanaged insurance plans. The column labeled "Number in 1 Year" adds up to more than 100 because the scenario assumes some children are represented in more than one row. For example, this scenario envisions 50 children who might undergo some specialized assessment by psychiatrists and psychologists in addition to subsequent treatment in some other modality.

The unit cost for each service, the number of units per user, and the projected annual costs are also calculated, yielding an estimate of $1.3 million or more than $18,000 per child. This would contribute an average of $129/EE/year to the employer's cost for psychiatric care.

Table 6.3. Two scenarios of 100 children and adolescents needing services

Scenario 1: No case management, traditional inpatient emphasis

Type of service	Unit of service	Cost per unit	Number in 1 year	Units per year	Estimated annual cost
Diagnostic assessment	Case	$600	50	1	$ 30,000
Inpatient hospital	Day	850	8	90	612,000
Residential treatment center	Day	500	6	120	360,000
Group home	Day	250	4	180	180,000
Day treatment	Day	150	10	48	72,000
Outpatient therapy	Visit	100	30	12	36,000
Receiving no treatment			30		0
					$1,290,000

Average annual service cost per child receiving care	$18,429
Average cost per employee for child/adolescent care	$129

Scenario 2: Individualized treatment with case management

Type of service	Unit of service	Cost per unit	Number in 1 year	Units per year	Estimated annual cost
Diagnostic assessment	Case	$500	50	1	$25,000
Inpatient hospital	Day	680	4	45	122,400
Residential treatment center	Day	400	3	60	72,000
Group home	Day	210	4	90	75,600
Therapeutic home	Day	210	4	120	$100,800
Day treatment	Day	135	24	48	155,520
Intensive family therapy	Visit	90	30	12	32,400
In-home services	Visit	200	20	10	40,000
				386	$623,720
Cost to manage all 100 cases		$3,154/week			$164,000
		Total costs			$787,720

Average annual service cost per child receiving care	$7,877
Average cost per employee for child/adolescent care	$79
Annual costs of scenario 1	$1,290,000
Annual costs of scenario 2	$787,720
Annual savings	$502,280
Annual savings per employee	$50

Scenario 2 assumes eight levels of community service, with intensive family therapy as the preferred mode of outpatient treatment. Aggressive case management and discharge planning to alternatives reduce the number of children and adolescents hospitalized and the lengths of the stays of those who are hospitalized. Instead of hospitalizing children and adolescents, they are seen in the home on a crisis intervention basis at a cost of $200 per visit. The total cost of this scenario represents an average of $7,877 per child served, with a contribution to the average EE/year of $79. This total cost includes the $164,000 required for case management for 100 children. Although these figures are used for illustration, they are representative, and even if they were somewhat modified, the conclusion would remain the same.

CONCLUSION

Managed care of psychiatric and substance abuse treatment is rapidly growing in both the public and private sectors, and there is no sign that this trend will abate or reverse itself. However, the challenge of efficiently providing appropriate, necessary care to all persons who need it, and not providing unnecessary or inappropriate care to others, still remains. This is no simple challenge because it includes a series of other specific challenges related to access and cost of care.

Access to insured care is presently dichotomized in our society between those with private insurance and those covered through public sector insurance such as Medicare and Medicaid. A recent survey estimated that 83% of U.S. children were covered by some form of private or public insurance (Bloom, 1990). This still leaves a shockingly large number of children uncovered, and with respect to psychiatric care, we can assume that a lot of the existing coverage is fairly limited.

Until we as a society are convinced that we can afford the cost of care as it is presently provided or delivered through existing mechanisms, we are unlikely to support more universal access to insured care. If we believe that we cannot afford the cost of care as currently delivered, then universal access to care will be delayed until cost-control mechanisms have been widely established and proven effective. In short, access limits will only be determined within the context of proven cost limits.

Quality must also not be sacrificed. Unfortunately, there are currently few persons who can even agree on how to measure quality. Without being able to measure it, we cannot determine whether it is being affected by any cost-control mechanisms.

Private sector employers who wish to maintain adequate mental health benefits will likely continue to explore optional, alternative services to replace expensive inpatient treatment. Insurance companies offering managed-care benefit plans on an insured basis are also likely to expand their preferred service provider networks to include these alternatives. The U.S. government and the Civilian Health and Medical Programs of the Uniformed Services (CHAMPUS) are also likely to expand the role of these mechanisms through their own domains. In short, the future of managed care and case management will be one of expansion, coupled with continuing tests of its effectiveness in maintaining or improving quality while controlling costs.

REFERENCES

Anderson, D. (1989). How effective is managed mental health care? *Business and Health, 7,* 34–35.

Bagby, N., & Sullivan, S. (1986). *Buying smart: Business strategies for managing health care costs.* Washington, DC: American Enterprise Institute.

Bloom, B. (1990). Health insurance and medical care: Health of our nation's children, United States, 1988. *Advanced Data from vital and health statistics, No. 188.* Hyattsville, MD: National Center for Health Statistics.

Broskowski, A. (1991). Current mental health care environments: Why managed care is necessary. *Professional Psychology: Research and Practice, Special Issue, 22,* 1–9.

Broskowski, A., & Marks, E. (1992). Managed mental health care. In T. Lentner & S. Cooper (Eds.), *Innovations in community mental health* (pp. 23–49). Sarasota, FL: Professional Resource Exchange.

Coile, R.C. (1991). Healthcare 2000: Role of managed care. In P. Boland (Ed.), *Making managed care work: A practical guide to strategies and solutions* (pp. 553–555). New York: McGraw-Hill.

Curtiss, F. (1989). How managed care works. *Personnel Journal, 68,* 38–53.

Feldstein, P., Wickizer, T., & Wheeler, J. (1988). Private cost containment: The effects of utilization review programs on health care use and expenditures. *New England Journal of Medicine, 318,* 1310–1314.

Foster-Higgins. (1989). *Health care benefits survey, 1988.* Princeton, NJ: Author.

Fox, D., & Neuschler, E. (1991). Managed care in Medicare and Medicaid. In P. Boland (Ed.), *Making managed care work: A practical guide to strategies and solutions* (pp. 557–573). New York: McGraw-Hill.

Frank, R., & Lave, J. (1992). Economics of managed mental health. In S. Feldman (Ed.), *Managed mental health service* (pp. 83–89). Springfield, IL: Charles C Thomas.

Goran, M. (1992). Managed mental health and group health insurance. In S. Feldman (Ed.), *Managed mental health services* (pp. 27–43). Springfield, IL: Charles C Thomas.

Hadley, T., Schinnar, A., & Rothbard, A. (1992). Managed mental health in the public sector. In S. Feldman (Ed.), *Managed mental health services* (pp. 45–59). Springfield, IL: Charles C Thomas.

Herzlinger, R., & Calkins, D. (1986). How companies tackle health care costs: Part III. *Harvard Business Review, 64,* 70–80.

Sullivan, C., & Miller, J. (1991). *The evolution of mental health benefits.* Washington, DC: Health Insurance Association of America.

VandenBos, G. (1983). Health financing, service utilization, and national policy: A conversation with Stan Jones. *American Psychologist, 38,* 948–955.

PROMOTING EFFECTIVENESS
Implementation and Accountability Issues

CHAPTER 7

Implementing and Monitoring Case Management
A State Agency Perspective

Lenore B. Behar

This chapter addresses the leadership role and responsibilities of state mental health agencies in implementing, monitoring, and refining publicly funded case management services for children with serious emotional disorders and their families. The initiation and assessment of high-quality, cost-effective case management services require state agency attention to planning, implementing, monitoring, and utilizing feedback about how case management services are working. This entire process is carried out within a conceptual framework that emphasizes the strengths of children and their families and takes a broader view of service than has been associated with traditional mental health services (Behar, 1986; Stroul & Friedman, 1986).

Emphasis on the provision of case management services to address the complex needs of children and their families has been part of the effort to improve child mental health services stimulated by the Child and Adolescent Service System Program (CASSP) described by Stroul (Chapter 1). In addition, the Robert Wood Johnson Foundation's Mental Health Services Program for Youth (MHSPY) placed considerable emphasis on case management services and provided grant funds for service coordination in eight states (Beachler, 1990). Substantial amounts of consultation and training to facilitate the utilization of Medicaid funding for mental health services, including case management, for youth with serious mental health problems were also provided by the MHSPY. The focus of this training was on strategies to increase the overall amount of children's mental health services by leveraging federal Medicaid funds.

As state mental health systems forged public policy with funding for implementation, they assumed the responsibilities associated

151

with the development of new concepts to ensure proper implementation and ongoing support. These responsibilities include: 1) changing philosophy and attitudes, 2) developing state policies and procedures, 3) training of staff, 4) financing case management services, and 5) program monitoring and evaluation.

CHANGING PHILOSOPHY AND ATTITUDES

However widely acclaimed, new concepts that require changes in functioning on the part of professionals also require a new set of attitudes. To implement case management services, changes are required in: 1) attitudes about families and their role in service planning and use; 2) attitudes about other agencies and their role in providing quality coordinated care, and entitlements; and 3) attitudes about one's own professional functioning and the sharing of the responsibility for service provision with others. The leadership role of the state is to communicate the reasons for these changes, the positive impact that such changes will make, and the importance of effecting change.

Attitudes About Families

As the family movement gains influence through organizations such as the Alliance for the Mentally Ill, the Federation of Families for Children's Mental Health, and other parent-run organizations, a new attitude is emerging among professionals. Professionals are developing revised views of parents, recognizing that the parents of children with emotional disorders are important partners in evoking positive change in their children and can be strong advocates for increased, appropriate services. The importance of parents and families has taken on a new meaning, and family strengths rather than family weaknesses have become the mainstay of treatment.

There is a growing recognition that separating children from their families in the name of treatment requires very careful assessment, especially in light of recent evaluation studies (Burchard & Clarke, 1990; VanDenBerg, 1993), which suggest that, with new treatment strategies, many children with serious disturbances can be treated at home. The idea of professionals providing intensive treatment services to help maintain children in their homes is expanding to include the idea that intensive services could and should include case management services provided in the home, as well as creative use of other sites outside the traditional clinic setting.

The provision of services in the home is bringing professionals directly in touch with the many struggles of families, including their need for other kinds of services such as nutritional counseling, food stamps, fuel, home repairs, job counseling, and so on. Many of these needs were formerly beyond the awareness and scope of the office-based practitioner. The emphasis on designing services to "meet the family on its own ground" is bringing into focus the need for professionals to gain a better understanding of ethnic and cultural beliefs, styles, and practices in order to relate better and provide more appropriate treatment to families outside the "culture" of the clinic.

New attitudes about families have emerged in local communities, at the state level and nationally, as the family movement has gained strength. However, this movement needs to be nurtured, and several states have provided technical and financial support to parent-run organizations. State agencies also have specific responsibilities to families under Section 1916(b) of the ADAMHA Reorganization Act (PL 102-321), which directs states to develop and implement comprehensive plans for service provision. This law furthermore requires states to include parents in planning councils and to ensure that they are represented in legislative testimony and in public hearings. The Education of the Handicapped Act Amendments of 1986 (PL 99-457) requires states to develop and coordinate services for children ages birth to 5 who have developmental or emotional problems or who are at risk for such conditions. This law provides an excellent blueprint for case management services. It requires case management services to include: 1) service coordination through an individualized family service plan (IFSP), 2) linkage of families to appropriate services, 3) coordination of the multiple services and agencies required by the family, 4) monitoring of the family's utilization of services, 5) monitoring of the effectiveness of services on the family's and/or child's problems, and 6) assistance to the family while in transition between services (Bailey, 1989).

The state agencies thus have the responsibility of encouraging local agencies to have parents participate in the service planning process and the advocacy process for their own children and broadening such participation for all children in need. Furthermore, the state agencies have the responsibility to encourage such participation in state-level activities as well.

Attitudes About Other Agencies

As in the adult mental health system, case management for children who have a serious mental health problem has been viewed as advantageous in coordinating services across the many agencies necessary to address the multiple problems of this population (Greenley

& Robitschek, 1991; Kane, Penrod, Davidson, Moscovice, & Rich, 1991; Klee & Halfon, 1987; Schoeneberg, 1987). Unlike the adult population, children with mental health problems frequently are tied legally to multiple agencies, including the (special) education system, the juvenile justice system, the public health system, and/or the welfare system. Frequently, multiple agencies involved with the same child must work together to help the child and his or her family. Most notable are the joint efforts needed between the mental health agency and schools, mental health and social services, mental health and juvenile justice, and, of course, mental health and substance abuse. Case management thus becomes a complex responsibility. On the one hand, diverse and independent agencies need to be coordinated; on the other hand, these agencies frequently are mandated to perform activities that incorporate some case management functions. Therefore, there is a need to clarify who is mandated to do what and who is responsible for what.

In addition to the responsibilities for coordination of care across agencies, case management for children who have a serious mental disability requires advocacy to ensure that children's rights are protected and that they have access to entitlements. Thus, this aspect of case management may promote conflict between agencies, those same agencies that are to be coordinated through case management.

Although much can be sorted out locally, the roles and responsibilities of the agencies need to be formally clarified at the state level. State initiatives that reinforce or reward joint efforts across agencies can promote cross-system understanding and enhance cross-system communication. Further, cross-training or joint training of the staff members of local agencies can be used to enhance interagency working relationships.

In addition to the promotion of new attitudes through the previously described mechanisms, the multiple state agencies involved with children and their families must model the kind of behaviors that reflect the new philosophy. Focusing on case management, examples should be set through: 1) the development of state-level interagency councils to address cross-agency issues, such as clarification of roles for case managers; 2) jointly sponsored, cross-agency training events; and/or 3) jointly funded local initiatives.

Attitudes About Professional Functioning

The acceptance of case management services as an important part of the treatment system has not been easy for some professionals. The incorporation of other professionals into the treatment process has been problematic for those who have functioned as the primary treatment providers and those who have assumed the total responsibility for treatment of the client, communication with the family, and coordination with the school or other involved agencies. For some service providers, the fulfillment of these multiple roles has been handled extremely well; for them, the problem has been recognizing that another professional can help and can essentially extend the services, freeing more of their time. Therefore, it becomes an issue of "letting go" of some of the responsibilities. For other service providers, the multiple roles have not been fulfilled and may have seemed superfluous to the doctor–patient relationship, based on the premise that the treatment process can go on without the extensions that case management can offer. For some clients and providers, this model may work well; for others, the absence of cross-agency coordination, advocacy, and supports provided through case management may weaken the effectiveness of the treatment process, or at least not strengthen it.

Over time, through exposure and training, service providers can come to recognize when case management adds strength to the treatment process and when it may not be necessary. As this service component becomes a legitimate part of the delivery system, the professional comfort level should increase, particularly if the benefits to the child and his or her family become apparent.

DEVELOPING STATE POLICIES AND PROCEDURES

Process

A major responsibility of the state agency is to develop policies and procedures for implementing services that ensure the consistency and quality of services across the state. However, states approach this task differently. Some states address this responsibility by developing such guidance as solely a state office responsibility and may have staff or contracted agents produce relevant materials, such as proposed standards for case management or training materials. Other states see developing programs and procedures as a joint responsibility to be undertaken with professionals from other state agencies and/or from local programs. Some pilot-test the policies and procedures in one area of the state, while others move statewide initially. Still other states require a formal public hearing before policies or regulations are instituted; others require a review of policies and procedures by representatives of other state agencies and/or of the local programs prior to implementation; and others promulgate policies without input from agencies, professionals, and citizens who may be affected.

The way in which a state approaches the implementation of case management services reflects the way the state is organized and its general way of doing business with professionals and clients. However, there may be room for more widespread participation in developing policies and procedures regarding case management services, as the provision of these services is sufficiently complex, involving the cooperation of other agencies, other professionals within the same agency, and families.

Although the quality of the policies and procedures might well be the same regardless of the mechanisms used to develop them, the acceptance of a new service or a new model of service implementation seems likely to be related to the amount of ownership that local service providers and local administrators have assumed. Clearly, policies or procedures can take he form of regulations that are somewhat arbitrarily foisted into the field and tied to dollars; thus, implementation may occur, but acceptance may be a whole other matter. The value of including stakeholders in the process is reflected in this well-known Chinese proverb:

> Tell me and I'll forget;
> Show me and I may remember;
> Involve me and I'll understand.

Although involvement of those affected by policies and procedures may be possible in many areas, the state agency may well find itself alone in negotiations regarding Medicaid reimbursement for services related to case management. In the past, some local agencies have had low awareness of or interest in developing or expanding case management services for children, focusing instead on services more directly related to treatment. When this is the case, the development or expansion of case management services might well be initiated by the state agency. The state agency's role is then to represent its constituency and, by making funding available, stimulate this area of service.

Content

The case management policies and procedures developed by the state of Louisiana (Louisiana Division of Mental Health, 1990) for both adults and children with mental health problems provides a comprehensive treatment of the topic. These policies and procedures address: 1) goals, 2) definitions, 3) target population, 4) priority groups, 5) philosophy, 6) staff credentials, 7) functions, 8) duties, 9) number of clients, 10) process for delivering services, 11) in-service training, 12) supervisory requirements, 13) case record content and maintenance, 14) fees, and 15) appeals and grievance procedures. These are the major categories covered. This list appears to address the major areas in which clearly defined policies and procedures are essential for implementing any new service.

Although there is room for variation within each of the previously listed policies and procedures, there appears to be a good amount of consistency. In keeping with CASSP philosophy, it appears that all states *establish goals* and *define case management* for children with emotional disturbance similarly, as a family-focused service designed to plan, organize, integrate, and monitor services into a comprehensive package. Additional purposes, goals, functions, or duties of case management include outreach, identification of resources, advocacy, and ongoing assessment of the appropriateness of services (Fox & Wicks, 1991). Substantial consensus exists on the topic of *target population,* with agreement that case management is a service for children and their families with complicated service needs. In other words, they need the services of multiple agencies or professionals, and they may have changing service needs that require ongoing assessment, planning, and integration. An example of the client with changing service needs is the hospitalized child needing aftercare planning and integration of services from the hospital and in the community.

Substantial agreement exists regarding number of clients, suggesting that the numbers should range from 14 to 20. It would seem that case management, as it has existed in other agencies, has had diminished effectiveness when too many clients (e.g., 50 or more) with serious problems are being dealt with, requiring a complex array of services.

There appears to be less agreement on, or perhaps attention to, credentials of staff and training and supervision of staff, seemingly because the skills needed cut across disciplines and because there is no widely available preservice training. However, a comprehensive training curriculum was completed in 1993, through the joint efforts of the state of North Carolina and the University of North Carolina (Behar, Zipper, & Weil, 1994).

Descriptions of needed skills for case management do exist in the literature. Roberts-DeGennaro (1987) discusses in greater detail the functions of the case manager within a model of social work practice. Weil and Karls (1985) provide descriptions of 15 different roles for case managers, and Bertsche and Horejsi (1980) define 13 basic tasks for case managers. Miller (1983) emphasizes that case management is a round-the-clock responsibility and not a nine-to-five office job. Dunst and Trivette (1987) have described four basic models of case management, all of which focus on enabling and empowering families. They offer 12 "principles of empowerment" applicable to all four models. State-level planners could draw on this growing literature and on focused surveys of front-line practitioners to articulate a case management model and the related skills.

In addition to addressing the previously mentioned categories, each state's plan for case management should emphasize the following: 1) the need to base service delivery on a sound model and on the description of alternative models; 2) clarification of the interface of case management with other services; 3) the need for a local quality assurance and quality improvement program; 4) the program standards and mechanisms for ongoing monitoring, evaluation, and feedback; and 5) the plan for influencing the curriculum of preservice academic programs to increase the production of professionals trained in the case management field.

The task of the state agency, in concert with representatives of other state agencies, local agencies, service providers, and parents, is to review existing information about service coordination, determine its appropriateness and applicability, and modify such information to serve as the basis for state policies and procedures. In this process, it is important to develop policies, procedures, standards, and rules and regulations that are clear, while maintaining a flexible atmosphere. Such planning should also include mechanisms for monitoring against the standards and regulations that are clearly defined and agreed upon by the participating parties.

TRAINING OF STAFF

The introduction of case management as a new service component requires retraining of existing staff, training of new staff, and restructuring of preservice training programs. There has been ample discussion of the need to train professionals in nontraditional methods within the continuum of care, including a focus on specific services such as case management, family preservation, and wraparound services (Allen, 1990; Behar, 1993; Behar, Lane, Thurber, Jolliff, & England, 1992; Callen, Johnson, Leon, Magrab, & Myers, 1990; Friedman, 1993; Munger, Behar, & Bainbridge, 1991; VanDenBerg, 1993; Chapter 10). There also have been a substantial number of professional articles and books written to provide orientation to case management, as well as to provide the basics of such services

(Allen, 1990; Ballew & Mink, 1986; Donner & Poertner, 1987; Dunst & Trivette, 1988; Miller, 1983; Ronnau, Rutter, & Donner, 1988; Santarcangelo, 1989; Weil & Karls, 1985).

However, there has been a notable lack of preparation for nontraditional services at the graduate level of studies in psychiatry, psychology, social work, and nursing, or in other fields producing mental health professionals. As a category within nontraditional services, case management singularly fares no better. Although case management for children with emotional disturbance is relatively new, such services have been promoted earlier for adults with long-term mental illness, for children with serious health problems, and for children in foster care. However, academic training in these areas is also sparse to nonexistent.

Thus, the state agency has two major responsibilities in the training arena: 1) to stimulate the relevant academic departments to revise their curriculum to include both classroom-based and field-based training, and 2) to ensure that appropriate in-service training and supervision are provided to professionals learning to be case managers on the job. In recognition of the difficulties inherent in accomplishing the former tasks and of the importance that they hold, major efforts to link the state agency staff and the university faculty have been undertaken by the National Institute of Mental Health (NIMH) together with CASSP and Georgetown University, by the National Association of State Mental Health Directors together with the University Professors of Psychiatry, and by the CASSP Research and Training Centers at Florida Mental Health Institute and Portland State University. Linkage and focus on the need for expanded academic training are important beginning steps toward producing better-trained professionals. However, changing deeply entrenched academic curricula and accompanying attitudes about their correctness are clearly long-term goals for most states and university systems that are working together.

Progress in training programs is being made in several states. Examples in North Carolina include a state-funded training program at the Orange-Person-Chatham Mental Health, Developmental Disabilities and Substance Abuse Program, which provides field experience for advanced graduate students in psychiatry, psychology, social work, and nursing. Funds are used to pay faculty at the University of North Carolina to leave campus and provide supervision in the field for their students at the mental health center, in the schools, in the courts, and in the county social services departments. Students are learning to assess children's functioning in environments other than offices. They are learning about the responsibilities and problems of the other agencies and about the support that these agencies can provide to children and their families, which appears to increase in effectiveness as agencies work collaboratively. They also are learning how to use services to avoid unnecessary hospitalizations. In order to learn about case management services, learning about the system of care and about the specific components of the system must occur. This program is described in more detail by Munger et al. (1991).

Specific focus on a curriculum for case management training for children's mental health services has been undertaken jointly by the North Carolina Child and Family Services Branch of Mental Health, Developmental Disabilities and Substance Abuse Services and the School of Social Work at the University of North Carolina. With the assistance of staff from two local CASSP projects, the Robert Wood Johnson project, the Fort Bragg Child and Adolescent Mental Health Demonstration, and parents from the North Carolina Alliance for the Mentally Ill–Child and Adolescent Network, a training curriculum has been developed. Bringing together the expertise of university faculty, parents, state agencies, and front-line service providers and supervisors gives a broad base to this 13-module training package, which is designed to be transported to many settings. The full curriculum has been pilot-tested with front-line service providers and graduate students, determining that it is useful both for in-service training and for preservice, university-based training. Upon its completion in 1994, the curriculum became available for use in training trainers and for distribution. In addition, trainee instruction was begun to develop each state's capacity for training. Further description of the curriculum can be found in Chapter 10.

FINANCING CASE MANAGEMENT SERVICES

Funding through CASSP has made case management services available in some states. The Consolidated Omnibus Budget Reconciliation Act (COBRA) of 1985 permitted states to fund targeted case management as an optional service under Medicaid. Case management can also be reimbursable under the rehabilitation option of Medicaid or reimbursable as an administrative service (Fox & Wicks, 1991). To enhance utilization, CASSP, through the Georgetown University Child Development Center, provided training and written information to states on strategies for gaining access to Medicaid to fund case management (Fox & Wicks, 1991; Fox & Yoshpe, 1987).

State agencies have given considerable attention to financing strategies, recognizing that service expansion cannot rely solely on state funding and that there are other potential sources of funds available. Through the efforts of the CASSP Technical Assistance Center at Georgetown University, information has been disseminated regarding the use of Medicaid funds for case management (Fox & Yoshpe, 1987). Similarly, since 1990, the Robert Wood Johnson Foundation's national program office has introduced substantial training for those states receiving grants through the MHSPY. CASSP and the State Mental Health Representatives of Children and Youth (SMHRCY) provided regional workshops on financing strategies using Medicaid and other federal entitlement programs in 1991. Furthermore, the implementation of PL 99-457 (updated by PL 102-119) has opened another avenue for funding the coordination of care.

It is clearly the state's responsibility to identify financing mechanisms for services and to assist local programs to access funds. The emphasis on financing case management services stems from the recognition that such services seem essential to improved outcomes for children, especially children with complex problems who use the public mental health systems. The attraction to use Medicaid has grown as case management has become a reimbursable service, either as targeted case management, as part of the rehabilitation option, as an administrative cost, as a collateral cost, or as part of the distributed cost of other services (Fox & Wicks, 1991). However, the use of Medicaid funding is dependent on the availability of state or local matching funds and some states have found creative mechanisms to identify existing funds to use as matching funds. Examples include certifying existing state mental health allocations as matching funds, using state funds allocated to other agencies (e.g., schools, juvenile justice programs) as matching funds, or using contributions from private service providers. Some of these approaches are easier to implement than others; some are more feasible than others depending on how the state is organized. Clearly, the area of matching funds is one for further exploration.

Certainly, case management for all eligible clients has received a major boost through the availability of Medicaid funds and, for children who are younger than 6 years, through the funding and requirements of PL 99-457 (updated by PL 102-119). However, the responsibility remains for state mental health agencies to identify other funds for those who are not eligible for Medicaid, those who are older than age 6, or those who do not meet the eligibility requirements of other federal entitlement programs.

Other approaches to funding case management services that appear worthy of exploration are the private insurance and managed-care industries, which are seeking to lower service costs without sacrificing quality. Case management, as a monitoring and utilization review function, has become part of the private insurance and managed-care approach (see Chapter 6). However, case management, in the broader sense, has much to contribute to these goals, not only through the monitoring function but also through the overall planning and coordinating functions, which appear to increase efficiency of service delivery. The Child and Adolescent Mental Health Demonstration at Fort Bragg, operated by the state of North Carolina for the Department of the Army, is beginning to show the usefulness and potential cost savings of this approach (Behar et al., 1992). States need, of course, to continue the quest for state dollars for those whose needs for case management services cannot be addressed by the previously described mechanisms.

PROGRAM MONITORING AND EVALUATION

Monitoring

The role of the state mental health agency in monitoring case management services is subsumed under the issues of monitoring services in general. The role of the state agency vis-à-vis the local service programs is complex, requiring the provision of technical assistance, assurance of training, identification of financing mechanisms, and development of policies, procedures, standards, rules, and regulations. Once these governing principles and practices are developed, these programs are required to be monitored and evaluated against them. It is indeed difficult to combine the roles of technical assistance and monitoring, but it is essential to the quality of services that external monitoring does occur and that it is used constructively.

The thin line that appears to separate the helper and oversight functions can be eliminated in the same way that quality assurance programs have been transformed to continuous quality improvement programs such as that adopted by the Joint Commission on Accreditation of Healthcare Organizations (JCAHO) (1992). These programs focus on changing the underlying motivation and attitude to improve functioning rather than to detect problems. The emphasis is to move from using policing mechanisms to using upgrading mechanisms. Such changes require attitudes that are built on the belief that professionals want to do a good job, are well trained and motivated, understand the issues, have nothing to hide, and are honest and responsible people.

The most critical issue in monitoring that approximates a continuous quality improvement effort is to have clearly defined criteria, agreed upon by both the reviewer and those being reviewed and reviewed according to agreed-upon methods. As noted earlier, jointly determined standards set the stage for this type of monitoring. The monitoring should serve to identify areas in which programs need to improve, in which they need assistance, and in which the state needs to put its efforts. State agencies and public or private clinics have developed variations on this theme predominantly for outpatient or other nonhospital settings. When such mechanisms are in place, part of the monitoring can take the approach of ensuring that the programs themselves have mechanisms to detect problems and mechanisms for self-correction.

An example of a mechanism for self-monitoring in case management services might be an internal check or tracking of timeliness of the case manager's response to calls from a client or a client's family. Tracking can be done by self-report, by a survey completed by clients or families, and by monitoring records. If delays beyond agreed-upon criteria are noted, the supervisor and staff together might review the glitches in the system or the overload in work that leads to such problems. This type of monitoring is problem solving as well and can lead to increased strengths in a program, rather than to the staff developing ways to avoid scrutiny. An external monitor can note the presence of such internal monitoring as one way the staff is working on continuous quality improvement.

Although on-site monitoring is important for many of the areas of interest, some monitoring can be done by reviewing reports and documents. An example of the latter could be a report of Medicaid revenues earned by a local program or a report of hospital utilization compared with a previous time period or compared with other programs of similar composition. By having the state and peer group review such reports, programs might be motivated to improve performance more than by sanctions and reprisals. Feedback would seem to be essential; hopefully, it would be timely, organized, attentive to strengths, and suggestive of improving areas of weakness.

Evaluation

The evolving changes in planning and programming for children and their families have emphasized the need for better evaluation of programs, particularly evaluation of the impact that these programs have on outcome. Case management is considered by some to be a relatively new and, thus, nontraditional service and, as such, it has been subject to scrutiny and/or criticism. To some, case management by someone other than the therapist appears to contradict their professional training and, therefore, approaches heresy. To others, it is viewed as the logical extension and massaging of important principles of mental health treatment to address the changing needs of the population for which we are responsible.

The role of the state agency in evaluation may be carried out best by encouraging independent studies by research institutes or by university-based professionals. Providing access for field-based research is an important contribution; this includes helping to bridge the communication gaps that may exist between those persons focusing on delivering services and those persons seeking reasonable controls in the system to implement an evaluation. Few states have the capacity themselves to do research studies. Encouraging independent studies by external evaluators fulfills an important function; providing funding or access to funding for such studies is equally important.

Evaluation studies of case management services for children with serious emotional disturbance are growing in number. However, few studies measure up to rigorous standards of methodology. Noteworthy is the work of Cantrell (1989), who reports on the findings of a 3-year project studying the development of case managers in ecological support roles. The work of Behar, Morrissey, and Burns (1990), through the North Carolina Division of Mental Health, Developmental Disabilities and Substance Abuse Services, carried out at the Robert Wood Johnson project site, is also noteworthy. Their work focuses on an evaluation of case management that compares the effectiveness of designated case managers with case management as a function provided as part of an interagency service team. The planned overall assessment of the eight Robert Wood Johnson MHSPY projects as described by Saxe (1993) should yield valuable information on the impact of case management services, which are central in all eight projects. Similarly, within the Fort Bragg Child and Adolescent Mental Health Demonstration in North Carolina, Bickman and his colleagues (Bickman, Heflinger, Pion, & Behar, 1992) studied the impact of the continuum of care on clinical outcomes and costs; within that project, the impact of case management services was assessed.

CONCLUSION

Clearly, by the year 2000, there should be substantial increase in the knowledge base regarding case management. This knowledge base should be used to improve the quality of services and to stimulate the development of new services. It should be noted that the focused and intensive program evaluations conducted by Behar et al. (1990) and Bickman et al. (1992) were initially stimulated by the state of North Carolina's interest in having its programs studied. These studies are more comprehensive and rigorous than the types of program reviews usually conducted by state agencies on the impact of service programs.

Case management for children who are seriously emotionally disturbed is newer than many of the services designed for this population, becoming a widely used service only since the mid-1980s. Much has been accomplished during these past years in establishing case management as the linchpin of the service system and in clarifying the major issues of this service. Ongoing reviews of service delivery, discussions with parents and families, and program evaluation should provide state mental health agencies with information to refine the policies and guidelines for implementation. The newness of this service component therefore offers a distinct advantage over more entrenched, traditional ways of serving children and their families in that it has the capacity to reshape and refine its characteristics.

REFERENCES

ADAMHA Reorganizaton Act, PL 102-321. (July 10, 1992). Title 42, U.S.C. 210 et seq: *U.S. Statutes at Large, 106,* 349-358.

Allen, M. (1990, Spring). Why are we talking about case management again? *The prevention report.* Oakdale: University of Iowa School of Social Work, National Resource Center on Family Based Services.

Bailey, D.B. (1989). Case management in early intervention. *Journal of Early Intervention, 13*(2), 120–134.

Ballew, J.R., & Mink, G. (1986). *Case management in human services.* Springfield, IL: Charles C Thomas.

Beachler, M. (1990). The Mental Health Services Program for Youth. *Journal of Mental Health Administration, 17,* 115–121.

Behar, L.B. (1986). A state model for child mental health services: The North Carolina experience. *Children Today, 15*(3), 16–21.

Behar, L. B. (1993). A need for public-academic collaboration in the training of child mental health professionals. In P. Wohlford (Ed.), *CASSP/NIMH conference proceedings on public-academic linkage.* Washington, DC: CASSP Technical Assistance Center, Georgetown University.

Behar, L., Lane, T., Thurber, D., Jolliff, L., & England, M.J. (1992, October). *A model managed care/continuum of care: The Fort Bragg demonstration project.* Paper presented at the annual meeting of the American Academy of Child and Adolescent Psychiatry, Washington, DC.

Behar, L., Morrissey, J., & Burns, B. (1990). *Assessing coordinated care for children and youth with SED.* Approved grant application, National Institute of Mental Health.

Behar, L.B., Zipper, I.N., & Weil, M. (1994). *Curriculum for case management in child mental health.* Raleigh: North Carolina Division of Mental Health, Developmental Disabilities and Substance Abuse Services.

Bertsche, A.V., & Horejsi, C.R. (1980). Coordination of client services. *Social Work, 3,* 94–98.

Bickman, L.B., Heflinger, C.A., Pion, G., & Behar, L. (1992). Evaluation planning for an innovative children's mental health system. *Clinical Psychology Review, 12,* 853–865.

Burchard, J.D., & Clarke, R.T. (1990). The role of individualized care in a service delivery system for children and adolescents with severely maladjusted behavior. *The Journal of Mental Health Administration, 17,* 48–60.

Callen, J.E., Johnson, D.L., Leon, G.R., Magrab, P.R., & Myers, H.F. (1990). *Policy recommendations from the national conference on implementing public-academic linkages for clinical training in psychology.* Washington, DC: Georgetown University Child Developmental Center.

Cantrell, R.P. (1989). *Development of case managers in ecological support roles.* Cleveland: Cleveland Institute for the Ecological Study of Children and Youth.

Donner, R., & Poertner, J. (1987). *Resource training manual for case management with adolescents with emotional problems and their families.* Lawrence: University of Kansas, School of Social Welfare.

Dunst, C.J., & Trivette, C.M. (1987). Enabling and empowering families: Conceptual and intervention issues. *School Psychology Review, 16*(4), 443–456.

Dunst, C.J., & Trivette, C.M. (1988). An enablement and empowerment perspective of case management. *Topics in Early Childhood Special Education, 8*(4), 87–102.

Education of the Handicapped Act Amendments of 1986, PL 99-457. (October 8, 1986). Title 20, U.S.C. 1400 et seq: *U.S. Statutes at Large, 100,* 1145–1177.

Fox, H.B., & Wicks, L.B. (1991). *Using Medicaid to finance care coordination services for children and adolescents with severe emotional disorders.* Washington, DC: Research Foundation for Mental Hygiene.

Fox, H.B., & Yoshpe, R. (1987). *An explanation of Medicaid and its role in financing treatment of severely emotionally disturbed children and adolescents.* Washington, DC: CASSP Technical Assistance Center, Georgetown University Child Development Center.

Friedman, R. (1993). Preparation of students to work with children and families: Is it meeting the need? *Administration and Policy in Mental Health, 20*(4), 297–310.

Greenley, J.R., & Robitschek, C.G. (1991). Evaluation of a comprehensive program for youth with severe emotional disorders: An analysis of family experiences and satisfaction. *American Journal of Orthopsychiatry, 61*(2), 291–297.

Joint Commission on Accreditation of Healthcare Organizations (JCAHO). (1992). *1993 accreditation manual for mental health, chemical dependency, and mental retardation/developmental disabilities services.* Oakbrook Terrace, IL: Author.

Kane, R.A., Penrod, J.D., Davidson, G., Moscovice, I., & Rich, E. (1991). What cost case management in long-term care? *Social Service Review, 6,* 281–303.

Klee, L., & Halfon, N. (1987). Mental health care for foster children in California. *Child Abuse & Neglect, 11,* 63–74.

Louisiana Division of Mental Health. (1990). *Case management policies and procedures manual.* Baton Rouge: Author.

Miller, G. (1983). Case management: The essential service. In C.J. Sanborn (Ed.), *Case management in mental health services* (pp. 3–16). New York: Haworth Press.

Munger, R., Behar, L., & Bainbridge, T. (1991, August). *An academic-community liaison to increase professionals' understanding of service continua: The child and youth demonstration project.* Paper presented at the annual meeting of the American Psychological Association, San Francisco.

Roberts-DeGennaro, M. (1987). Developing case management as a practice model. *Social Casework, 68*(8), 466–470.

Ronnau, J., Rutter, J., & Donner, R. (1988). *Resource training manual for family advocacy case management with adolescents with emotional disabilities.* Lawrence: University of Kansas, School of Social Welfare.

Santarcangelo, S. (1989). *Case management for children and adolescents with a severe emotional disturbance and their families.* Montpelier: Vermont Department of Mental Health Children and Adolescent Service System Programs.

Saxe, L. (1993, March). *Evaluation of the Robert Wood Johnson Mental Health Services for Youth Program.* Paper presented at the annual meeting of the Society for Research in Child Development, New Orleans.

Schoeneberg, L.A. (1987). *The effectiveness of case management in serving severely emotionally disturbed children and adolescents.* Unpublished doctoral dissertation, Florida Institute of Technology, Melborne.

Stroul, B.A., & Friedman, R.M. (1986). *A system of care for seriously disturbed children and youth.* Washington, DC: CASSP Technical Assistance Center, Georgetown University Child Development Center.

VanDenBerg, J. (1993). Integration of individualized services into the system of care for children and adolescents with emotional disabilities or neurobiological disorders. *Administration and Policy in Mental Health, 20*(4) 247–258.

Weil, M., & Karls, J.M. (1985). *Case management in the human services.* San Francisco: Jossey-Bass.

CHAPTER 8

Using Case-Level Data to Monitor a Case Management System

John D. Burchard, Betsy Hinden, Michelle Carro, Mark Schaefer, Eric Bruns, and Nancy Pandina

Of all the failures of which state human services bureaucracies have been accused, the failure to produce seemingly endless and occasionally meaningless streams of paperwork has not been listed. In fact, human services agencies are rather well known for collecting detailed process information about how and to whom services are provided. However, what generally has been lacking is an approach to information management that focuses more heavily on the relationship between a service and its outcome.

The approach to information management that the authors are advocating is similar to the one that guides many successful businesses. It is an approach that relies heavily on the behavior and attitudes of the consumer. In general, it involves obtaining information from the consumer that helps shape a product or the delivery of a service. It also involves outcome information pertaining to its utilization and usefulness. For example, before a fast-food establishment introduces a new product, information relevant to "consumer buying behavior" may be obtained through market surveys of consumer demographics, interests and attitudes, consumer hot lines, or free or cost-reduced samples of the service or product. The information helps the organization better understand the relationship between the services and/or products they provide and the people they serve. Once the information has been gathered, time and money are spent organizing the data into charts and graphs that require a minimum of interpretation and that help the organization predict whether the services or products will have a desirable influence on the buying behavior (but not necessarily the health) of the consumer.

The bottom line, however, are the outcome data. Are consumers buying the service or product? Are they satisfied? Do they believe it is helpful? Can they suggest ways to improve the service or product? Depending on the degree of competition, timely answers to these types of questions can make the difference between success and failure.

The authors of this chapter believe there is a critical need for a more consumer- and outcome-based information management system in the field of children's mental health. In recent years, a number of studies and government reports have documented current deficiencies in child and family mental health, education, and related services in the United States (Knitzer, 1982; Office of Technology Assessment, 1986). It has been estimated that two thirds of the 3 million youth with severe and persistent emotional and behavioral problems do not receive the services they require (Knitzer, 1982). Services have been found to be not only inadequate, but also inaccessible, inappropriate, and often untimely. Our currently overloaded and understaffed service systems are forced to operate on "shoe-string" budgets; this necessitates a triage model, that is, services are not provided until a child has become so unmanageable that removal from the home and placement in a highly restrictive hospital or residential treatment program seems to be the only alternative. Indeed, from 1980 to 1985, the incidence of residential treatment for children and adolescents rose from 33,000 to 169,000 (Kiesler, 1993). Although many of these children might otherwise have been served effectively in less restrictive, more normalized settings, such services are either unavailable, inaccessible, or unknown to the families who need them. Hence, our children are frequently underserved, overserved, or lost indefinitely.

Many factors have contributed to the current crisis in children's mental health services; however, it is the authors' observation that inadequate and irrelevant public agency information systems have contributed to this decline. The information available to children's service agencies falls far short of what is needed to understand how our services affect children and their families and how consumers believe their services can be improved. Although many agencies and programs are improving their ability to report the number of individuals served and the type, intensity, and cost of services provided, they are unlikely to have any objective information related to successful goals or outcomes. Few agencies report objective data on the behavioral and emotional adjustment of the children they have served, for example, how many of the children are engaging in less severely problematic behaviors today than 1 month, 2 months, or 1 year ago? Even fewer agencies have any objective follow-up data on what happens to children after they leave services. In fact, not many agencies can provide reliable information on the whereabouts of the children they stopped serving 1 year ago. In most cases, agencies do not know whether the children are living in the community, going to school, working, or serving a jail sentence. Yet, most agencies will attest that their services are intended to have a long-term impact on the children and families they serve and that it does matter which children make it and which do not. These same agencies would also say that it would be helpful to know more about the relationship between services and outcomes.

CHALLENGING THE ETHIC OF INTRINSIC GOODNESS

If it is true that services can be improved through an information management system that focuses more on the consumer and service outcomes, then why have methods to gather and assimilate such information not been developed or implemented? Identifying sources of resistance to such an evaluation system might be illuminating and helpful. In 1983, Reginald Carter, Director of Planning and Evaluation for the Michigan Department of Social Services, wrote *The Accountable Agency*, to help public agencies improve services through accountability. According to Carter, one of the primary obstacles to any effort to determine the effectiveness of a social service is the "ethic of intrinsic goodness." Originally defined by Dr. William Benton, the ethic was described as follows:

> Since their inception in the United States, personal social services have tended to be encapsulated in an ethic of intrinsic goodness. Perhaps, due to their philanthropic origins, social services have been widely viewed as a symbolic commitment of a society to do good. As a result, the extent of a society's commitment has traditionally been measured in the size of the investment in programs to meet the economic and social needs of deserving individuals, families and communities. That is, the more we would spend on social programs the better. (Benton, 1981, p. 7)

In essence, the ethic of intrinsic goodness eliminates the need to determine service outcomes because, as the ethic states, simply providing the service is sufficient.

In the field of children's mental health services, the presumption of intrinsic goodness is currently being undermined by two important developments. The first is a decline in the resources available for children's mental health services. This development is the result of the increasing federal deficit, the existing recession, and

corresponding taxpayer revolts. Thus, because there are fewer resources, the criteria for obtaining money is shifting from intrinsic
goodness to documented effectiveness.

The second challenge to the ethic of intrinsic goodness is the
development of competing service technologies, particularly for children exhibiting the most severe emotional and behavioral problems.
Until recently, there was a strong correlation between the severity
of a child's problem behavior and the restrictiveness of services.
Children who engaged in severe thought disorders, aggression,
drug and alcohol abuse, or suicidal gestures were most likely to be
placed in secure residential treatment programs, usually far from
their homes and communities. Recent qualitative data from the authors' own research suggest that comparable children do at least as
well, if not better, when individualized or "wraparound" services
are provided in the child's community (Burchard & Clarke, 1990).
The existence of two very different strategies for serving the same
type of child prompts an important question: Which one is "intrinsically good?" The authors know of no better way to answer this question than to systematically compare the two types of service on the
basis of their outcomes.

An obstacle to agency accountability has been the limited usefulness of the program evaluation research conducted in the past.
Part of the limitation in usefulness has resulted from an inability to
conduct the most powerful experimental design. In order to infer a
cause–effect relationship and thus prove that a service has a particular impact on a child, the research design must include the following
(Carter, 1983): 1) random assignment of subjects, 2) experimental
and control groups, 3) a sample large enough to draw reliable statistical inferences, and 4) data having high validity. For a variety of
reasons, few of these conditions can be achieved in public agencies.

In addition to not being able to conduct a true experiment, Carter (1983) and others have identified several limitations in the quasi-
experimental research designs that have been conducted: 1) most
quasi-experimental studies are costly and take several years to complete; 2) the data are collected at relatively remote intervals and important information is missed between collections; 3) by the time the
results have been determined, things have changed and the results
no longer apply; 4) argumentation (based on subjective experience
or constituent testimony) is more powerful than intermittent, wa-
tered-down scientific data; and 5) most program evaluations are one-
shot efforts that lose the historical context.

Given these limitations, Carter (1983) advocates for an information management system that is based on objective outcome data
collected on a regular basis. He lists the benefits as follows: workers

experience increased morale as a result of knowing which clients were helped, the public has increased confidence in government when they know that programs are effective, and public administrators have confidence in the extent to which services are successful. Over time, such information provides a baseline for assessing new program initiatives that determine whether they are more or less effective than former programs. Better public relations also result when increased client impact information enables an agency to respond more accurately to the news media.

In the remainder of this chapter, the authors describe several components of an information management system that is responsive to the concerns and issues just expressed. They believe it is the beginning of a data collection system that will enable agencies to assess outcomes in an objective, relevant, and timely manner. The information management system is referred to as the Vermont System for Tracking Client Progress (VSTCP) and is based on a collaboration between the Department of Psychology at the University of Vermont and the Vermont State Departments of Mental Health and Mental Retardation, Education, and Social and Rehabilitation Services (i.e., the child welfare agency).

To determine the progress that is being made by a child and his or her family who are receiving mental health services, the authors believe it is necessary to collect ongoing data in the following areas: behavioral adjustment of the child, type and magnitude of services, restrictiveness of services, cost of services, and consumer satisfaction. This chapter also describes and illustrates data collection techniques that relate to the adjustment of services throughout the lifespan of the child, the restrictiveness of residential services, and the day-to-day adjustment of the child.

A key person in the utilization of the outcome measures described is the case manager. At least in Vermont, the case manager plays a role similar to that of the air traffic controller. The authors believe case managers' effectiveness can be enhanced if they are provided with a comprehensive picture of the significant behaviors, events, and services that have occurred in the children's past as well as periodic information concerning the children's adjustment to current services. Therefore, the data collection instruments are reviewed and exemplified with respect to their benefits to case managers.

LIFE EVENTS TIMELINE

The Life Events Timeline was developed to address the need for a simple, understandable approach to displaying important aspects of a child's and family's history. The timeline was initially applied to individual case studies of children in out-of-state residential programs to enable a better understanding of the events that preceded the out-of-state placement and to facilitate the identification of services that might have prevented the placement. Timelines are also being used in the development and evaluation of individualized treatment plans. In addition, researchers have expressed interest in using them to track service utilization over time.

The Life Events Timeline consists of six timelines placed in a single visual field to display the occurrence of significant events, services, and behaviors. For example, the first timeline, placed at the top of a piece of paper, depicts the approximate onset of significant problematic behaviors across the child's life span (e.g., hyperactivity, assault, suicidal gestures). A second timeline placed directly under the first illustrates the onset or occurrence of significant events in a child's and family's life, including, but not limited to, family births or deaths, judicial restraining orders, parental separation or divorce, unemployment, and substantiated physical or sexual abuse. A history of services provided for the child and family is then presented on subsequent service-specific timelines (e.g., child/family, educational, or residential services). The sixth and last timeline displays the estimated costs of the three types of services.

Figure 8.1 provides an example of a Life Events Timeline for a 17-year-old boy referred to as Brian. Because the purpose is to illustrate a technique for reviewing previous services and outcomes, Brian's case is only summarized. (For a more detailed account of the case see Schaefer, Burchard, & Rick, 1990.)

Brian was born in New England, and he and his family have lived in a small town since his birth. He is the second of four children with one older brother, one younger brother, and one younger sister. Brian's parents married shortly after finishing high school, and they have been largely unemployed since that time, although Brian's father has worked sporadically. Nine months after Brian's birth, his older brother was removed from the home and placed for adoption by the state child protection agency due to physical abuse by Brian's father. During subsequent years, the father physically abused the mother and the children; there is no indication of any state intervention.

At the age of 9, Brian disclosed to his mother that he and his younger brother had been sexually abused by one of their father's friends. Their mother reported the abuse to child protective services, who substantiated that both boys had been sexually abused repeatedly over the previous 3 years. The child protection agency believed that Brian's mother showed appropriate concern for both boys and

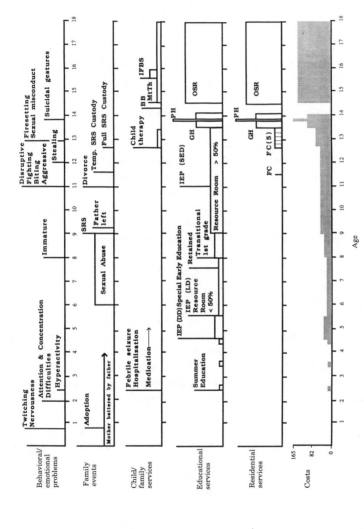

Figure 8.1. Life Events Timeline. (SRS, Social and Rehabilitation Services; BB, big brother; M&TH, therapy for mother; IFBS, intensive family-based services; IEP, individualized education program; DD, developmental disability [classification]; LD, learning disability [classification]; SED, severe emotional disturbance [classification]; GH, group home; PH, psychiatric hospital; OSR, out-of-state residential program; FC, foster care.) (Adapted from the computer program management system of the Vermont System for Tracking Client Progress.)

that she was able to protect them from further abuse. Thus, after recommending that she seek counseling for her sons, they closed the case. Shortly after this investigation and the subsequent conviction of the offender, Brian's father left the family and divorced Brian's mother. In retrospect, Brian's mother said she was devastated by these events and was unable to gather the personal resources necessary to seek appropriate treatment for her sons. Thus, counseling to address the sexual abuse was never provided for Brian or his family.

By the age of 13, Brian was exhibiting extremely disturbing behaviors such as stealing, fire setting, and sexual misconduct. As a result, he was removed from his home, taken into state protective custody, and placed in a series of foster homes, each of which was unable to cope with his increasing behavioral problems. After a suicidal gesture, he was sent to a psychiatric hospital for a more comprehensive evaluation, where it was recommended that Brian be sent out of state for long-term residential treatment.

The Life Events Timeline shown in Figure 8.1 documents, on six separate timelines, the significant events just described. The uppermost axis portrays the onset or occurrence of significant behavioral and emotional problems. The second timeline contains information concerning important family events that may have influenced Brian's development. The third timeline, and probably most significant axis from the standpoint of proactive, preventive services, shows the occurrence (and nonoccurrence) of child and family services. As can be seen, aside from medication for Brian's hyperactivity, Brian and his family received very few services in spite of the increasing severity of their problems. The next two axes present, respectively, a history of the educational and residential services received by Brian. The last axis shows the estimated costs of services on an annual basis, which in this case were as high as $60,000 per year.

Figure 8.1 illustrates how the positioning of multiple timelines on a single piece of paper can provide the case manager with an instructive and relatively comprehensive case history of the child's and family's past experiences with the service delivery system. Relevant behaviors and events are presented contextually with meaningful estimates of the onset, duration, intensity, and cost of services. Services that have been provided are readily identified, those that coincide with improvements can be distinguished from those that have not, and the case managers and other decision makers have a broad, descriptive baseline for evaluating subsequent changes in services.

During their development, Life Events Timelines were constructed manually using graphic arts and page design software. Recently, VSTCP has developed a menu-driven program, the Data Entry and Graphic Programs, that allows one to enter clients' case history information into a database and automatically produce timelines on demand. Although this program greatly facilitates the process, the time required to collect and enter timeline data is still extensive. Nonetheless, the authors believe that the time and effort can be justified for those children receiving intensive, costly services.

THE RESTRICTIVENESS OF RESIDENTIAL SERVICES

A second technique used to measure the progress of a child receiving mental health services involves tracking the restrictiveness of a child's residential services. Although it is only one aspect of a child's adjustment, residential restrictiveness is a critical variable in determining the success of a service delivery system. Increased restrictiveness has traditionally been associated with poorer child adjustment. If a child is receiving services in a residential treatment center, it is important to show progress with respect to the emotional and behavioral problems that led to that child's admission. However, the treatment process is not complete until the child is functioning at an acceptable level within a more normative, community-based environment.

Robert Hawkins and his colleagues at the University of West Virginia and the Pressley Ridge Schools in Pennsylvania have developed an instrument to measure the restrictiveness of residential placements for children (Hawkins, Almeida, Fabry, & Reitz, 1992). The restrictiveness of 27 different settings was rated by 159 child-care providers and administrators who were familiar with these settings. Based on the results, a quantifiable, equal-interval scale was established. This scale ranged from the least restrictive living environment (independent living by self = .05) to the most restrictive living environment (jail = 10.0). The authors have adapted Hawkins's scale to quantify and track, retrospectively, the restrictiveness of residential placements in which a child has resided from birth to the present. Future changes in placement may be added to the graph on an ongoing basis.

The method for tracking residential restrictiveness is illustrated through a second case presentation shown in Figure 8.2. Because the purpose is to illustrate the authors' methodology, the case is

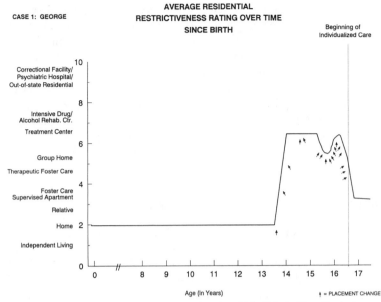

Figure 8.2.   Average residential restrictiveness rating since birth. (Adapted from Harrington, Schaefer, & Burchard, 1991.)

summarized. (For a more detailed presentation of this case, see Harrington, Schaefer, & Burchard, 1991.)

The subject, who is referred to as George, is a 17-year-old male. George has an extensive history of residential placements, beginning at age 14. According to his parents' report, George exhibited disturbing levels of "excitability and overactivity" by the age of 2. As he grew older, he became increasingly aggressive, destructive, and self-injurious, both at school and at home. As a result of these escalating behavior problems and George's unmanageability, his mother relinquished custody of George to child protective services when he was 13; a series of residential placements ensued.

As Figure 8.2 illustrates, George was placed in 18 different residential settings. The most restrictive placements included several out-of-state residential treatment centers and psychiatric hospitals. However, at the time that the graph in Figure 8.2 was constructed, George had returned to Vermont and was living in a supervised apartment in a community and was receiving extensive individualized, wraparound services.

The history of George's residential placements was determined through reviews of agency case files and interviews of service providers familiar with his case. A cursory review of George's placement history shows that George's life has been extremely unstable and that he did not respond well to most of his placements. This graph not only displays what some have referred to as the "multiple placement disorder" (K. Dennis, personal communication, 1992), but it also can serve as a baseline for determining whether progress is being made with new services and treatment changes. Although this graph does not provide a comprehensive picture of the progress that is being made by a child, placement restrictiveness and stability are meaningful indicators that can be used to help the case manager establish accountability. The graph in Figure 8.2 is provided as a means of viewing a child's placement history in terms of residential restrictiveness. The residential services axis of the Life Events Timeline displays placement restrictiveness in the same way. Thus, residential history graphs can be created manually using graphic arts software or automatically as part of a Life Events Timeline using the VSTCP Data Entry and Graphic Programs. Both methods allow for regular updating as a child changes placements. In addition, the VSTCP software allows the data entry menus to be customized to match an agency's particular residential setting.

THE WEEKLY ADJUSTMENT INDICATOR CHECKLIST

An empirically based measure of a child's daily adjustment is probably the most relevant evaluation of a child's progress because it reveals the immediate and long-term impact of services. The Weekly Adjustment Indicator Checklist (WAIC) was developed to measure or "track" the occurrence of specific behaviors and events that relate to placement failure. It consists of 23 "indicators." Sixteen of the indicators refer to negative behaviors or emotions, six refer to positive behaviors, and one refers to the occurrence of parental contact for children not living at home. The 16 negative indicators were selected by service providers and were judged by child-care professionals and laypersons in the community to be those behaviors that are most likely to place a child at risk for removal from the community. The WAIC is shown in Figure 8.3.

The WAIC is designed to be filled out by the child's primary caregiver and should take no more than 3–5 minutes to complete. Using a criteria of 85% confidence, the caregiver indicates on which days each particular behavior or event occurred during a given week. Brief definitions of each indicator are included on the checklist and a user's guide is available for further scoring instructions.

WEEKLY ADJUSTMENT INDICATOR CHECKLIST

ID# _____

Week starting _____ (Month/Day/Year)

days child not observed _____

Directions: Please indicate according to your best judgment on how many days this week the following behaviors or events occurred. Respond on the corresponding line: 0-7 days.

1. **SELF-CONFIDENCE** How many days did the child or youth appear self-confident in his or her activities for more than 85% of the time? _____ days

2. **COMPLIANCE** How many days was the child or youth's response to requests and general activity acceptable 85% of the time? _____ days

3. **PEER INTERACTIONS** How many days did the child or youth have good peer/sibling relations 85% of the time? _____ days

4. **SCHOOL ATTENDANCE** How many days did the child or youth receive credit for school attendance? How many school days were there this week? _____ days / _____ days

5. **VOCATIONAL INVOLVEMENT** How many days did the child or youth work for pay or receive training for work skills? _____ days

6. **PHYSICAL AGGRESSION** How many days did the child or youth hit, strike, bite, or scratch a person with intent to harm them? (Includes hitting with an object.) _____ days

7. **PROPERTY DAMAGE** How many days did the child or youth damage property on purpose? _____ days

8. **THEFT** How many days did the child or youth take property without permission? _____ days

9. **RUNAWAY** How many times did the child or youth run away? (If the child or youth ran away for several days, this should be counted as one event.) _____ days

10. **ALCOHOL/DRUG USE** How many days did the child or youth use illegal drugs or alcohol without permission? _____ days

11. **SEXUAL ACTING OUT** How many days did the child or youth engage in inappropriate sexual behavior which was displayed publicly or directed toward another person? _____ days

12. **EXTREME VERBAL ABUSE** How many days did the child or youth speak to another person in an extremely malicious, abusive, or intimidating manner? _____ days

WEEKLY ADJUSTMENT INDICATOR CHECKLIST, Side 2

13. **SAD** How many days was the child or youth sad, withdrawn, or depressed to a degree which significantly interfered with participation in an important activity? _____ days

14. **ANXIOUS** How many days was the child or youth fearful, anxious, or worried to a degree which significantly interfered with participation in an important activity? _____ days

15. **SELF-INJURY** How many days did the child or youth attempt to harm him or herself nonaccidentally? _____ days

16. **LIFE THREAT** How many days did the child or youth threaten or engage in physical assault in a manner which you believe was life threatening? _____ days

17. **SEXUAL ABUSE/ASSAULT** How many days did the child or youth attempt to force him or herself on another person sexually? _____ days

18. **SUICIDE ATTEMPT** How many days did the child or youth attempt to commit suicide? _____ days

19. **FIRESETTING** How many days did the child or youth set a fire without permission or set a fire in a manner which could have resulted in property damage or harm to others? _____ days

20. **CRUELTY TO ANIMALS** How many days did the child or youth torture, kill, or behave very cruelly toward any animal on purpose? (Does not include hunting with permission.) _____ days

21. **POLICE CONTACT** How many days did the child or youth have contact with police concerning his or her negative behavior? _____ days

22. **PARENT CONTACT** How many days did the child or youth have contact with his or her natural or adoptive parent(s)? (Includes letter, telephone call, or personal visit.) _____ days

23. **POSITIVE BEHAVIORS** What were some of the most positive things the child or youth did this week?

_____

_____

GENERAL COMMENTS _____

_____

Figure 8.3. The Weekly Adjustment Indicator Checklist. (From the University of Vermont. [1993]. Vermont System for Tracking Client Progress, Burlington, VT: Author; reprinted with permission.)

The information provided by caregivers is entered into a continuous computer database that is part of the VSTCP Data Entry and Graphic Programs. Every 2 months, bar graphs are generated, reflecting the weekly rate of occurrence for each behavior or event that has occurred at least once for each particular child. The graphs, which can accommodate up to 18 months of data, are sent to case managers and caregivers and provide feedback regarding the effectiveness of services provided. Changes in the child's adjustment can be identified visually, and case managers can adjust services accordingly. Figure 8.4 is an example of the bar graph that was produced from 1 year's worth of WAIC data on a 15-year-old girl referred to as Samantha.

Samantha was removed from her mother's custody before she was 2 years old as a result of neglect and probable abuse. She was placed in two foster homes and adopted at age 5. She was the victim of sexual abuse in all these placements. By the time she was 10, Samantha's behavior was so problematic that her adoptive parents were unable to manage her alone. She was extremely aggressive with peers and adults, indulged in repeated and prolonged temper tantrums, inappropriate sexual behavior, suicidal and self-injurious gestures (e.g., biting and swallowing broken light bulbs and other sharp objects), and smearing of feces and menstrual blood. Her thinking was incoherent at times, she was rejected by her peers, and she suffered from a very poor self-image and depression. She was placed in a restrictive, residential treatment facility for children and youth where she remained for 6 months before beginning a series of unsuccessful placements in group and foster homes.

When Samantha was 14 years old, she was removed from a group home and was placed in a therapeutic (specialized) foster home where she began receiving individualized, wraparound services. Her caregivers began completing the WAIC at this time. The type of feedback that is provided to the case manager is exemplified in Figure 8.4. As the bar graphs illustrate, Samantha periodically was anxious and depressed, engaged in some self-injury, although only during the first 3 weeks of the year, and exhibited physically aggressive behavior that diminished over time. Not shown are the graphs that illustrate a rapid decline in property damage and theft during the first few weeks of data collection and improvements in self-confidence, compliance, peer interactions, and school attendance. The data for that year also reflected an increase in contact with her adoptive parents.

The data from the WAIC are also consolidated into groups of indicators and plotted on a monthly basis and presented graphically

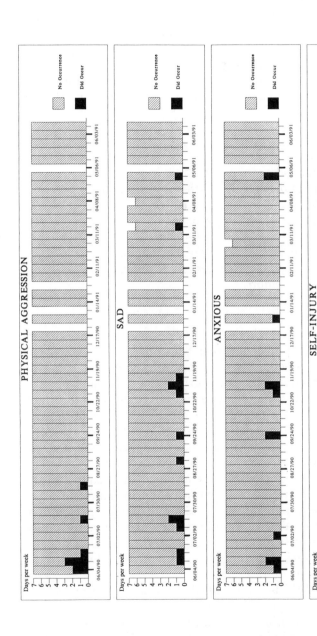
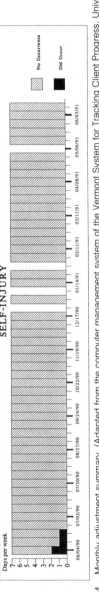

Figure 8.4. Monthly adjustment summary. (Adapted from the computer management system of the Vermont System for Tracking Client Progress, University of Vermont, 1993.)

with residential restrictiveness data and placement change. The VSTCP Data Entry and Graphics Programs can automatically produce these monthly adjustment summaries from the same behavioral databases accessed to create the weekly bar graphs. This method of data presentation can incorporate up to 3 years of data. An example of a monthly adjustment summary for Samantha is shown in Figure 8.5. Negative indicators are grouped into the following categories:

Severe negative	*Moderate negative*
Physical aggression	Alcohol/drug use
Property damage	Extreme verbal abuse
Theft	Sad
Runaway	Anxious
Life threat	Self-injury
Sexual abuse	Sexual acting out
Fire setting	Cruelty to animals
Suicide attempt	
Police contact	

The data shown in Figure 8.5 provide extensive empirical documentation of the improvement that Samantha has shown over a more than 2-year-period. Critical at-risk behaviors have either declined or have been eliminated, and positive behaviors have increased. In addition, Samantha has moved gradually into a more normalized living environment. The graphs also enable the case manager to see important relationships across indicators. For example, increases in moderate negative behaviors appear associated with changes in the living environment. The specific behaviors that contributed most to these increases were anxiety ("anxious to a degree that significantly interfered with participation in important activities") and extreme verbal abuse ("speaking to another person in an extremely malicious, abusive, or intimidating manner"). Such information enables the case manager and the service providers to better understand Samantha and contributes to more effective and more proactive crisis planning in the future.

Because the WAIC is usually filled out by a single caregiver and reflects only his or her perspective at a given point in time, the reliability of the instrument has been difficult to establish. Two preliminary studies with small numbers of subjects conducted in residential settings resulted in favorable inter-rater and test–retest reliability coefficients. Additional data on the reliability of the instrument are

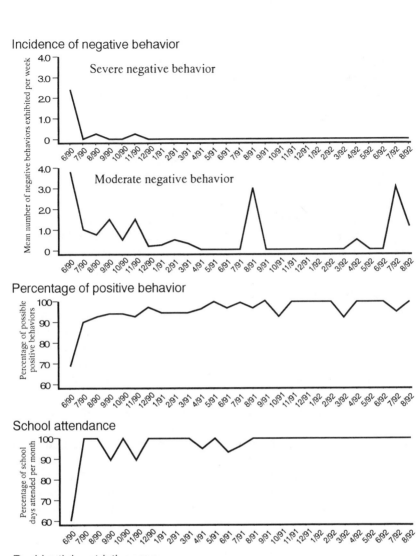

Figure 8.5. Monthly adjustment summary. (Adapted from the computer management system of the Vermont System for Tracking Client Progress.)

currently being obtained. In addition, good agreement between WAIC scores and future residential restrictiveness has been found (Yoe, Bruns, & Burchard, 1993), supporting the validity of the instrument.

The WAIC is being used in several other locations in the United States and, in some instances, the procedure has been somewhat modified. For example, the adjustment data are collected on a monthly rather than on a weekly basis, and the data are being provided by clinicians or case managers instead of primary caregivers. Although the authors believe the instrument is likely to be most reliable when administered daily or weekly by the primary caregiver, these other systems seem to be working quite well and have the potential to provide meaningful and useful data.

CONCLUSION

For years, services for children have survived and been funded on the basis of the presumption of intrinsic goodness. Because helping children is intrinsically the good thing to do, little emphasis was placed on determining whether the services really made a difference. However, as the resources for services have become more limited, the question of service effectiveness has become more prominent. Service agencies are increasingly being asked to document the accountability of their efforts.

This chapter describes and illustrates several methods for collecting data that display and assess a number of critical aspects of the relationship between services and client outcomes. Although the information provided by these methods does not present a complete picture of the progress of a given child, it does enable case managers and administrators to see more clearly whether progress is being made in the most critical at-risk areas. It also provides an empirical basis for trying to determine whether behavior change is a function of the services that were provided. The data can also guide efforts to improve services within a larger service delivery system.

In addition to the methods previously described, the authors have used Youth and Parent Satisfaction Surveys to assess the quantity and type of services provided, the youth's satisfaction with those services, and the youth's sense of involvement and unconditional care in the service delivery process (Rosen, Heckman, Carro, & Burchard, 1994). Such information provides an additional method for assessing service effectiveness and provider accountability.

For both ethical and practical reasons, the authors believe that human services must be as responsive to the needs and demands of its stockholders, investors, and consumers as are any product-oriented corporations. It is their hope that the methods described in this chapter will increase accountability, effectiveness, and the overall quality of the mental health services provided for children and their families.

REFERENCES

Benton, W. (1981, August). *The ethic of intrinsic goodness*. Paper presented at the International Council on Social Welfare, Ontario, Canada.

Burchard, J.D., & Clarke, R.T. (1990). Individualized approaches to treatment: Project Wraparound. In *Proceedings: Children's mental health services and policy: Building a research base* (Vol. 3, pp. 57–63). Tampa, FL: Mental Health Institute.

Carter, R.K. (1983). *The accountable agency*. Newbury Park, CA: Sage Publications.

Harrington, N., Schaefer, M.C., & Burchard, J.D. (1991). A case study of the use of individualized care to reintegrate a youth with serious emotional disturbance into the community. In A. Algarin & R.M. Freidman (Eds.), *Fourth annual research conference proceedings: A system of care for children's mental health: Expanding the research base* (pp. 127–140). Tampa: Florida Mental Health Institute, Research and Training Center for Children's Mental Health.

Hawkins, R.P., Almeida, M.C., Fabry, B., & Reitz, A.C. (1992). Restrictiveness of living environments for troubled children and youths: A simple measure for program evaluation, policy planning, and placement decisions. *Hospital and Community Psychiatry, 43*, 54–59.

Kiesler, C.A. (1993). Mental health policy and the psychiatric inpatient care of children. *Applied and Preventive Psychology, 2*, 91–99.

Knitzer, J.K. (1982). *Unclaimed children*. Washington, DC: Children's Defense Fund.

Office of Technology Assessment. (1986). *Children's mental health problems and services—A background paper* (ATA-BP-H-33). Washington, DC: U.S. Government Printing Office.

Rosen, L.D., Heckman, T., Carro, M.G., & Burchard, J.D. (1994). Satisfaction, involvement, and unconditional care: The perceptions of children and adolescents receiving wraparound services. *Journal of Child and Family Studies, 3*, 55–68.

Schaefer, M.C., Burchard, J.D., & Rick, K. (1990). A case study of a child in out-of-state residential care: An in-depth analysis of what didn't work. In A. Algarin, R.M. Friedman, A.J. Duchnowski, K.M. Kutash, S. Silver, & M.K. Johnson (Eds.), *Proceedings of the 3rd annual conference on children's mental health services and policy: Building a research base* (pp. 211–226). Tampa: Florida Mental Health Institute, Research and Training Center for Children's Mental Health.

University of Vermont. (1993). *Weekly adjustment indicator checklist*. Vermont System for Tracking Client Progress. Burlington, VT: Author.

Yoe, J., Bruns, E., & Burchard, J. (1993, March). *A comparison of child adjustment instruments for children at risk*. Poster presentation at the 6th Annual Research Conference: A system of care for children's mental health: Expanding the research base, Tampa, FL.

CHAPTER 9

Case Management to Assure Quality Care in Multiagency Systems
Building Standards of Practice into a Computerized Clinical Record

Robert F. Cole

Case management for families and children with emotional disorders is a developing field of increased complexity. Case managers must coordinate efforts with five categorical agencies—child welfare, mental health, health, education, and juvenile justice—as well as broker and monitor services to assist families and children. If the efforts of the five responsible agencies can be combined into one, the coordinating center of this effort would be the common plan of care for an individual child. Case managers are the designers, orchestrators, and keepers of this plan. The computerized clinical record is a tool to assist case managers to achieve efficient and effective operation of the system of care so that children and families receive what they need to live successfully in the community.

This chapter reports on the development of a computerized information system designed to support case managers in multiagency systems as they go about their daily business by automating essential parts of their work. This system, CareTrack, has been designed and developed based on a vision rather than on a practice. It was conceived by a group of people who shared a vision of a reformed system of care whereby the efforts of the five categorical agencies could be combined to provide intensive treatment to children with the most serious mental and emotional disturbances in the context of their home and community. This is not only an information system project but also part of a new vision of case management expanded to include new roles and functions. It also extends the content of the traditional case record information to include clinical documentation that meets the requirements of clinical quality assurance, as well as the encumbrance of funds (but not the accounting of expenditures) and the monitoring of services, service outcomes, and service expenditures.

This effort stems from the experience of those involved in the planning and development process of the Mental Health Services Program for Youth (MHSPY), an initiative of the Robert Wood Johnson Foundation to support state and community partnerships in eight sites in developing systems of care for children and youth with applications required for this serious emotional disturbance. Forty states prepared the applications required for this program, and 12 were funded to advance their plans. At the end of the first development year, the need for an automated case-tracking system became apparent to the eight sites chosen for full implementation. In order to address this need, the National Program Office, established by the Foundation at Prudential's Group Medical Department to provide direction and technical assistance to the sites, organized a "design seminar" to bring together 24 professionals from the sites who represented the various public agencies responsible for children with serious emotional disturbance. Prudential's technical design staff assisted a 2-day process through which the group examined the information needs of case managers.

The CareTrack system is the first step in a 4-year process through which some of the MHSPY sites will try to develop an automated clinical record consolidating the efforts of all the responsible agencies into a coherent package of care for the child and his or her family. This requires the translation of the languages of the various service traditions so that information can be used by the five categorical agencies making up the system of care. It is not a computerized billing system or a data collection device for research activities, but rather it attempts to support case managers in their job. Prior to describing the automated record-keeping system, the case management system for which the automated clinical record-keeping system was developed is described.

CASE MANAGEMENT IN A MULTIAGENCY SYSTEM OF CARE

Consideration of the needs of children with serious mental and emotional disturbances and their families and the daunting complexity of the agencies that have nominal responsibility for them has brought leaders in the field of child mental health to frame solutions and initiatives in the context of a multiagency system of care. This has been true of the National Institute of Mental Health (NIMH)

Child and Adolescent Service System Program (CASSP), which has developed a theory and planning methodology that has been applied in virtually all the states and demonstrated in model program initiatives such as Ventura County, California, and those developed under the *Willie M.* (1980) consent decree in North Carolina, ordering the state to provide services to youth who have serious disturbances and who are violent. This decree preceded the development of CASSP.

Policy Structures for the Locally Organized System of Care

There are certain policy structures, joint actions taken by responsible categorical agencies at the state and local levels that are prerequisite to the development of a community-based organized system of care to serve children with serious mental and emotional disturbances (Figure 9.1). First, there is some sort of *state compact* among the state categorical agencies that facilitates regulatory flexibility and formulates a coherent joint financing policy to support integration of effort at the local system level on behalf of these children. Second, at the level of the local operational counterparts of these central bureaucracies, there is an *interagency consortium* that formalizes their agreement to pool efforts to serve these children and identifies governance structures through which their collaboration is carried out.

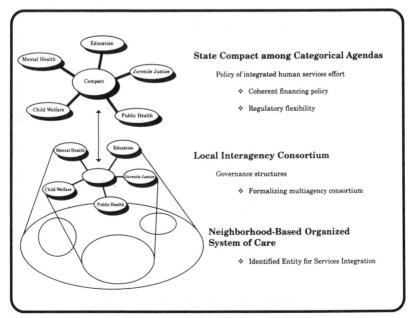

Figure 9.1. Policy structures for the locally organized system of care.

Finally, the system of care is organized through an *identifiable entity*, probably on a scale that is limited to maximize effectiveness and community ownership, with some version of unitary case management and flexible service capacity so that services can be individualized to meet the unique needs of a given child and his or her family. These policy structures are basic to the conceptualization of the system of care by NIMH's CASSP and have been addressed in each of the sites of the MHSPY.

Participants in the Multiagency System of Care: From the Family Outward

A system of care should be built around individual children and their needs. This ensures that the clinical judgments made on behalf of children and their families are not conditioned by the needs of institutions or programs. Consequently, the participants in the system of care are viewed, in terms of some order of influence, as the concentric layers of the famous onion (Figure 9.2). The *child's family* (or surrogate family) is the first layer, most intimately involved and directly responsible; the *case manager*, as broker of the system on the family's behalf, is next; the *clinical team*, representing formal participation of responsible agencies and long-term guidance, follows; the *provider agencies* are next, charged with the performance of a specific strategy; and, finally, the *public systems* representing the consortium

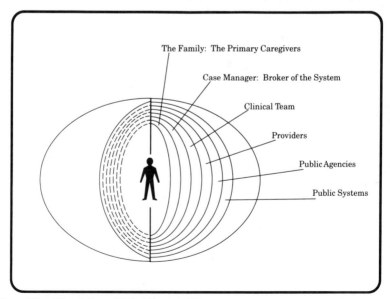

The Family: The Primary Caregivers

Case Manager: Broker of the System

Clinical Team

Providers

Public Agencies

Public Systems

Figure 9.2. Actors in the multiagency system of care.

of operating categorical agencies compose the outer layer. Some discussion is necessary to peel away these layers and to consider the complex formalities and relationships. Because we are dealing only with a metaphorical onion, we have the luxury of peeling from the inside out.

The Family: The Primary Caregivers Two implicit assumptions need to guide the development of an ideal case management system. First, it is possible to provide *intensive care* to children with serious mental disturbance in the natural setting of their home and community; and second, the most important asset for a child with a serious mental disability is a *close relationship with his or her family* (or surrogate family), no matter how stressed or in pain they may be at any given time.

The family unit, then, must be the primary object of therapeutic attention and, individually or as a group, family members must become primary participants and, as soon as possible, leaders in the treatment process. It is assumed that the treatment process will accompany the child's developmental process. The definition of the client as the individual child, as individual sibling children, or as the family unit as a whole is a matter of the clinical conceptualization of the case and should be reflected in the record.

The Case Manager as Broker: The Task of Orchestration The case manager in this system serves as a broker of services and resources on behalf of the child and his or her family. Different systems of care will structure the case management role in different ways depending on resources and culture. Clinical or administrative functions may be assigned to the case manager in varying degrees. Ideally, terms such as *family advocate* or *care coordinator* will be used to avoid the impression that the child or family is a "case" or that they should be "managed" (see Hobbs, 1982).

In case management, what is managed depends on your viewpoint. From the often officious perspective of human services agencies, the difficult situations experienced by children with emotional disturbances and their families are best described as "cases" that, of course, should be "managed." In fact, from a viewpoint closer to the family, the term *case* might just as well connote the complex of agencies and resources that must be marshaled to the benefit of the child and his or her family. In this sense, the constant in the case management function is the *activity of orchestrating* or *mobilizing* all the resources of the community to the service of the troubled child and his or her family. *Case managers manage the system.* Even though they may appear to be in a subordinate role in the various agency hierarchies, they "manage up."

The Clinical Team: A Long-Term Resource for Child Development For children for whom mental or emotional disturbance threatens to result in a lifetime disability, a stable interdisciplinary team must be formed and committed to stay with children throughout their developmental years. The case manager orchestrates the assembly of such a team, maintains its involvement with the child and his or her family, records its deliberations in the clinical record, and informs it of measured progress through monitoring the outcomes of the services. When the child is stabilized and growing and the family feels confident, the team can fade to the background. But in cases of great severity, it should be possible to reconvene the team as a familiar panel of experts to support the child and his or her family as they are confronted with the problems that may arise as the child's development proceeds.

The primary purpose of the clinical team is to formulate clinical judgments (i.e., informed and expert judgments made on behalf of patients). Obviously, the child and his or her family should be appropriately involved in the clinical team's deliberations and be an integral part of its consensus-building process, which results in the plan of care. The clinical team should try to attain a kind of independence and objectivity that focuses only on the patient's interest. There is no place for vested interest of a particular provider to promote a particular service or program for either theoretical or financial reasons; nor is there a place for a responsible public system to shift the responsibility of costs to another system. But, nonetheless, the availability of financial resources and the designation of responsibility must be considered as much as any other resource or responsibility.

This kind of objectivity and detachment is not easy to achieve, especially in the complex environment of public entitlement agencies with broad and often conflicting authorities. These agencies must be represented on the clinical team if they are to integrate their financial efforts to support care or extend their professional resources to provide care. An important role must also be maintained within the clinical team for the clinical consultants who are not service providers with a specific interest in the particular case. Skillful case managers orchestrate their contribution in order to attain the necessary objectivity and detachment needed for successful treatment and care.

Service Providers, Agencies, and Public Systems Finally, the three outer layers of the system of care are composed of service providers, agencies, and public systems. Service providers are organizations or individuals who provide direct care to the child and his or her family. A mental health center or child guidance clinic might be an example of a service provider, as well as community-based non-profit agencies that provide day or rehabilitation services, in addition to group or solo clinicians. Some local agencies may provide some services directly, even though they serve as designated representatives of public systems, and they may contract with or buy other services from other providers, such as a family and children's agency that works largely under contract with the public child welfare agency.

Agency refers to local entities or organizations that represent the public systems either as field offices, designated authorities, primary contractors, or official local administrators. *Agency* usually connotes the entity responsible for buying or paying for services recommended by the clinical team, such as a school district's special education program, the local child welfare office, or a juvenile court probation program with purchase-of-service dollars for individual children.

Public systems are the major entitlement agencies created by public laws specifying roles and responsibilities, including the administration of entitlement programs whereby citizens with defined characteristics and needs are entitled to certain publicly funded benefits. Child welfare, education, mental health, public health, and juvenile justice are the basic public systems responsible for children with severe emotional and behavioral disorders. Public systems always have central state bureaucracies, usually with federal counterparts, and they are manifested and represented in various ways in a given locality by different kinds of agencies.

The Configuration of Organizations within the System of Care

The configuration of the organizations making up the system of care is important to the functioning of the case management system. These configurations allow for considerable variation but are constant elements of the governance of a given system (Figure 9.3).

First, at the level of the local jurisdiction there is some kind of joint interagency agreement(s) among the responsible categorical agencies to work together on an agreed-upon target population of the most troubled children. This agreement constitutes a multiagency consortium, and the joint multiagency work that is done under it is overseen by an interagency steering committee. The steering committee might constitute designated managers from each system or be the executive committee of the multiagency consortium.

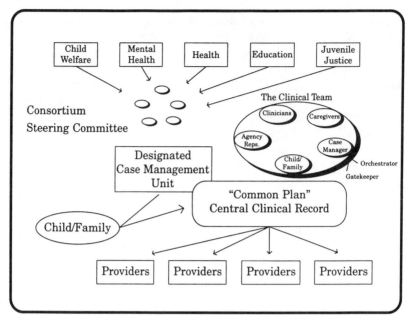

Figure 9.3. Configuration of the locally organized system of care.

Second, the multiagency consortium must identify one group of case managers located in one of the agencies or in a neutral place to whom a target population of children with severe needs and their families are assigned and for whom the participating agencies share responsibility. These case managers are expected to take the lead role in fulfilling the case management function even though other agency case managers may need to keep open records on the case to meet a given agency's requirements. These case managers should receive central clinical supervision and training and should have direct access to independent clinical consultation.

Third, the casework unit must maintain a *central clinical record* or *file* for each child and/or family under its care. This will include the constantly renewed plan of care by which the cooperative efforts of all responsible agencies and caregivers are organized around a coherent clinical strategy. The central record also should contain *first-level clinical documentation* for third-party payors, especially Medicaid, in order to maximize service provision flexibility by maintaining clinical justification and the rationale for the whole service package. Detailed clinical notes would, of course, be maintained, defining specific treatment and charting progress by each provider. The central record will keep track of the *eligibility status* of the child and/or family under all entitlements and potentially be the vehicle for the organization and management of service delivery. The central record also will serve as the hub from which *quality assurance* activities, *consumer satisfaction,* and *cost-management operations* can be organized. Furthermore, the central record will generate documentation of *service system accountability* and *outcome effectiveness* to guide the actions of the multiagency consortium. The participating agencies may have regulatory requirements to maintain certain records, but the central clinical record should be considered the operating document of all the agencies' integrated efforts on behalf of the child and/or family (Table 9.1).

THE PHYSICAL PLANT: A TANGIBLE DESCRIPTION OF THE AUTOMATED CLINICAL RECORD SYSTEM

The automated clinical record system, CareTrack, was designed based on the case management system described. CareTrack assumes that a unit of case managers is set up by the multiagency consortium in one central place, either in a neutral place or attached to an operating agency designated by the consortium. CareTrack would be directly available to the case managers; from three to six workers might work with one IBM-compatible personal computer (386 with 80-megabyte hard drive) loaded with the commercially available relational database management software called "Paradox," a product of Borland International, Inc., and the CareTrack application software. (Note: CareTrack has been upgraded to Paradox 4.0 and can be used on a local area network [LAN].) Clerical staff may assist the case managers with some data input, and a designated systems administrator could provide support, manage file security, and develop and maintain the information look-up tables (computer files used for reference purposes), especially those that contain provider and service information specific to the jurisdiction.

Through CareTrack, the computer serves, by analogy, as an extension of the social worker's traditional filing cabinet. Hard-copy (paper) files are not eliminated, but certain summary reports (e.g.,

Table 9.1. The common plan: Functions of the central clinical record

- Coherent clinical strategy
- First-level clinical documentation
- Eligibility status for all entitlements
- Hub for quality assurance activities, consumer satisfaction, and cost management operations
- Documentation of service system accountability and outcome effectiveness

Plan of Care Summary, Case History Summary) produced by Care-Track can be inserted regularly into the record with the signatures of responsible clinicians. Forms are minimized and used for routine information with which clerical staff might assist, that is, most data can be collected on a steno pad in the field and entered directly by the caseworker.

CareTrack is not a billing system or an accounting system. It is presumed to be able to stand alone in the endless variety of administrative structures typical of a multiagency system of care. It can be related to other computer systems by cross-walking (computer matching of files of various systems). For example, CareTrack files and a community mental health center's billing system could be compared. CareTrack plans of care may also be used to "encumber" funds, and a voucher processing module can be developed that provides an accounting record of expenditures against purchase-of-service contracts. Similarly, a running record module can be developed to record the family advocate's contacts with the child and his or her family for billing purposes. CareTrack provides individual records for quality assurance purposes, as well as the linking of actions under a family-centered clinical strategy.

It is anticipated that CareTrack's data structures are comprehensive enough to produce any aggregate reports (or even individualized reports) required by the various oversight public system agencies. Furthermore, it is extremely important that a "substitution agreement" be negotiated from the outset so that case managers can be relieved of duplicative recording requirements. CareTrack's provisions to maintain confidentiality should meet all reasonable standards. Personal identifiers are contained within the local office, either on a specific personal computer or within the multi-user LAN. A LAN is a system by which individual computers can work with one another. Access to individual files is restricted to the assigned caseworker and his or her supervisor, and security is maintained by a system administrator. Transfer utilities, or computer programs that select only certain information from a file, allow the centralization of case data filtered of personal identifying information. Unduplicated case numbers reference casework sites within states, and identification keys are held and maintained within the local casework units.

Basic Concepts of CareTrack Data Structures

CareTrack uses five basic concepts to organize clinical record information: people, events, community resources, the plan of care categories, and the unique nomenclature or language used by each system of care.

People   Information is collected about all persons significant to the child's history, development, and treatment, including family and significant others. CareTrack stores a special file on each person who is relevant to the child, including family members, friends, more distant relations, foster families, and other significant caregivers. The case manager can arrange this information in a *genogram* identifying the immediate *significant sphere* of personal relationships or outlining the family history to assist in the presentation of the case in the clinical case conference.

Events   Events serve as the building blocks of the case history. CareTrack classifies the events according to a taxonomy or system of classification of all possible events (which is available in the program's information look-up tables). The general categories of the taxonomy identify each event as either an occurrence in the child's behavior or the family's or community's life or as a response or intervention on the part of the various community service systems. Two levels of subtypes specify the events according to different types. A partial outline of the branches of the taxonomy is demonstrated in Figure 9.4.

The profile of each event allows for a great degree of detail, dates, places, service providers, estimated costs, particular circumstances, interpretation of meaning, and significance. Unlimited event records can be filed and the whole event history summarized

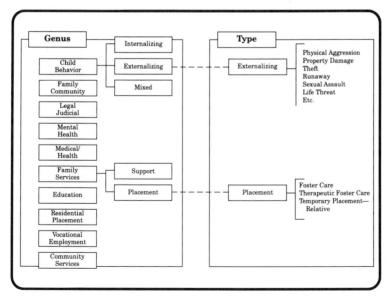

Figure 9.4.   The events taxonomy.

in a one-page *time bar report* (discussed as follows), which facilitates the worker's presentation to the clinical case conference.

Community Resources   Profiles of all providers and relevant agencies in the community are contained in the CareTrack look-up tables. These are computer files that are a ready information resource for the caseworker and a direct aid in drawing detailed repetitive information into the record with minimum keystrokes. Information in these profiles is detailed, including specific services and service provider identification. Each contract has different public agencies, service rates, service units, and revenue sources covering each service.

Plan of Care   The plan of care is CareTrack's basic clinical document that directs and controls the course of treatment. Each edition of the plan is archived or saved automatically as it is replaced by development of a current edition. The plan of care outlines relevant treatment issues (e.g., strengths, problems, needs), specific clinical goals, prescribed services to meet the goals, and expected measurable outcomes related to each goal. It provides the framework by which the caseworker monitors both the provision of services and the achievement of measured outcomes in monthly progress reports entered into CareTrack.

Language of the Local System of Care   CareTrack allows each site to enter its own terminology as used in the local system of care, defining the significant policy issues relevant to the particular community. These terms and categories are contained in the look-up tables, which are used to categorize treatment issues, presenting problems, clinical goals, service definitions (linked to state billing codes), measurable outcomes, and so on. This allows the system of care to use its own words for goals that are compatible with the clinical training and supervision approach taken in the particular locality. The same is true with the words for presenting problems or measurable outcomes. This means that when reports on children for whom "completion of schoolwork" may have been set out as a measurable outcome are tallied, the improvement under one strategy or another can be compared. The ability of the system of care to put its own categories on the look-up tables makes it possible to get computer access to aggregate data that are directly relevant to the system.

THE CASE PROCESS

CareTrack supports a case manager in taking a case through the following process (Figure 9.5). Referral information is received by the interagency consortium through procedures that are specified in a given system. Usually it includes identifying information, a current summary of the case history, descriptive information about members of the child's family and other significant people in the child's life, information about the different agencies that are involved with the child and his or her family, insurance carriers, and a short narrative defining the presenting situation that led to the child's referral. The case will be accepted or referred to another agency based on guidelines provided by the interagency consortium's steering committee and, if accepted, assigned to a given caseworker. Once assigned, the caseworker prepares the case for the clinical case conference at which the clinical team completes the plan of care; the plan of care is authorized (i.e., its prescribed expenditures are approved by the designated manager of the agency responsible for each service) and then activated. The lead clinician signs for the whole team. At this point, the caseworker sets about enrolling and engaging the child and his or her family in the various services prescribed in the plan. Each month the case manager monitors the provision of services and records progress reported by the various service providers against predefined outcomes. Each quarter (or sooner, if necessary), a new edition of the plan of care is prepared with the help of the clinical team in a periodic clinical case conference. Annually, there is a for-

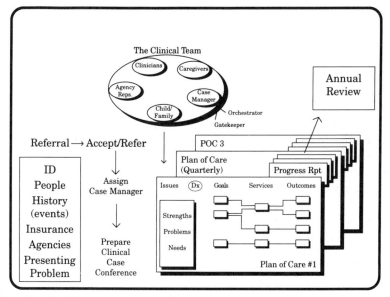

Figure 9.5. Model for case processing pathway.

mal clinical review at which long-term goals are set. The cycle continues until it is appropriate to discharge the child and his or her family from services.

The details of this process can be understood through a discussion of the initial development and preparation of the case, the structure of the plan of care, the programmatic and financial monitoring of the case, and the analysis and review of the performance of the whole system of care based on the records of each individual case.

Case Preparation

Upon being assigned the case, the caseworker prepares it for presentation to the clinical case conference. This involves much direct work with the child and his or her family as well as with other involved agencies, caregivers, and service providers, and specialists and experts who may be needed to perform assessments or administer tests. The history of the child and his or her family is developed by building around the events gathered in the referral process to include the child's whole life and developmental history. CareTrack helps to summarize this story by providing the caseworker with a time bar report, which visually separates the story into the dimensions of the child's and family's experiences, along with the events involving each of the public systems. Working from the time bar report, the caseworker could easily construct the kind of visual summary of the case history that has been presented by Burchard's "multiaxial timeline" (Burchard et al., 1991) (Figure 9.6).

Information about the people in the child's life is provided as the caseworker learns more about the family members and their resources and ties to the community. CareTrack assembles this information in summary reports to assist the caseworker in developing genograms to chart family patterns and relationships and in identifying the child's sphere of significant relationships for consideration by the clinical team. The caseworker gathers all the clinical assessments that may be done in preparation for the clinical case conference as well as information from other perspectives, such as past service providers and potential future service providers. CareTrack provides various places to record this information. The different sections of the plan of care might be drafted in this process, anticipating issues and exploring possibilities that might be further discussed in the clinical case conference.

Structure of Plan of Care

The automated plan of care is the center of the clinical record and follows a very standard format modeled on the quality assurance

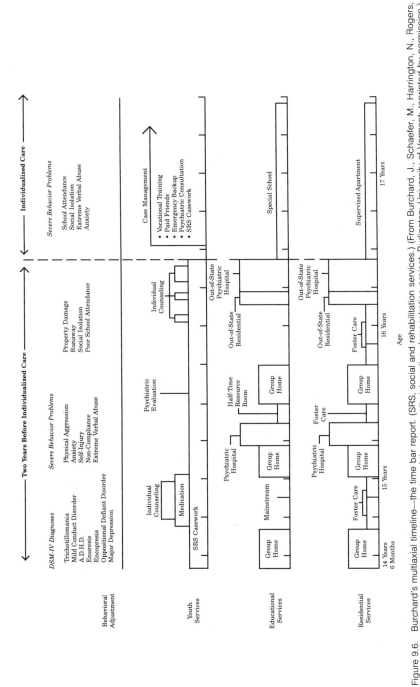

Figure 9.6. Burchard's multiaxial timeline—the time bar report. (SRS, social and rehabilitation services.) (From Burchard, J., Schaefer, M., Harrington, N., Rogers, J., Welkowitz, J., & Tighe, T. [1991]. *An evaluation of the community integration demonstration project*. Burlington: University of Vermont; reprinted by permission.)

practice standards of eminent psychiatric training institutions and national accrediting organizations. The four basic components of the plan of care allow the construction of straightforward clinical strategies, as well as the construction of those that are more complex.

Treatment Issues: Strengths, Problems, and Needs The presenting situation of the child and his or her family can be described by a series of "issues" screens. These consist of a "headline" descriptive statement, a two- or three-sentence description, and a code taken from the locality's customized look-up table. Cumulatively, the issues statements prepare a logical context for the actions to be taken in the plan.

Diagnosis and Assessment: Clinical Insights and Functional Assets/Deficits The automated record provides a format to record a complex, five-axis diagnostic analysis using the categories of the *Diagnostic and Statistical Manual of Mental Disorders*, 4th revised edition (*DSM-IV*) (American Psychiatric Association, 1994), which can be taken from the system's look-up tables. There is a format for a diagnostic summary to be written and signed by the lead clinician, as well as for revision of medication information. The scores of the North Carolina Functional Assessment Scale are built into the system and can be recorded; there are also open fields in which to record scores on other standardized functional assessment instruments.

Clinical Goals: Focusing the Treatment Effort and Prioritizing the Agenda An itemization of clinical goals consisting of a numerical ordering, a headline description, a two- or three-sentence descriptive definition of the goal, and a code taken from a customized look-up table is included in the record. There should be a logical connection from the goals to the presenting information in the treatment issues (strengths, problems, needs), as well as an automated connection from the services to the service outcomes. This is described as follows.

Clinical Strategy: The Package of Services Making up the Intervention Plan Finally, CareTrack lists the clinical strategy in terms of a series of services, hopefully in a coherent package. Each service is prescribed in a defined time period in terms of specified units, and it is possible to identify the proposed service provider with the details derived from look-up tables. Each service must be connected to one or more of the clinical goals and, for each goal, a measurable outcome must be defined, thus defining the format for the caseworker to monitor the progress of the service provision process.

After the plan of care is formulated in the clinical case conference and the caseworker has secured the approval (or *authorization*) of the responsible administrators to pay for the services, the plan of care is activated, that is, it is finalized by CareTrack and made part of the permanent archive as the first edition of the plan of care. The contents of the first edition are copied into an open "next edition," which can then be edited and modified after the next 3-month period (or sooner, if necessary), when the clinical team reconvenes to assess the progress of the service program and formulate the next edition of the plan of care. In the meantime, with the first edition activated, the caseworker proceeds to enroll the child and his or her family in the planned services.

Monitoring Clinical Progress and Financial Expenditures

On a monthly basis, CareTrack provides reports for the caseworker to systematically monitor both the clinical progress and the financial expenditures that have been projected in the plan of care. The system's progress report can be printed as a report to which information can be added and then entered into the computer. This provides a format that the caseworker can use as he or she contacts each service provider to determine what units of service have been delivered and how the child and his or her family are faring. As delivered service units are reported, CareTrack automatically tallies expenditures and estimates the revenues paying for those expenditures since that information was entered (from look-up tables) at the plan of care's inception and confirmed at enrollment. The caseworker is also able to discuss the child's progress in terms of the measurable outcomes specified in the plan of care and to record progress in both descriptive and numerical terms.

Monitoring System Performance

Finally, CareTrack makes it possible for supervisors and administrators, as well as the interagency consortium steering committee, to monitor the performance of the system of care as a whole, based on the recorded experience of individual children. It is possible to track expenditures against plan-of-care encumbrances even before bills are submitted, to track progress toward opening new sources of revenue, to identify eligibility potential that should be followed, and even to identify effective service delivery patterns.

CONCLUSION

The very effort of developing CareTrack lends clarity to the problem of providing services to children and youth with serious mental and emotional disturbances and their families. Supporting through automation the work of case managers operating in a multiagency system of care to serve this most needy target population of troubled and troubling children, the automated clinical record forces examination of the intricate details of what "intensive treatment in normal settings" means. The information system has required its designers to think around the corners of the dauntingly complex interrelationships among categorical agencies, to translate between the different voices and dialects of their disciplines and traditions, and to discover the common ground of their efforts and responsibilities in the individual child's treatment plan. Inevitably, there remain some familiar but still unanswered questions concerning the integration of human services, substance and accountability in service delivery practice, the balance of clinical judgment and financial accountability, and both the role segmentation of the case management function and its necessity to the organization of care. Such questions point to the central policy issues for children with mental and emotional disturbances and their families.

The first question is in regard to human services integration. Can we, indeed, treat children with serious mental illness without intensive efforts of all the responsible public agencies? Or, by way of corollary, can the mandates of any categorical agency be achieved without an integration of effort? It is hard to imagine that we can do so without interagency coordination and integration of effort orchestrated by the case manager through a common plan.

Second is a question regarding substance and accountability in service delivery practice. Can we effectively treat children with serious mental illness without meeting standards of accountability comparable to medical quality assurance standards? The problems these children present do not lead us to believe so, and this places an unprecedented challenge upon our programming in home and community settings.

The third question concerns the balance of clinical judgment and financial accountability. On the one hand, can a child with serious mental illness be effectively treated without the directive guidance of sound clinical judgments? On the other hand, can effective financial decisions be made if cost-cutting concerns lead to the neglect of good clinical judgment? The soundest economies are achieved through the effective exercise of clinical judgment, and the case management function, with ready command of all its information, can best integrate clinical and financial management.

Finally, there is a question regarding the segmentation of case management roles and the necessity of the organization of care. Should the case manager serve as an advocate, a clinical therapist, a gatekeeper, or an organizer? Clearly, the case management function is broader than the several possible roles a worker might assume in a given system of care. But the constant is that the overall organization of care achieved by an individual or the interaction of players who share aspects of the case management function is *sine qua non* for the effective treatment of a child with mental and emotional disturbance and the support of his or her family.

REFERENCES

American Psychiatric Association. (1994). *Diagnostic and statistical manual of mental disorders* (4th rev. ed.). Washington, DC: Author.
Burchard, J., Schaefer, M., Harrington, N., Rogers, J., Welkowitz, J., & Tighe, T. (1991). *An evaluation of the community integration demonstration project*. Burlington: University of Vermont.
Hobbs, N. (1982). *The troubled and troubling child*. San Francisco: Jossey-Bass.
Willie M. v. Hunt, Civil No. C–C–79–0294, slip op. (W.D.N.C., February 20, 1991; *See* 657 F. 2d 55, 4th Cir., 1981).

TRAINING AND SUPERVISING SERVICE COORDINATORS

CHAPTER 10

Issues and Principles of Training for Case Management in Child Mental Health

Marie Overby Weil, Irene Nathan Zipper, and S. Rachel Dedmon

When there are multiple problems and stresses for children and their families, they frequently need case management and services from multiple agencies. For example, a child may have lost a parent through death or divorce; a child may have experienced prolonged sexual or physical abuse; or biological factors may have had an impact on personal and social development with results that produce serious and complex behavioral and emotional difficulties. Such personal and familial difficulties may be exacerbated by poverty, substance abuse, family stress, and other factors. Family disruption from within by divorce or externally from state intervention aimed at protecting children also may complicate the difficulties experienced by a child and intensify problematic emotional and behavioral responses to stresses and daily life situations. When children need mental health support, intervention, or treatment, they and their families should be connected with services of the child mental health system.

CASE MANAGEMENT IN CHILD MENTAL HEALTH

To provide services in a supportive and empowering manner, service providers need to work together to coordinate services and meet the multiple needs of children and their parents for information, support, advocacy, intervention, and treatment. Case management is a method of service provision that seeks to guarantee that children and their families receive the services and supports they need through a process of interaction, with a key service provider

211

and other members of a service network, that is effective, supportive, and empowering. For families, involvement in a case management program should mean that they have a case manager/key service provider who is committed to streamlining the service system
and ensuring that the child gets the services, opportunities, and
supports needed for optimal development.

Case management involves: outreach and problem identification, assessment of the child's needs for treatment and services, assessment of family needs, development of a service plan by the family and case manager, linking the child and his or her family to
needed services and support systems, service coordination and assessment, monitoring of problems in service provision for the child,
advocacy for the child and family in the service network and community as needed, and evaluation with the child and family of outcomes of treatment and service provision (Weil, 1985b). As Figure
10.1 illustrates, in working with children and their families, there
is a dual process of building a parent–professional partnership and
developing interprofessional collaboration for effective service coordination.

The case manager's primary goals are to help the family solve
problems and to ensure that the child is effectively connected to
needed programs and services. The term *case management* is not felic-
itous. It may sound like a technical and impersonal approach, but
the practice should be built on a strong, supportive relationship with
the child and family and involves important steps in service delivery
and coordination that can help to attain desired goals and build a

Steps in the Case Management Process	Client Identification and Outreach	Assessment	Service Planning	Service Implementation	Evaluation at Client Level & System Level	
Case Management Activities	Sharing and Exchange of Information					} ACTIVITIES
	Linking and Service Coordination					
	Service Monitoring					
Interactive Processes	Parent–Professional Partnership	(enablement, empowerment, and advocacy)				} PROCESSES
	Interprofessional Collaboration	(coordinated assessment and evaluation; joint planning and decision making)				

Figure 10.1. The case management process in child mental health. (Adapted from Weil, M.O., 1985b.)

family-centered and responsive service system for children with mental health problems. By definition, case management is needed when multiple services are utilized to coordinate the work of multiple professionals and community support and advocacy programs for families. Service coordination is the middle part of the case management process; it ensures that service providers work toward the same goals, do not "trip over" each other, respect each other's areas of expertise, and work together to support the child and his or her family. In service coordination, the case manager and parents, foster parents, or guardian assess the services that the child is receiving and "troubleshoot" to solve problems as they arise. When problems are identified in this troubleshooting and monitoring process, the case manager and family move into advocacy work. With or without problems, the case manager and family continuously evaluate the service system and the progress and outcomes of treatment and intervention.

Case management and its service coordination component are therefore critical processes in ensuring that children get the services they need and that families are engaged and empowered in the service provision process (Weil, 1985a). All too frequently, in the past, children have not received all the services that they needed, and families often felt excluded from the decision-making and problem-solving processes. Service providers in different agencies have not communicated effectively with each other or coordinated their efforts toward common goals for the child and family. From the recognition that service systems have frequently not met their responsibilities for coordinated intervention and treatment and have not been "family friendly," demonstration programs have increasingly focused on developing best practices in case management and service coordination to see that the child mental health system connects families effectively with other community services. This connection requires that the case manager assist the family with information about other services and how to use them, and that the case manager orchestrates collaboration and coordination among various service providers to see that they all focus on the goals of the service plan and work with the parents and child in a mutual problem-solving partnership.

The number of children recognized as needing multiple services has greatly increased in recent years, and with that increase has come an escalating demand for carefully coordinated services that are tailored to meet the needs of the child and family. It is now recognized that what is needed is a comprehensive, family-centered, community-based system of services for the families of children who have emotional or behavioral disorders, or other serious problems or vulnerabilities (Friesen & Koroloff, 1990). In order to assist case managers and families to develop partnerships to improve services for vulnerable children and children with disorders, training is needed to practice working together and solving problems.

This chapter discusses the development, implementation, and evolution of a curriculum for training for case management in child mental health and the model for curriculum development that guided the process. The curriculum, entitled Case Management for Children's Mental Health: A Training Curriculum for Child-Serving Agencies (Zipper & Weil, 1994), is described, along with competencies needed for practice in this field. Issues of training implementation are presented and directions for preservice and professional education are also discussed. Finally, the chapter concludes with a set of training principles designed to be applicable throughout the United States, which guided the North Carolina Child Mental Health Curriculum Development and Training Project. These training principles can provide useful guidance to both states and agencies engaged in improving services to children and their families through staff training in case management, collaboration with families, service coordination, and cross-system service integration. State and local information that needs to be added to ground the curriculum in specific service contexts is also noted.

This curriculum, now available throughout the United States, was developed in North Carolina by way of a collaborative process involving child mental health practice demonstration sites, the Child and Family Services Branch of the North Carolina Division of Mental Health, Developmental Disabilities and Substance Abuse Services, and the School of Social Work at the University of North Carolina at Chapel Hill. The project was initiated in response to the increasing needs for the following: 1) case management knowledge and skills development among child mental health practitioners, 2) development of collaboration and service coordination skills among all practitioners in the child- and family-serving systems, and 3) development of effective parent–professional partnerships to meet the needs of children with emotional and behavioral difficulties more effectively.

The momentum in mental health services for children, as well as in education and health services, is to shift from child-focused to family-centered services. Early Intervention legislation mandates parent involvement in case management. For example, the 1986 amendments to the Education of the Handicapped Act (Part H of PL 99-457) and the Individuals with Disabilities Education Act (IDEA) of 1990 (PL 101-476) mandate that states electing to participate provide services for children with disabilities and/or developmental delays between birth and age 3 and their families, in relation to the concerns, resources, and priorities of the family. Current trends in child welfare emphasize family support, in-home services, and family preservation. The focus of intervention in all these fields is converging toward a common family-centered perspective. With the increasing overlap in the populations served by these systems, child mental health practitioners need to be prepared to use a family-centered intervention approach with children and their families who have serious problems, including reactions to family disruption.

Case management is an effective way to assure the coordination of services provided by multiple agencies. The lack of service coordination has been one reason for the shortage of services to children with serious emotional problems and their families (Friesen, 1993). In the field of early intervention, in which case management is now known as service coordination, it is a mandated service (Zipper, Weil, & Rounds, 1993). In mental health, case management can ensure that wraparound services tailored to their specific needs are available and accessible to children and families (Behar, 1986). Earlier approaches to case management with children in the mental health system, however, were extrapolated from the case management models developed for adults. A new focus on the specific developmental, treatment, and intervention needs of children and the concerns of their families is required to build a system that integrates services in an effective, empowering model.

Such an approach should acknowledge not only those issues unique to children's mental health, such as children's manifestations of emotional disorders, but also changes in family structure and the increasing diversity of the population. Like adults, children can experience emotional problems ranging from mild adjustment reactions to psychoses. Children's problems, however, are heavily influenced by their stage of development, family interactions, and other environmental factors. Children and adolescents served through the mental health system reflect our national diversity in terms of culture, race, ethnicity, sexual orientation, and economic status. Furthermore, children live in various types of home environments including two-parent families, step- or blended families, single-parent families, same-sex parenting partners, with other relatives, or in adoptive or foster families. When children are not able to live in a family setting, they may be placed in group homes, residential settings, or hospitals.

Families are also characterized by differences in material and supportive resources. For example, those using the child mental health system in the United States are representative of the full range of families. They may also be poor, rich, working-class or middle-class families. They may be families characterized by severe conflict and disruption or families recognized in their community as highly functional and supportive. They may be families in which all members have experienced severe trauma and stress. They may also be families whose children have serious problems, such as schizophrenia or major affective disorders, and whose behaviors, therefore, are as likely to affect family dynamics as to be affected by them (B. Friesen, personal communication, October 22, 1993). Case managers and others involved in service provision need to be sensitive to all these issues, while also recognizing the special role of prevention in child mental health—to deter the development of more serious difficulties and to offset additional problems.

A pressing need exists for appropriate preservice education and in-service training for child mental health practitioners, including case managers, and for other workers in the public and voluntary child- and family-serving systems. Training is needed to ensure that practitioners are prepared to address increasingly severe presenting problems among children—ranging from schizophrenia to violent acting-out behaviors—and to provide family-centered and effectively coordinated services. Traditional psychotherapy may not be useful in families with complex problems, particularly when it is offered in isolation from other services (Schorr, 1988). Education and training for child mental health workers cannot afford to concentrate on the development of child diagnostic and treatment skills without an equal focus on service coordination and an ecological perspective on children and their families. In developing appropriate training, it is also necessary to address these variations and the unevenness of case managers' and others' preparation for their complex tasks. Case managers in child mental health are recruited from a variety of disciplines. In current practice, there is tremendous variation in case managers' educational level and field of specialty, as well as in their prior work experience.

In this chapter, principles for training child mental health case managers are drawn from the examination of best practices and from the experiences in the curriculum development process undertaken in North Carolina to build a state-of-the-art and future-focused model for family-centered practice in child mental health. Curriculum development for Case Management for Children's Mental Health (Zipper & Weil, 1994) was funded by the Division of Mental Health Developmental Disabilities and Substance Abuse Services of the State of North Carolina with funds from the Robert Wood Johnson Foundation, the Child and Adolescent Service System Program (CASSP) demonstration programs, and the Civilian Health and Medical Program of the Uniformed Services (CHAMPUS) child mental health demonstration project at the Rumbaugh Clinic at Fort Bragg. The Annie E. Casey Foundation provided funding for training trainers and for national dissemination of the curriculum. The content of the curriculum is focused on competencies needed by case managers for effective service to children who have emotional or behavioral problems and their families. It places a major emphasis on families and family decision making, and case managers' roles, as well as intensive work on service coordination and teamwork with other service providers. In addition to describing the curriculum, this chapter presents strategies for training implementation and directions for preservice and professional education. Survey responses from a sample of CASSP agencies about their perspectives on case management training are also incorporated. These surveys were completed by a group of CASSP directors at their annual meeting in North Carolina in November 1991.

CASE MANAGEMENT FOR CHILD MENTAL HEALTH: A TRAINING CURRICULUM FOR CHILD-SERVING AGENCIES

In North Carolina, child mental health case management training is being implemented through a contract between the state's Department of Human Resources, Division of Mental Health, Developmental Disabilities, and Substance Abuse Services, and the School of Social Work at the University of North Carolina at Chapel Hill. The model established a collaborative process for content development involving the State Division of Mental Health Children and Youth Program, three demonstration child mental health programs, child mental health advocacy organizations, and project faculty at the School of Social Work. Using this process, a training curriculum emphasizing experiential interactive learning was developed for child mental health case managers and personnel in other child- and family-serving programs. Concurrently, project faculty have been engaged in incorporating principles of case management practice into the School of Social Work's child mental health curriculum. As a result, there will be congruence between the child mental health intervention models taught in preservice education at the university and those taught in agency-based in-service training throughout North Carolina.

In-service training must respond to both the priorities of policymakers and the practice needs and experiences of child mental health case managers and supervisors. The curriculum development project included these groups as partners in a collaborative planning and piloting process (Figure 10.2).

When agreement was reached with state child mental health personnel on major topic areas, social work faculty drafted broad goals and operationally defined objectives for specified curriculum modules. These were reviewed and critiqued by demonstration site staff, state office personnel, and representatives of advocacy organizations for children with mental health needs and their families. When this review was completed, project faculty at the School of Social Work formulated content and training activities to meet agreed-upon goals and objectives. Case vignettes were provided by site representatives to ensure that training activities reflected current practice conditions. The curriculum has been pilot-tested at program sites, and evaluations were completed by case managers and supervisors. The evaluations, together with direct feedback on the activities, guided final module revisions in preparation for statewide implementation and national availability.

The curriculum is applicable to case management and service coordination in child mental health and other child- and family-serving systems. The collaborative process by which content was determined represents the consumer, as well as those involved in policy planning and service delivery. The three demonstration projects are representative of state-of-the-art child mental health case management approaches; a Robert Wood Johnson pilot project that models interagency and interprofessional collaboration between the mental health system and other service providers in rural areas; a CHAMPUS-funded demonstration project serving children and their families at a large military base; and CASSP model demonstration projects serving young children and their families in urban areas. The training modules address the competencies needed by case managers for effective practice in the child-serving system.

Curriculum Content

The curriculum begins with an introduction to case management in the child-serving system and basic competencies for case management grounded in a focus that encompasses a mental health perspective on the child, his or her family, and the service network. This curriculum focuses on competencies in three major areas: 1) building a partnership with parents (or adults responsible for the child); 2) competencies related to the child's or adolescent's need for support, development, and treatment; and 3) competencies for planning, coordination, collaboration, and intervention in the ser-

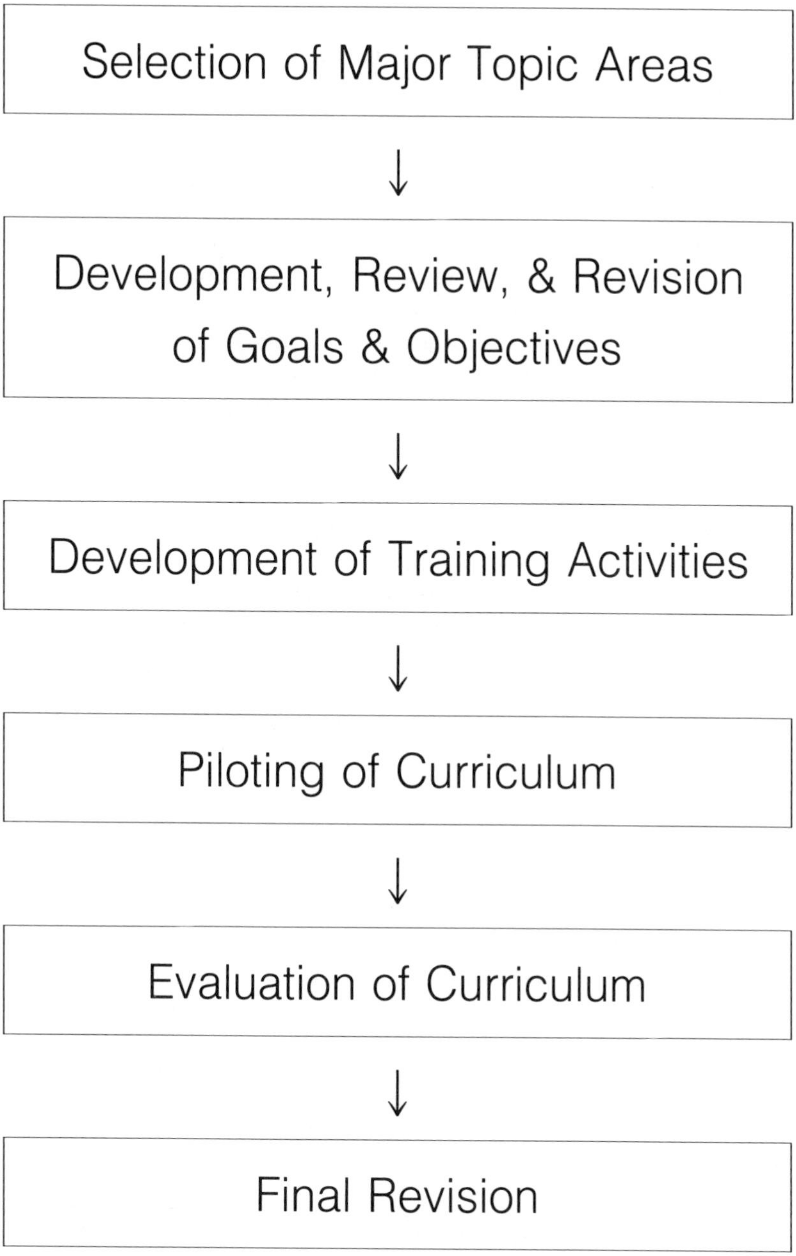

Selection of Major Topic Areas

$\downarrow$

Development, Review, & Revision of Goals & Objectives

$\downarrow$

Development of Training Activities

$\downarrow$

Piloting of Curriculum

$\downarrow$

Evaluation of Curriculum

$\downarrow$

Final Revision

Figure 10.2. The curriculum development process.

vice system. Activities focused on developing these competencies are woven throughout the curriculum. Major parts of the curriculum focus on the roles of case managers, the process of case management, and the functioning of the child-serving system. One module engages participants in analyzing the system of services (and service gaps) in their state. A second critical module focuses on collaborating with families and a third on collaborating with other service providers. These modules are particularly important because case managers often have to interpret reasons for assessments and serve as a liaison between parents and other professionals. Another module deals with the complexities of assessment and intervention in child mental health, which case managers need to understand whether they function primarily in a treatment role or primarily as service brokers and coordinators.

Some case managers work with ongoing teams; others must develop an intervention team for each child served. Many clinicians, however, have had very little training in teamwork. Consequently, one module focuses on developing teams and facilitating team functioning. This module stresses that case managers have a critical role to play in facilitating team planning, goal setting, and conferences, and that, increasingly, they need to assist other service providers in working with parents as team members.

The curriculum encompasses a number of special issues and concerns. One key module deals with cultural diversity among families and focuses on helping participants demonstrate sensitivity and competency in multicultural practice. Because of the rapid development of legislation and programs for infants and young children that have an impact on the child mental health system, the curriculum includes a module on early intervention for very young children. One module of the curriculum focuses on crisis intervention, one concentrates on survival skills for case managers, one addresses the roles of parents as advocates for their children, and another module deals with special issues of supervision and cross-agency service integration. The modules included in Case Management for Children's Mental Health (Zipper & Weil, 1994) are presented in Table 10.1

Training the Trainers

The curriculum model calls for a "train the trainers" approach in which university faculty and practice-based trainers are paired in preparation for implementation of the curriculum, involving parent advocates and additional experts as appropriate to address regional concerns. As Table 10.2 illustrates, university- and practice-based training faculty bring complementary expertise to the training enter-

Table 10.1.   Case management for child mental health: A training curriculum for child-serving agencies

Curriculum Modules
I. Introduction to Case Management
II. The Basics of Case Management
III. The Service System in Our State
IV. Diversity and Cultural Competence
V. The Case Manager, the Process, and the Child-Serving System
VI. Case Management Functions and Process: Collaborating with Families
VII. Case Management Functions and Process: Collaborating with Service Providers
VIII. Crisis Intervention
IX. A Mental Health Perspective on Assessment and Intervention
X. Developing Teams and Facilitating Team Functioning
XI. Service Coordination in Early Intervention
XII. Parents as Advocates and Case Managers
XIII. Survival Skills for the Case Manager
XIV. Supervision and Cross-System Management

From Zipper, I. N., & Weil, M. (Eds.). (1994). *Case management for children's mental health: A training curriculum for child-serving agencies.* Raleigh: North Carolina Division of Mental Health, Developmental Disabilities, and Substance Abuse Services; reprinted by permission.

prise. Their teamwork is a means through which the curriculum training process models collaboration.

The Annie E. Casey Foundation funded a national series of "training of trainers" in the fall of 1994, in preparation for implementation of the curriculum. In these workshops, participants from throughout the nation worked together to practice training activities

Table 10.2.   Using complementary expertise and modeling collaboration

University-based training faculty	Practice-based training faculty
Theoretical perspective	Practice perspective
Information on national trends in services for children	Information on local developments and implementation in services for children
Knowledge about organizational development and interorganizational relationships	Knowledge about state and local service network
Information on current research and theory development	Experience with implementation of local demonstration projects
Knowledge of adult learning principles	Knowledge of staff and staff responsibilities

from the curriculum and consider its adaptation to local conditions. In June 1994, at a CASSP Conference in Traverse City, Michigan, the curriculum developers provided a workshop that demonstrated application of the curriculum to a variety of state-based specific training needs. From the North Carolina experience in training, the team recommended that all states adopting the curriculum employ a partnership of university- and practice-based trainers and include parents and leaders of local advocacy groups as trainees and participants. This combination will ensure that theoretical perspectives on exemplary practices are conveyed in the context of the realities of family-centered, community-based practice and that the principal stakeholders—parents, service providers, and the community support system—are engaged as a team in the training process. To teach collaboration, it is best to model effective collaboration.

CASE MANAGEMENT COMPETENCIES: VALUES, KNOWLEDGE, AND SKILLS

The case manager involved with a child and his or her family has a principal responsibility to work with and support both in their involvement in the service system. As illustrated in Figure 10.3, the child and his or her family are the center of this network and the case manager has the role of assisting to connect the family and child to services, advocating for their needs, and working with them

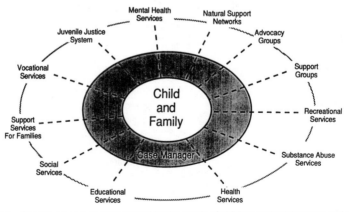

Figure 10.3. Service network to meet mental health needs of children and adolescents and their families. (From Zipper, I.N., & Weil, M. [1994]. *Case management for children's mental health: A training curriculum for child-serving agencies* [Module III]. Raleigh: North Carolina Division of Mental Health, Developmental Disabilities and Substance Abuse Services; reprinted with permission.)

to monitor and evaluate the effectiveness of services. A wide range of professionals, support or advocacy groups, and community-based services may be involved with the child and his or her family. Figure 10.4 illustrates the variety of professionals who may be involved in service coordination for a child involved in the mental health system and its community-based network. The child and his or her family are at the center of the collaborative, interprofessional, community-based network. The case manager strives to ensure that the family's involvement with a multiplicity of staff from different programs is a smoothly running system rather than a complex maze.

Understanding and effectively coordinating services tailored to the needs of an individual child and her or his family within the complex child-serving system is a central task for the case manager. Although the child and his or her family are always at the center of the service system, case managers in child mental health must have a tripartite focus to meet their service needs effectively. Case managers must focus careful attention on: 1) the child, 2) the family, and 3) the service system. The child's needs for treatment and support for development are paramount. The case manager needs to develop an effective planning and problem-solving partnership with the parents, foster parents, or guardians of the child, and must be ever-vigilant to ensure that other service providers are fulfilling their commitments to the child and his or her family. Facilitating good

Collaborators for Case Management in Child Mental Health

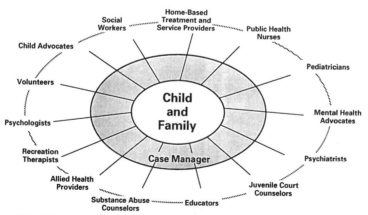

Figure 10.4. Collaboration for case management in child mental health. (From Zipper, I.N., & Weil, M. [1994]. *Case management for children's mental health: A training curriculum for child-serving agencies.* [Module III]. Raleigh: North Carolina Division of Mental Health, Developmental Disabilities and Substance Abuse Services; reprinted with permission.)

working relationships between the parents and other service providers is part of the case manager's responsibility, as is working with the parents in service monitoring and evaluation, to see that the child's needs are being met. This tripartite focus of the case manager is illustrated in Figure 10.5

Eligibility for services is determined by the child's needs, but the case manager must focus equally on the partnership with the parent or responsible adult and on service coordination and collaboration among service providers, as well as on the child. The interactions between the case manager and each focal point affect all other interactions. This tripartite focus necessitates that child mental health case managers have a variety of competencies to carry out their roles. Characteristics of effective case managers that have been suggested have often focused on interpersonal and attitudinal qualities (Bailey, 1989). In addition to such qualities, effective case management requires a specific value base, knowledge relevant to the population to be served and to the service system, and skills needed to provide the service, including relating to children with mental health needs, engaging in partnerships with their parents or other responsible adult, and facilitating interprofessional collaboration. In this curriculum model, values, knowledge, and skills are addressed to build needed competencies.

Values

An ecological perspective on the child, family, and community that involves examining the broad environment to understand difficulties

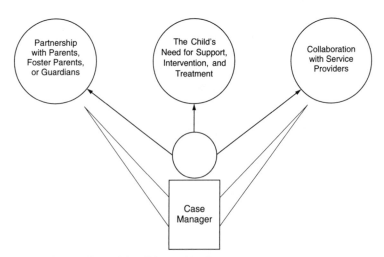

Figure 10.5. Tripartite focus of the child mental health case manager.

as well as to intervene is essential to effective case management. In fact, systems theory, which considers the interrelationships among various aspects of the environment, has been called the conceptual foundation of case management practice (Roberts-DeGennaro, 1987). Case managers who understand the powerful role that informal and formal supports can play in enhancing individual and family functioning will expend the time and effort needed to find and enlist such supports. Case managers who believe that community-based services are the most relevant and appropriate for children with emotional or behavioral problems will provide the intense involvement needed to ensure that agencies, organizations, and individuals collaborate to support and preserve families.

Involvement with families who are under stress, whose resources are strained, or whose actions may not always appear to be in the best interests of the child, requires a firm commitment to a family-centered approach to service delivery and a commitment to family preservation. Some families may not be able to consistently provide an environment conducive to their child's development and will need considerable support if efforts at family preservation are to succeed. Case managers need to believe that families want what is best for their child. Families should be valued for knowing their child better than anyone else, although they may not always fully understand the child's behavior.

Case managers need to value family preservation to the point of providing intensive support and intervention to help keep the family intact in times of crisis. Wraparound services can provide a means of multiple intervention and help to prevent crises. However, there are obviously times when keeping the family together is not possible, as in instances when the child's safety cannot be ensured in the home even when intensive services have been provided. In such situations, when placement is needed, the case manager, guided by the belief that the child's natural family is the home of choice for the child, will work with the family and other service providers toward family reunification when that is possible. This may entail advocating on behalf of the child and his or her family for services that may be inaccessible or unavailable.

Case managers need to value the basic integrity of children and adults and respect the cultural, racial, and ethnic and social class differences among families. They also need to appreciate families' varied coping styles, recognize that all families sometimes have difficulty coping effectively under stress, and believe that families generally have the capacity for positive change. An increasingly viable means to act on these values is to assist families in joining parent

support groups, parent advocacy groups, and parent-organized concrete services (Friesen & Koroloff, 1990).

Case managers, frequently privy to strictly confidential information, must be keenly sensitive to client confidentiality, while recognizing the tensions inherent in working with multiple members of a
family and service providers in multiple agencies. For example, parents and adolescents may provide very different information, making it hard to come to a common understanding of the problem and
to agree on intervention options. Other organizations may have realistic needs for information in order to provide relevant, appropriate
services. Sometimes, the need to protect the child supersedes the
parent's right to confidentiality, especially in adhering to federal and
state laws that mandate reporting of suspected child abuse or neglect. These realities mean that case managers sometimes face difficult ethical dilemmas in working with families. They need to value
clients' rights to confidentiality, while understanding the complexity
of the issues.

Working with families from an empowerment perspective involves promoting the family's ability to utilize its existing strengths
to meet its needs (Dunst, Trivette, & Deal, 1988). Case managers
working from this perspective believe that community-based family-
centered services are the most relevant and appropriate for children
and their families. These values were identified by a sampling of
CASSP program directors as most basic to effective case management (Zipper, Weil, & Rickenbaker, 1992). Case managers using this
perspective will value their partnership with the family and perceive
that partnership as egalitarian, collaborative, and open (Collins &
Collins, 1990). In addition, they will value the empowerment that
families gain from interaction with other service providers and with
other parents in groups that provide support, education, and/or advocacy (Friesen, 1993).

Case managers need to value interprofessional collaboration as
a means of problem solving. They should respect the expertise
brought by professionals from various disciplines in the mental
health system and elsewhere in the public service network. Understanding and valuing the basic functions of the components of the
public child-serving system can help case managers interpret the
policies and practices of these agencies to both parents and children
and increase the likelihood of effective service coordination. Increasingly, children with multiple difficulties are related to several systems—mental health, child welfare, juvenile justice, and/or special
education (Glisson & James, 1992). Building case management positions that can function interorganizationally, developing collabora-

tion, and managing conflict are major points of value, knowledge, and skill. In addition, case managers should value and promote collaboration with private sector agencies and service providers.

Despite the extent of problems and disruption seen in some families, it would be inappropriate to focus on family maintenance without committed efforts toward improvement of family functioning to prevent additional problems. Case managers, therefore, must appreciate that a broad perspective on and commitment to prevention is essential to good case management.

Knowledge

Case managers need to understand the process and function of case management and their role vis-à-vis the family and service providers, as conceptualized in the particular case management model used by their agency (Weil, 1985b). They need specific information about relevant legislation and about state, local, and organizational policies affecting children and families. Case managers need information about agency policies relative to confidentiality to guide their actions as they encounter the ethical dilemmas that can be expected. They need to know how to access the local network of services for children ages birth to 18 years, such as those services provided in child-care and preschool settings, the school system, social service agencies, medical and health services, substance abuse programs, religious and spiritual settings, and community organizations. They need to know how to assess and improve interorganizational relations and build service networks (Glisson & James, 1992; Weil & Karls, 1985).

Case managers need information about the functioning of families, including how stress can affect the family system and how the family system affects its members. To play a vital role in the broad child mental health system and to ensure effective service to families, cases managers need an understanding of the total intervention process from assessment to termination. Even though they may not be solely responsible for any one part of the process, they are responsible for the implementation and facilitation of the total plan.

Moreover, case managers need information on assessment strategies; they need to know what information they are expected to gather as part of an assessment and when changes in behavior or circumstances warrant reassessment. They need to know enough about children's development and about emotional and behavioral problems to understand the common manifestations of those disorders frequently seen in children served by the mental health system. When case managers also function as psychotherapists, they should know how to design and offer family-centered intervention. When the therapy is provided by another professional, the case manager needs to be familiar enough with therapy and intervention models to help interpret the treatment process to the family and to take part in evaluating progress in therapy.

There will be times when keeping the family intact, although a valued concept, is neither safe nor wise for the child or another family member. Thus, the case manager needs to know how to assess the nature of a crisis and how to determine when a child needs to be moved to a safer place or a different level of service. This involves knowing when and whom to call to arrange for intensive crisis intervention and child protective services involvement, or placement in a group home, residential treatment center, or hospital.

The case manager needs to know about all levels of mental health service, including home- and community-based intervention, day treatment and residential care, and hospitalization; how to determine when a transition is appropriate; and how to access a new level of service when needed. Medication is needed by some children being served by the mental health system, and the case manager should be familiar with primary medications used, frequent side effects, and reactions requiring medical evaluation. The case manager needs to know not only when intervention goals have been met, but also some of the common reactions that children and their families experience with the termination of treatment.

Skills

Case managers' skills must be based on values consistent with effective practice and grounded in the case management model specified in their agency. The particular model obviously will shape training priorities for skill development, although some skills are basic to all models. For instance, broad skills in communicating with others are essential. Case managers need skills in communicating with children, adolescents, parents, grandparents, and surrogate parents from different cultures and classes, and with professionals who have varying roles, expertise, responsibilities, and levels of authority.

Child mental health case managers should function from a family empowerment perspective to enable parents to support their child's development and to represent family interests to other service providers. Case managers need specific skills in working with families in preparation for assessment: involving them in the development of the treatment and intervention plan, reframing issues, working through crises, and helping families to maintain motivation at predictably difficult times. Case managers will also be engaged in capacity building, skill development in problem solving, and decision making with the family.

In addition to parents, the most effective advocates for children with mental health needs often have been mental health professionals (Knitzer, 1982). Case managers, as service coordinators, are in a unique position to identify service gaps. In order to address these gaps, they will need skills in advocating for particular children and families. They also will need skills in advocating for services, which may involve facilitating the formation and functioning of advocacy groups.

Case management programs rely on different models for service planning. Although all case management models involve interprofessional collaboration, sometimes including private sector service providers, the direct involvement of different professionals will vary. The case manager may relate interdependently to the family and to a number of different professionals (including those in public and nonprofit agencies, and in private practice), and develop an integrated service plan based on the information provided. More typically, the case manager is responsible for assembling relevant professionals to work with a particular family or for collaborating with an existing team. Where decisions are made in a group context, the case manager needs specific skills in group facilitation (Nash, 1990; Nash, Rounds, & Bowen, 1992), particularly when the interprofessional team functions much like other task groups to gather and process information needed to solve problems and make effective decisions (Toseland & Rivas, 1984).

In working with the school, the case manager needs to be able, with the family, to help school personnel understand the child's mental health assessment and his or her strengths and needs. In working with psychotherapists, the case manager needs skills in relating to therapists from different disciplines and an understanding of the therapists' methods and approaches to treatment. It is particularly important that the case manager work with the therapist and the family to clarify their perspectives and interests and to understand the parents' goals for their child. In some instances, the case manager will need to educate family members about the process of therapy and assist them in monitoring how therapy is progressing and determine when the goals that have been set for the child have been achieved.

Regardless of the case management model employed, all case managers need skills in assessment, information gathering, problem analysis, planning, negotiation, collaboration, problem solving, decision making, and advocacy (Zipper et al., 1993). All case managers need skills in documentation and record keeping. In addition to involvement in the case management process and the service system, all will be involved in transitions to different levels of service, termination, and evaluation of client outcomes. Case managers need skills for these complex functions. Respondents to the survey of CASSP directors indicated that case managers further need empathy and flexibility to carry out their roles, and they need to be "unflappable" (Zipper et al., 1992).

Because of the stigma sometimes still attached to mental health services, it is important that case managers be able to interpret those services to others. In this way, case managers can provide an important bridge between the family and the mental health system, and between mental health and other service providers within the service network.

IMPLEMENTATION OF CASE MANAGEMENT TRAINING

In-service training is more than attending conferences or informational briefings (Wray, 1989). Training must be carefully planned to ensure that it matches the needs and experiences of training participants as well as the priorities of case management supervisors and program administrators. Information about the case management program is needed in several broad areas: the client population, service system, practice setting, and the local case management model. Information is also needed about the agency's administrative structure, the history of the program and its relationships within the service network, supervisors' and managers' performance expectations and training priorities, typical caseload size, supervision and support available to case managers, and particular areas of concern. During the training needs assessment process, trainers may become aware of systemic problems that may impede case managers' effectiveness or efficiency. They can help identify such systemic issues and ways in which these barriers may undermine the achievement of case management goals and bring them to the attention of agency administrators (Austin, Brannon, & Pecora, 1984).

Trainers

The survey of CASSP directors indicated that little training is available for child mental health staff and that, where in-service training is available, it is generally provided by supervisors and state-level consultants (Zipper et al., 1992). To be effective, case management trainers need considerable substantive knowledge about the child-serving system, mental health practice with children and their families, the increasing need for service network collaboration, and other topics included in the case management curriculum. They need up-to-date information and understanding of family-centered approaches to intervention with children, emerging in such areas as early intervention, family preservation, public social services, substance abuse, and education, as well as in child mental health. Trainers also need specific knowledge about case management practice and interprofessional collaboration. Since the case manager's role depends, in large part, on the chosen case management model, trainers must understand how case managers derive their authority in the context of the chosen case management model. They must understand the implications of different model options for the authority and roles of the case manager and for the skills needed to carry out case management.

Experience indicates that in light of the variety and complexity of topics and skills to be addressed, an interagency team model is most effective for case management training for children's mental health. Workers across the child-serving system can learn to collaborate and establish more positive working relations through interagency team training. The combination of university- and practice-based trainers should provide grounding in both content and practice realities. The training context provides an ideal opportunity to model collaboration among parents and service providers. Specifically, parents and professionals can serve as cotrainers for case managers. Parents bring a wealth of experience to help case managers understand what it means to be a family member with a child who has a serious emotional disorder. This parent–professional collaboration can provide an opportunity to demonstrate parental expertise, professional respect for parental roles, and ways for parents and professionals to work collaboratively toward established goals.

The trainers' knowledge of relevant issues must be coupled with specific training and group facilitation skills. Trainers need to use different roles as appropriate to the content and the context, moving easily from the role as expert on content to the role of group facilitator, structuring and managing group activities while attending to differential responses of group members.

Training will be guided by the various skills and information needed in the particular model of case management being implemented locally (i.e., whether case managers have a dual role as both case manager and psychotherapist, whether they are expected to facilitate team decision making, and to what extent they monitor services provided by others). Trainers need to understand the implications of these case management models and practice variations in order to structure training that is relevant to local conditions. Trainers should ensure that training reflects sensitivity to the perspectives of families and to family diversity as well as to the roles of the various professionals engaged in working with children and their families in child mental health and the larger child-serving system.

Training Strategies

Training for adults should utilize adult learning models based on the primary principle that participants, as adults, are responsible for their own learning (Bruner, 1968; Knowles, 1970). Training should provide opportunities to develop abilities in observation, to reflect on and analyze practice, and to engage in experiential/active learning activities (Weil, 1977). The inclusion of a variety of experiential activities allows participants to build on their own knowledge and skills, and provides opportunities for practicing collaborative problem solving (Zipper et al., 1993).

Models for training adults should be grounded in the developmental interests and self-concepts of adults as expressed in active, self-directive learning styles. The interests of adult learners are shaped by their roles and responsibilities. Activities in which participants take on the roles of family members and other service providers can assist participants in their own process of understanding others' roles and clarifying their own.

Training exercises should provide opportunities for building on existing skills and experience, for using new knowledge, for practicing newly developed skills, and for engaging in collaborative problem solving. They should build on the varied experiences of training participants (Rothman, 1973).

A combination of teaching and learning modalities is useful to ensure that: 1) the method matches the particular content presented, 2) training builds on participants' own skills and experiences, and 3) a stimulating learning environment is maintained. Modalities appropriate to case management training include minilectures, small- and large-group discussion and exercises, and use of instructional materials, such as videotapes, to stimulate discussion. Raising questions for group consideration can serve to reframe and organize issues for participants. Group problem-solving activities focused on work with the child and his or her family and on promoting interprofessional collaboration are particularly effective when structured around practice-based vignettes. Case studies can provide an effective means for sharing common ground to analyze various aspects of service provision (McWilliam, 1992; Zipper, 1993).

Training exercises designed to develop ways of conceptualizing the service continuum and identifying the components of the local service network provide case managers with working guidelines to strengthen practice and facilitate service coordination. Experience indicates that consideration of systemic problems that become apparent in this training context can provide a valuable opportunity for collaborative problem solving. By including professionals from multiple agencies in the training experience, the promotion of collegial relationships among service providers and the development of service system problem-solving approaches may be facilitated.

Training Evaluation and Follow Up

Training evaluation is shaped by the needs assessment process. Outcome-oriented training objectives should be formulated based on specific identified needs. The evaluation instrument should measure the attainment of specified objectives. Ideally, values, knowledge, and skills related to the objectives should be measured before and after participation in the training experience. Where time and fiscal constraints limit the feasibility of such comprehensive evaluation, the evaluation should focus on measurement of outcome objectives (Zipper et al., 1993).

Follow up is an important aspect of training. When feasible, follow-up contact with participants can provide trainers with information that can be useful for confirming the curriculum, as well as for updating and strengthening it. In some instances, trainers can also function as consultants for programs and training participants, assisting agencies in strengthening practice and interagency collaboration.

DIRECTIONS FOR PRESERVICE AND PROFESSIONAL EDUCATION

Although there is ample evidence that in-service training is needed for case managers in child mental health and the larger child-serving system, it is equally evident that preservice preparation is important to efficient service delivery. Since master's degree–level social workers are frequently employed in case management and supervisory positions, the preservice educational program for that profession is examined in the following paragraphs.

Teaching models are needed to educate social workers to perform effectively as case managers in child mental health (Kurtz, Bagarozzi, & Pollane, 1984). To develop appropriate preservice education models, professional school faculty need to stay in touch with the innovations that are evolving in the field (Wray, 1989) and design a plan of study that incorporates the theory-based in-service content identified in this chapter. As an example, the collaboration leading to the Case Management for Children's Mental Health (Zipper & Weil, 1994) curriculum, as described earlier, has resulted in a revision of the specialized child mental health courses at the University of North Carolina at Chapel Hill School of Social Work.

Foundation social work courses reflect generalist practice, and students are introduced to varying levels of service as well as to a variety of service systems. This broad stroke is important to future case managers who will fulfill many roles and coordinate services of multiple agencies. Traditional social work foundation courses also provide such valuable content areas as: systems theory; organizational behavior; child, adolescent, and adult developmental theory; social policy, history, and change; methodology, including case management; practice skills, such as interviewing and record keeping; procedures for evaluation of practice; and examination of the effects of diversity (e.g., race, gender, sexual orientation, disabling conditions).

A family-centered methodology course is needed that addresses general practice and includes comparison of various models on theoretical perspectives, applications, and techniques. The specialized courses in child mental health should include the following: 1) a broad policy course that addresses not only mental health policy, but also those policies and services that influence the welfare of children in areas including health, education, and public social services; 2) a human behavior course that focuses on emotional and behavioral problems of children, provides grounding for that part of child assessment that may include a mental disorder, and recognizes that diagnoses are both fluid and reflective of more than just the child's behavior; 3) a child mental health practice course that gives equal emphasis and status to case management and psychotherapy, with consistent attention given to individual and family strengths and prevention strategies; 4) an evaluation of practice course that focuses equally on clinical and program evaluation; and 5) a field placement in a state-of-the-art child mental health program using a model of service that provides the student with opportunities to serve both as a therapist and as a case manager, to serve as a team member and a team leader, and to work in partnership with parents and in collaboration with community service providers. An additional course focused on interprofessional collaboration and cross-system case management would be valuable. With this preservice preparation, the hiring agency will need to provide only site-specific and model-specific content to prepare the new worker for practice.

Training Principles

The principles that have guided the North Carolina model for in-service training and preservice education outlined in this chapter involve various aspects of case management training, from the initial needs assessment through evaluation. They are summarized in the statements that follow:

1. Training should have a tripartite focus on the child, the family, and the service network.
2. Training should address the child's needs for improved personal, family, and community functioning based on an ecological perspective.
3. Training should address the development of a partnership between the family and the case manager that is designed to promote improvement in the child's functioning and to support the family and/or responsible adult.
4. Training should address skills needed for interprofessional and interagency collaboration in the service network and for working with advocacy and parent groups.
5. Training should use adult learning principles to address the values, knowledge, and skills needed for family-centered and community-based case management with children and their families.
6. Training should be grounded in relevant federal and state legislation, in local agency policies and procedures, and in an understanding of exemplary practices for children and their families.
7. Training should include content on case management roles, functions, and process.
8. Training content on family-oriented mental health assessment, diagnostic criteria, and mental health intervention should be examined from the case manager's perspective.
9. Training should include attention to the diversity among families in terms of culture, race, ethnicity, sexual orientation, and socioeconomic status.
10. Training should address the complex legal and ethical issues of confidentiality and child and parental rights.
11. Training should present prevention as an important aspect of case management services, with a focus on all levels of prevention.

12. Training should stress the need for wraparound services for children across systems and categorical programs.
13. Training should deal with issues of transition of children and their families among service programs and eligibility classifications.
14. Training should focus on collaboration among public agencies, with special attention placed on the child welfare system and on effective, congruent models of service between public and private sector service providers.
15. Training should promote understanding of the local model of case management, capitalize on opportunities to learn about the service network, and provide opportunities for practicing collaboration with service providers from multiple agencies, disciplines, and professions.
16. Skilled trainers, practitioners, and parents should work as co-trainers to ensure effective presentation of theoretical material, practice realities, and family issues.
17. Training should involve collaboration between university and agency personnel in design, implementation, and evaluation to ensure the development of exemplary practices in the state and to ensure congruence between preservice training and in-service education.
18. Training and preservice education should present case management as a skill on a par with psychotherapy in the child mental health field.

CONCLUSION

Training in case management in child mental health will be essential in building family-centered, community-based, child-serving systems. These systems will be grounded in wraparound services geared to the particular needs of the child and his or her family, rather than categorical services delineated by agency function. The effort to tailor services to meet the needs of particular children and their families will increase the importance of case managers in creating, arranging for, and coordinating services. Collaboration among service providers is critical to the success of family-centered services. Collaboration among service providers is critical to the success of family-centered services. The case manager plays a key role in ensuring this essential collaboration. Carefully designed preservice education and in-service training programs are critical elements to ensure that case managers in child mental health are prepared to build and provide leadership in community-based and family-centered services to meet the needs of children and their families.

REFERENCES

Austin, M.J., Brannon, D., & Pecora, P.J. (1984). *Managing staff development programs in human service agencies.* Chicago: Nelson-Hall.

Bailey, D.B. (1989). Case management in early intervention. *Journal of Early Intervention, 13*(2), 120–134.

Behar, L. (1986). A state model for child mental health services: The North Carolina experience. *Child Today, 15*(3), 16–21.

Bruner, J. (1968). *Toward a theory of instruction.* New York: Norton.

Collins, B., & Collins, T. (1990). Parent and professional relationships in the treatment of seriously emotionally disturbed children and adolescents. *Social Work, 35*(6), 522–527.

Dunst, C.J., Trivette, C.M., & Deal, A.G. (1988). *Enabling and empowering families.* Cambridge, MA: Brookline Books.

Education of the Handicapped Act Amendments of 1986, PL 99-457. (October 8, 1986). Title 20, U.S.C. 1400 et seq: *U.S. Statutes at Large, 100,* 1145–1177.

Friesen, B. (1993). Creating change for children with serious emotional disorders: A national strategy. In T. Mizrahi & J. Morrison (Eds.), *Community organization and social administration: Advances, trends and emerging principles* (pp. 127-146). New York: Haworth Press.

Friesen, B., & Koroloff, N.M. (1990). Family-centered services: Implications for mental health administration and research. *Journal of Mental Health Administration, 17*(1), 13–25.

Glisson, C., & James, L. (1992). The interorganizational coordination of services to children in state custody. *Administration in Social Work, 16*(3/4), 65–80.

Individuals with Disabilities Education Act, PL 101-476. (October 30, 1990). Title 20, U.S.C. 1400 et seq. *U.S. Statutes at Large, 104* (part 2), 1103–1151.

Knitzer, J. (1982). *Unclaimed children: The failure of public responsibility to children and adolescents in need of mental health services.* Washington, DC: Children's Defense Fund.

Knowles, M.S. (1970). *The modern practice of adult education.* New York: Association Press.

Kurtz, L.F., Bagarozzi, D.A., & Pollane, L.P. (1984). Case management in mental health. *Health and Social Work, 9,* 201–211.

McWilliam, P.J. (1992). The case method of instruction: Teaching application and problem-solving skills to early interventionists. *Journal of Early Intervention, 16*(2), 360–373.

Nash, J. (1990). Public Law 99-457: Facilitating family participation on the multidisciplinary team. *Journal of Early Intervention, 14*(4), 318–326.

Nash, J., Rounds, K., & Bowen, G. (1992). Level of parental involvement on early childhood intervention teams. *Families in Society, 73*(2), 93–99.

Roberts-DeGennaro, M. (1987). Developing case management as a practice model. *Social Casework 68*(8), 466–470.

Rothman, B. (1973). Perspectives on learning and teaching in continuing education. *Journal of Education for Social Work, 16*(2), 39–52.

Schorr, L.B. (1988). *Within our reach: Breaking the cycle of disadvantage.* New York: Doubleday.

Toseland, R.W., & Rivas, R.F. (1984). *An introduction to group work practice.* New York: Macmillan.

Weil, M.O. (1977). *Practicum in law and social work: An educational program in interprofessional collaboration.* [Doctoral dissertation, Graduate Center, City University of New York]. Ann Arbor, MI: Ann Arbor Dissertation Publications.

Weil, M.O. (1985a). Historical origins and recent developments. In M.O. Weil & J. Karls (Eds.), *Case management in human service practice: A systematic approach to mobilizing resources for clients* (pp. 1–28). San Francisco: Jossey-Bass.

Weil, M. O. (1985b). Key components in providing efficient and effective services. In M.O. Weil & J. Karls (Eds.), *Case management in human service practice: A systematic approach to mobilizing resources for clients* (pp. 29–71). San Francisco: Jossey-Bass.

Weil, M.O., & Karls, J. (Eds.). (1985). *Case management in human service practice: A systematic approach to mobilizing resources for clients.* San Francisco: Jossey-Bass.

Wray, L. (1989). Local issues in case management. In M.H. Linz, P. McAnally, & C. Wieck (Eds.), *Case management: Historical, current and future perspectives.* Cambridge, MA: Brookline Books.

Zipper, I.N. (1993). The go-between. In P.J. McWilliam & D. Bailey (Eds.), *Working together with children and families: Case studies in early intervention* (pp. 203–216). Baltimore: Paul H. Brookes Publishing Co.

Zipper, I.N., & Weil, M. (1994). *Case management for children's mental health: A training curriculum for child-serving agencies.* Raleigh: North Carolina Division of Mental Health, Developmental Disabilities and Substance Abuse Services.

Zipper, I.N., Weil, M., & Rickenbaker, T. (1992). *Executive summary: Survey of CASSP directors on training for case managers in child mental health.* Unpublished manuscript, University of North Carolina, School of Social Work, Chapel Hill.

Zipper, I.N., Weil, M., & Rounds, K.A. (1993). *Service coordination in early intervention: Parents and professionals.* Cambridge, MA: Brookline Books.

Parent–Professional Collaboration for Public Sector Training for Children's Intensive Case Management
A Case Study

Norma Radol Raiff, Marilyn Henry,
and Connie Dellmuth

In recent years, an understanding of the imperative for parents and community system collaboration to meet the special needs of children and adolescents with serious emotional problems has gained wider acceptance by families, service providers, program administrators, and senior planners. This principle, which is a cornerstone of the Child and Adolescent Service System Program (CASSP) systems approach to service delivery (Stroul & Friedman, 1986), upholds family members' contributions as key informants, long-term case managers, and advocates for their children (Hatfield & Lefley, 1987; Intagliata, Willer, & Egri, 1988).

Different models exist to build collegial relationships and to introduce the family perspective into service design and delivery. Approaches include intensive training (Vosler-Hunter, 1989) and self-instructional materials (Kelker, 1988) to sharpen parent dialogue with professionals, and research-based scales and questionnaires intended to sensitize professionals to family-centered practice (Abel-Boone, Sandall, Loughry, & Frederick, 1990; Bailey, 1991; Dunst & Trivette, 1988; Dunst, Trivette, & Deal, 1988; Winton & Bailey, 1990). The family perspective is also institutionally recognized in federal programs, such as CASSP (Stroul & Friedman, 1986), and in professional policies (National Association of Social Workers [NASW], 1984). As a result, family members are increasingly represented on planning committees and advisory boards, as members of gatekeeping teams such as local Interagency Children's Services Councils (Garland, Woodruff, & Buck, 1988), and as evaluation partners (Malekoff, Johnson, & Klappersack, 1991).

While these approaches focus on the service relationship, a second direction for partnership is that of the Public–Academic Liaison (PAL). Proposed by the National Institute of Mental Health (NIMH) in 1988, the PAL tries to strengthen mental health academic and public service sector linkages, primarily through research collaboration (Bevilacqua, 1991). In Pennsylvania's curriculum venture, a university-based academic center was introduced as a third member of an expanded family–professional team—one with the potential to link parent voices and mental health policy intention to academic expertise in curriculum design and state-of-the-art research on youth with emotional disabilities. This public sector partnership was assembled as a first step in devising ways to answer the flood of original and pragmatic questions raised by newly hired case managers working in a rapidly expanding community-based public program.

A tripartite relationship between an academic setting, the public sector, and families holds the promise of building manpower, knowledge, and long-term program effectiveness. Extracurricular assistance is often needed when graduate or undergraduate programs do not yet provide the body of knowledge needed to work in newer helping settings. When public practice is involved, the state Office of Mental Health (OMH) is responsible for spelling out training guidelines that are philosophically and practically compatible with staff's projected role and program philosophy. Partnerships between family groups and the university are also a way to disseminate family-centered expertise to the professional literature through the academic sector's commitment to publication. Since family members are the ultimate consumers and judges of how well child training programs succeed in preparing staff, recruiting parents as curriculum consultants helps to ensure that the focus and the materials are acceptable and useful.

CASE STUDY IN PARENT–PROFESSIONAL COLLABORATION

Background

In 1989, the Pennsylvania OMH was awarded an Alcohol, Drug Abuse and Mental Health Administration (ADAMHA) "States Helping States" contract (AD-CE-89-0028) to develop a curriculum to train intensive case managers (ICMs) to work with families of children and adolescents with serious emotional disturbances. From its inception, the OMH viewed children's intensive case management as but a single component of a comprehensive approach to children's programming. The CASSP vision of a system of care provided a set of organizing values for which intensive case management was the complementary "hands and feet" of service implementation.

The ADAMHA grant specified the development of a week-long training package that included trainer's and trainee's materials, a videotape, and a resource guide. To accomplish this, the OMH developed a working partnership between itself and the Parents Involved Network of Pennsylvania (PIN of PA), a statewide association dedicated to advocating on behalf of the needs of families with children who have serious emotional disturbances, and Western Psychiatric Institute and Clinic/University of Pittsburgh Medical Center (WPIC/UPMC), one of the state's three public academic psychiatric training centers.

The immediate goal was to determine what it would take to initially prepare child mental health ICMs to do their job. In Pennsylvania, a child ICM normally has a caseload of 2–4 consumers, is expected to provide a face-to-face contact with the child at a minimum of once every 2 weeks, and serves children who have a mental health diagnosis and who are either participating in several child-serving systems or who meet local priority guidelines. The small caseload reflects the fact that services can be provided to other individuals to assist in family case management efforts. A baseline expectation was that the material would be respectful to the family and CASSP perspectives, and would incorporate a seminal paper previously developed by a state CASSP task group (Pennsylvania Office of Mental Health [PA OMH], 1990). The curriculum was also to address cultural diversity and was to be developed through linkages to a state CASSP Subcommittee on Minority Initiatives.

The new curriculum was expected to build on existing state training developed to prepare "generic" case managers working with adults or with a mixed age range. The preexisting training model was based on one of four widely recognized approaches to mental health case management (Robinson & Bergman, 1989). Commonly referred to as the strengths approach or the resource acquisition model, it is most associated with the work of Rapp and his associates at the University of Kansas (Chamberlain & Rapp, 1983; Sullivan, 1992; Weick, Rapp, Sullivan, & Kisthardt, 1989). Systematic linkages between the earlier and the emerging "child" curriculum were seen as essential to developing a continuum of learning. This was also done to ensure that case managers working in a single agency, especially in rural areas that might not have resources for a full-time child worker, would be able to communicate and problem solve using similar vantage points.

The project's immediate goals were to: 1) identify educational priorities and content; 2) locate key informants and useful published and unpublished materials; and 3) design an integrated teaching approach to showcase the contributions of family members, the major youth-serving systems, and academic faculty.

Pennsylvania Office of Mental Health, Division of Children's Services Pennsylvania's OMH has been an early and committed advocate for the expansion and coordination of innovative children's services throughout the Commonwealth. CASSP was introduced in Pennsylvania under OMH auspices in the spring of 1986. The first four county projects were implemented by the following year. At the time of the ADAMHA grant, 35 of the state's 45 county mental health/mental retardation programs had been funded. These programs provided a pool of program administrators and county and statewide advisory committees knowledgeable about local needs who were potential consultants to the training project. At that time, it was projected that all county programs would have CASSP programs by June 1992.

Pennsylvania's CASSP program strongly reflects the federal position regarding a needed system of care for children and adolescents. Statewide "principles of service" include:

1. A commitment to children and adolescents living in families
2. The primacy of permanency planning
3. An emphasis on the family setting as the first focus of treatment
4. The need for a rich array of child and family services to avoid out-of-home placement
5. Family and child involvement in service planning
6. The need to tailor service decisions to the uniqueness of the child or adolescent and his or her family
7. Coparticipation by all community service systems involved with the child and his or her family in placement, program, funding, and discharge responsibilities
8. The primary role of family and community as being responsible for the child
9. The child's and family's right to case management services to ensure coordinated, time-limited, and therapeutic services to children
10. The right of each child to have an advocate

Support for the development of a culturally competent system of care is a second Pennsylvania CASSP initiative and is closely intertwined with the global principles of parent–professional collaboration. Cultural competency in child case management is viewed as crucial to program success. It is operationalized as the incorporation of practice principles that recognize the role of norms, values, beliefs, and stressors unique to the family's culture. Practice is expected to start with acceptance of the importance of culture and the need to adapt services accordingly. This includes acknowledgment of the family, as the culture defines it, as the locus of support and as the preferred point of intervention. Cultural responsiveness also means appreciation for the role of the family, community, church, and other natural systems as primary supports and resource bases. Ideally, a responsive practice incorporates cultural preferences as a means of reinforcing self-determination in service planning, linkage, and referral; highlights the need for cultural "location" as part of assessment in order to understand acculturation and assimilation concerns and dynamics; views individuals in the context of their cultural memberships and experiences; matches people's needs with their help-seeking behaviors; and acknowledges that cross-cultural dynamics must be adjusted to and accepted. In brief, the family–case manager collaboration was understood to mean working both with the strengths unique to each child and family and with the strengths of the culture (Bazron, 1989; Cross, Bazron, Dennis, & Isaacs, 1989).

It is within the context of these twin CASSP thrusts that the subsequent development of Pennsylvania's Curriculum for Children's and Adolescent's Case Management must be understood.

Parents Involved Network of Pennsylvania PIN of PA, incorporated in December 1989, is a statewide parent-run organization of parents and other interested persons, focused on child mental health issues. PIN's mission is to address the unique needs of children and adolescents with emotional or behavioral problems by providing education, information, support, and advocacy for children and their families. The goals include:

> to provide a centralized resource for education, information and referral; to take a leadership role in the development of a public policy agenda for children's mental health issues; to promote a full range of high quality services for children and adolescents and their families, including 1) community-based services in the least restrictive setting, 2) early intervention/prevention services, and 3) family support services, including support for siblings and respite services; to promote the de-

velopment of parent self-help/advocacy groups; and to promote collaboration among the child-serving systems, which include parents, mental
health, education, child welfare, juvenile justice, and drug and alcohol.
(Fine & Borden, 1989, p. 68)

The organization consists of a state coordinator, a board of directors, and four regional coordinators. There are approximately 28
parent support groups statewide. Annual meetings were held in
1990 and 1991 to provide parents and professionals an opportunity
to network in regional workshops and to access information through
additional workshops and a resource table. PIN's model of parent
support groups and advocacy training have also been disseminated
nationally (Corp & Kosinski, 1990; Fine & Borden, 1989, 1991).

PIN parents have made significant contributions on councils
and advisory groups across Pennsylvania. Through participation in
a parent–professional subcommittee of the CASSP Statewide Advisory Committee, PIN was instrumental in helping to develop the
state's child case management plan. Ultimately, PIN representatives
participated in the child curriculum's development as analysts and
provided input about needed curriculum revision. As cotrainers they
assisted with presentations and experiential exercises, and helped
to identify local and regional family speakers and panelists. More
important, PIN parents contributed to the curriculum's vitality
through real-life modeling of the respect and value of parent–professional training partnerships.

*Western Psychiatric Institute and Clinic/University of Pittsburgh
Medical Center* WPIC/UPMC is a uniquely situated university-
based psychiatric hospital whose mission includes direct patient
care, research, and training. As part of the Division of Public Psychiatry, WPIC is a regional training institute and provides ongoing consultative and continuing education services to the 23 counties of
western Pennsylvania, almost one third of the state.

WPIC has been involved with generic statewide ICM training
since 1987. Certification of training attendance is a statewide staffing
prerequisite. Between 1987 and 1992, WPIC provided basic training
to more than 350 adult and child ICMs, supervisors, county-level
administrators, family members, and consumers. Since 1989, and as
a result of this project, more than 250 direct and administrative staff,
child advocates, and interested family members have participated in
the newly designed child ICM training. WPIC also offers advanced
"alumni" workshops on specialized topics and provides program
consultation and many other types of community and state hospital-
based training programs for the public sector. This regional service

helped to ensure access to front-line case managers, senior administrators, and other staff.

Formal Process

The project's first task was to identify the most needed competencies to help staff work with family members and personnel in the major youth-serving systems (i.e., mental health, public welfare, juvenile justice, mental retardation, drug and alcohol). An extensive computerized literature review found comparatively few skill-related training materials. Although mental health case management has been written about extensively, most of the information focuses on questions of service definition (Anthony, Cohen, Farkas, & Cohen, 1988; Bachrach, 1989) and program outcomes (Baker & Weiss, 1984; Bigelow & Young, 1983; Bond, Miller, Krumwied, & Ward, 1988; Borland, McRae, & Lycan, 1989). Even more important, the models of service delivery were almost unanimously keyed to adult consumer needs and issues. In addition, with few exceptions (Hunter College School of Social Work, 1990; Ronnau, Rutter, & Donner, 1988), most training packages are adult focused.

To address this gap, the partnership began by identifying alternative information sources known through earlier community outreach, such as family members, academic faculty, and CASSP and case management personnel. The inclusion of both child case managers and their supervisors and several of the most expert adult case managers as key informants was a first step. Persons were nominated from the collaborators' firsthand knowledge of exemplary programs or at the suggestion of state and regional OMH staff. The rationale for this broadened pool was that adult service workers often intervened with dependent youth in a family and that mixed groups of clients often existed. CASSP directors and members of advisory committees were also asked to identify resource personnel and family informants. Finally, PIN's extensive contact and membership networks were solicited for input and process evaluation.

The partnership developed four strategies to cast a representative information net and to provide early consumer and field staff sanction: 1) key informant workshops, 2) open-ended interviews, 3) development and revision of a list of basic competencies, and 4) constituency review.

Key Informant Workshop   The process was initiated using a key informant approach that recruited CASSP and child system staff and administrators, PIN representatives, family members, and academic colleagues to brainstorm during an introductory 2-day working session. This orientation featured an overview of the state's approach to intensive case management and established a shared set of academic and parent-driven concerns. This by-invitation meeting used lists initially provided by the county and regional OMH, PIN, and county- and state-level CASSP advisory committees.

Informants were asked to pinpoint training needs and identify resource materials in their own programs that they felt case managers would have to master to do a good job. The intent was to discover priority topics and program regulations and policies that would affect ICM referral, linkage, and monitoring. Workshop members were also asked to provide continuing assistance to the project, to offer access to their system's resources, and to continue to identify and recruit knowledgeable key informants. Some were also asked to write, review, or present components of the subsequently developed training modules.

Open-Ended Interviews One of the challenges confronting the project was the absence of a substantial body of published knowledge regarding the specific skills and knowledge required by child case managers. As a corollary, there was almost no information about how to modify the standing generic curricula to include the perspective of the child in the family and the child in the many systems of care. Wide differences in age, in child disabilities, in the way that families saw themselves as their child's case manager or advocate, and in community resource structures made it essential to identify the most commonly recurring case management themes.

To accommodate these issues, a strategy of interviewing key informants about actual situations was selected. An open-ended, direct questionnaire was developed that asked respondents to discuss "typical," and "most difficult," or "most rewarding" situations and to identify needed knowledge areas. The questioning sequence was reviewed by the collaborative team and pretested initially with expert regional child case managers and supervisors. PIN and statewide CASSP helped expand the interviewee pool by identifying additional regional and statewide informants and continuously providing project outreach. The former provided needed access to private individuals who might otherwise have remained unconnected or who might have felt uncomfortable about discussing their situation. OMH and regional CASSP staff were especially valuable in initiating statewide contacts outside of WPIC's immediate geographic region.

This snowball technique was established about one third of the way through the project and remained active until the final report. Thirty tape-recorded interviews with family members and child

ICMs and their supervisors were transcribed and analyzed to highlight recurring practice issues. These appropriately disguised materials were eventually used as illustrative content and exercises in the curriculum and in a subsequent training videotape.

Specification of a List of Family-Centered Case Management Competencies The development of a series of competency statements was the next step. It demanded a new strategy that could discover which child ICM skills, values, and functions were considered essential, and how to phrase statements that family members would find acceptable and view as mirroring their priorities.

A written questionnaire was developed from three sources: existing state ICM practice regulations cited in the State Mental Health Bulletin, the CASSP concept paper, and the practice literature. Respondents were asked to rank competencies and to add to a list of anticipated best practices that related to philosophy of treatment, family approaches, strengths-based assessment versus deficits assessment, crisis precipitants and interventions, childhood developmental stages, major child psychiatric diagnoses and treatments, case management interventions and home- and community-based practices, organization and system protocols, and respectful CASSP-based case planning. This list of competencies was continuously revised and expanded based on continuing respondent input. The questionnaire was disseminated for reaction purposes and was not meant as a random survey. Respondents included members of the key informant panels, workshop participants, and academic colleagues with special interest in child mental health case management.

The emphasis was on discovery and on the cementing of the working relationship among the field itself, the university, and the parents in the design of useful statements of function. Writing and selection of specific competency items was intended to stimulate input and to identify additional content inadvertently excluded.

The process was deemed pragmatically complete during a joint WPIC/OMH negotiation session. Because the training was introductory, most of the content dealt with orientation and front-end issues related to state guidelines, knowledge awareness, sensitization to family and cultural issues, initiation and development of a multisystem service plan, and the necessity of planned case feedback and review. The extensive list of competency statements was then organized and turned over to other training colleagues who were responsible for incorporating the statements in preliminary curriculum modules. Over time, modules and components were produced by the senior author and members of WPIC's children's outpatient and inpatient services, an expert ICM supervisor, an out-of-state consultant, and staff from Eastern Pennsylvania Psychiatric Institute/Medical College of Pennsylvania and Hershey Medical Center (the state's other psychiatric training institutes). Special credit must also be given to the Families as Allies Project, Research and Training Center on Family Support and Children's Mental Health, who displayed a true collaborative spirit by permitting the use of exercises included in their handbook, *Working Together* (Vosler-Hunter & Exo, 1987). Although the finished material was reviewed by the OMH and PIN, responsibility for the final product resided with WPIC.

Constituency Review The final strategy, conducted simultaneously with the first three, was intended to preview and gain sanction from other constituents who had strong vested interests in seeing that the curriculum was philosophically accurate and pragmatically and humanistically applicable. This approach consisted of connecting with organized groups who expressed either a concern or a general desire to help with input and provision of information.

WPIC again used a community consultation model to generate proposed curriculum presentations and asked OMH's help in scheduling. These marketing and review sessions included a working outline, an overview of the module sequence, and a description of the philosophy, and were provided to many administrative and professional audiences. In all cases, the offer was made to continue discussion on an individual basis. This approach often resulted in the useful dividend of recruiting other informants to more extended involvement in the collaboration.

Informal Processes

Although the knowledge search was complicated and systematic, it represented only part of the dynamics of a partnership that all persons believed to have been extremely fruitful and without major disruption. During interviews and even after, the authors were often asked about how the process was developing and to comment on anticipated interpersonal and ideological barriers. It was the authors' experience, however, that this was a truly collaborative relationship strengthened by the following:

1. *Preexisting OMH commitment to CASSP principles of the parent partnership* Pennsylvania OMH had successfully introduced CASSP to many counties in the state and was a tireless advocate for the CASSP vision prior to the project's initiation. The principle of parent representation and involvement was already cemented in OMH ad-

visory committee guidelines and in OMH's principles paper, which established a framework for competency development. An established corps of CASSP staff and supporters were available to act as key consultants and to link agents to other parents and program resources. OMH continued to strengthen and fund PIN of PA throughout the life of the project and beyond, thereby reinforcing that organization's growth and development and its availability as a consulting resource.

2. *Initiation by trusted mediators* The request to build a training partnership originated with OMH staff whose previous work with WPIC and PIN had cemented that liaison's reputation as being fair, interpersonally skilled, and willing to lead as well as listen. Each of the parties in the marriage (WPIC and PIN) extended initial trust to the other based upon confidence in the arrangements broker (OMH). Net widening (e.g., expanding the consulting base) was accomplished using the same principle of sponsored access, with trusted agency informants being asked to invite newcomers to the planning table for frank discussion.

3. *Open communication and a nontraditional approach to work* Each partner developed a personal and professional commitment to an extraordinary investment in time and personal access. Home and office telephone numbers were shared, and it was not uncommon for extensive dialogue to occur after-hours and on an ongoing basis. Substantial personal travel was also arranged, with participants meeting at other prearranged conference sites and at highway rest areas that criss-crossed the state.

4. *Network expansion* Ownership without exclusion became a project hallmark. Input and commentary were continuously solicited with ongoing efforts to ensure those offering feedback that suggestions would be honored if possible and that time would be taken for explanations and consideration of alternatives. As the curriculum progressed and was redefined, an array of options was incorporated in the training material giving later trainers and presenters latitude; for example, case studies based on frequently reported scenarios were provided, however, guest presenters and parents were encouraged to introduce special issues of personal or regional concern.

5. *Respect for specialized expertise coupled with a willingness to cross boundaries* Each partner recognized that the other had expertise but not necessarily a monopoly over accomplishment, and each was willing to make suggestions and to persist while signaling when perceived positions were essential. This willingness to prioritize positions and to remain flexible included a commitment to try to under-

stand the other's request, to consider alternative options, and to incorporate strongly held positions whenever possible. Different points of view were respected and not personalized.

One example involved the introduction of psychiatric content into the curriculum. Although there was some feeling that this was a lower priority, the academic liaisons were able to provide compelling feedback from early training sessions that front-line staff considered this to be essential content that was not provided in their college preparation. Besides advocating to "start where the audience was," the training institutes made a commitment to identifying psychiatric personnel who would be family friendly and up-to-date and to providing handouts that staff could use for supplemental background reading and as a resource to share with family members.

The status of potential child abuse and neglect was another uneasy issue. The planners were initially ambivalent, believing that the topic detracted from the profamily message; at the same time, field workers were repeatedly bringing this up as a source of professional strain. At the family group's recommendation, the topic was incorporated in "train the trainer" materials so that trainers would be able to knowledgeably comment during discussion and group exercises if the subject was audience initiated. A representative from the Child and Youth Service was asked to briefly discuss mandated reporting as part of program description, and the decision was made to address the broader subject of job-related stressors and stress management techniques.

CONCLUSION

The child ICM curriculum was pilot-tested in May 1990 and was revised and taught in the fall of that year. It consisted of 10 modules, each one-half day in length (see Table 11.1). Its critical core rests on the parent–professional partnership and the CASSP system of care values, as movingly described by a parent-trainer:

> Many years ago, when my son was little I started on what turned out to be a long-term process of looking for, finding, gaining access to, evaluating, and making decisions about specialized types of services for my child who had emotional problems. This process was complicated, at times overwhelming and frustrating. It required a commitment of energy and a tremendous amount of time, persistence and at time just sheer stubbornness. I also had to learn a lot of new things . . . [about] laws, regulations, and procedures in special education, mental health, children and youth and eventually juvenile justice. . . . I became aware that although I saw my child as one person, he would be compartmentalized and labeled by each different environment he was in,

Table 11.1. Modules for children's ICM

Part I: Introduction and training resources for lead trainers
        A. Introduction for lead trainers
            1. Curriculum design strategies
            2. Training approaches
            3. Matrix of training techniques
        B. Training resources
Part II: Training Modules
        Module I: What makes children's ICM different from adult ICM?
        Module II: Parent–professional collaboration
        Module III: Understanding family strengths
        Module IV: Features in implementing strengths assessment with children and adolescents in the context of the family: Balancing strengths and risks
        Module V: Features in service planning: Support for the family and child
        Module VI: The ICM and the mental health system: Understanding common diagnostic terms and their implications for accessing services
        Module VII: The children's intensive case manager and the system of care: Education and special education
        Module VIII: The children's intensive case manager and the system of care: Children and youth, juvenile justice, mental retardation, drug and alcohol
        Module IX: "Putting it together": Practicing children's ICM interventions
        Module X: Combating job-related factors which may contribute to stress and burnout

and I would be the one to portray him as a whole child to countless individuals. In short, I became my child's case manager.

Today, my remarks about case management are focused on values and attitudes and the importance of understanding their role in the development of a partnership model of case management services. Over the past 13 years I have been struck by the number of times I have been told that what I held important was unimportant and dismissed; and my values which have been an integral part of my family for years and years were viewed as problems and labeled accordingly.

The key to case management services for children and their families is partnership—parents, child, and professional collaboration. It means developing a model based on individual and family strengths. It also means respect for the child within the context of his/her family and a respect for the family taking into account the differences which exist within a family and the differences in values and life style among families whose children have emotional problems. This is a model of cultural competency in the broadest sense of the term. Without this focus, case management services will be but one more service added to the list of services parents may already be receiving. (Borden, 1990)

Presenters in the ICM training have included representatives from all the partnerships that built the curriculum: administrators, parents, academic faculty, highly experienced child ICMs and their supervisors, and representatives of the CASSP system of care. The authors continue to build new collaborations by recruiting presenters on an ongoing basis. As individuals grow more experienced and comfortable in these roles, they often rotate assignments or assume greater training responsibility. The role of the parent cotrainers has been greatly expanded beyond the introductory modules to which their participation was initially limited.

Careful attention continues to be paid to include, as trainers, persons of various cultures who are parents and/or professionals in children's services. A highlight of the initial sessions was a spontaneous role play in which two case managers enacted a good-natured, culturally competent, community-based encounter for the edification of their compatriots. Nonetheless, it has been clear that supplementary diversity training is necessary and that offerings on this topic have to be provided above and beyond the ICM initiative.

Training has continued with some modifications. A major factor in providing for continuity was PIN's willingness to persevere as a training partner. Not only has PIN continued to take responsibility for the module introducing the parent–professional partnership, but the lead PIN function has expanded to include cofacilitation and commentary on *all* modules, not just the introductory segments. As regional training teams have grown more comfortable with their partnership dynamics, the give-and-take of the experience has been enhanced.

In addition to augmenting the parent–cotrainer function, increased outreach has been undertaken to include parent ICM recipients as workshop panelists and as part of the training audience. They provide a real-life quality to the presentations and can share what has actually worked or not worked for them. Central and regional OMHs continue to actively encourage county mental health/mental retardation (MH/MR) program administrators to identify and, in some cases, to financially sponsor family attendance. In one county, this took the form of underwriting a family's hotel bill and providing an ICM for support and accompaniment. The authors have continued outreach to professionals who are parents of children with serious emotional disturbance in the hopes that their presentations will help erase "we"/"they" perceptions.

Greater efforts have also been made to recruit parents and professionals of various cultures as cotrainers, panelists, and audience members. During the second year, the OMH conducted regional

CASSP workshops on culturally competent practice with families of color, thus expanding knowledge and helping the authors to identify other stakeholders who might participate in ICM training sessions.

Regional CASSP personnel continue to assume increased responsibility for linking to key players in the child-serving systems. They assist by contacting parents and local resources and by actively recruiting knowledgeable persons whom they consider to be strong speakers.

The modules continue to be dynamically reworked in response to participant evaluation. Training time has been shortened to accommodate funding cutbacks and staff preferences, and currently runs between 3 and 3½ days. All child ICMs and their supervisors are mandated to attend within 6 months of hire.

One of the project's most important outcomes is that the generic curriculum is no longer "for adults only" but has been revised to anticipate the child case manager's needs. All case management training, whether generic or "alumni," now purposely incorporates child-focused material; child cases and parent concerns are routinely presented. As a result of the consciousness-raising lessons of this experience, the training institutes now incorporate child topics throughout the training cycle. This is a needed first step in building continuing training support for a children's mental health agenda that includes not only ICM but also other new trusts designed to support families and to build responsive family resources.

REFERENCES

Abel-Boone, H., Sandall, S.R., Loughry, A., & Frederick, L.L. (1990). An informed, family-centered approach to Public Law 99-457: Parental views. *Topics in Early Childhood Special Education, 10*(1), 100–111.

Anthony, W.A., Cohen, M., Farkas, M., & Cohen, B.F. (1988). Clinical care update: The chronically mentally ill: Case management—More than a response to a dysfunctional system. *Community Mental Health Journal, 24*(3), 219–228.

Bachrach, L.L. (1989). Case management: Toward a shared definition. *Hospital and Community Psychiatry, 40*(9), 883–884.

Baker, F., & Weiss, R.S. (1984). The nature of case management support. *Hospital and Community Psychiatry, 35*(9), 925–928.

Bailey, D.B. (1991). Issues and perspectives on family assessment. *Infants and Young Children, 4*(1), 26–34.

Bazron, B. (1989). *The minority severely emotionally disturbed child: Considerations for special education and mental health services: A task force report*. Washington, DC: CASSP Technical Assistance Center, Georgetown University Child Development Center.

Bevilacqua, J. (1991). The NIMH public-academic liaison (PAL) research initiative: An update. *Hospital and Community Psychiatry, 42*(1), 7.

Bigelow, D.A., & Young, D.J. (1983). *Effectiveness of a case management program.* Unpublished manuscript, Graduate School of Nursing, University of Washington, Seattle.

Bond, G.R., Miller, L.D., Krumwied, R.D., & Ward, R.S. (1988). Assertive case management in three CMHCs: A controlled study. *Hospital and Community Psychiatry, 39*(4), 411–418.

Borden, J.R. (1990, September). *The role of values and attitudes in developing collaborative case management services: A parent's perspective. Module I. What makes children's ICM different from adult ICM?* Presentation at first Child Case Management Training, Pennsylvania Office of Mental Health, Harrisburg.

Borland, A., McRae, J., & Lycan, C. (1989). Outcomes of five years of continuous intensive case management. *Hospital and Community Psychiatry, 40*(4), 369–376.

Chamberlain, R., & Rapp, C. (1983). *Training manual for case managers in community mental health.* Lawrence: University of Kansas, School of Social Welfare.

Corp, C., & Kosinski, P. (1990, February). *Parents Involved Network, Delaware County, Pennsylvania chapter: A self-help, advocacy, information and training resource for parents of children with serious emotional problems.* Paper presented at the third annual research conference of the Florida Mental Health Institute Research and Training Center for Children's Mental Health, University of South Florida, Tampa.

Cross, T.L., Bazron, B.J., Dennis, K.W., & Isaacs, M.R. (1989). *Towards a culturally competent system of care: A monograph on effective services for minority children who are severely emotionally disturbed.* Washington, DC: CASSP Technical Assistance Center, Georgetown University Child Development Center.

Dunst, C.J., & Trivette, C.M. (1988). An enablement and empowerment perspective of case management. *Topics in Early Childhood Special Education, 8*(4), 87–102.

Dunst, C.J., Trivette, C.M., & Deal, A. (1988). *Enabling and empowering families: Principles and guidelines for practice.* Cambridge, MA: Brookline Books.

Fine, G., & Borden, J.R. (1989). Parents Involved Network project: Support and advocacy training for parents. In R. M. Friedman, A.J. Duchnowski, & E.L. Henderson (Eds.), *Advocacy on behalf of children with serious emotional problems* (pp. 68–77). Springfield, IL: Charles C Thomas.

Fine, G., & Borden, J.R. (1991, February). *Parents Involved Network project: Outcomes of parent involvement in support group and advocacy training activities.* Paper presented at the fourth annual research conference of the Florida Mental Health Institute Research and Training Center for Children's Mental Health, University of South Florida, Tampa.

Garland, C., Woodruff, G., & Buck, D.M. (1988, June). *Division of Early Childhood white paper: Case management.* Unpublished manuscript, The Council for Exceptional Children, Reston, VA.

Hatfield, A.B. (1981). Families as advocates for the mentally ill. A growing movement. *Hospital and Community Psychiatry, 32*, 53–55, 641–642.

Hatfield, A.B., & Lefley, H.P. (1987). *Families of the mentally ill: Coping and adaptation.* New York: Guilford Press.

Hunter College School of Social Work. (1990). *Training: Children's intensive case management schedule.* Unpublished manuscript, Hunter College, New York.

Intagliata, J., Willer, B., & Egri, G. (1988). The role of the family in delivering case management services. In M. Harris & L.L. Bachrach (Eds.), *Clinical case management* (pp. 39–50). San Francisco: Jossey-Bass.

Kelker, K.A. (1988). *Taking charge: A handbook for parents whose children have emotional handicaps.* Portland, OR: Portland State University, Research and Training Center to Improve Services for Seriously Emotionally Handicapped Children and Their Families.

Malekoff, A., Johnson, H., & Klappersack, B. (1991). Parent–professional collaboration on behalf of children with learning disabilities. *Families in Society, 72*(7), 416–432.

National Association of Social Workers (NASW). (1984). *NASW standards and guidelines for social work case management for the functionally impaired: Professional standards (no. 12).* Washington, DC: Author.

Pennsylvania Office of Mental Health (PA OMH), Division of Children's Services. (1990). *Pennsylvania case management services for children and adolescents who are emotionally disturbed and their families.* Unpublished manuscript, Harrisburg, PA.

Robinson, G.K., & Bergman, G.T. (1989). *Choices in case management: A review of current knowledge and practice for mental health programs.* Washington, DC: Policy Resources.

Ronnau, J., Rutter, J., & Donner, R. (1988). *Resource training manual for family advocacy case management with adolescents with emotional disabilities.* Lawrence: University of Kansas, School of Social Welfare.

Stroul, B., & Friedman, R. (1986). *A system of care for severely emotionally disturbed children and youth.* Washington, DC: Georgetown University Child Development Center.

Sullivan, W.P. (1992). Reclaiming the community: The strengths perspective and deinstitutionalization. *Social Work, 37*(3), 204–209.

Vosler-Hunter, R. (1989). *Changing roles, changing relationships: Parent professional partnerships on behalf of children with emotional disabilities.* Portland, OR: Families as Allies Project, Research and Training Center on Family Support and Children's Mental Health.

Vosler-Hunter, R., & Exa, K. (1987). *Working together: A training handbook for parent–professional collaboration.* Portland, OR: Portland State University, Research and Training Center to Improve Services for Seriously Emotionally Handicapped Children and Their Families.

Weick, A., Rapp, C., Sullivan, W.P., & Kisthardt, W. (1989). A strengths perspective for social work practice. *Social Work, 34*, 350–354.

Winton, P.J., & Bailey, D.B. (1990). Early intervention training related to family interviewing. *Topics in Early Childhood Education, 10*(1), 50–61.

Creating and Maintaining Support and Structure for Case Managers
Issues in Case Management Supervision

Cathy Roberts Friedman and John Poertner

The 1980s were years of rapid expansion in the use of case management. On the one extreme, the concept of case management has been presented as a panacea and, on the other extreme, it has been used to describe a multitude of system problems. The ambiguous use of the term to describe a range of generic functions for different populations has created confusion for both professionals and consumers.

For the purpose of this chapter, the authors review their version of the role and functions of case management. The primary job of a case manager is to assist the child to live in a family environment while being educated in the most typical situation possible. This is accomplished through the development and implementation of an individualized service plan for the child and his or her family that will achieve these outcomes and that is agreed upon by the key participants. The case manager serves as an advocate for the child and his or her family, ensures communication among all service providers, and makes certain that the plan is based on a strengths-based ecological assessment. The case manager also guarantees that the plan is adjusted as needed and assists the child and his or her family in acquiring the skills needed to advocate effectively for themselves.

In the program that one of the authors directs, the target population is youth who have been identified as having severe emotional disturbances, who require intensive case management services by a multi-agency staffing committee. These youth have typically been involved with the system for many years. They are frequently considered to be at a "dead end" and, in many cases, the youth and the family have given up hope.

The case managers typically have at least a master's degree and about 20 youth clients. After receiving a referral, the case manager makes contact with the youth and his or her family, develops a relationship, and identifies the strengths, goals, and needs of the youth and his or her family in educational, vocational, housing, family supports, legal, social, medical, cultural, spiritual, financial, emotional, and behavioral areas. The case manager also has access to flexible funds that enable him or her to purchase and/or create supports that are believed to be needed to achieve the desired goals.

The community in which this program exists has established a multiagency community team to review the needs of children who have serious emotional problems for whom current services are inadequate. This team is broadly representative of community constituents involving the schools, child welfare, the juvenile court system, and other child-serving agencies. The case management program operates almost as an extension of this team, even though the program is a part of the community mental health center under contract with the public mental health authority.

Major supervisory responsibilities are to provide support and direction to case managers. Although this is the case for any supervisor, there are several features of case management for children who have emotional disorders that makes these responsibilities especially challenging. First, case management for children who have serious emotional disturbances and their families is relatively new. There are few precedents for it within sponsoring organizations. Therefore, it is not likely to be well understood by key program or administrative staff.

Second, case management emphasizes outreach into the community (homes, schools, etc.). Since agencies are often less experienced with outreach programs, they are often concerned about the cost effectiveness of such outreach efforts or are concerned about the risks to the case manager.

Third, case management is a program that serves a high-risk population and seeks to serve that population in a different manner. Therefore, case managers must have flexible hours so that they can work with children and their families when they are available after school or after work. In addition, case managers frequently need to be available around the clock on an as needed basis.

Fourth, the financing of case management services can be extremely complex. As more and more agencies seek to use Medicaid services to fund case management, a more solid financial base may be developed. However, this financial base requires extensive paperwork and derives from a medical model. Case management is a holistically oriented service rather than a traditional medical service. Effective case managers are often notorious for action rather than meticulous record keeping. Furthermore, increasing numbers of case management programs are recognizing the advantages of flexible funds. As advantageous as such funds are, they typically represent a special challenge for fiscal staff.

Fifth, within case management, it is clear that case managers must have their first allegiance to the youth and the family. Although it may be argued that other service providers subscribe to this same practice, the commitment of case managers to their clients must be unequivocal. Among other things, this means that effective case managers must not hesitate to advocate actions that make it possible for the youth to be served in a normal environment even if it is contrary to the desires of others in the agency.

The characteristics of case management for youth who have serious mental disorders presents a challenging context for supervision. The literature on supervision of case management is of little help. No model of case management has demonstrated effectiveness in keeping children who have emotional disturbances in family settings. Although there is some evidence that supervision can positively influence client outcomes (Harkness, 1987), no model of supervision has proven to be any more effective than any other model in terms of outcomes for clients. Therefore, the ideas presented in this chapter are those that the authors have found to be important in helping case managers to do their job. The supervision topics to be addressed include:

1. Selection and training
2. Caseload size
3. Enhancing case managers' power and authority
4. Creating a supportive climate
5. Participatory supervision
6. Maintaining relationships within the agency
7. Maintaining relationships among agencies

SELECTION AND TRAINING

One of the most important responsibilities of a program supervisor is to select the right person for the job. In some communities, in which case management is a new concept and the program is small, even a single improper selection of a candidate may be enough to destroy the program or at least set it back several years.

Drawing on the experience of the authors, Table 12.1 lists key attitudes, skills, and knowledge of an effective case manager working within a program serving children who have serious emotional disturbances and their families. This list emphasizes a combination of clinical knowledge and skills, systems knowledge, and a set of attitudes.

In terms of recruitment, there is little in the list that is specific to one mental health discipline; therefore, recruitment efforts are broad. To attract good candidates, recruitment efforts emphasize the creativity in the position, the opportunity to do something innovative, and the challenge of serving the target population.

Individuals who have demonstrated commitment to youngsters and their families in prior work are strong candidates. Moreover, these candidates must also be able to form supportive relationships with parents and youth. Applicants whose experience has been with agencies that are more accustomed to blaming parents may find it difficult to make the transition to collaborative relationships. Involving parents in the selection process can help identify those candidates who can develop these necessary relationships.

Table 12.1. Key attitudes, skills, and knowledge of an effective case manager

Attitudes	
Sense of humor	Mature
Likes people	Steady
Cares for other people	Flexible
Values consistent with the work group	Risk taking
Skills	
Negotiation	Communication (oral/written)
Leadership	Questioning authority
Listening and using feedback	Motivating others
Interpersonal influence	Working independently
Reframing	Attending to details
Decision making	Advocacy
Problem solving	Assertiveness
Task analysis	Persistence
Conflict management	Teaching
Knowledge	
Child service system	Mental health clinical diagnosis

For the sake of brevity, the list of knowledge areas is limited to topics not previously identified. Each attitude and skill requires related knowledge.

Given that case management is a new role, it is unlikely that new staff will be experienced at this function; therefore, training is important. During initial training, it is desirable to avoid presenting the case manager with a full caseload. Cases can be added as the case managers acquire the knowledge to fulfill their responsibilities.

Just as the case manager must ensure that a thorough assessment of a youth and his or her family is completed so that a customized service plan can be developed, the supervisor must be committed to an individualized training plan for each case manager. In some cases, this may result in specialized readings or individualized instruction. In other cases, it will involve an initial apprenticeship period during which the new case manager works closely with the supervisor or an experienced case manager. These joint activities must be accompanied by opportunities for the supervisor and the case manager to discuss what has taken place.

In a new or very small program, opportunities to learn from experienced case managers may be limited. Also, at the beginning of a new program the supervisor may have responsibilities that cut across several programs and may have little or no direct experience in case management. In these situations, supervisors need to recognize their limitations (time or experience) and use experienced case management supervisors as consultants.

There is always the need for ongoing training. Probably the most important developments in the children's mental health field include emphasizing the need for multiagency community-based systems of care, carrying concepts of individualized care to new heights, redefining relationships among parents and professionals, and recognizing the need to become culturally competent. In most cases, these changes require not just new knowledge, but also major shifts in attitudes. It is essential that case managers understand these trends and are prepared to implement them. Conferences, readings, and visits with other programs are all mechanisms for carrying out this ongoing training.

CASELOAD SIZE

The question asked most frequently of and by case management supervisors is: How many is the ideal number of clients? All the characteristics of case management for youth who have serious emotional disorders make it difficult to answer this question. There are several factors to consider and different approaches to determining the number of clients that is best for each case manager.

A major factor affecting the determination of the appropriate number of clients is the level of intensity needed by the youth and his or her family. In general, as the seriousness of the problems increase, the level of intensity increases and caseloads need to be smaller. Also, for youth who are in their own homes or in a foster home in the community, the day-to-day level of support needed will be greater than for youngsters who are being served in hospitals or in residential treatment programs. Furthermore, in the absence of formal services, where there is an even greater need for arranging informal supports, the time required to organize and supervise such efforts increases.

Another consideration is one of cost effectiveness. If the individualized service plan that is developed, monitored, and coordinated by the case manager is the last step before the youth ends an expensive residential placement, then considerations of cost effectiveness alone call for a smaller number of clients in order to maximize the likelihood of success.

In establishing the appropriate number of clients, it must be recognized that the case manager must identify and work with key people who have an influence on the youth. Each case can easily involve 10–15 players. This includes parents, siblings, step-parents, grandparents, boyfriends, girlfriends, teachers, principals, neighbors, staff of residential programs, foster parents, protective service providers, outpatient therapists, judges, coaches, spiritual leaders, and employers. In addition, individuals who provide respite to the parents, or who act as a therapeutic friend for the youth, as a tutor, or as a family therapist require attention. After all, there is considerable investment of time spent in the recruitment of these people, ensuring that they are properly trained and supervising their work with the family.

Given the number of potential participants and the work involved in ensuring that the individualized treatment program is applied properly for youth who are at risk of out-of-home placement, 10–12 clients are recommended. It should be noted, however, that these are recommendations based on program experience. No research exists on the relationship between effectiveness and number of clients in children's mental health.

Given the complexity of the issue of the appropriate number of clients, an approach used by one of the authors is to focus on the time spent with youth and their families. The program has a standard of 50% of case management time spent with children and their families. When time spent with youth and their families falls to less than 50%, discussions with the case manager focus on removing obstacles to meeting this standard. Frequently, this discussion uncovers cases that have stabilized or cases that can be closed. In either instance, new cases can be assigned. Focusing on time is a useful, pragmatic way to obtain a good mix of clients.

During the course of working with the youth and his or her family, the case manager seeks to help the youth and his or her family develop resources and enhance their ability to be their own advocates. As the situation for the youth and his or her family stabilizes and as the ability to advocate for oneself increases, the case manager diminishes his or her involvement and prepares to close the case. The time frame for this shift varies for each youth and family. For some youth who have had no contact with their family for years, and for youth with particularly serious difficulties and their families, even after several years it may be counterproductive to close the case. In determining whether to continue or discontinue case management services, some of the considerations are as follows:

1. In the last 3 months, have there been any events that the youth and his or her family were unable to handle by themselves?
2. Have the youth and his or her family demonstrated the skills needed to navigate the "system" without assistance?
3. Can the youth and his or her family be served appropriately through the more "routine" services?
4. Are the youth and his or her family aware of and do they make appropriate use of natural supports as well as supports within the service system?

ENHANCING CASE MANAGERS' POWER AND AUTHORITY

In most systems, case managers have no formal authority to make decisions. It is still a rare occurrence for case managers to have the funds to purchase what families need to provide care for their child or to purchase what youth need to live in the community. Frequently, budgetary constraints dictate that case managers are drawn from a variety of entry-level professionals with bachelor's degrees. Consequently, in a meeting with a judge, guardian *ad litem*, psychiatrist, school principal, and child welfare worker, the case manager is frequently seen as the person of lowest status.

The case manager's power derives from relationships and knowledge. It is the supervisor's job to provide the skills needed by case managers to build and maintain relationships with youth, parents, and other team members. The supervisor monitors these relationships to ensure that they are producing desired results.

Relationships The most significant impact a case manager can have on a youth or family is developing a positive relationship as a supportive ally and as an advocate. This relationship builds on the respect and understanding of each person's role and function. The case manager begins to build expectations with the first contact. When there is trust and dependability, there is a basis for sharing and taking risks.

Relationships are as important with child welfare workers as with a youth's grandmother. Developing a trusting relationship with other service providers, such as child welfare workers, involves such tasks as getting to know them as individuals, knowing and respecting their role in the system, recognizing their individual strengths, and rewarding them for their good work. All this implies spending time with them to develop this relationship. If there is trust and respect, the myriad of people involved with the client will work harder and maintain the investment required to assist the youth and his or her family. The relationship determines how much cooperation the case manager will obtain. For example, if the case manager has a relationship with the crisis unit staff then, when there is a need for the youth to be seen, the staff will see him or her without many of the usual hassles.

Knowledge of Youth and Family Caregivers Knowledge is power. When a case manager completes a holistic strengths assessment, few other people will know as much about the child and his or her family. For example, school personnel concerned with the classroom behavior of a child are searching for methods of controlling the troublesome behavior. The case manager knows that one of the child's strengths is his or her intense interest in science. This information is used to increase the time the child spends on science as a means of replacing the troublesome behavior. The case manager's power and credibility are enhanced through the success of the child and the decrease in problems for school personnel.

Most youth with serious emotional disturbances or their families have never had a holistic strengths assessment. This is an assessment of the child's strengths across life domains, such as education, recreation, health, affection, and self-definition. Since this type of assessment is unusual for these children, it is unlikely that a case manager will have this skill when hired. Consequently, the supervisor becomes responsible for training the case manager to conduct this type of assessment.

Knowledge of Policies   Knowledge of policies, administrative rules, or laws that govern services is a valuable tool when there is reluctance from individuals in the system to provide the necessary flexibility to allow the child or his or her family to have the needed accommodations. Often there are informal practices that inhibit the provision of services; however, when case managers know the policy, they can advocate more effectively. For example, if a child is expelled from school for an extended period of time and the case manager knows that school policy forbids such expulsion, he or she can use the policy to have the child reinstated.

Interpersonal Influence Skills   The power to influence people is essential. In some situations, the case manager's ability to *influence* the judge to allow the child to live at home is the only power he or she has. Simons (1982, 1985) has identified many useful interpersonal influence skills. These skills are an important base of knowledge for supervisors and case managers. It cannot be assumed that case managers have learned or refined these interpersonal influence skills. Supervisors must continually assess case managers' use of these skills and provide guidance when needed and rewards when they are used well.

CREATING A SUPPORTIVE CLIMATE

The case manager's agency and office can be a supportive, comforting, and energizing place or it can contribute to the general lack of clarity, confusion, and turmoil of difficult case situations. For example, after visiting with a child being placed in still another living arrangement, meeting with a family caregiver about an emotional situation in the home, or meeting with a judge about not placing the child in a juvenile detention facility, the case manager needs a supportive environment. Support is experienced in a variety of ways and comes from many different sources. What the supervisor observes and how he or she responds are important. Supervisors can help create and maintain a supportive environment by using or changing aspects of organizational culture. This includes conscious use of cultural elements such as norms and values, stories, symbols, and rites and rituals (Enz, 1988).

Norms or Values   When people are working together they share the same norms or values. Norms are the "shoulds" that people express about situations. What should this child do? What should the judge do in this case? What should the parents receive? The answers express values or norms that direct individual behavior.

A work group does not come to a commonly shared and practiced set of norms automatically. For example, one of the authors visited a case management group in which the supervisor expressed the value of keeping children at home whenever possible. When the case managers were asked to share a recent success story, half of them told of a recent institutional placement of a child. Although it is sometimes necessary for a child to be placed outside the home, child placements would not be expressed as success stories if the value of keeping children at home were shared by the staff. There was an apparent contradiction between the group's behavior and the value expressed by the supervisor. In a group that is practicing the value of keeping youth at home, the stories would be about those youth successfully maintained at home and the heroic efforts of staff and caregivers that were aimed at keeping the youth at home.

Individuals acquire the norms that they operate from in a variety of ways including life experience, education, training, and the workplace. The supervisor is key in defining, shaping, and maintaining organizational norms. One case manager mentioned that the multiple demands of all the people involved in a case often became overwhelming and confusing. She said that when she came back to the office it helped her to see a poster on the wall that stated the values of the unit. This is a simple way to define and communicate a group's values. Of course, a poster is not enough. The supervisor who is establishing or maintaining a common set of norms must use a variety of methods to accomplish this end. For this supervisor, nearly every interaction is an opportunity to reinforce the norms of the group. These responses range from having the group define the six or seven most important norms for working with children and their families, posting the norms on the wall in the case managers' work area, including the norms in written materials about the program, telling stories in the work group that illustrate service providers' practices linked to the norms, and rewarding service providers for these practices.

Symbols   A powerful way to communicate and maintain values is through symbols. Symbols are objects that are used to represent something abstract such as a value or norm. Visit a nearby church if you have any doubt about the power of symbols to communicate. In the case management group that listed their top values for working with children and families on a poster, the poster was a symbol, as are agency documents and report forms. For example, when a monthly report package for a community mental health center contains several pages of data on income and nothing else, the values of this center are clear.

Language is another powerful set of symbols. If the value of a case manager is to involve family caregivers and the phrase "dysfunctional family" is used on a consistent basis, it is likely that families will be seen by case managers as dysfunctional. It is also likely that the use of this term will set the norm for not involving families in a meaningful manner. If the supervisor talks about the heroic efforts that family members make to maintain their child at home, staff are more likely to involve family members.

Stories   Stories are another powerful use of language. Anthropologists listen to stories for a culture's heroes or models to identify norms. These models indicate how one "should" act. In the case management group, the heroes are identified in the stories that staff tell about themselves, children, and families. Stories about what children and their families have achieved demonstrate what is possible and what staff are working toward. Too often, organizational groups tell stories about impossible clients or staff. These people are models in the sense of the identification of values, but the difficulty is that the models are negative. Negative stories produce negative expectations for clients and staff. For example, a youth with a severe emotional disturbance was frequently in trouble in his classes because he was always drawing futuristic helicopters rather than doing the required work. This was labeled by a variety of professionals as an obsession or delusion. The mother with the assistance of the case manager was eventually able to convince the teachers and the youth to use his interest in drawing as a reward for exhibiting required behavior for a period of time in the classroom. Over time, school personnel were able to see his interest in designing helicopters as a real interest and as a strength. The youth was then allowed to attend normal science and math classes and eventually was removed from special education classes. In high school, the youth was in accelerated science classes and made the honor roll. This story is a powerful way to communicate the many features of working with children and caregivers, including the possible positive consequences of viewing behavior as normal, working from a strengths perspective, and the importance of persistence and a long-term perspective.

Every supervisor can tell positive stories about clients and staff. These stories demonstrate what is possible. Supervisors can listen for new success stories to keep staff rewarded and focused. If a case manager hears success stories about families, he or she will have concrete examples of what is possible. If a case manager has success with a judge and his or her supervisor uses that story to illustrate what is possible he or she will feel rewarded, his or her behavior will be reinforced, and others may learn by example.

Rites and Rituals This refers to all formal and informal interactions in an organization. The "employee of the month" is an example of a ritual for recognition of good work. The coffee break and the conversation that accompanies it is an example of an informal ritual. It is easy to construct formal events that honor the person who has the most success obtaining goals or involving families. Although the informal events are less recognized, they may be as important. The hastily made certificate because Judge Jones finally agreed to a treatment plan at home or the regularly stated "good job getting that resource for Mrs. Jones" may be more important than the formal events. The supervisor cannot overuse positive feedback. Frequent positive feedback is critical for reinforcing organization norms, values, and behavior.

PARTICIPATORY SUPERVISION

One traditional model of mental health supervision involves 1 hour of individual consultation each week. However, as agencies respond to increasing demands, many lack such time and use a group supervision model consisting primarily of the supervisor passing on the latest policy guidelines. This situation is not empowering of the case manager. Therefore, one of the authors has been involved in developing an empowering model of supervision (Ronnau & Page, 1991). Empowerment refers to case managers' acquiring alternative actions when they are experiencing difficulty in a case. Case managers report this to be energizing and helpful. The essential elements of this model are as follows:

- Focusing on situations in cases where case managers are having difficulty
- Clarifying the situation
- Brainstorming alternative actions and resources
- Emphasizing informal and normal community resources
- Having a minimum of three possible actions before the group moves on
- Celebrating failure
- Feedback from the group on the supervision session

The model is operationalized when the supervision session begins on time and is conducted in a location where group norms are reinforced through charts and posters. Workers receive an agenda that reinforces the norms of the group and the session. The emphasis is on situations in cases where case managers believe they have no options, and it is important to start where the worker feels "stuck." The value of this approach is in acquiring alternatives for action.

When a worker expresses a difficulty, the supervisor does not suggest alternatives but begins by helping to clarify the situation. Clarification involves asking questions about the goal for the case and the tasks that the child and his or her family are working on to achieve the goal. Frequently, when case managers have difficulty they lose perspective, and a review of goals and tasks brings clarity to the situation. For example, a worker may say that he or she is not certain what to do next about the Smith family. The supervisor asks questions such as: What is your goal for John? What is John's mother saying she needs to care for John at home? What does John say he needs to be successful at home or school? What are John's strengths? What are Mrs. Smith's strengths?

The next step is facilitating the group in brainstorming. Traditionally, brainstorming involves generating a list of alternatives without evaluation. There is a difference in this model. The person presenting the obstacle is asked to evaluate the alternatives for his or her appropriateness with the case, the service provider's abilities, and the service provider's style. The service provider presenting the situation is the expert on the situation and the only person capable of evaluating alternatives. Similarly, if an alternative is something that the service provider does not have the skills or desire to do, it is unlikely that he or she will try and should be relieved of that expectation. In the Smith example, the questions of clarification identify that the service provider is having difficulty helping meet Mrs. Smith's need to have John adequately supervised after school and before she gets home from work. The group identifies eight or nine options of which the service provider agrees that there are three that she is comfortable with and will explore this week. These include involvement in the YMCA, enlisting the help of a neighbor who is a retired social worker and has expressed interest in helping, and the use of a formal attendant care program.

When resources are needed, there is emphasis on generating informal, normal community alternatives. To help children and their families function in the community in normal environments, it is necessary to focus on normal resources. Often when workers believe that they have no options, it is because they can only see the need in terms of formal services that do not exist, are too expensive, or do not have room for another client. This can result in unnecessarily placing a child in an out-of-home placement for lack of a better resource. The focus on informal resources raises the possibility that the need can be met in another way. In the Smith case, one of the first suggestions was the use of attendant care as a formal service. Through the process of examining informal resources, the ideas of the YMCA and the neighbor were identified and explored. The service provider agreed to explore these informal resources before she relied on attendant care.

An additional requirement is that each service provider presenting a situation obtain a minimum of three alternatives and know the specific action required for each before the group goes on to the next case. In some cases, this requires the group to generate many alternatives before three acceptable ones are identified. Consequently, not every client is discussed; however, this is not a problem. If each service provider leaves the session with a minimum of three alternatives for difficult situations, the work of the group will continue. Although some clients consume a great deal of time, service providers report that the generation of alternatives is helpful in other cases. Some supervisors are initially uncomfortable with not covering each case because they believe that they need information on each case. If the group operates with an information system, the supervisor has all the case information needed and does not have to use the supervision session to obtain information. (See Rapp & Poertner, 1992, to develop such an information system.)

Frequently, a service provider is stuck on a case because what he or she tried did not work. In this model of supervision, such failure is celebrated. It is a tenet of this model that failure is essential to learning. If it was known for certain what needed to be done in each situation, case managers would not be needed. Case managers need to be creative and take risks in their efforts to assist children and their families. This creativity and risk taking is not likely to occur if service providers fear failure. Certainly boundaries need to exist so that the child and his or her family are not endangered. However, there are many situations in which greater risk taking has the potential of assisting children, families, and case managers.

Sessions end with service providers completing a simple checklist of expectations for the session. Supervisors know from their experience how the session went. However, it is important to obtain the service providers' perspective to ensure that everyone is sharing the same point of view. Conducting supervision sessions following this model is an efficient use of time. More can be accomplished in 1½ hours with seven people than in 7 hours of individual supervision. Similarly, service providers report that the model is effective.

They report leaving these sessions energized and hopeful, which is the central goal of the model.

MAINTAINING RELATIONSHIPS WITHIN THE AGENCY

Although case managers must retain their primary commitment to youth and their families, the supervisor can help case managers recognize the importance of maintaining good relationships within their own organization. The case management group needs to be a legitimate part of the agency. To assist children and their families, service providers may need resources from other programs within the agency. There may be individuals within the agency that have formal or informal decision-making authority over access to services or the placement of the child. There may be individuals in the agency who do not operate from a strengths perspective or who blame family caregivers for the difficulties experienced by the youth.

Supervisors confronted with the task of developing supportive organizational relationships may need a variety of strategies to accomplish this goal. Two related strategies are involvement and education. It is the supervisor's role to ensure that other agency staff are involved with the program and informed about it. This requires frequent meetings to educate staff about the program and to give them a sense of involvement and ownership. They may be involved in suggestions about referral processes, methods of sharing information, or assisting orienting new case managers to the agency.

Case management services of the type the authors are describing for children and their families are relatively new to many mental health agencies. This makes educating other staff an essential supervisory task. The educational process helps staff in other groups to understand the program's objectives, the reasons it is needed, the approaches that are used, and the rationale for its unique features. As part of the educational process, the program supervisor may want to invite agency staff to visit other case management programs and/or bring information about other programs and their procedures to the agency.

Having parents assist with the educating of other staff is a helpful technique. Parents' stories about their struggles in caring for the child and acquiring assistance are powerful in helping others understand the stresses and strains of caring for a youth who has serious emotional problems. Beyond educating, parents are also resources for influencing others. Parents can often influence agency policies or procedures that a case manager has difficulty changing.

Another aspect of developing relationships within the agency is the supervisor being proactive in identifying potential conflicts and problems. For example, confusion on the referral process can produce conflicts that are not really personal but appear that way. This may result in a debate over the necessity of placing the child out of the home. The supervisor may be able to avoid these conflicts by being direct and straightforward in identifying the problem and working with others to identify a satisfactory solution. An appropriate balance must be established both by case managers and the supervisor between internal public relations, without which the program could not survive, and advocacy for children and their families.

Another strategy for developing and maintaining a positive relationship within the host agency is to ensure that credit for success of the case management program is shared by the agency in general. This sharing can take place through appropriate gestures of thanks within the agency or through acknowledgment of the support of the agency by external sources. A parent who has had success with case management and who thanks an agency administrator builds support. If an organization sees case management as a source of favorable recognition in the community or in the specialized professional community, then it is likely to provide needed support to the case management program.

MAINTAINING RELATIONSHIPS AMONG AGENCIES

It is not unusual for a case manager to receive a case that, in addition to the child and a caregiver involves:

- Numerous family members
- A mental health therapist
- A psychiatrist
- A child welfare case worker
- A guardian *ad litem*
- A juvenile judge
- A special education teacher
- A court service officer

If the family includes more than one child in need of services, the number of people and variety of professionals increases dramatically. The case manager must maintain a focus that is helpful to the child and the family caregiver, as well as maintain ongoing relationships with other professionals. The supervisor must make certain that the case manager has these skills. One important aspect of maintaining relationships among agencies is to be sure that case managers focus on knowing what is required from each person involved in the system to assist children and their families. In the middle of a crisis with a child, it is easy to forget what a particular person in the system needs to do to benefit the child and his or her family. In these situations, the supervisor helps the case manager gain clarity and specificity. This assistance can be accomplished by: 1) helping the case manager identify each key person involved with the child, and 2) identifying the minimal behavior required for the child and/or family caregiver to receive what they need. The focus here is on helping the case manager to specify what is needed in terms of behavior and sort out the difference between nice and necessary. For example, although it might be nice, easy, or convenient if the child welfare worker wrote a reintegration plan with the caregiver, visited the caregiver once a week, and signed the voucher for respite care, is this the minimum behavior required for success?

Specific and reasonable expectations are necessary first steps but are not enough to maintain relationships among agencies. The case manager must also exercise those interpersonal influence skills identified by Simons (1982, 1985). This suggests that supervisors support case managers in developing and practicing these skills.

Supervisors can also sense potential problems among agencies through the collective number of clients of each case manager. When concerns arise across cases, the supervisor can intervene at the community or system level with the same attention to minimal behavior and interpersonal influence skills. For example, when several case managers report a particular juvenile probation officer to be difficult to influence, the supervisor may need to intervene directly. This includes identifying the behavior required of the probation officer and developing strategies to influence his or her behavior.

CONCLUSION

It is extremely difficult to help youth with serious emotional disorders remain in family settings in the community and participate in normal community activities. The supervisor may play a key role in ensuring that case managers achieve this outcome with children and families. This chapter provides supervisors with tools in seven areas that, in the authors' experience, are critical to providing the support and structure needed by case managers. Naturally this effort begins with selection and training, where clear expectations must be established. These expectations include the philosophy or set of attitudes of the unit as well as a way of doing the job that differs greatly from the normal way of doing business. These issues are addressed in the selection of case managers and in their training.

Case management with children with serious emotional disorders is difficult and time-consuming, involving many individuals and agencies. Consequently, it is essential to consider caseload questions and to find ways in which supervisors can enhance the power and authority of case managers. Overwhelmed and impotent workers can be inadvertent agents of disaster for children, families, and themselves. Developing a supportive and participatory environment can be central to helping case managers maintain energy and enthusiasm. Consciously using elements of organizational culture is a useful tool, as is assuming that case managers know best and should be involved in assisting each other.

Finally, this chapter considers the establishing and maintaining of relationships within and among agencies. Supervisors need skills in organizational influence to provide leadership and direction in these complex areas. Case management for children with serious emotional disorders is new and complex, and consequently it is not always adequately addressed within more traditional agencies. In addition, another case manager in a community increases the number of professionals involved in a youth's life. Supervisors must devote time and attention to these two constituencies.

The job of a case management supervisor is large, complex, and difficult. Supervisors assist children with serious emotional disorders through the work of case managers. When the supervisor's job and the case manager's job receive equal attention, the field of children's mental health will produce the results we all want for children and families.

REFERENCES

Enz, C.A. (1988). *Power and shared values in the corporate culture.* Ann Arbor, MI: UMI Research Press.

Harkness, D.R. (1987). *Social work supervision in community mental health: Evaluating the effects of normal and client focused supervision on client satisfaction and generalized contentment.* Unpublished doctoral dissertation, University of Kansas, Lawrence.

Rapp, C.A., & Poertner, J. (1992). *Social administration: A client-centered approach.* New York: Longman.

Ronnau, J., & Page, M. (1991). *Training manual for family advocacy services.* Unpublished manual, University of Kansas School of Social Welfare, Lawrence.

Simons, R.L. (1982). Strategies for exercising influence. *Social Work, 27*(3), 268–274.

Simons, R.L. (1985). Inducement as an approval to exercising influence. *Social Work, 30*(1), 56–68.

STATE-OF-THE-ART PROGRAMS
Examples from the Field

CHAPTER 13

New York's Family-Centered Intensive Case Management Program

Caren Abate, Lydia Brennan, and Barbara Conrad

Family-centered intensive case management represents an innovative approach to serving children with serious emotional disturbances and their families (Evans, 1990). It is an example of the strengths model of case management in that it not only addresses the needs and problems of children and their families, but also emphasizes their strengths and interests. It is unique because it provides intensive and individualized services to children with serious emotional disturbances and their families by focusing on the development of the families' social network and by providing families with the skills and supports necessary to care for a child with a serious emotional disturbance (see Table 13.1).

In the development of a comprehensive, community-based system of care for children and youth with serious emotional disturbances and their families, the New York State Office of Mental Health (OMH) established an array of new programs between 1987 and 1990. The Family-Centered Intensive Case Management Program was established as part of the OMH's research and demonstration grant through the National Institute of Mental Health (NIMH). The case management project was funded through a combination of the targeted case management Medicaid option, the research and demonstration grant, and state funds. The grant funded training, data collection, parent–advocate position, and other program enhancements, such as respite, family recreation events, and the parent support groups. State funding provides the flexible service dollars that are associated with the program. The case management positions are funded with state and Medicaid funds. Children who are eligible for the program are between ages 6 and 12 years, reside within a specific service area, have a *DSM-IV* (American Psychiatric

277

Table 13.1. Family-centered intensive case management

- Support from a parent advocate and family-centered intensive case manager (ICM) team
- 24-hour-a-day/7-day-a-week response capability
- Planned and emergency respite care
- Parent skills training for natural parents
- Parent support groups
- Comprehensive family and child needs assessment
- Case management and linkage to needed services for the family unit
- Flexible service dollars to purchase individualized services and/or to develop new programs and services for the collective group of family-centered intensive case management clients
- Home visits by the parent advocate and family-centered ICM, both scheduled and on an emergency basis
- Client and system advocacy
- Psychiatric consultation
- Family recreation events

Association, 1994) diagnosis and serious behavioral and/or emotional difficulties, have been placed outside the home, or are at risk of being placed outside the home due to behavioral and/or emotional difficulties. It must also be determined that a situation that would endanger the health and well-being of the child does not exist within the home.

Several assumptions were made in the development of the Family-Centered Intensive Case Management Program model. First was the assumption that because children with serious emotional disturbance and their families often require numerous services provided from a variety of agencies, an effective service intervention must not only address the needs of the child, but also the needs of the entire family, including siblings.

The second premise was that parenting a child with a serious emotional disturbance is a stressful, challenging job, and that families, including the siblings of the child, are often isolated and stigmatized. Many parents lack the support and skills needed to parent and advocate for a child with a serious emotional disturbance. The program is built on the belief that parents can benefit by obtaining respite, forming partnerships with other parents, gaining information, and learning new skills related to their child's disability. It also acknowledges that transportation and child care needs must be addressed in order for parents to participate in support groups and training opportunities. Furthermore, as these parents gain skills and knowledge, they may be interested in broader system change activities on a local or state level.

Third, communities often lack the array of services and funding flexibility to meet the individualized needs of children and their families. Traditional funding streams and the need to generate revenue often limit services flexibility in providing in-home and community-based services to children and their families (Surles, Blanch, Shern, & Donahue, 1992). A capitated Medicaid rate and flexible service dollars were two strategies used to ensure that services focused on meeting the individualized needs of children and their families.

Finally, there was the belief that parent advocates, individuals with experience in parenting a child with a serious emotional disturbance, can work with professionals to provide supportive services to families. Parent advocates can also represent the collective group of children and their families by advocating on both a local and state level for needed reform. They can help policy makers better understand the needs of children and their families and confront existing barriers to accessing services. This systems change must occur if case management is to be an effective service intervention for children and their families.

THE PROGRAM MODEL

The focal point for family-centered intensive case management services is the family and the goal is to keep the child in "natural environments"—family, school, and community. In order to accomplish this goal, the family-centered intensive case manager (ICM) and parent advocate work with a group of eight families that have a child with a serious emotional disturbance. Each group has access to trained respite caregivers that provide planned, emergency, or crisis respite to the families in the program.

Parent support groups are available for the provision of peer support with specific meeting times determined by the families. Transportation and specialized child care are provided on-site to facilitate parental participation, but attendance is voluntary. Skills training and the implementation of different behavioral interventions that can be used effectively with children are available to families on an individual basis. In addition, at least three family recreation events are planned each year based on the desire of the families in the program.

The family-centered ICM is not limited in the amount of time spent with individual children, families, or other service providers, nor are the recipients limited as to to where services are provided—in the home and in the community. A reduced case manager–child ratio (1:8) provides ample time to address child and family needs on an individualized and intensive basis. Flexible service dollars (approximately $2,000 per child/per year) are available to case managers for the purchase of individualized services. In some instances, service dollars are used to develop new programs and services that can benefit all children in the community with serious emotional disturbances.

ELEMENTS OF FAMILY-CENTERED INTENSIVE CASE MANAGEMENT

After a child and his or her family are determined to be eligible for the program, a visit to the family's home is scheduled, and a detailed family assessment is completed by the case manager, parent advocate, and the family. The family is asked to identify what they need for their child to remain at home. Information collected includes a complete family and social history, history of services utilized, and satisfaction with those services. To measure a child's functioning, the Child Behavior Checklist (Achenbach & Edebrock, 1983) is completed as a measure of the child's capacities from the parents' perspective.

After several meetings, an initial family service plan is developed. In its development, all family members are asked to identify the strengths and weaknesses they see in themselves and in their family. They are also asked to identify what changes they would like to see in how their family functions. The result is a family service plan that links family members to needed services (e.g., mental health, vocational, social services, alcohol/substance abuse treatment, recreational).

Six-year-old Joe was referred and accepted into the program by the school psychologist. At school, he is frequently aggressive with peers and adults. When angered, he will hit, kick, or throw things, and he was recently suspended from school for throwing a chair at a teacher. At home, Joe is physically aggressive and sexually inappropriate with his parents and siblings. It recently became known that Joe was sexually abused by a male babysitter, and when taken for treatment to a local mental health clinic, the family was told that he could not be treated because of his acting-out behavior.

Joe's family consists of his mother, Karen, age 31; his father, Mike, age 35; his sister, Emily, who appears to be very withdrawn; and his stepbrother, Billy, who was abused by his natural father. Billy has severe learning disabilities and behavioral problems. At school he is frequently oppositional and belligerent. At home he has a difficult time obeying rules and is in frequent conflict with Joe.

Their fights often become extremely violent, and Karen fears one of them might be seriously hurt.

Mike makes only $24,000 a year and is supporting four children from a previous marriage. He is concerned about the possibility of losing his job. The family lives in a two-bedroom apartment and is under severe financial stress due to Mike's child support payments, medical bills, and a loan to an untrustworthy family member. There is marital conflict concerning the best way to discipline the children.

For Joe's family, some of the priority needs included: different living arrangements, help with finances, adequate medical and dental services, counseling for Joe to deal with the sexual abuse and other issues, parenting skills and support for Karen and Mike, evaluation of Emily's behavior, a school assessment for Billy, marital counseling for Karen and Mike, and increased recreational opportunities for Karen and Mike as a couple and for the family as a whole.

The service plan is developed with concrete steps designed to assist the family in meeting the goals that they have set for themselves. One identified goal was to increase quality time spent as a family. The specific steps identified to meet that goal included arranging work schedules to plan a family night out and creating a list of family activities that all members enjoyed. The plan also outlined how some of the flexible service dollars would assist the family with the cost of the activities.

The family-centered ICM is responsible for linking the family to needed services and coordinating planning meetings with family members and additional service providers. This ensures that everyone knows about the service plan and is working to achieve the same goals. Karen agreed to schedule an appointment for Joe at the mental health clinic and call the case manager if any stumbling blocks emerged. The case manager would maintain contact with the mental health therapist to ensure that services were coordinated and appropriate.

Service plans are reviewed at least every 3 months for the first year and modified as needed. The object of the team meeting is to reach agreement with the family, service providers, and family-centered ICM as to goals, the steps needed to reach the goals, and a definition of success. Discharge from the program is recommended when the child has functioned successfully in the family, at school, and in the community for 3 months. Discharge is a joint decision between the family, case manager, and other service providers based on significant improvement in the child's functioning.

Although the individual needs of families may differ, a basic set of services is provided: 24-hour-a-day, 7-day-a-week crisis intervention; in-home and out-of-home respite services; flexible service dollars; parent support group; recreation events for children and siblings; and linkages to services that are needed by the child and his or her family. The key is treating each child and family individually and wrapping services around them, rather than fitting them into a predetermined, inflexible package of services.

Flexible service dollars are used by the case manager for individual family and child services purchased using vouchers. During the first 6 months of the program, of all families served, 55% of service dollars were spent for economic purposes (e.g., paying a utility bill, installing a telephone, buying food), 22% were spent to address recreation and social needs (e.g., camp scholarships), 9% for school/vocational needs (e.g., school supplies, vocational program), and 6% for clinical needs (e.g., rewards for token economy). The only requirement is that the use of the service dollars must relate to meeting a goal in the family's service plan. To date, 58% of service dollars have been used to address child-specific needs and 42% have been used to address parent or family needs. Service dollars may also be used for the collective group of clients.

Basic 24-hour, 7-day-a-week crisis services are provided to each family. These services can range from the parent advocate providing a listening ear after a bad day to physical intervention in the home by the case manager. Parents in the program have identified the ability to have easy access to staff who listen and respect them as one of the most important and supportive aspects of the program.

Out-of-home respite involves placing the child with a specially screened, trained, and certified family. The stay can range from 1 to several days and is designed to provide parents with a much needed break from the stress of raising a child with a serious emotional disturbance. Respite families are paid a $300 per month retainer and $40 per day when a child is in the home. A specified amount of respite is not provided to each family; rather, the amount is based on the needs of the family. Respite workers are trained using the Rest-A-Bit Training Manual (Donner, 1988). In-home respite has been preferred and used most frequently by the families in the Family-Centered Intensive Case Management Program.

Parent support groups are available at each site; however, development of some of these groups has proven to be challenging. These challenges include geographic distances between families living in a rural county, the diversity of the families socioeconomically and culturally, and finding a time that is convenient for most families to participate. What has proven to be helpful is providing transportation and respite, having the parents set the agenda for the meetings, and focusing on positive events.

Parenting skills training and education are provided individually with each family. Helping families develop and implement plans to structure a child's day, to use reward systems that work, and to make the child's day predictable are some of the areas of focus. The plans are worked out in advance of a crisis situation and revised as needed. Confidence building is critical and the parent advocate provides support and encouragement as the family learns and practices new skills.

Family recreation events are planned by and for the families. Summer picnics, a back-to-school barbecue, and a Halloween party are just some of the events that have been planned. These events help to break down the isolation experienced by many families with children who have serious emotional disturbances. Activities for the children in the program and their siblings have also been a success. The latter involves the development of Sibshops (sibling support groups), which combine fun, recreational games with other supportive activities (Meyer, Vadasy, & Fewell, 1986).

Advocacy in the Family-Centered Intensive Case Management Program is carried out at both the case and class levels. Case advocacy has most frequently involved helping a family to understand and negotiate the education system. In one instance, the case manager and the child's parent convinced special education not to place a child in the fifth grade for the third time. Advocacy at the class level involves parent advocates serving on mental health planning committees, testifying at public hearings, and/or meeting with local policy makers. Through these activities, parents being served in the program learn how to advocate for their child.

ROLES OF THE CASE MANAGER AND PARENT ADVOCATE

The family-centered ICM is required to have a master's degree in the human services field with 2 years of experience working with children with serious emotional disturbances or a bachelor's degree with appropriate experience. The ICM assesses the needs of the child and his or her family, participates in service planning, coordinates and monitors services and the use of service dollars, assists in the development of formal and informal support systems, and works as an advocate both at the case and class level.

Planned activities include home visits with families, parent training and support groups, frequent contact with service providers, and recreational activities with the families. Unexpected activities, ranging from calling seven different dentists in the area before finding one who will treat a particular child to spending the night with a family in crisis, are also part of the job. The key to the job is flexibility. Case managers must be able to do whatever needs to be done, whenever it needs to be done. This may mean working nights and weekends and using a great deal of creativity.

Family-centered ICMs receive 10 days of generic case management training over the course of 10 weeks that focus on such things as the role of the case manager, advocacy skills, understanding child and family service systems, entitlement programs, and how to translate child and family needs into resources and services. Ongoing training on a variety of child and family topics is also provided throughout the year. Clinical supervision, regular contact with other case managers in the region, and psychiatric consultation on specific cases are also provided. In addition, family-centered ICMs are on-call to respond to family crises on a rotating basis with other case managers in the region.

The parent advocate position is a sign of the changing view of parents' involvement in mental health services (Friesen & Koroloff, 1990; Lourie & Katz-Leavy, 1991). The requirements for parent advocates is that they are the parents of a child with a serious emotional disturbance and that they are empathic, understanding, and able to communicate effectively with other parents. The role of the parent advocate is to help the case manager conduct home visits, advocate at the case and class level, train respite caregivers, and educate the community about children with serious emotional disturbances and their families. In addition, the parent advocate coordinates the support group and provides a "human touch" by helping other parents understand that there are others out there with the same frustrations and fear. The parent advocate contacts and follows up with parents who have missed parent support group meetings and helps make arrangements so that they can participate. Most important, the parent advocate is there to lend help with an open ear and an open mind.

Parent advocates and case managers receive training on the role of the parent advocate, on how to start and implement parent education/support groups, on how to implement Sibshops, on how to teach parenting skills to other parents, and on how to train respite caregivers. Additional training on such topics as understanding the special education system have also been helpful, and regular contact with parent advocates from other programs for mutual support and team building is essential.

CONCLUSION

Joe and his family are still receiving services from the Family-Centered Intensive Case Management Program. School outbursts and physical aggression at home have diminished for both Joe and Billy. Both boys are involved in after-school recreation programs. Emily is seeing a therapist to deal with her feelings of anger. Unfortunately, Karen and Mike have separated, and his whereabouts are unknown. Karen is working very hard to keep the family together and the parent advocate is working with her on better ways to discipline the children, helping with child care arrangements, and managing finances.

Although the long-term outcomes regarding the Family-Centered Intensive Case Management Program are not yet available, there is evidence to suggest the efficacy of the services. With few exceptions, the majority of the children in the program continue to live at home. Parent satisfaction with the program has been unequivocally positive. Parents in the program say that they are "listened to" for the first time. Although family-centered intensive case management will not eliminate the need for residential placement, it offers one strategy to help preserve and support families while maintaining children at home.

REFERENCES

Achenbach, T.M., & Edebrock, C. (1983). *Manual for the Child Behavior Checklist and Revised Child Behavior Profile.* Burlington: University of Vermont, Department of Psychiatry.

Donner, R. (1988, June). *Rest-a-Bit: A training program for respite care providers.* Topeka, KS: Families Together.

Evans, M. (1990). *Outcomes of two intensive service programs for children* (Grant No. MH48072-02). Washington, DC: National Institute of Mental Health.

Friesen, B.J., & Koroloff, N.M. (1990). Family-centered services: Implications for mental health administration and research. *Journal of Mental Health Administration, 17*(1), 13–25.

Lourie, I., & Katz-Leavy, J. (1991). New directions for mental health services for families and children. *Journal of Contemporary Human Services, 72*(5), 277–285.

Meyer, D., Vadasy, P., & Fewell, R. (1986). *Sibshops: A handbook for implementing workshops for siblings of children with special needs.* Seattle: University of Washington.

Surles, R., Blanch, A., Shern, D., & Donahue, S. (1992). Case management as a strategy for systems change. *Health Affairs, 11,* 152–163.

CHAPTER 14

Family Advocacy Services
A Strengths Model of Case Management

John Ronnau

This chapter describes family advocacy services, a strengths model of case management that was developed at the University of Kansas, School of Social Welfare.[1] The model has been implemented over the past several years in various settings, including a state psychiatric hospital, community mental health centers, and state human services departments. The psychiatric hospital setting data compiled from using this model are used here.

The family advocacy services model is described by means of a framework consisting of the goal, problem definition, assumptions regarding community structure, focus of intervention, target population, the basic elements of service, assumptions regarding clients and client roles, and the roles of case manager, or "family advocate."

DEFINITION OF THE PROBLEM

The strengths model of case management is designed to help youth with serious emotional disabilities live successfully in their communities. This help is provided not only to the youth but also to their schools and adult caregivers, whether they be group home staff or family members. The success of the youth is often dependent upon the knowledge, energy, and commitment of the significant adults in their lives. The impact of severe emotional disturbance on children can be devastating but the consequences do not stop with the individual. The demands made on parents who care for these children are extensive (Moroney, 1981; Thompson & Doll, 1982; Willis, 1982). The effects of family stress were clearly evident in Edward's case, a

---

[1] The model is described in detail in the publication, *Training Manual for Family Advocacy Services* (Ronnau & Page, 1991). Material from that manual and its predecessor, *Training Manual for Family Advocacy In-Home Services* (Ronnau, 1989b), provide the basis for this chapter.

16-year-old youth who had spent approximately one half of his life in a psychiatric hospital for aggression, violence, and depression.

> When Edward was released his mother reported being at wits end due to his lack of basic independent living skills, which he had not developed as a hospital patient. Edward would even follow his mother to the bathroom because he didn't know what to do without constant supervision. As his mother put it: "The young man has lived in a controlled environment for ten, eleven years . . . they tell him when to get up, when to eat, when to go out and play, when to relax, when to study; and all of a sudden he's out here and is having to make decisions." (Ronnau, 1989a, p. 371)

The problems experienced and the behaviors exhibited by youth with emotional disturbances are referred to in the strengths model as disabilities. This terminology is selected because it is less stigmatizing and discouraging than the typical mental illness labels. The concepts of normalization, mainstreaming, and reasonable accommodations are important foundations for this approach.

GOAL OF THE STRENGTHS MODEL

The goal of family advocacy services is to assist youth with emotional disabilities to live in family environments and be educated in normal settings. In keeping with the strengths model, normal environments for youth are described as:

- Being most family-like (ideally, the youth's family itself)
- Involving community activities (e.g., YMCA, YWCA, community sports programs, church activities, Boy Scouts, Girl Scouts, youth symphony)
- Including mainstreaming school attendance and usual school activities

Community Structure

In keeping with the philosophy of accommodation, the entire community is looked on as a potential resource to meet the needs of youth with emotional disabilities and their caregivers. The assumption of the strengths model is that most persons in the community, given appropriate information and support, want to cooperate to meet the needs of these youth and their families.

For those services that exist but are not accessible to the family due to political or policy problems, the family advocate will play a role in building bridges to allow access. For example, a supervisor of an afterschool swimming program refused to admit an adolescent out of fear that he or she could not manage the "crazy kid" with the conduct disorder. But after the family advocate provided specific information about the youth's condition (with the parent's permission), along with reassurance and offers of support, the supervisor admitted the youth to the program. In addition, the family advocate may attend the youth's first one or two swim sessions to help relieve everyone's anxieties.

Edward's stepfather provides another good example of the importance of access to normal community resources for his son.

> When he was younger getting him into Boy Scouts would have been a good thing . . . stuff where you can get him with other people and at least have the possibility of making some friends and more contact and a more acceptable type of structure than running around breaking windows on garages. We're talking about positive role models; some way for the kid to learn different ways to behave. (Ronnau, 1989a, p. 372)

When such needed services do not exist, the family advocate will play a role in developing them. For example, when after school care was a problem for a caregiver, the case manager and parent identified a retired social worker who was available to provide this supervision. The joint efforts of the case manager and the caregiver created a resource needed to allow the youth to live at home.

Focus of Intervention

Family advocacy services are focused on helping *both* the youth with emotional disabilities and their caregivers. Research conducted with the strengths model has shown that these caregivers, most often the youth's family, are a key to the success of the youth in the community (Ronnau, 1989a). The family's cooperation and participation is a major factor in the long- and short-term success of any treatment plan (Hobbs, 1975). The family is the primary link between the continuum of services that the child or adolescent will need (Lourie & Katz-Leavy, 1987). It is virtually impossible, and often counterproductive, to work with the child in isolation from the family; to help the child you must help the family. The younger the child with the emotional disability, the more the focus must be on involvement of the family.

The important role that family caregivers play in the success of these youth in the community is emphasized by a special education teacher who was asked what Ralph, a 16-year-old who has spent 2 years in the psychiatric hospital due to "multiple placement failures" and a diagnosis of "depressive and affective disorder," needs to live successfully outside the hospital. The teacher stated, "In order for him to be successful in school and outside of the hospital he would probably have to have a very stable home environment. That would be number 1 . . ." (Ronnau, 1989a, p. 459). In other words, youth need an individual who will provide the care and direction required to become a functioning adult member of society.

Target Population

Although diagnoses give the broad parameters of the characteristics of children with severe emotional problems, they really say very little about them and they certainly do not prepare family advocates for the types of individuals they will encounter. These youth share the existence of an emotional disability, yet each one is unique. The following are examples of adolescent clients.

> Lisa is a 13-year-old residing at the state hospital. She is the only child of her 30-year-old single mother with whom she lived before her admission to the ward. Lisa was placed in the hospital because of her frequent runaway attempts and her inability to respond to her mother's authority. She receives excellent grades in school and finds it easy to make and maintain friendships. She was diagnosed a Conduct Disorder by the attending psychiatrist. Lisa feels her problems stem from boredom. Her mother works, takes night classes, and is seldom home.

> Joe is a 16-year-old male. He is a tall boy with a large build. He lives with his mother and his half brother Sam. Joe's problems started in school when his grades began to fall. He also become involved in alcohol and marijuana use. In February, Joe was admitted to the adolescent acute psychiatric unit after making a suicide attempt. Joe had taken three over-the-counter sleeping pills. Joe reportedly speaks to God and hears voices telling him what to do. Joe has been depressed for some time and according to his therapist seems to suffer from a sense of failure. Joe reports his problem as being a lack of peer relationships, and he hopes that case management will be able to provide this for him.

The most important point to remember about these youths is that although their disabilities do present problems in their lives, they also possess many strengths. Building on these strengths often minimizes the scope of their problems in other areas. For example, facilitating the socially acceptable activities that Joe enjoys (strengths) often counteracts the boredom and alleviates the problem. Joe's dream of becoming a pilot led to his involvement in a model airplane club. His physical aggression was channeled into a martial arts class at the YMCA.

ASSUMPTIONS UNDERLYING THE STRENGTHS APPROACH

The strengths model is guided by four principles. These principles serve as a compass and as guideposts for the design and implementation of the model. The four principles that guide the family advocacy model are as follows:

1. An active role by the family caregivers is essential for enabling the child to live in a normal environment.
2. Society should accommodate the needs of families who care for children with emotional disabilities.
3. Caregivers themselves are the best informants regarding their own needs and the needs of their child.
4. Family caregivers have strengths.

Seven implications for practice that follow from these principles also are listed as follows. They should serve to guide the case management process as well.

1. The relationship between the caregiver and the service provider is the key to making the helping process work.
2. The family system is used to identify caregiver strengths, not problems.
3. The family caregivers determine what they need to provide care.
4. The emotional and physical needs of caregivers must be met.
5. Family caregivers should be provided as much information as they want about their child's disability.
6. Family caregivers are met where they want to be met, usually in normal community environments such as the home or school.
7. Family and community strengths are used to acquire normal resources to assist in providing care.

Assessment

If an active role by family caregivers is essential, then developing a relationship with the youth and caregiver is the first task of the case manager. However, the case management process is not as linear as this implies. The relationship, assessment, and objective-setting processes may all occur at the same time. A caregiver may be exhausted from providing care (the caregiving in this case is a strength), and expresses this need for help. The case manager recognizes the caregiving as a strength and assists the caregiver with obtaining relief from caregiving. The caregiver sees that the case manager can be helpful and their relationship develops. This much more fluid process with blurred boundaries between relationship building, assessment,and objective setting is the normal case management process.

Based on a mutually beneficial relationship, it is during the assessment process that the strengths of the caregiver and the youth are identified and used to establish and work toward goals. In the case of the youth, it is what the youth does well that is his or her strengths. It is what the youth says he or she needs to be successful in a family environment and school that becomes the focus of work between the youth and the case manager. One youth enjoyed drawing futuristic pictures of helicopters. His liking of science was identified as a strength and his stated desire to learn more about science became the basis for setting objectives.

In the case of the family caregivers, the assessment process used in the strengths model is based on the family system conceptual framework developed by Turnbull, Summers, and Brotherson (1984). This framework consists of four components: family resources, family interaction system, family life cycle, and family functions. The family can be thought of as a system whose primary job is to meet the needs of its members (Caplan, 1976; Leslie, 1979). The purpose or output of family interaction is to produce responses to fulfill the needs associated with family functions. The family functions component of the systems framework represents the different categories of needs the family is responsible for addressing. According to this systems framework, the seven functions that families fulfill are affection, education, domestic needs, health, economic, recreation, and socialization (Turnbull et al., 1984). An assessment tool built around these seven family functions is used by family advocates to identify the youth's and caregiver's strengths. The tool is nothing more than a depiction of the family system so that, as the caregiver and the case manager use the family system to identify strengths parts of the family system, areas of strengths will not be forgotten.

Since the assessment process recognizes that families are systems and, therefore, complex and multifaceted, it is easy to identify strengths in all families. A unique feature of this assessment is that *only* strengths are identified. Some assessment processes talk about identifying strengths and then go on to focus on existing problems. This assessment process uses the caregivers' strengths to assist them to acquire what they need to provide care to the youth experiencing difficulties. This assessment process does not identify and address problems in the family system. The families' needs are those things they say they need to provide care for the youth in the family setting. It is this list of strengths and caregiver-identified needs that sets the stage for mutual objective setting. For example, a case manager identified a long list of strengths with a caregiver. Among these strengths were her ability to learn quickly and be persistent in her efforts. The caregiver identified a need to learn a behavior management method to care for her son. Based on her strengths, the case manager located a school psychologist who was particularly good at designing and modifying behavior management systems. The mother quickly learned the system and easily understood how to make changes as required by her son's behavior.

Two additional uses of the strengths are: 1) using the inventory of strengths to recognize what the caregiver has accomplished and thereby build the caregiver's confidence and self-esteem, and 2) representing or interpreting families to other service providers. Normally, service providers are caught up with problems and rarely focus on the strengths of the caregiver or the youth (Saleebey, 1992). When providers come to know the strengths of the caregiver and youth, they can begin to use these strengths to assist the youth to live a more normal life. These last two uses are illustrated in the following case example:

> Ronnie's mom was discouraged because she had to call the police to help during her son's violent episodes. Her confidence was boosted when the case manager reminded her that the time between episodes had increased significantly, thanks to the family's behavior management plan. The case manager also reminded Ronnie's teacher that his grades and attendance had improved.

Families caring for youth with severe emotional disturbances are used to having their problems and deficits pointed out. A major difference in the family advocacy model is that an even greater emphasis is placed upon finding and using the family's strengths, especially during the assessment process.

Planning

Planning is the process by which youths, their caregivers, and the family advocate decide which objectives to work on. All objectives must meet the following standards:

- Stated in positive terms
- Family and/or youth oriented
- Realistic and achievable
- Measurable and observable
- Focused on resource acquisition (not behavior or psychological changes)

It is typical for professionals working with youths with emotional disabilities to want to help by attempting to change behavior. But objectives, such as "May will stop arguing with the math teacher" or "Jose will stop fighting with his brother," will only make the youth defensive and further erode self-esteem. Instead, resource acquisition objectives, such as "May will get a tutor to help with her math" and "Jose will enroll in boxing lessons at the YMCA," are much more likely to stop the problem behaviors and have more positive long-range effects. It is important to note that resource acquisition objectives such as these are only formulated *after* learning *from* the youths what it is they want as well as identifying their strengths and using these strengths to establish resource acquisition objectives.

The following are examples of objectives that were set and achieved with adolescents who have received family advocacy services. These objectives clearly illustrate the practical and focused nature of the planning process. Each of these was developed by the youth, based on a strength of the youth, and is resource acquisition focused.

- Write a plan to purchase a coat.
- Ask school advisor about more mainstreaming hours.
- Ride the bus alone for one stop.
- Find five possible part-time jobs in the classified ads.

Setting objectives with caregivers is a similar process. Caregivers frequently have conflicting information about the child's situation from different professionals and express a need for "knowing" what is really wrong. The case manager can frequently assist the caregiver to acquire this information and, thereby, strengthen the caregiver–case manager relationship.

Setting objectives by building on strengths of caregivers is illustrated by the mother who was a nurse and needed to obtain a variety of services for her son. In discussion with the case manager about who needed to accomplish which tasks to obtain the services, the mother commented that many of these were things she did when she was a practicing nurse. She had given up working as a nurse to provide care to her son and no longer considered herself as a competent professional. The case manager recognized the mother's competence as a nurse and suggested that she approach service providers in the same way she did as a nurse, only this time it was to obtain the needed care for her son rather than for a patient. The objectives written for the plan of care were easily written as the mother recalled her work as a nurse. It was not long before the mother was writing plans of care prior to the case manager arriving for their appointment and they were simply discussing the plan as written.

Beth, a ninth grader, has been in the hospital for 1.5 years for depression and suicide risk. Beth's mother listed the following when asked to comment about the benefits of case management for her family. The practical nature of this list is a good example of the results of the planning process:

- The family advocate tried to get everybody together.
- The family advocate was somebody I could call and talk to if I had a problem.
- The family advocate provided alternative ways to handle problems.

Another unique feature of this model of case management is the mutual determination of the tasks needed to obtain the agreed-upon objective—who will accomplish which task and by what date. The case manager does not assume that the caregiver cannot identify and accomplish the necessary tasks, nor does the case manager assume that the caregiver can do it all. This is mutually determined so that the plan of care includes a list of objectives and tasks, notations on who will complete the tasks, and the dates by which the tasks will be completed. This plan of care becomes the basic document that structures the work between the caregiver and the case manager.

Advocacy

Workers often need to be advocates on behalf of their clients. Advocacy, in the form of informal interpersonal negotiation, may serve to remove barriers that prevent a client from receiving entitlements or other needed services. At times, simply making service providers aware of the barriers that prevent the client from utilizing services may lead to an improvement of the situation. However, stronger measures may need to be taken by the family advocate, including enlisting the support of supervisory or administrative-level staff within their own agency or making use of more formal channels, such as the State Protection and Advocacy Office, which may provide a professional advocate to attend school or treatment team meetings on the family's behalf (Intagliata, 1982).

In keeping with their roles as advocates, when asked to identify benefits of case management for their clients, family advocates stated that one of the benefits was that case management was able to be involved with the family even when the family was not receiving other services. Also, the case manager was somebody that they (clients) both could identify as a link. That is, there was somebody who would be involved with and make contacts for the child and his or her family.

When asked to talk about the benefits of case management, Edward, an adolescent client, also referred to the advocacy function.

Yeah, she's helped me. Especially when I got out, she's been working with me on community things. Like now, we're working on the bus schedule system and before we were working on a job again, working on my track, activities, and stuff like that. So she really is a big help. . . . She talks to my parents and stuff like that. So everybody knows about it. (Ronnau, 1989a, p. 436)

As the family advocate works with the family in caring for a child with emotional disabilities, it is inevitable that gaps in the service system will be identified. The advocate may discover that the community is lacking some of the basic services that the family needs, such as support groups and respite care. In such a case, the family advocate should document the need for the missing services and inform other key persons in he community of these service gaps (Intagliata, 1982).

Evaluation

The primary client outcomes tracked in the strengths model and, therefore, the primary measures of success are the child's living arrangements and educational status. Since objectives are the building blocks to achieve these ends, the number of objectives set and achieved are also used as evaluation measures. In the mutual process that occurs between the supervisor and the family advocate, expectations for the number of objectives to be set and achieved are determined. The expectation could be, for example, one objective per week for the adolescent and two for the parents, depending on their needs and abilities.

Since one of the standards an objective must meet is to be measurable, evaluation largely consists of determining whether the objective was actually achieved. Determining success is a mutual process between the youth and the caregiver. When an objective is achieved, it is cause for celebration; when it is not, no one is to blame. The focus is always on what has been learned, not on blaming the youth or caregivers for failing. The following example shows how objectives can be changed to meet the person's needs:

Thirteen-year-old Jose was continually getting into fights at school. The family advocate went to great lengths to help him meet the objective of joining the Golden Gloves group at the YMCA, but Jose did not show up for the boxing lessons. He confided in the family advocate that he really didn't like to fight but felt compelled to do so since other boys were "looking at him" in a sexual way. Jose went on to divulge the sexual abuse he had experienced as a young boy. Clearly, the focus on fighting was inappropriate but this could not be known until Jose disclosed his previous abuse. Consequently new objectives related to Jose learning about his experiences and his sexuality were needed and were set to obtain the help that Jose needed.

ASSUMPTIONS REGARDING CLIENTS AND THEIR ROLES

A basic tenet of the strengths model is that it is not beneficial to blame families. The heart of the family advocacy process is the relationship that is developed among the family advocate, the youth, and the family caregiver. Mutual trust and respect are among the characteristics that must be present in the relationship if the goal of keeping the youth in the community is to be attained. The worker's attitude toward the caregivers and the youth is especially important to the establishment of this relationship. This is not a hierarchical "worker as expert" model. The strengths model simply will not work unless the family advocate sincerely believes that youths and their caregivers can be full partners in the helping process, with the potential to learn and change. The following example illustrates how family advocates use the strengths of family caregivers to encourage and involve them in the process:

> Eileen was feeling discouraged because she could not afford to move from low-rent housing and she knew that she was not providing a safe environment for her family. She also felt guilty for her own past drug usage and its effect on the family. She called herself a "terrible mother." The worker endeavored to be specific in her praise of Eileen such as her completing her college junior year and her mitigation of some difficulties by constructively changing some parenting approaches. (Ronnau & Page, 1991, p. 12)

ROLES OF THE FAMILY ADVOCATE

The major role of the family advocate in the strengths model involves assessment, teaching, brokering, and advocacy. Because being a family advocate is challenging and complex, it is assumed that service providers will be trained professionals in the field of social work or another closely related field.

The service provider's primary attention, especially in the early stages of the helping process, is paid to identifying the family's strengths and needs. Using the strengths approach does not mean that a client's problems are denied. For example, some youngsters with emotional disabilities may need long-term therapy or even medication to help manage their disability. The distinguishing characteristics of the strengths approach is that the strengths of the family and the youth are even more zealously assessed than their weaknesses and they become the means for solving the family's problems.

As a teacher, the family advocate educates agency personnel, mental health and medical professionals, and other service providers in the community about accommodating families who have children with emotional disabilities. In addition, the family advocate helps the youth learn independent living skills and helps family members meet their caregiving needs. Examples of the independent living skills that case managers have helped adolescents learn include:

• Riding the bus
• Making change
• Selecting clothes for purchase
• Using the library
• Filling out a job application
• Doing the laundry
• Interacting with strangers
• Saying what they want from others

Family members have been helped to:

• Obtain respite care
• Join a support group of other parents who have children with emotional disabilities
• Get back into their bowling league for relaxation
• Talk to teachers about how their child is treated at school

The family advocates are trained and reminded to always gear their teaching toward empowering the clients to do for themselves. Supervisors continuously ask family advocates, "Will the clients be able to do this for themselves when you are gone?"

As a broker of services, family advocates play an important role in helping the family to find and use the resources they need. When services in a community are fragmented and categorized, parents become frustrated, discouraged, and fatigued. When family members burn out, the child will most likely be put back in the hospital. The worker's role as a broker can greatly supplement the family's efforts.

Workers using the strengths approach are reminded not to focus on using formal community resources. An adolescent with emotional disabilities may need outpatient therapy at the community mental health center, may need medical or dental care, or may need to reenter the hospital for a short time. These services are important. In the long run, however, it is the informal resources that will sustain us—friends, neighbors, grandparents, aunts, uncles, cousins, retired teachers, coaches, and church volunteers, to name a few. These informal resources can be enlisted to provide specialized supervision after school until a parent returns from work, to teach youths to play a sport, to work on cars, to learn about cosmetology,

or to join a summer recreation league. These are examples of resources actually acquired by family advocates using the strengths
approach.

The role of advocate is implemented as family members are
helped to articulate their needs and as community members are per-
suaded to make accommodations. As advocates, service providers
help to build bridges where there were once barriers keeping youths
and their families from getting the help they need.

REFERENCES

American Psychiatric Association. (1987). *Diagnostic and Statistical Manual of Mental Disorders (third edition–revised)*. Washington, DC: Author.
Caplan, G. (1976). The family as a support system. In G. Caplan & M. Killi-lea (Eds.), *Support systems and mutual help: Multidisciplinary explorations* (pp. 19–36). New York: Grune & Stratton.
Hobbs, N. (1975). *The futures of children*. San Francisco: Jossey-Bass.
Intagliata, J. (1982). Improving the quality of care for the chronically men-tally disabled. The role of case management. *Schizophrenia Bulletin, 8*(4), 655–674.
Leslie, G.R. (1979). The nature of the family. In G.R. Leslie (Ed.), *The family in social context* (4th ed., pp. 3–23). New York: Oxford University Press.
Lourie, I.S., & Katz-Leavy, J. (1987). *Severely emotionally disturbed children and adolescents* (Report). Washington, DC: National Institute of Mental Health.
Moroney, R. (1981). Public social policy: Impact on families with handi-capped children. In J. Paul (Ed.), *Understanding and working with parents of children with special needs* (pp. 97–120). New York: Holt, Rinehart & Winston.
Ronnau, J. (1989a). *An exploratory multiple-case study of what adolescents with emotional disabilities need to live in the community*. Unpublished doctoral dis-sertation, University of Kansas, Lawrence.
Ronnau, J. (1989b). *Training manual for family advocacy in-home services*. Law-rence: University of Kansas, School of Social Welfare.
Ronnau, J., & Page, M. (1991). *Training manual for family advocacy services*. University of Kansas, School of Social Welfare, Lawrence. (This project was partially supported by the Research and Training Center on Family Support and Children's Mental Health, NIDRR Grant #122B9007-90, Port-land State University.)
Saleebey, O. (1992). *The strengths perspective in social work practice*. New York: Longman.
Thompson, E.H., & Doll, W. (1982). The burden of families coping with the mentally ill: An invisible crisis. *Family Relations, 31*(3), 379–388.
Turnbull, A.P., Summers, J.A., & Brotherson, M.J. (1984). *Working with fam-ilies with disabled members: A family systems approach*. Lawrence: University of Kansas, Research and Training Center on Independent Living.
Willis, M.J. (1982). The impact of schizophrenia on families: One mother's point of view. *Schizophrenia Bulletin, 8*(4), 617–619.

Therapeutic Case Management
Vermont's System of Individualized Care

Suzanne Santarcangelo, Nancy Birkett,
and Nancy McGrath

Therapeutic case management, wraparound, and *individualized* services
are all terms in Vermont's system of care, which combines a philosophy of delivering children's mental health services with specific clinical skills and interagency policies and procedures. Individualized
wraparound approaches involve a total commitment to the child and
his or her family (Burchard & Clarke, 1990). The underlying elements include unconditional care, flexibility, creativity, child- and
family-centered services delivery, strengths-based assessment, and
interagency collaboration. These elements are at the heart of the
therapeutic case management model.

Therapeutic case managers must be able to combine the skills
associated with child, family, and environmental assessment; treatment team development and facilitation; service development; therapeutic intervention; progress evaluation; child- and family-centered
care; and advocacy. This combination of skills must be provided
within the context of outreach service delivery.

This chapter attempts to illustrate the interface between philosophy and skills as it is embodied in Vermont's model of therapeutic
case management. An overview of the target population, community connections, and treatment teams is presented. The chapter addresses assessment, developing a treatment plan, developing individualized programs and resources, establishing a trusting and
helping relationship, and developing transition plans. It also discusses proactive planning for crisis. Finally, there is a section on

---

All quotes from parents, grandparents, or adolescents in this chapter were obtained through interviews, group discussions, and panel discussions conducted by
the authors as part of their research.

service delivery, monitoring, and coordination, and a general discussion of Vermont's model follows.

It is important to note that the processes described in this chapter are not always linear in sequence. In order to be responsive to the unique and changing needs of a child or his or her family, the therapeutic case manager and treatment team must constantly assess, reevaluate, and adjust treatment interventions and service delivery, based on the input of the child and his or her family. The process is best considered circular and fluid, as opposed to linear and rigid.

SYSTEMS OVERVIEW

Target Population

Vermont's system of care has emphasized family preservation and the integration of children and adolescents into their communities whenever possible. This includes the reintegration of children and adolescents into their home communities from intensive residential facilities both in and out of Vermont. This emphasis on community reintegration was the catalyst for the development of the therapeutic case management program. Because of the diverse family circumstances of the individuals who are served, the term *family member* refers to individuals in biological, adoptive, or foster families. Family members are recognized as the experts in knowing their child.

It was widely recognized that children should not have to be removed from their families, prompted by a lack of comprehensive services in the community, in order to get effective mental health treatment. Heightened awareness of this problem led the state of Vermont to seek an alternative system to sending children out of state, as well as create an avenue to bring children home from such placements. Therapeutic case management was that alternative. Due to limited staff and financial resources, specific target groups were prioritized as a strategy for the development of therapeutic case management.

The first priority group included children and adolescents referred to, currently placed in, or at risk of placement in intensive residential programs both in and out of state. The second priority includes children and adolescents who are at risk of being placed outside their natural or foster home, or out of district. The third priority includes children and adolescents who are referred to local interagency teams to resolve problems. The fourth priority includes all other children and adolescents with a severe emotional disturbance requiring multiple services.

Vermont's focus remains with the first priority group at this time. Once increased funding for therapeutic case management positions can be obtained and interdepartmental policies can be streamlined, it is anticipated that phase-in of other priority groups will proceed.

WHERE TO START

Community Connections

The role of the therapeutic case manager in Vermont is to create an interagency treatment team and develop individualized treatment services that are responsive to the unique strengths, needs, and potentials of the child, his or her family, and the community.

Due to behavioral problems and multiple placement changes, many of these children and adolescents have become disenfranchised from their homes, schools, families, and communities. In order to reconnect children with their families and communities, the therapeutic case manager uses natural supports in the community and/or services provided by existing agencies. Natural supports that have been accessed in Vermont include local YMCAs, libraries, the United Way, and employment programs, as well as family, friends, neighbors, and church groups. In one instance, a local church donated space to the community mental health center to conduct a cooking course for adolescents preparing for independent living. In a spontaneous gesture of appreciation, this group of adolescents offered to reconstruct the church gardens. Thus, volunteer work can easily serve as another strategy for community integration. These community experiences can be used to provide youth with a sense of belonging, productivity, and self-worth. For example, one adolescent who graduated from the program stated, "The [treatment] team was very supportive, they helped me develop a network that still supports me, I'm trying to give back what I can."

Organized services may include counseling, school-based services, family education programs, parent support groups, and specialized treatment, such as substance abuse and sex offender programs. The therapeutic case managers must work closely with school staff to ensure that educational programs complement and coordinate with other community-based interventions. Often, this may require weekly meetings that gradually diminish in frequency (e.g., monthly) once all services, roles, responsibilities, and treatment strategies have been clearly defined. Therapeutic case managers are team leaders, accountable for coordinating and ensuring appropriate and timely services for the child/adolescent and his or her family. To achieve this, the child and his or her family are included in every aspect of treatment planning, service implementation, and assessment of program effectiveness. That is, the model relies most heavily on a team-based approach.

Treatment Teams

> No one ever looked at who I am, found out what my needs are, and asked me what I want, I'm involved in decisions on an equal basis. (adolescent)

> It's a good feeling. . . . It is cooperation. We work as a team. The team respects our feelings and actions. (grandparent)

> The team provides me with the information I need to make daily decisions. (foster parent)

Because the therapeutic case manager acts as one member of an interdisciplinary team, decision making is determined by treatment team consensus. The membership of a child's treatment team is highly unique to that child and his or her family. In all cases, the team includes a representative from each agency with which the child is involved (e.g., child welfare, education, mental health, vocational rehabilitation, probation and parole). Additional members may be invited by the child, his or her family, or the therapeutic case manager. They may include relatives, past or present caregivers, neighbors, or other members of the community (e.g., clergy, police officers, judges, doctors). The treatment team process is not without challenges.

> Initial team meetings can be intimidating especially when all the attention is focused on you and your child's deficits. (parent)

> Because my daughter is on her own, and I have other children at home it's hard to balance the amount of time I give this . . ., court hearings, family and team meetings . . . and still take care of my life and other child. (parent)

Because of the comprehensive focus of treatment and the reliance of treatment on existing community resources, it is essential that the therapeutic case manager develop and maintain effective interagency and caregiver relationships. This is necessary to provide the child with the best possible opportunities for successful community living. In practice, this involves scheduling team meetings; updating members on significant life events occurring between scheduled meetings; and being available to brainstorm and discuss day-to-day events and interventions with the child, family, or school.

Depending on the child's and family's needs and the composition of the treatment team, the case manager's role in monitoring progress and service delivery, in facilitating communication among team members, and in advocating on behalf of the child may vary in proportion and intensity. Roles and responsibilities are defined by the team based on each member's strengths, interests, and role in the overall child care system. For example, in a situation in which a child or adolescent is involved in the court system and their guardian *ad litem* or parole officer is a member of the treatment, the team may delegate all judicial functions to that member. In a situation in which there is no guardian *ad litem*, the team may petition the court to appoint one or decide that the therapeutic case manager take on that role.

It has been the authors' experience that developing strong interagency relationships on a treatment team may be cumbersome at first (e.g., scheduling meetings, defining roles). However, it ultimately serves to streamline the process of service delivery and strengthen the community commitment to that child or adolescent. Many members are relieved to view themselves as partners with the child, his or her family, and other service providers, rather than the sole authority or person responsible for "doing it all." Investing time in the development of the team pays off during subsequent months and years of service delivery.

The development of an effective treatment team relies on knowing the child, his or her family, and community resources. This can be accomplished through a comprehensive assessment process and through building trusting relationships with the child and his or her family. This chapter illustrates how this unfolds in the therapeutic case management process.

Assessment

Therapeutic case management in the community requires a comprehensive view of the child and his or her family's strengths, needs, and potentials. In order to accomplish this specific task, it is necessary to include assessment, relationship building, treatment planning, and individualization. Examples of each of these undertakings are provided in the following paragraphs.

Assessments may be both formal and informal. Assessments help to establish child- and family-centered goals, which then serve as the foundation for service planning. Comprehensive assessments provide information for development of comprehensive service goals, and involve multiple tasks. The first is to determine the child and his or her family's current strengths and needs. This often includes informal discussions with the child, his or her family, and other caregivers or professionals in the child's life. Questions focus on who the child is, where he or she has been, and what his or her dreams are for the future (O'Brien & Forest, 1989). It is important to note that this information gathering includes hearing, seeing, and feeling the tone of voice, gestures, and thoughts expressed by each individual. Often, this requires attention to small details, such as off-hand comments, exaggerated statements, and sense of humor.

It has been the authors' experience that clinic-based assessments can be intimidating. Thus, a more informal exploratory, story-eliciting approach is preferred by many case managers. Successful settings may include home visits, relaxed play activities, and car rides. During such discussions, the case manager learns the family's value system, strengths, and potentials. Such an approach also allows time for the therapeutic case manager, child, and family to engage in and begin to establish a therapeutic relationship.

No standardized assessment tool exists in the therapeutic case management system. Therapeutic case managers are advised to talk with the key players in the child's life. This includes the people with whom the child spends most of his or her time (e.g., siblings, teachers, parents, coaches, tutors, babysitters) and the people who will be spending most of the time with the child (e.g., new classroom teachers, job coaches). This may involve as many as 10 interviews, 20 minutes to 1 hour in length. These interviews serve as an introduction for the therapeutic case managers and allow them to begin to assess the child's and community's strengths and needs. These assessment interviews are held in the first 2 weeks of receiving the client referral.

The second level of assessment involves a close look at the community. This includes social and cultural environments and community resources, both formal and informal. Community strengths (number and types of resources) are also examined.

The therapeutic case manager must assure that all formal assessments (e.g., medical, psychiatric, psychosexual, neurological, psychological) have been performed. The treatment team's decision to pursue more formal and/or standardized assessments is based on the adequacy of information in the child's records, as well as the child's specific diagnosis or medical condition. The task at this point is to schedule a treatment team meeting. Future discussions then turn to what the child and his or her family need to realize their potentials.

PUTTING THE PIECES TOGETHER

Developing a Treatment Plan

Once assessment information has been collected and relationships and treatment team membership have been established, the therapeutic case manager then facilitates a team discussion of the specific services and supports that will be put in place to help the child succeed in the family setting and in the community.

The information gathered through the assessment process is translated into service needs during this discussion. For example, children with peer relationship problems living in geographically isolated areas may require peer tutors at school, out-of-home respite options geared toward participation in group activities or in school sports, and transportation; older adolescents with limited independent living skills may require a shared living situation with a mentor (e.g., an adult who can serve as a job coach and as a daily living skills teacher).

Professional service providers must also be appropriately "matched" to the child. In one example, it was determined that an intensive dental treatment was too intrusive for a severely traumatized child. The therapeutic case manager elicited support from the treatment team to pursue a second opinion. A second service provider was located whose techniques were less intrusive and traumatic. In another example, an adolescent was characterized by professional service providers as being resistant to therapy (i.e., never showing up). During the assessment interview, it was also learned that he was often abused in a small "office-like" room. On a separate visit with the therapeutic case manager, the boy confirmed a fear of small rooms. A therapist was located who did outreach work, therapy was resumed, and "sessions" were held during walks in the park.

Similarly, paraprofessional support is matched to the child's individual needs. Some staff work specifically with family members on reunification, while others provide back-up or 24-hour coverage to children or adolescents who are experiencing a crisis. In all cases, respite services are provided. Respite options are created for both the child and primary caregiver, ranging from peer support to trained respite workers in the child's home to out-of-home respite families or placements.

Once established, the treatment plan is reviewed and revised on an ongoing basis, approximately every 3 months, through regularly scheduled team meetings. This allows for the evolution of an individualized plan based on the unique and changing needs of each child and his or her family. One parent states, "People listen to me and my son . . . they are always creative and flexible in coming up with new strategies to help him."

Developing Individualized Programs and Resources

Individualized programs start with the therapeutic case manager and treatment team brainstorming interventions and creating strategies to meet the needs of the child and his or her family. This may include enhancing therapeutic opportunities through the flexible use of existing funding resources or personnel from relevant agencies (e.g., having a traditionally school-based aide start the day at a child's home and establish a "morning routine" for the child and his or her family prior to arriving at school). In situations in which a specific service does not exist, the therapeutic case manager and treatment team develop the service. One professional housemate comments, "It's important to individualize and try new things because every one is different, there are no recipes."

Individualization may be accomplished by expanding existing programs as well as creating new ones. Examples include training a family member or friend to provide respite services, training peers to provide crisis support, and using martial arts training to enhance self-esteem, feelings of safety, and self-control. This type of individualization is accomplished through the use of flexible, creative funding strategies. Flexible funding is a necessary and integral part of providing wraparound services in the community. One strategy employed in Vermont was the establishment of "Flex Funds." Up to $1,500 per child is available to therapeutic case managers to use for the individual needs of each child. There are three criteria for accessing these funds. First, the child or adolescent must be receiving therapeutic case management services. Second, the request must be for creative, nontraditional activities that would enhance therapeutic efforts. Third, there must be no other way to financially support the activity. Some examples include: funding to have a tattoo removed, allowing the adolescent to put past experiences to rest; reimbursement to a potential employer to support salaries for youth during a trial period of work; funding to divide one bedroom into two in order to create private space for siblings; health club memberships; weekend retreats for older adolescents; and so on.

A small amount of flexible funding has helped therapeutic case managers gain the trust of the children they serve (e.g., by listening and acting on their individual requests), empower the families they work with (e.g., by helping relieve day-to-day stresses), and develop partnerships with local community members (e.g., by supporting vocational experiences in local businesses for children and adolescents). These funding mechanisms, in conjunction with other interagency policies, have given therapeutic case managers an avenue to creatively respond to the unique and changing needs of each child, family, and community.

Establishing a Trusting and Helping Relationship

In order to maintain team cohesiveness, the therapeutic case manager must maintain ongoing regular contact with the child, his or her family, and significant others in a supportive and helpful manner.

> We knew that no matter what happened, all we had to do was yell "help." (grandparent)

> The therapeutic case manager allows me time to vent. They are sometimes the mediator between me and my housemate . . . this support is crucial. (professional housemate)

> When you do something wrong it's remembered longer than when you do something right, they are helping me deal [with my reputation] and be part of the community. (adolescent)

This trusting relationship is perhaps the most essential element in defining the service as "therapeutic." The flexible and intensive hours committed to each situation allow the process of discovery to unfold between case manager and family, avoiding the artificial restrictions of a 50-minute hour or monthly meeting. Two- to three-hour home visits are not unusual. One parent confesses: "This is the first time [since my daughter was in the state's custody] that someone could devote time to us and her . . . [it is also] the first time someone has attempted to help her gain skills, not just contain and house her."

Just as the therapeutic case manager must recognize the strengths and needs of each child and his or her family, therapeutic case managers must learn the strengths and limitations of every player in order to maximize the benefits of their strengths. For example, a child placed in a mainstreamed school was assigned to a first-year teacher. The first-year teacher had high expectations for the students as well as for his own performance. Being faced with a mainstreamed student who was labeled "seriously emotionally disturbed" heightened the teacher's anxieties about his own ability to teach. This was uncovered in the assessment interview process. The treatment team, which included the teacher, decided to maximize the student's opportunity to succeed by having the therapeutic case manager visit and observe the classroom and meet separately with the teacher on a weekly basis. It was important for the therapeutic case manager to understand the teacher's own expectations and challenges in the context of a child with intense special needs and to respond to them supportively.

Developing Transition Plans

At different points in life, every child will experience transitions. Transitions occur among services (e.g., moving to a new school or new community) as the individual moves into adulthood and/or toward independent living. The therapeutic case manager will ensure the development of a service plan that will be needed and that will provide for the continuation of existing services. For example, one grandparent comments: "We plan to move [out of state]. This means another transition, but the team is right on top of it, already exploring what is available out there, so that it can be set up and ready to go once the move is a reality."

Academic transitions can be particularly stressful when children are faced with new teachers, schools, and peer groups. The therapeutic case manager and treatment team take proactive steps to ease this transition. For example, the creation of a portfolio was employed in one situation. A representative sample of academic achievements, as well as personal and artistic interests, was developed with input from the child to be included in the transcripts sent to the new school. Packets may also include letters of introduction from current teachers. These letters communicate learning styles, academic and social strengths, challenges for the student, and recommendations for classroom accommodations (e.g., peer tutors and support within the school).

EXPECT THE BEST, PREPARE FOR THE WORST

Practice Planning for Crisis

A major factor in the success of individualized services is proactive planning to prevent and respond to crises. Children and adolescents who are reintegrated or diverted from residential placements do not miraculously leave their challenges behind, nor are they suddenly bestowed with a new repertoire of positive coping skills. Crises and setbacks are expected. Therapeutic case management services attempt to "decatastrophize" crises and to use the situation as a positive opportunity to teach the child, adolescent, or family new coping skills. Although crises present challenges, they also present rich opportunities for change and the learning of new skills. In situations in which safety may be a concern, concrete plans of action are developed by the treatment team in order to provide an effective crisis response. Crisis or safety plans may focus on feelings of emotional security (having someone to check in with at various times of the day) and physical safety (having prearranged a "crisis" bed to go to). Such plans help to instill confidence in both service providers and service recipients.

The foundation of proactive crisis planning involves an understanding of what defines a crisis for the child, his or her family, and other service providers. For example, a crisis for a child or family may not be a crisis at school, or vice versa. To gather the information needed for proactive planning, it is helpful to ask each person, "What's the worst thing that could happen, at home, to your classroom, in the community, at work, and so on?" (Tannen, 1991).

A primary task of the treatment team is to prevent and/or diffuse crises. However, this task is undertaken with the awareness that some crises and setbacks are inevitable. With successful proactive planning, these crisis situations can be used for learning new skills and breaking old patterns (Wells, 1991). Hence, crisis plans are crucial to individualized services.

Crisis plans often reflect several levels of intervention. First, in the case of a violent child, the crisis plan may call for a prearranged cueing system (e.g., cards, hand signals) that allow the child to communicate increased anger, frustration, anxiety, or aggression. The child is taught to cue an identified crisis person (selected with the child's input) whenever he or she feels a threshold loss of control. This person is then available to help the child process the situation, which may involve leaving the area.

If the situation escalates beyond the control of one individual, the next level may involve accessing more staff support. In the school, this may mean the principal, janitor, or another teacher. In the community, the crisis plan may involve the case manager, crisis outreach workers, the police, or other designated support personnel. Again, support persons must be prearranged and selected with child input (Hamilton, 1991).

The third level may involve a predetermined amount of time in a safe environment. This could range from an emergency respite home to a staff secure environment or juvenile detention facility.

The individual elements of a crisis plan are always tailored to each child's situation and needs. The goal of these plans is to provide consistency, security, and support to the child and his or her family. The underlying assumption of this planning is that services should be unconditional as well as individualized.

> The therapeutic case manager helped put [my daughter's] crisis into perspective for me. (parent)

> It put tools at hand [to help us deal with our granddaughter]. (grandparent)

> I feel like I have the information I need to deal with it. (foster parent)

> Knowing I have respite available helps me through the difficult times. (foster parent)

KEEPING THE PIECES IN PLACE

Once a treatment plan has been developed, service providers have been recruited, and the roles and responsibilities of team members have been defined, the tasks of the therapeutic case manager move toward coordination, monitoring of progress, day-to-day advocacy, and maintenance of communication. These functions are delineated in the following paragraphs.

Providing, Monitoring, and Coordinating Services

After all supports and resources are identified, the therapeutic case manager takes the lead in ensuring that all services are provided in a coordinated, well-integrated manner. This includes maintaining ongoing communication with all involved individuals.

In the initial stages, this may require daily phone calls or meetings to refine and implement individualized education programs (IEPs) and treatment plans. This communication is important in maintaining the flexibility and effectiveness of services. Over time, the frequency of formal meetings typically decreases to one per month. However, ongoing informal communication with all team members is maintained by the therapeutic case manager.

> As a parent I always felt part of the team . . . they shared information. (parent)

Our case manager is constantly in touch with the school. She comes to the house once a week to do things with my granddaughter. (grandparent)

They're honest, up-front, that's important to me. (adolescent)

Advocating

Advocacy may happen in a variety of forums. Within the legal system, the therapeutic case manager may provide expert testimony on the efficacy of community-based services for youth. With other agencies, the therapeutic case managers ensure that information is up-to-date and accurate and that treatment decisions are driven by team consensus. Advocacy also happens with other professionals in the community (e.g., doctors, dentists). The goals of these advocacy efforts are specific to each situation. In some circumstances, therapeutic case managers intervene on behalf of the child or family when services are not being delivered in a timely, efficient, or assessable manner; while in others, they may help the family to gain access to additional information or interpret highly specialized or complex material (e.g., legal, medical).

Education and Public Awareness

The therapeutic case manager, in conjunction with the individual treatment teams, local interagency teams, and advocacy organizations, provides ongoing education to parents, the professional community, and the general public. This general education relates to the community integration of children with severe emotional disturbances. Strategies to promote public awareness include attending school board meetings, providing teacher in-service training, participating in advisory boards, and presenting programs to service and civic groups.

CONCLUSION

The Vermont model of therapeutic case management closely parallels other models of case management that are emerging nationally for children and adolescents experiencing a severe emotional disturbance and their families. However, there are several elements that are distinct (Family Impact Seminar, 1992). For example, therapeutic case managers assume a more proactive role than is described in available literature. All individualized plans include the provision of respite services for both the child and caregiver. In addition, proactive plans to prevent and plan for crises are also required.

Also, three functions have been added to Vermont's model that are not clearly delineated in others (Family Impact Seminar, 1992). First, interventions and creative strategies to overcome policy and obstacles and individualized services where none were previously available through existing resources have been developed. Second, ongoing education and public awareness efforts for parents, professionals, and the general public related to community-based services for children and adolescents experiencing severe emotional disturbances are being promoted. Third, the child is being involved in every aspect of service delivery.

The third distinction relates to the target population phase-in plan and caseload considerations (Family Impact Seminar, 1992). Specifically, it is acknowledged that therapeutic case management services should be available to all children and adolescents who have multiple service needs. However, limited resources make it necessary to target priority groups as a strategy for implementation. As a result, the development of therapeutic case management services in Vermont is occurring over several phases. Caseload considerations have also led to a clear limitation on the number of children that a therapeutic case manager can serve at any given time. Current experience in Vermont suggests that effective therapeutic case management requires a minimum of 7–10 hours per week per client. The volume of therapeutic case management time depends on the intensity of the child's and family's needs and the availability of resources. The average number of clients for a therapeutic case manager is 4 in the initial stages of community integration, with a maximum of 12 clients at any given time. After 3 years of operation in Vermont, no therapeutic case manager has had more than seven children and adolescents as clients at any one time. Although these distinctions give uniqueness to Vermont's model, they do not preclude its generalization to other states' or children's service systems.

We have begun to break out of a pattern of treatment that alienates children and adolescents from their families and home communities. Work remains to be done to streamline interagency financing procedures and to evaluate clinical outcomes for children and their families.

As we maximize and blend funds between the Departments of Social and Rehabilitation Services, Education, and Mental Health and Mental Retardation, continued dialogue with Vermont children, adolescents, families, and service providers will be essential. The development of a streamlined, responsive system capable of meeting each child's and family's unique needs and potentials will always be our goal. As one adolescent proclaims: "I'm treated like I'm somebody, that's really important to me. . . . They took a big risk putting me in this program and it means a lot to me, because I'm able to be a person, not a file, a big file!"

REFERENCES

Burchard, J. D., & Clarke, R. T. (1990). The role of individualized care in a service delivery system for children and adolescents with severely maladjusted behavior. *Journal of Mental Health Administration, 17*(1), 48–60.

Family Impact Seminar. (1992). *Family centered social policy: The emerging agenda.* Washington, DC: American Association for Marriage and Family Therapy, Research and Education Foundation.

Hamilton, R. W. (1991). *Self-control training and crisis management planning for children and youth with severe behaviors.* Unpublished report, Burlington: Center for Developmental Disabilities, University of Vermont.

O'Brien, J., & Forest, M. (1989). *Action for inclusion.* Toronto, Ontario, Canada: Frontier College Press.

Tannen, N. (1991, May). *Guidelines for implementing an individualized plan of care for children and adolescents experiencing a severe emotional disturbance and their families.* Unpublished report, Waterbury: Vermont Department of Mental Health and Mental Retardation.

Wells, P. (1991, July). *Understanding crisis: What it means for each child.* Workshop Presentation, Waterbury: Vermont Department of Mental Health and Mental Retardation.

CHAPTER 16

Transitional Case Management

Lisa K. Armstrong

Adolescence is a period of change in the physical, emotional, developmental, familial, environmental, cultural, educational, and vocational arenas of life. The transition from adolescence to adulthood requires the youth and his or her family to adjust to a multitude of changes surrounding progress toward independence. This transition occurs throughout the youth's life, beginning near birth and continuing beyond adolescence.

Such normal transitions are more difficult if the child has an emotional disturbance. Frequently, the youth's normal opportunities to learn independent living skills have been disrupted. It has not been unusual for systems serving youths to ignore these transitions. Youths often have been expected to move from living in a 24-hour-per-day, highly structured environment to independence without any advanced preparation. The youth's 18th birthday becomes a date that automatically signals this transition, regardless of his or her skills. The youth is expected to go from a service system that identifies the youth and requires him or her to receive services to one in which he or she must seek out services. Only recently have mental health service systems for youth recognized the need for attending to these transition needs. In an ideal system, attention to independent living skills would be part of formal service delivery from an early age.

This chapter is a description of a transitional case management program. This program is an example of the type of transitional services that need to exist for all youth. As a developing model it may be incomplete; however, it represents a state-of-the-art program that is constantly changing. This program description includes the discussion of issues involving the differences between adult and youth systems, family needs, community expectations, and youth's emo-

The author would like to thank Catherine and Robert Friedman for their assistance with this chapter.

317

tional needs. The program components and implementation issues necessary for a successful transition program for youth who are diagnosed with an emotional, behavioral, or mental disturbance are discussed.

DEFINITION OF TRANSITIONAL CASE MANAGEMENT

Transitional case management addresses the transitional needs of individuals 16–25 years of age who have an emotional, mental, or behavioral disturbance. Case managers must recognize the need to develop community living skills from an early age; however, current system inadequacies and resource constraints require the focus to be on older youth.

In this program, transitional case management is a continuum of intensive and holistic services provided to youths, their families, the community, and significant others in order for individuals to learn to live in the least restrictive environment (LRE) and to be reintegrated into the community from out-of-home placements. The community reentry process from out-of-home placements involves learning independent living skills and assisting youths and their families to maximize their individual strengths. When youths learn to recognize their symptoms and stressors, they have more control over their choices and behaviors. In addition, youths are educated about their symptomatology and stressors, which have historically resulted in hospitalizations, multiple rejections, and failures. Case managers creatively assist transitional youths to learn to make decisions and to take responsibility for their lives.

When developing transitional case management programs, it is important to focus on the youths' strengths and goals. The aim of this type of case management is to build on such strengths and to help youth live optimally in the community by securing a social and recreational life, a safe living environment, employment, good health, integrated self-concept and sexual identity, transportation, and a network of support. The program helps youths begin to take steps toward meeting their needs and making their dreams become realities. Many times, the transitional case management program is the initial step to help youths learn to laugh, play, believe in themselves, and recognize that they have the power to achieve their own personal goals, not only the goals designated by others. When needed, the transitional case management program assists youths and their families to communicate. Often, multiple placements have disrupted communication between youths and other family members. To assist in understanding the importance of transitional case management, one young man's life story is used as an example:

Allen is an 18-year-old Hispanic male who was referred to the transitional case management program at the age of 17. Allen was in a residential treatment program when the referral was made by a children's case manager. Allen had received outpatient, crisis stabilization, and residential treatment since the age of 5 for depression, temper tantrums lasting for 2–3 hours at a time, physical aggression toward females (i.e., punching them in the face), suicide attempts (i.e., overdosing on over-the-counter medications and cutting his wrists), paranoia, and rapid mood swings. Allen was placed in the foster care system at the age of 4 due to severe sexual molestation and physical abuse by his mother and her two boyfriends. Allen had 30 foster home placements, 2 state hospitalizations, and 2 residential treatment placements. Allen's last contact with his family was 4 years ago. Allen has two younger male siblings also placed in foster care.

SYSTEMS IMPACT ON YOUTH

It is important to recognize the different assumptions and available services associated with the child and adolescent system when compared with the adult system. Allen lived in the child welfare, education, and legal systems, where he was taught to be dependent on adult caregivers for shelter, food, health care, entertainment, education, socialization, problem solving, and decision making. Allen's life was planned by people who were bound by agency, education, and legal policies surrounding their missions to protect him from further abuse and harm, to educate him in school slots for adolescents who have disabilities, and to keep him in designated environments. Allen had had an average of four foster care workers per year due to the foster care system's high turnover rate. Therefore, there was no consistent guardian to make decisions about Allen's life.

Trust and reliability were not words or concepts that Allen learned from the adults who made the decisions in his life. When entering the adult systems and "society," Allen was a "system product" filled with painful memories of multiple placements, multiple rejections, multiple perceived failures, and the distinct feeling of being alone. Because adolescent placement funding stopped on the day that Allen turned 18 years old, he had to leave the residential psychiatric facility where he had lived for 2 years. The psychiatric residential service was designed for dependent adolescents, not young adults struggling for life control and independence.

As a young adult, Allen is expected to be independent (not dependent on adult caregivers), to be employable, to make decisions based on multiple choices, to know how to structure his day, and to know the mechanics involved in caring for himself in normal life domains (e.g., financial, physical, mental, emotional, vocational, medical, educational, and legal). The majority of youths with emotional disabilities who have been dependent on the system have difficulty adjusting to the multiple changes and expectations that occur when they reach 18 years of age. For those youths who did not have the benefit of early transitional services,the transitional case managers are the anchors that will help the youth adjust to and cope with making choices.

THE TRANSITIONAL CASE MANAGEMENT PROCESS

The transitional case management process involves the major components of choosing services, the transitional tour, family involvement, assessment and life planning, and defining expectations. The transitional process is individualized and can take some youths 4–5 years to complete. Transitional case managers need to have a consistent plan for services to be offered and tasks to be completed by the youths, but not a limited time frame for youth to either accept services or complete essential independent living tasks.

Choosing Services

Many of the youths who have been referred for transitional case management services have clinical or children's case managers from the mental health or child welfare system. Clinical case managers introduce the youth to the transitional case managers. The youth is given the choice of whether or not to participate in the transitional program. The option of participation is often the first opportunity the youth has had to decide which services he or she will accept. The referred youth must request transitional services after the initial visit with the transitional case manager, which includes the explanation of transitional services, residential options he or she will have as an adult, and behavioral indicators that are necessary for him or her to be discharged into the community from residential treatment programs, or admitted to community residential settings that are designated for adults. Transitional and clinical case managers begin to visit the youth and his or her family together after the youth has requested transitional services. This case management team assists the youth and his or her family to gradually become familiar with the people who will be working with them in the transition to adulthood and into the adult mental health system. In some instances, the transitional case manager has to join the clinical case manager on several visits before talking about the transitional program because of the youth's attachment to the clinical case manager and his or her fear of change.

In the experience of the program described in this chapter, transition tends to be more successful if transitional case managers work with the youth and his or her family at least 6 months prior to the youth's 18th birthday or prior to the move to an independent living residence. The youth who has not developed a relationship with the transitional case manager before his or her 18th birthday usually drops out of the transitional program within 2–3 months after reaching adulthood. In Allen's case, the children's case manager remained the only consistent person for Allen; he had not learned to trust others. The transfer from the children's case manager to the transitional case manager occurred over a period of 1 year.

Transitional Tour

All persons requesting transitional services receive a tour of their living, educational, vocational, recreational, medical, and psychiatric options. A transitional tour not only provides youths and their families with a concrete picture of adult placement choices, but also decreases the anxiety involved in making multiple changes. No one is placed in an unknown or unseen setting with strangers unless he or she becomes homeless and an emergency placement is needed.

The transitional tour gives the individual an opportunity to choose where he or she is going to live and attend school after his or her discharge into the community or upon his or her 18th birthday. The case manager visits the youth immediately before the tour and gathers information on the youth's perceptions, fears, goals for adulthood, and dreams. The tour focuses on the task of making decisions about placement, school, and family involvement.

To facilitate Allen's tour arrangements, the child welfare foster care system paid for a round-trip plane ticket from his residential placement to his home community. The residential facility provided a day pass for Allen to go with the clinical case manager and foster care worker to visit potential adult placements. A visit with his grandmother (at a local restaurant) was arranged per Allen's request. This linkage to his family before community discharge was motivating to Allen.

Family Involvement

Families are involved in the transitional program and the adult services orientation even if their children are in institutional settings. The families usually appreciate being involved. They are invaluable assets to the case managers as historians, system survivors, and committed partners through the transition process. Not all families acknowledge the youth's freedom to direct his or her life; the adolescent's goals are given priority in the transitional program even when he or she is in conflict with his or her family's goals. To assist family members in the transitional process, a monthly support group is offered.

Assessment and Life Planning

Assessments are comprehensive, holistic, and ongoing with the youth, his or her family, placement personnel, and community service providers. Neighbors, clergy, professionals, educators, and other significant persons are resources to help complete realistic, strengths-oriented assessments of the youth and his or her family. Transitional life planning is based on strengths and dreams, not problems or pathological histories contained in clinical records.

Successful transitions occur when case managers acquire information from all possible sources to understand and appreciate the adolescent's history, culture, family relationships, strengths, limitations, current level of functioning, coping "survival" skills, spirituality, and dreams. It is important to know the number of residential placements each youth has experienced because it may be an indication of the potential number of adult placements the youth will experience. For example, one youth moved every 8 weeks. In that youth's experiences, trusting an environment for more than 8 weeks had historically represented further rejections, insecurity, and abandonment. From this youth's perspective, it was better to reject people and situations and to be in control than to be emotionally controlled by others.

The assessment of the youth's relationships is an important factor in linking individuals to appropriate community resources, recreation, employment, and wraparound workers. To accomplish this, it is important to discover ways to form relationships, develop trust, and obtain accurate information from youths and their families. Trust is not an immediate need or expectation of the transitional case management staff. Honesty, patience, and a sense of humor are the components necessary to complete ongoing assessments and to build the bridges to trust and adulthood.

> In Allen's situation the case manager met with Allen monthly while he was in a psychiatric treatment facility. Allen's grandmother and mother were seen by the case manager on several occasions to gather information about Allen and his family from the family members' perspective. Once Allen came to the community the case manager met with Allen four to five times per week. Allen and the case manager ate lunch together, walked in Allen's neighborhood, and shopped for basic necessi-

ties. Through these activities the case manager assessed Allen's level of independent living skills, ability to communicate needs, and awareness of how to protect himself (i.e., locking doors, walking across streets, and not talking to strangers about personal information).

It was important to establish boundaries with Allen but also to develop a team approach in which Allen knew the case manager cared about him as an individual, not as a severely emotionally disturbed client. It was important to acknowledge Allen's strengths and his need to test the case manager's trust, nonjudgmental attitude, and "no rejection" philosophy.

Defining Expectations

The majority of transitional youths have difficulty adjusting to the multiple changes and expectations that occur on their 18th birthday. Transitional case managers assist the youths to adjust to and cope with the power of having choices about school, work, residence, play, and relationships.

Allen's case manager assisted him in understanding society's expectations. For example, once he was legally an adult, Allen's physical actions toward other people would no longer be tolerated or justified because of his childhood history of abuse, abandonment, mental illness, and rejection. If Allen broke the law he would be placed in a jail not a juvenile detention center. Allen learned the differences between the child and adult systems as well as the different consequences of his behavior. The transitional case manager assisted Allen's family and other community providers to set realistic expectations for Allen by understanding where he was developmentally and emotionally.

It is important to expect and permit youths to rebel and make mistakes as "normal" adolescents.

Allen's history of aggression made him ineligible for placements in licensed boarding homes and the adult residential treatment systems; therefore, he was placed in a furnished apartment in the community. Allen initially did not know how to cook, clean, shop, budget, or ride the bus; he had never lived by himself.

Wraparound workers (respite workers and in-home therapists services) are also helpful in the transitional process.

In Allen's situation, wraparound workers were provided to help him learn to be independent and self-sufficient. Flexible funds were used to purchase the necessities for his apartment. The case manager helped Allen obtain disability benefits, food stamps, access to special education services, a psychiatrist, an in-home therapist, and membership in the local YMCA. Allen purchased a key ring for this first key in his life, night lights for his apartment, a wallet for his identification, and a bike for transportation. The transitional case manager was flexible and creative with Allen's treatment and service planning because Allen's history, needs, strengths, limitations, and dreams were understood. The case manager involved Allen in the monthly treatment team meetings and worked with him to identify potential motivators for achieving his goals.

Case managers also need to assist youths and their families to rebuild their relationships in an adult-to-adult manner. Allen was assisted in reestablishing links to his family and in setting realistic expectations about these relationships.

> Allen and the case manager had several visits with his family. Allen learned to independently visit his mother and grandmother by using the community's bus system. Initially, Allen saw his family weekly and talked enthusiastically about the visits. At the end of 2 months, Allen and the case manager were able to talk about his anger toward his mother's abuse and rejection. With the wraparound workers and case manager assistance, Allen learned to set realistic expectations of family members and to have confidence in his resilience to survive without his family meeting all his emotional needs.

Allen realized that he wanted only monthly contact with his mother due to his intense anger about her abandonment and abuse of him. He decided to have dinner once a week with his grandmother whom he believed cared about his current status and dreams. Also, the in-home therapist met with Allen and his grandmother on a monthly basis. With his case manager's assistance, Allen was reunited with his brothers.

Transitional Coverage

Transitional professionals need to begin working with youth as early as possible and be prepared to assist and provide support at all times. Transitional programs have to provide 24-hour coverage for youths, their families, and others involved with the youth. Some individuals need either telephone contact or visits with their transitional case managers on a daily basis. Twenty-four hour coverage with the assistance of beepers provides a continuum of care that is consistent with the needs of the youth.

Transitional case managers monitor the youth wherever they reside (i.e., a residential treatment program 4 hours away, a family home, or jail). For example, individuals who are in state hospitals are seen monthly, as the case managers actively participate in treatment team meetings with the state hospital and residential treatment staff.

Youths who are currently linked to the transitional program or who are on the waiting list for services are encouraged to attend a monthly transitional support group. The group focuses on issues of community reentry, fears, dreams, independence, and relationships with persons who have not been mental health consumers. The group assists youths in developing a support system and in feeling that they are not alone in their struggle to make it in the adult world.

Transitional Staff Expectations

Transitional case managers need a high energy level, clinical skills, and a sense of humor. They need to be patient, flexible, and know how to advocate for individualized services. Case managers should enjoy having multiple job responsibilities and spending the majority of their time in the community. Case managers should be familiar with both the adolescent and adult system personnel and resource options.

Case managers also have a role in educating their agency and community service providers on transitional issues. Often, service providers are fearful of youths' histories and levels of functioning. Honesty, endurance, and assertiveness are necessary characteristics of individuals working with multiple transitional resources.

Being able to set limits with individuals and having empathy (i.e., the capacity to cry with youths and their families) are other important characteristics of transitional case managers. It is necessary to understand the liability issues, funding sources, policies, and paperwork involved in the provision of transitional services. Liability issues surround not only high-risk youths but also the use of contracted employees (i.e., wraparound workers). Wraparound workers sign annual contracts that stipulate monthly attendance at treatment team meetings and weekly telephone contacts with the case managers. Volunteers and other program staff involved with youths need to be trained and have annual local, state, and federal law enforcement checks.

CONCLUSION

Transitional case management is part of a continuum of care that provides community-based, accessible, flexible, and creative services for youths, institutions, crisis stabilization units, and the community. The transitional program described in this chapter has about 20 youths who are diagnosed as having an emotional, mental, or behavioral disturbance. The transitional youth's requests for services lead to comprehensive assessments, trust and relationship building, family involvement, and individualized life planning. Life planning revolves around the adolescents' and families' strengths, goals, dreams, and holistic needs. Youths are assisted in making decisions about their residence, recreation, social, legal, cultural, psychiatric, and educational domains as adults. As youths experiment with life choices they are not rejected for their rebellions, behaviors,or noncompliance with traditional outpatient and case management services. Transitional case management services are flexible, accessible 24 hours per day, and as intense as the youths and their families need them to be.

Ideally, case managers are creative, adaptable, and energetic. A sense of humor and clinical skills are essential in coping with multiple crises, fluctuating individual and family needs, and agency/community policies. Together, dedicated case managers and youths in transition have torn down the invisible walls of childhood institutionalization and the dreams of youths and their families have become realities.

Parents as Case Managers

Susan Ignelzi and Beth Dague

Parents have to be recognized as special educators, the true experts on their children; and professional people—teachers, pediatricians, psychologists and others—have to learn to be consultants to parents. (Hobbs, 1978, p. 65)

Despite the relative newness of the formal service strategy known as "case management," families have traditionally performed many service coordination functions to attempt to secure and manage appropriate services for their relatives who need assistance. For example, Seltzer, Ivry, and Litchfield (1987) found that relatives of elderly persons who needed a variety of formal agency services performed at least one case management function at the time of requesting formal services. These informal helping activities of family members, including families with children who have emotional disorders, have generally not been taken into account in formal case management programs.

This lack of recognition of the family's role in service delivery has begun to change, however, with the increasing acceptance of a family-centered approach to service delivery and as service providers are learning to work in partnership with families. Family members are beginning to be formally acknowledged for their service contributions, and in some states and communities they are being specifically recruited, trained, and, in some cases, remunerated for their service provision roles.

In this chapter, the authors examine the unique requirements of case management for children with emotional disorders and identify a variety of ways that family members have participated in service development and reform for these children. The authors argue that employing parents as case managers either for their own or other children is a logical next step, and they discuss a variety of issues related to implementing this innovation.

The emergence of case management since the mid-1980s has had a major effect on how social, medical, and mental health services are offered. Case management evolved in response to the need to coordinate formal services and a concern about delivering human services in an efficient and cost-effective manner. Case management in children's services can be defined as a process and series of actions designed to ensure that children with serious educational, physical, medical, or mental health needs receive the services, treatment, care, and opportunities to which they are entitled in a supportive, effective, and cost-effective manner.

The overall concept of case management is essentially the same for adults, children, and adolescents, but the implementation is different for children because of the following major considerations:

1. Children and adolescents are part of a system, or systems, that includes the family. Case management must address the requirements of the family, and the legal mandates of the various child-serving systems.
2. The rapid change that characterizes children's development calls for a case management system that is flexible and responsive to the needs and choices that children have as they grow and change.
3. The mental health system is only one of several child-serving systems involved in a child's life. Various child-serving systems provide a variety of services, including the resolution of questions surrounding a child's custody and family confidentiality issues, which need coordination through multiple system case management. Coordination and collaboration are required with these other systems, which include child welfare, mental retardation and developmental disabilities, juvenile court, and education systems. Many of these agencies also provide some case management services to families.

Because childhood encompasses more developmental stages and corresponding changes than does adulthood, it is extremely important that a child and adolescent case management system be theoretically based on a developmental model. A developmental case management model offers program options that take into account the youth's stage of development, focusing on assessments and services that are considered developmentally appropriate. The concept of developmental appropriateness means that services are designed using knowledge about typical developmental phases of children within specific age ranges. Individual appropriateness involves a response to each child as a unique person with individual growth patterns. The knowledge of these two dimensions provides a framework from which the case manager prepares and plans for appropriate services.

This developmental approach can be contrasted with the medical model, which has had a significant impact on thinking in the field of children's mental health. While the developmental model focuses on assessing the developmental stage of the children and structuring educational, therapeutic, and rehabilitative services to promote growth, the medical model is based on diagnosis, treatment, and cure (i.e., on identifying and eliminating or reducing the effects of disease or pathology). Thus, the medical model is not always applicable to children with emotional or behavioral disorders, as there is no magical cure for disorders such as conduct disorders, adjustment reaction to adolescence, or autism. This model has also been criticized for increasing dependence and relying on institutional care rather than on community-based care.

NEW ROLES FOR FAMILY MEMBERS

Since the mid-1970s, there has been a refocusing on the family's role in the care of children and adolescents. With the emphasis on reducing institutional care and serving children in their own homes and communities, the pivotal importance of the family and of supporting the entire family have become widely accepted as fundamental principles in the children's mental health field. These changes have been stimulated by policy changes such as PL 94-142 (the Education for All Handicapped Children Act) of 1975, which requires that parents be a part of the educational planning process for their children; PL 99-457 (the Education of the Handicapped Act Amendments of 1986), which mandates that parents of young children with disabilities participate in service planning, and the ADAMHA Reorganization Act of 1992 (PL 102-321), which requires family involvement in the development of state mental health plans.

In addition to policy initiatives, the advocacy of family members has been the key to promoting change. As Friesen and Koroloff (1990) point out, "one of the most important factors in expanding roles for parents, reducing stigma, and securing more support for family programs has been the development of an articulate parent voice" (p. 19). Family organizations such as the National Alliance for the Mentally Ill–Child and Adolescent Network and the Federation of Families for Children's Mental Health have developed a vision of what community-based systems should include and have emphasized the importance of a central role for families in service planning and evaluation. Many families and service providers in the field of mental health and in other disability fields share a vision of a family-centered system. Such a system would be responsive to the needs of all family members, providing family support services to help families successfully cope with the challenges of raising a child with disabilities (Friesen & Koroloff, 1990).

As a family-centered philosophy has steadily gained acceptance, state and local planners, policy makers, medical and mental health service providers, and families are still exploring the implications of adopting a family-centered approach. The philosophy of family-centered care involves a collaborative partnership between parents and professionals in the continual pursuit of being responsive to the strengths, needs, hopes, dreams, and aspirations of families with children who have emotional disorders. A partnership approach means that professionals and the community share the family vision of the child's future and work with the family to accomplish that future. In a family-centered system, parents have many opportunities for involvement and freedom of choice about how they will be involved. Three of the most common ways that family members have participated in shaping or providing services are self-help or support activities, family advocacy, and the development of family–professional partnerships.

Self-Help

Self-help has often consisted of three elements for family members. They are as follows:

- *Emotional support,* which means learning that they are not alone, that they are not to blame, and that they have the power to make things better.
- *Self-education,* which involves learning about their child's mental health problems, treatment issues, and methods of coping successfully with a child who has mental health or other problems.
- *Advice,* which requires gathering practical knowledge on what resources are available in the community and how to deal with the education systems, courts, child welfare, and a host of other topics.

Advocacy

In addition to helping and supporting each other through self-help, a number of parents become involved in improving the services their son or daughter receives. Frequently, once parents identify and accept that there is a mental health problem, significant behavior problem, or other problem area, they become interested in improving the children's mental health system and providing a better community-based system of care. It is this energy and spirit of advocacy that has moved the system of care ahead in many states and communities. Parents may serve as advocates either for their own or other children, or they may focus their energy on the political arena and the professional community.

Family–Professional Partnerships

When families realize their child has an emotional disability, they nearly always seek the help of a mental health professional. Children and adolescents with emotional disorders are so difficult and baffling to deal with that professional help is often necessary. In seeking appropriate help and following through to see that the child or adolescent receives services, the parents or other family members enter into relationships with professionals. The family's involvement with the formal service system typically extends for many years and may involve a large number of professionals. Parents typically have a variety of positive and negative experiences with professionals. For example, in many cases, parents and professionals have developed partnerships, with parents frequently taking on the responsibility for developing this partnership. Parent self-help and support, parent advocacy, and parent–professional relationships are natural steps for parents in moving through this system of care.

THE NEXT LOGICAL STEP

As these new roles of active parent involvement have evolved, the next logical step for parents has been that of providing paid direct services either for their own children with emotional disorders or for others. Although the authors did not find any published reports describing programs in which parents served as paid case managers in children's mental health, a number of precedents from other fields are described in the literature. For example, Moyers (1989) describes a program in Orange County, California, in which parents may take a free course, serve an apprenticeship, and function as a parent program coordinator before becoming a case manager at the Developmental Disabilities Center. Moyers cites the legislation, the California Welfare and Institutions Code, Section 4648(a), that makes it possible for parents to become case managers: "Nothing shall prevent a person with developmental disabilities or such person's parents, legal guardian or conservator, from being the program coordinator of the person's individual program plan, if the regional center director agrees that such an arrangement is feasible and in the best interest of the person with developmental disabilities" (p. 20). Moyers also describes a project that exists in three Minnesota counties that was adapted from the Orange County, California program, in which in addition to training and support, parents in the project receive $40 a month to act as case managers for their sons and daughters.

The early childhood and developmental disability arena has led the way in utilizing the skills and abilities of parents in working with other parents. Hausslein, Kaufmann, and Hurth (1992), describing the progress toward family-centered services promoted by Part H of the Individuals with Disabilities Education Act (IDEA) (PL 101-476), state that the most exciting move for parents under Part H is the expanded variety of roles that they might assume. For example,

- First and foremost, parents are there for the long haul as their own child moves through the service system.
- Second, parents are the primary decision makers about services needed for their child and themselves. They establish what their concerns, priorities, and needs are.
- Some parents may become official service coordinators or co-care coordinators for their own children (a possibility under the recent reauthorization of Part H that had been precluded by earlier regulations).
- Parents may teach professionals and other parents to become service coordinators.
- Parents may advocate for better integration and more family-centered practices among health, education, and social services designed to support infants, toddlers, and their families.
- Parents may participate in the development of service coordination policy through participation in local or state Interagency Coordinating Councils. (Hausslein et al., 1992, p. 11)

In communities, one way of applying the family participation litmus test is to discover ways in which communities and programs have developed fiscal incentives for families. Paying families to provide services for themselves or other community family members is one measure of the program commitment to parents, and paying a family for services provided by that family legitimizes and validates their skills. It also allows the family to become a recognized member of the treatment team, a real service provider. However, when paying a family, we need to be careful that the method of reimbursement does not affect the family's eligibility for other support services or entitlement programs.

EMPLOYING PARENTS

Although providing reimbursement to parents for direct services to families is relatively new, some states and communities have developed a variety of methods to engage parents in paid services. In developing creative opportunities for parents, consideration must be given to the following values and principles:

1. The training and skill development for parents and professionals alike must share a set of core values and principles about families, children, and services. Most parent programs suggest successful completion of a parent mentoring program prior to paid employment for the parent.
2. Consistent supervision and support to parents performing paid tasks to ensure success for families and the paid provider is an essential component.
3. Federal, state, and local regulations regarding standards of performance in providing services to families in community-based programs may need to be waived or made flexible enough to allow parents to be paid service providers.
4. Changes in benefits status for a parent whose income increase results in a loss of medical or other public benefits must be avoided. State policy changes or waivers may be necessary.
5. There must be respect for parental choice in deciding when and if they choose to provide services for their own child or another child. There must be flexibility to allow a parent to respond differently over time depending on the family's circumstances.
6. Respect for cultural sensitivity of the family as a service provider and as a service receiver is an essential component of the training program and throughout service delivery.

There are many areas of the United States where reimbursement already is being paid to parents for services provided to other families. Table 17.1 identifies some existing ways in which parents act as paid service providers for their own or other children. The list of parent roles and the locations that employ parents and other family members is growing every day.

As local and state systems have moved toward paying parents as legitimate paraprofessionals, some obstacles have been encountered. The most obvious obstacle is the direct confrontation between the fiscal and service side of the public service equation. Many described an initial "we can't do that" response from the fiscal office when approached with the first family member who was to be paid for providing case management services for his or her own or an-

Table 17.1. Parents as paid service providers

Type	Location
Direct pay	
Parent mentors	Canton City Schools, Canton, Ohio Child & Adolescent Services Center Canton, Ohio
Parent collaborators	Finger Lake District, New York
Parent case managers	KIDS, Columbus, Ohio Family Liaisons, Montana
Early intervention	California, Colorado, Minnesota, North Carolina, Ohio
Parent advocates	KIDS, Columbus, Ohio
In-home support staff	Positive Education Program, Cleveland, Ohio Child and Adolescent Service Center, Canton, Ohio
Respite providers	Easter Seals, Canton, Ohio Vermont Respite Program, Vermont
Service planners, managers of family cash grants	Illinois, Ohio, Virginia
Indirect pay	
Payback voucher Co-op programs	Positive Education Program, Early Intervention, Cleveland, Ohio
Voucher programs	Franklin County Alcohol and Drug Addiction Services Board, Columbus, Ohio

other's child. However, education about the legal mandates of parent involvement for the fiscal officers and county auditors often addresses their concerns so that fiscal mechanisms to pay parents can be established. A second issue is the possibility that paying parents may disrupt or suspend entitlements that the family may be receiving. Some states have addressed this issue with waivers for parents, while others have developed voucher systems.

Training for parents and the professional and paraprofessional staff of any community appears to be an essential ingredient for successful programs. Training programs need to specifically address supervision and support for parents as paid staff. In addition, the training program should include mediation skills that will eventually be needed as parents and professionals confront genuine differences of opinion. Professionals also may need training and support in understanding the value of collaborative approaches to working with parents as partners.

Most communities have had more success in paying parents for services provided to children other than their own. The ethical and auditing problems surrounding the provision of services to one's own child have proven to be difficult. Furthermore, many parents prefer to serve families other than their own, because they can be more objective and can limit and manage their involvement in ways they cannot with their own children. What is most important is that parents be given the option to decide when services are provided and who will provide these services to their family. As one parent eloquently stated:

> First, parents need to be aware of the wholeness of their lives, their values around other responsibilities, relationships, and dreams, and figure out what role case managing their child will and can play. They need to be fully supported in the decision they make regarding the amount of their commitment and given tremendous flexibility in the response they give in the long term and the short term. Secondly, parents need as much mentoring and teaching as they desire from experienced parents. Not many of us knew in the beginning how to be involved in a pro-active way. Sure, we knew what dates to show up at meetings and to pay the bills that came in. But I imagine that a lot of us learned from an experienced parent how to make the right phone calls, to write an IEP [individualized education program], to say no, or to demand the services that our children were entitled to. I learned a great deal from hearing how dynamic parents got what they needed. And I learned a lot from parents who were willing to say that they didn't always do it all, that they slacked off when they could, that they decided they had more than they could possibly do, so they either skipped out on the expectations or got someone else to do "their" job for them! (Wagner, 1992, p. 1)

The ebb and flow of each family's situation also affects the parent's ability to act as a paid service provider to another family. For this reason, it is essential that programs build in flexibility and support for parent employees.

CONCLUSION

In this chapter, the authors have set forth some opportunities and challenges for parents and professionals to work together as service providers. If we are going to view parents as service providers, the mental health system, as we now know it, needs to change. This change will begin with a change in perspective, from a view that blames parents to one that sees parents as vital contributors to the system of care. We will also need to implement a family-centered perspective that recognizes the family as the constant in the child's life and honors the parents' central roles as decision makers.

Change in organizations, systems, and society is rooted in individual personal change, in the ways people think and behave. In the real sense, systems do not change, people do. State and local planners, policy makers, and service providers from child-serving agencies must take responsibility for this change. Professionals must become aware of families' needs, learn how to provide for these needs, and open the treatment arena so that parents can join them side-by-side as paid service providers.

REFERENCES

ADAMHA Reorganization Act, PL 102–321. (July 10, 1992). Title 42, U.S.C. 201 et seq: *U.S. Statutes at Large, 106,* 349-358.
Education for All Handicapped Children Act of 1975, PL 94-142. (August 23, 1977). Title 20, U.S.C. 1401 et seq: *U.S. Statutes at Large, 89,* 773–796.
Education of the Handicapped Act Amendments of 1986, PL 99-457. (October 8, 1986). Title 20, U.S.C. 1400 et seq: *U.S. Statutes at Large, 100,* 1145–1177.
Friesen, B.J., & Koroloff, N.M. (1990). Family centered services: Implications for mental health administration and research. *Journal of Mental Health Administration, 17*(1), 13–25.
Hausslein, E.B., Kaufmann, R.K., & Hurth, J. (1992). From case management to service coordination: Families, policymaking, and Part H. *Zero to Three, 12*(3), 10–12.
Hobbs, N. (1978). Perspectives on re-education. *Behavior Disorders, 3*(2), 65–66.
Individuals with Disabilities Education Act of 1990 (IDEA), PL 101-476. (October 30, 1990). Title 20, U.S.C. 1400 et seq: *U.S. Statutes at Large, 104,* 1103–1151.
Moyers, A.J. (1989). Parents as case managers. *New Ways,* pp. 20–21.
Seltzer, M.M., Ivry, J., & Litchfield, L.C. (1987). Family members as case managers: Partnership between the formal and informal support networks. *The Gerontologist, 27*(6), 722–728.
Wagner, C. (1992). Unpublished manuscript (untitled). Research and Training Center on Family Support and Children's Mental Health, Portland State University, Portland, OR.

The Illinois Family Assistance Program for Children with Mental Disabilities

Kenley Wade, Mary Lou Hicks,
Robert Goerge, and Ruth Osuch

Recently, Illinois joined the ranks of other states in addressing the needs of families with children who have emotional and developmental disabilities by establishing a special family support program. In 1990, the Illinois legislature passed the Family Assistance Law for Mentally Disabled Children (PA 86-921). The purpose of this law is to strengthen and support families who provide care within the family home for children whose level of emotional disorder or developmental disability constitutes a risk of out-of-home placement. The Illinois Family Assistance Program (FAP) provides a monthly cash stipend to eligible families equivalent to the amount of the Supplemental Security Income (SSI) benefit for a single individual. The family is allowed to use the stipend at their own discretion, as long as it is for the benefit of the family member with the disability. The purpose of this chapter is to describe the nature and background of family support programs, the various aspects of the cash subsidy model in Illinois, and lessons learned from the first year of implementation.

BACKGROUND

Family support programs for children with disabilities and their families have emerged over the past 15 years as a way to enhance the capacity of parents in their child-rearing roles, to enhance the overall quality of family life, and to prevent a premature or unwanted out-of-home placement. To date, 41 states have developed programs with a specific focus on supporting families who are providing care at home to a child with a disability (Knoll et al., 1990). Twenty-three of these states offer some form of financial assistance to families.

The recent attention given to family support represents a departure from traditional human services in several ways. From an economic perspective, family support programs represent a savings from costly institutional care (Agosta et al., 1991). From a policy perspective, family support programs are a shift away from service models, in which the child was seen as the target of intervention and parents were passive recipients of a predefined package of services, to newer innovative strategies in which parents retain primary control (Singer & Irvin, 1988). Moreover, past programs tended to be episodic, crisis-related services, whereas family support programs center on prevention and offer a continuum of services. Family support programs are beginning to recognize individual family needs and to view parents as active partners in securing services for their children. Part of the rationale for such a program is to empower families to meet their own needs. Empowerment is based on the premise that family needs are unique, that these needs are best identified by the families themselves, and that the best way to meet these needs is to support families' participation in securing goods and services (Dunst, Trivette, & Deal, 1988).

Family support programs can be categorized into three models: 1) cash subsidy programs that provide money directly to families for the purchase of services or habilitation materials, 2) supportive programs that provide direct services to families from providers contracted by the state, and 3) combination programs that offer both cash subsidies and direct services (Human Services Research Institute, 1984). With the signing of PA 86-921, the Illinois Department of Mental Health and Developmental Disabilities (DMHDD) began administering the FAP on October 1, 1990, the first cash subsidy to families in the United States to include children who have emotional disorders along with children who have developmental disabilities.

VALUES AND PRINCIPLES

One distinction a cash subsidy program has from other family support program models is parental control over decisions regarding the purchase of services and items to meet the needs of their child (Krauss, 1986). The FAP offers parents the maximum amount of freedom in terms of choosing how to best meet the specialized needs of their child and the overall needs of the family. The underlying assumptions behind the cash subsidy model are that families are in the best position to identify their needs and, more important, that the needs among families are so unique that no one service model exists to meet this diversity. These assumptions are in keeping with the values and principles contained in the Illinois State Mental Health Plan for children and adolescents. One of the values is that services should be child centered (i.e., designed to meet the needs of children and their families), with the needs of the child and his or her family dictating the type and mix of services. The principles that guide the service system include family empowerment and family focus; that is, empowering families to set their own goals and decide on services to be received, while also focusing on the need to preserve the integrity of the family through their participation in the planning and delivery of services.

INITIAL IMPLEMENTATION

The start-up of the FAP involved two major activities. One was the establishment of three committees whose tasks were to set guidelines and recommendations and oversee general activities. The second activity was the development of outreach efforts in order to recruit potential applicants.

A project director was appointed from DMHDD's executive staff to chair the three major committees established to assist with implementation of the FAP. The first committee was actually a working task force composed of staff from all sectors of the DMHDD's central administration. This task force identified all the steps required to implement the legislation as well as the policy and procedure issues to be addressed. The other two committees were advisory to the project. One committee was composed of parents, consumers, and advocates, and the other was composed of service providers and associations. Procedures, such as the selection of participants and policies regarding income maximums for participants, were developed by the task force and reviewed by the advisory committees. This comprehensive review process served to establish credibility and trust in the actions taken to implement the program.

In developing the outreach plan, one issue that DMHDD struggled with was whether to inform as many potentially eligible persons as possible, which could create a demand greater than the available funding (the FAP only had funding for 284 families), or whether to reasonably limit the outreach effort in order to disappoint or reject fewer applicants. This consideration was complex given that many of the persons eligible for this program are already in jeopardy of losing the services they receive due to government funding concerns, have been turned down in the past for services similar to family supports, and may be distrustful of programs that appear "too good to be true." However, DMHDD developed an extensive plan to contact numerous agencies (public and private) and professional organizations. The project director was primarily responsible for contacting the various agencies regarding the goals of the programs, application procedures, and materials necessary to recruit applicants. Some of the activities included attending press conferences, being a guest speaker on one of the local Chicago radio stations that targets the African American population, and meeting with many of the executive directors and key staff of the state departments to inform them of the program.

In order to make the application process accessible to the greatest number of people, an aggressive outreach plan was developed. It included the following:

- *Two press conferences*—One conference took place in Chicago, which is the major media market in Illinois and has the largest population, and one in Springfield, which is the Illinois state capitol and included participation by the sponsoring legislator, Representative Lee A. Daniels.
- *Other publications*—Contact was made to provider associations, professional associations, consumer groups, and advocate organizations that publish newsletters, and articles were distributed for inclusion in their next editions.
- *Agency contacts*—The DMHDD director made personal contact with the directors of the other state agencies to secure their cooperation and the DMHDD project director met with administrative and program staff in key agencies to explain the program.
- *Direct mail*—A brochure (printed in both English and Spanish), which was targeted toward families who have children with emotional disorders or developmental disabilities, was produced. The brochure included the application form as a perforated tear-off card to serve as a self-mailer to the DMHDD central office. Letters along with brochures were sent to groups, agencies, and individuals, asking them to help reach families who might benefit from the program.

From the mass direct mailing process, DMHDD received 4,268 postcard applications of which 618 were duplicates or were received after the cut-off date. From the 3,650 application cards that were received within the specified time frame, 284 families were selected at random to be in the first group for additional screening and 313 families were selected to be in the second group, as alternates. The information on the postcard application from the brochure included the child's name, gender, race, type of disability, date of birth, Social Security number, name of parent or guardian and complete address, phone number, income level, whether the child lives at home or plans to return home, and whether the child is a foster child.

Having a child in an out-of-home placement did not preclude a family from applying for the FAP. In fact, if a family who had a child in placement was selected, they could receive a one-time payment equal to double the monthly stipend ($814) to assist with preparations to return their child to their home.

The program consists of a cash subsidy equivalent to SSI, currently $407 a month, and optional service facilitation of up to 20 hours per year. The program was funded to provide stipends to 284 families, one half of whom were to include children with emotional disorders and the other half of whom were to include children with developmental disabilities. Families who were selected via the random drawing were then instructed to submit clinical material regarding their child's disability to a professional examiner for review.

ELIGIBILITY

There is considerable concern with the dispensing of public funds, specifically, that objective criteria should be established to determine program eligibility. Eligibility criteria answer such questions as: "Who is the target population?" and "For whom are services being directed?" Moreover, they are useful criteria for program evaluation. Eligibility criteria allow for an examination of program equity—"Did the program serve those for whom it was intended?" The FAP has four broad eligibility criteria: 1) the child must meet the clinical definition of "severe" emotional disorder or "severe" developmental disability, 2) the child must be living at home or the family must make arrangements to have the child returned home if the child is currently in an out-of-home placement, 3) the family income cannot exceed $50,000, and 4) the family must reside in Illinois.

The DMHDD recruited and selected a number of examiners across the state who were paid to conduct the eligibility reviews. Parents were also free to select an examiner if the person met the criteria established by the DMHDD. If their child's disability met the standards addressed by the program, along with the nonclincial criteria (e.g., income, residency), the family was enrolled in the program.

The FAP is clearly targeted for families who have children with "severe" disabilities. Verification of three of the four criteria relies on fairly straightforward, factual information. The clinical criteria with its emphasis on the severity of a child's disability, however, is subject to multiple factors. Along with age and diagnosis, functional levels of behavior and developmental stages were included by DMHDD to describe the target populations and to operationalize protocols and procedures regarding severity of disability. These protocols were developed in the form of checklists for each diagnostic category to determine program eligibility. In fact, the clinical criteria for a child with a "severe" emotional disorder is provided as an example of how the DMHDD operationally defined one such diagnostic category.

Diagnosis

A primary diagnosis must meet the *DSM-III-R* (American Psychiatric Association, 1987) criteria of a mental disorder with onset in childhood or adolescence (excluding v-codes, adjustment disorders, mental retardation when no other mental disorder is present, or other forms of dementia based upon organic, physical, or alcohol/substance abuse disorders).

Although diagnosis alone cannot be used as a basis for defining long-term mental illness or severe emotional disturbance in children, certain diagnostic categories are most often associated with it. They include childhood schizophrenia, schizophrenia of adult-type manifesting in adolescence, pervasive developmental disorders, and other emotional/behavioral disorders that fulfill the disability and duration requirements of this definition, such as affective disorders and certain disorders with severe medical implications.

Disability

The child must meet *DSM-III-R* Axis V criterion of severe functional impairment (a score of 40 or below on the GAF or Children's GAS) and be experiencing significant limitations of major life activities in his/her capacity for living in a family or family equivalent *and* in two or more of the following areas (not to include impairment in function due to physical or environmental limitations):

1. Self-care at an appropriate developmental level
2. Receptive and expressive language
3. Learning
4. Social interaction and self-direction, including behavioral controls, decision making, value systems at an appropriate developmental level

SERVICE FACILITATION/CASE MANAGEMENT

The FAP is part of the Illinois law (PA 86-921) that created a similar program for adults, the Home-Based Support Services (HBSS) program. In the enabling legislation, case management was specifically required for adults who were selected for participation. This requirement for adults is included because, instead of a cash stipend, adults receive an array of services equal to the value of three times the monthly SSI benefit. Therefore, case management is mandated in order to assure that someone is responsible for "managing" the planning and delivery of services.

For families with children in the FAP, the legislation simply requires the DMHDD to advise them regarding other services that may be available for their child. There is concern that making the service facilitation component mandatory in the same manner as it is for adults would restrict parents' use of the subsidy and prevent maximum empowerment. Consequently, service facilitation is optional for families. The function of service facilitation is to make families aware of local support resources including in-home services, crisis intervention, respite care, and other mental health or developmental disability services. Each family who was approved for the FAP could receive up to 20 hours of service facilitation paid for by DMHDD. If the family wanted additional hours beyond those paid by the DMHDD, they were free to purchase them from their stipend. The DMHDD established criteria for service facilitators and recruited them through the existing community-based mental health agencies. Information regarding their availability was provided to approved families.

To date, only 40 of the 200 approved families have requested service facilitation from DMHDD. The low level of requests for this service raises several issues. First, some of the families do not think that they require this service. Second, the way in which this service was presented to families and the actual services provided may account for the lack of interest. Finally, many families have only been receiving the stipend for a few months and this service may not become a priority for them until other, more concrete needs have been addressed.

OBSTACLES AND LIMITATIONS

There were some initial obstacles to overcome, even as the legislation was being considered. Some of the child-serving agencies expressed concern about awarding a cash stipend to parents of children with emotional disorders and, to a lesser degree, parents of children with developmental disabilities. The opposition had two premises: first, there should be some control over what families could purchase with the stipend, and second, parents of such children lacked the judgment to spend the funds appropriately. The point of view of DMHDD and the consumer and advocate groups did not support these premises. The DMHDD's position, as well as the legislative sponsor, Representative Daniels, was that these parents were certainly capable of managing an additional $407 per month on behalf of their child. Previously, other states have used an unrestricted cash stipend process without negative consequences. Finally, it would run counter to the principle of empowerment for families if DMHDD retained control over how the funds could be used.

Another obstacle was the general policies of other financial assistance and taxing entities (i.e., Aid to Families with Dependent Children [AFDC], SSI, state income tax, and federal income tax). It was important to ensure that there were no penalties attached to receipt of the cash stipend. The DMHDD, through the implementation task force, tackled these policy and legal issues by assigning one of its attorneys to the task. The outcome was that the Social Security Administration (SSA) and the Illinois Department of Public Aid agreed that the cash stipend directed toward the care of the child with a disability would not be considered income in their financial means test for SSI or AFDC benefits eligibility. Similarly, the Illinois Department of Revenue and the Internal Revenue Service agreed that the stipend was not income and would not be taxed.

The primary program limitation is simply that funding is available for so few families. At $407 per month for 284 families, the program is funded at less than $1.5 million per year. Given the current fiscal environment (i.e., major revenue shortfall due to a sagging economy), the best the program will be able to do is to try to maintain the current level of participants.

EVALUATION

The legislation that established the FAP also included a mandate that the programs undergo formal evaluation. The Chapin Hall Center for Children at the University of Chicago was selected to conduct the evaluation of the FAP. The Chapin Hall evaluators examined three major areas of the FAP: 1) the outreach efforts, 2) the families who applied, and 3) the needs and characteristics of families. This description of the FAP includes excerpts from their reports. Unfortunately, the second phase of the evaluation will not occur because of funding limitations identified previously. However, we have the benefit of the findings from the first phase of the evaluation.

Outreach Efforts

The different state agencies, special interest organizations, and service providers viewed the FAP with varying degrees of interest. A number of issues illustrate both the successes and the shortcomings of the outreach efforts by the department. First, the lack of time given to DMHDD and provider agencies to orient their staff, notify families, and assist with the application process was a critical factor. In addition, the shortage of time did not allow DMHDD to follow up with the agencies to discuss the progress of their outreach plan. DMHDD launched their intensive recruitment efforts in early June, which left only 7–8 weeks for the information to reach eligible persons in time to submit applications. Program planning had begun much earlier and, accordingly, some of the agencies were well informed of the program and its goals before the recruitment period.

Second, there was confusion among the agencies about a one-time family support grant that was available the previous year (fiscal year 1990) and the ongoing FAP, which began in fiscal year 1991. Tied to this issue was confusion about the way that the adult program was administered differently than the child program. Although the application processes were similar, it was clear to the service providers that the actual program services were very different. Some agencies may have had less interest in families becoming eligible if it meant losing them as clients, since eligible families with children could choose to purchase services from non-DMHDD provider agencies.

Third, the outreach plan was not successful in recruiting applicants who did not already have an affiliation with a service system or an advocacy organization. These applicants would have had a lesser chance of hearing about the program than families who are known to the various agencies. The extent to which the outreach efforts captured families who typically "fall through the cracks" versus "veteran" families is unclear. The results from the family survey indicate that parents of children with developmental disabilities were more likely to have heard about the program through their child's school, while parents of children with emotional disorders were more likely to have heard about the program through a social service agency. Finally, DMHDD relied heavily on state agencies to disseminate information at the local levels. Greater participation seems to have occurred with the agencies who provide direct services to the applicants.

Overall, the outreach plan submitted by the DMHDD was thorough and comprehensive in nature, yet the number of persons who applied to the program was quite small. It is unclear if families of children with developmental and emotional disabilities were discouraged from applying for reasons other than lack of awareness. For example, one of the program's eligibility criteria is that the emotional or developmental disability be severe in nature. The DMHDD emphasized in both written and verbal communication that the applicant's disability must be severe. This criterion may have discouraged professionals and potentially eligible families from applying if they were led to believe that their child's limitations were not severe enough to qualify.

The outreach plan was intended to provide equal access across the state for program applicants, thereby ensuring an equal chance for selection. It is clear that efforts were taken to notify various interest groups and public service agencies. In spite of this effort, much work was needed to reach the families at the local level.

Families Who Applied

The families who applied to the FAP were predominantly those who identified their children as having developmental disabilities rather than emotional disabilities, 85.4% and 14.6%, respectively. Slightly more than one half of the children were male (58.8%) and boys were more likely to have a diagnosis of a "severe emotional disability" (64.8%) than girls (35.2%). A greater proportion of the African American families applied under the "severe emotional disorder" category than other racial groups. Overall, children with an emotional disability were older than children with a developmental disability. There was also, however, variation among the other regions of the state in the ages of the children who applied.

The reasons for these differences are unclear. Given that the majority of African American children are from the city of Chicago and poverty areas, these children may be at greater risk of experiencing an emotional disability. Comparisons of children who applied to the program versus the general population of children with emotional and developmental disabilities are unavailable. Other reasons for this include issues of protection with respect to labeling, accuracy of the diagnostic tools, and the constant shift in definition.

The response rate to the FAP is a complex phenomenon to examine. It is a function of DMHDD outreach efforts, families' connections with service systems (i.e., local special education districts, state government programs), and human behavior (i.e., the motivation to submit the application). A more detailed study of the participant population may provide additional information on these important issues.

Needs and Characteristics of Families

It is clear that respite care is a strong need felt by families who have children with both developmental disabilities and emotional disabilities. This need is great for both groups, but particularly for the families of children with emotional disorders, for whom this service is almost nonexistent. Both the availability and accessibility of respite care needs to be expanded. The availability of this resource may improve family functioning, provide parents with an opportunity to seek employment, and forestall out-of-home placements.

Parents of children with developmental disabilities seem to have a greater involvement with parent organizations. The findings in this report would suggest that social support and affiliation with a parent organization can promote coping capabilities, reduce overall family need, and alleviate some of the negative impacts associated with the care of their child (Goerge, Osuch, Costello, & Tan, 1991). The availability of such organizations for parents of children with developmental disabilities is one factor. The lack of these same resources for parents of children with emotional disorders, the parents' outreach efforts, or the general acceptance of belonging to such a group are salient issues that warrant further study.

Finally, families who are anticipating an out-of-home placement appear less connected to a support network, experience more stress concerning their child, and report a higher level of need. Support networks in the form of support groups and advocacy organizations need to be developed and need to employ aggressive outreach strategies. Policy makers and professionals need to become more aware of the positive effects derived from informal support and help families strengthen existing networks and work creatively to develop new ones.

CONCLUSION

Programs designed to meet the needs of families who have children with disabilities continue to evolve, influenced by policies that address residential care, the availability of community-based mental health services and educational programs, and economic factors such as housing and employment. The Illinois Family Assistance Law addresses some of these concerns.

Yet, the question remains—if the authors had this to do over again, what would they do differently? One thing the department would do differently is to provide clearer descriptions of the populations of children to be served. The declaration on the self-mailer postcard of the "type of disability" created a problem when some parents indicated "severe emotional disorders," which under clinical review were determined to be developmental disabilities (i.e., autism, mental retardation). Therefore, for children and adolescents served by the mental health service system, the department would place more emphasis on the definition of "severe emotional disorders." Second, the outreach effort would be changed in a manner that would separate the application process (i.e., one brochure/application for children with emotional disorders and one for children with developmental disabilities). Third, a step would be added to the screening process, preceding the random selection, that would serve as a preliminary assessment of the child's disability. In this way, the problem of misdirecting an application (i.e., emotional disorder vs. developmental disability) would be eliminated. Finally, the department would consider decentralizing the screening, assessment, and selection process to community-based mental health agencies, after policies and procedures had been developed (collaboratively) at the state level.

Problems, obstacles, and limitations aside, the development and implementation of the FAP reinforces some of the precepts and principles to which DMHDD is committed. One precept is that if we work collaboratively, even in the context of temporary coalitions, we will achieve a positive outcome. In the case of the FAP, advocates, families, consumers, legislators, service providers, and DMHDD worked together to produce a different way to help families who have children with disabilities. The principles of empowering families and maintaining a family focus on service system development were also sustained within this program. Representative Daniels took the lead in assuring that families had full discretion and authority in determining how to spend their cash stipend for the benefit of their child. One example of maintaining a family focus was the establishment of a separate family advisory committee whose input was direct and not filtered through or influenced by other entities. Overall, the FAP is a successful venture. The challenge for the future is to ensure that DMHDD has learned something from its development and will exercise the same courage and initiative to create more collaborative opportunities to move the service system to the next plateau.

REFERENCES

Agosta, J., Knoll, J., Freud, E., Osuch, R., Deatherage, M., White, C., Rabb, B., & Godfrey, T. (1991). *Four pilot family support programs funded by the Illinois planning council on developmental disabilities: Evaluation findings.* Cambridge, MA: Human Services Research Institute.

American Psychiatric Association. (1987). *Diagnostic and statistical manual of mental disorders* (3rd ed., rev.). Washington, DC: Author.

Goerge, R., Osuch, R., Costello, J., & Tan, I. (1991). *Analysis of the first survey of families* [Report]. Chicago: Chapin Hall Center for Children.

Dunst, C.J., Trivette, C.M., & Deal, A.G. (1988). *Enabling and empowering families: Principles and guidelines for practice.* Cambridge, MA: Brookline Books.

Human Services Research Institute. (1984). *Supporting families with developmentally disabled members: Review of the literature and results of a national survey.* Cambridge, MA: Author.

Knoll, J.A., Covert, S., Osuch, R., O'Connor, S., Agosta, J., & Blaney, B. (1990). *Family support services in the United States: An end of decade status report.* Cambridge, MA: Human Services Research Institute.

Krauss, M.W. (1986). Patterns and trends in public services to families with a mentally retarded member. In J. Gallagher & P. Vietze (Eds.), *Families of handicapped children: Research, programs and policy issues* (pp. 237–248). Baltimore: Paul H. Brookes Publishing Co.

Singer, G., & Irvin, L. (Eds.). (1988). *Support for caregiving families: Enabling positive adaptation to disability.* Baltimore: Paul H. Brookes Publishing Co.

CURRENT RESEARCH AND FUTURE PROGRAM DEVELOPMENT

Case Management Research
Issues and Directions

Barbara J. Burns, Elizabeth Anne Gwaltney,
and G. Kay Bishop

The roots of case management were identified as early as 1863 in the formation of the Massachusetts Board of Charities, the early settlement houses, and the Charity Organization Societies (Weil & Karls, 1985). In the 1900s, federal and state legislation, as well as private sector policies, have more clearly defined this expanding field. The Education for All Handicapped Children Act of 1975 (PL 94-142), the Community Mental Health Centers Act (PL 88-164) (supplemented by Part F in 1972 to support services for children and adolescents), the State Mental Health Services Comprehensive Plan (in the Omnibus Health Act, PL 99-660), and federal Medicaid statutes are among the earlier systemic approaches that helped to clarify the role of case management. More recently, the National Institute of Mental Health (NIMH) Child and Adolescent Service System Program (CASSP) and the Mental Health Services Program for Youth (MHSPY) of the Robert Wood Johnson Foundation have similarly addressed the service system as a whole. Overall, a focus on coordinating services, developing a continuum of care, promoting accountability, and provision of case management has emerged. Children with serious emotional disturbances (SEDs) have been targeted for coordinated service delivery as they often present multiple service needs in the areas of mental health, education, social service, juvenile justice, and health (Behar, 1985; Knitzer, 1982; Looney, 1988; Stroul & Friedman, 1986, 1988).

Although such legislation and policy recognize the need for case management and may even mandate it for purposes of funding and system development, no definitions and service description are provided, even in PL 99-660 (Robinson & Toff-Bergman, 1989), but this is beginning to occur under PL 99-457 (the Education of the Handicapped Act Amendments of 1986). No consensus definition is evident in the human services literature. In practice, case management varies in form and function and may be defined by the system or systems in which it is provided (Intagliata, 1982).

What then is case management? Is it a process, a person, a therapeutic relationship, a team, a system of care, or coordination within a continuum of care? Who is and who is not a case manager? Without falling into unprofitable semantic debate, some agreement needs to be reached if research is to be feasible and if valid comparisons are to be made. Examination of models of case management and the functions of case management may yield more insight.

In the mental health field, available research literature on case management focuses on adults with severe and persistent mental illness. The structure of case management services studied has varied greatly based on local and diverse service systems. The Program in Assertive Community Treatment (PACT) developed by Stein and Test (1980), a team approach in which professionals share responsibility for case management and client service needs, is one of the few community-based models of care that has been successfully tested and replicated through clinical trials (Taube, Morlock, Burns, & Santos, 1990). Results of studies on clients served by PACT teams have consistently shown lower hospitalization use and improved functioning; also, costs were not greater than for clients served by traditional hospital services (Weisbrod, Test, & Stein, 1980). This model does more than provide case management services; it encompasses the full range of direct and support services needed by the client. Because case management is so intricately involved in a community support system of care, it is difficult to determine which facets of the PACT model make a difference (Taube et al., 1990).

Other studies of case management for adults (Bond, Miller, Krumwied, & Ward, 1988; Franklin, Solovitz, Mason, Clemons, & Miller, 1987; Goering, Wasylenki, Farkas, Lance, & Ballantyne, 1988) have raised the issues of consistency of implementation of case management services, diffusion of activity between control and experimental groups, and the environmental context of case management operation as serious factors to consider in subsequent studies. Rubin (1992), in a review of eight recent outcomes studies on case management, states, "claims that case management has been empirically demonstrated to be effective appear to be premature" (p. 148). Further refinement of research should address some of the uncertainties of the first generation of case management studies. Hargreaves and Shumway (1989) offer direction for the second generation, suggesting multicommunity randomized controlled trials in which both the model of case management and the nature of the service system environment are varied. In the child mental health system, similar questions about the nature of case management have been raised, but descriptive reports from current studies are only now beginning to appear in the literature. Models of continuity of child mental health care have paralleled adult services to a considerable extent. Yet, there are factors that create differences in the service systems, as well as developmental needs of children and adults, that may not allow findings from adult studies to be directly transferable to children's services.

Variations in the locus of major components of service delivery and composition of the service system are two factors of note. In the adult system, the key services issue is determining which format of service delivery yields the most effective outcomes for clients. A community mental health system usually includes components such as inpatient treatment, residential care, day treatment, and outpatient services. A multidisciplinary team usually encompasses a full range of support and treatment services. For adults, which method works best? Although significant credence is given to support needs that extend beyond the formal mental health system (i.e., entitlements, psychosocial rehabilitation, supportive housing, peer and family support), the community-based models of service are generally funded by mental health dollars, administered through mental health or contract agencies, and include a variety of services, both treatment and support, provided by mental health staff. Other agencies do not, as a rule, provide significant amounts of direct services to adults with severe and persistent mental illness, even though the need for this exists, especially in the areas of housing, health, and rehabilitation.

With children, a different situation exists. An infant's needs are unlike those of the troubled teenager; also, the needs of a young adult in transition may be distinct from those of the adult or elderly person with chronic mental illness. A multitude of agencies and staff may be involved on a regular basis, and each agency may be providing extensive direct services to the child or youth and his or her family. Each agency may also feel responsible for the overall circumstance of the clients for either legal or professional reasons. In essence, there may be several treatment plans, individualized education programs (IEPs), or service plans in existence for an individual child and family. Each agency identifies service needs while being administered and funded quite separately. Children are *always* subject to multiple agencies and legislative mandates, and have only the legal status of a dependent. They may be wards of the court, foster children, or subject to parental control.

The school system interacts with the child or youth on an almost daily basis. This is a complex bureaucracy not included in the adult system of care. Public Law 99-457 requires special education services for children and youth with SED. However, access to adequate and appropriate provision of such services varies dramatically from one state to another and from one school district to another within states (Singer & Butler, 1987).

Often, the juvenile justice system is also integrally involved with the child and his or her family in a direct service way. In the juvenile justice system, a treatment and rehabilitation orientation is intended to assist the child to live a life free of criminal activity. In North Carolina, juvenile court counselors are often strong advocates for their clients when few other professionals still see a possibility of rehabilitation.

The child welfare system, especially the child protective services agency, is also frequently involved with children who have SED and their families and, often, placement in residential or foster care is administered and funded by the Department of Social Services (DSS). The DSS may have legal guardianship of children and function in the role of *parens patria* when children are removed from the home, either for protection from abuse or for needed psychological treatment, or both. Many children under DSS supervision/custody have experienced serious life traumas or neglect and, thus, have serious emotional and/or psychological complications.

To date, clinical observation of model services has suggested that individual case managers may be the appropriate choice in children's services (Behar, 1985). For example, the Willie M. program for seriously disturbed and assaultive children and youth in North Carolina has included case managers since its inception. This program, which provides services in the mental health system when such children were previously handled by juvenile justice and not treated, has been cited as a national model (Beachler, 1990). However, the variations previously noted in service delivery and composition of the system raise questions as to what form of case management may be most appropriate. For example, will team case management or individual case managers work better in a system that has extensive interagency service delivery and responsibility (Berkowitz, Halfon, & Klee, 1992; Kaufman, 1992)? There is still a virtual absence of well-controlled studies of case management in the children's mental health field. Research is needed to determine which models of case management are effective and which work for different subgroups of children and youth with SEDs.

For both adults and children, case management is seen as a way to overcome fragmentation of services, provide coordination, and offer a continuum of care. Reviewing the extant literature on case management and developing a typology of approaches, Robinson and Toff-Bergman (1989) note, however, that *none* of the approaches described address the needs of children and youth with SED.

> In fact, the basic precepts of the intensive case management models may run contrary to the needs of children and youth. For example, the philosophy of intensive case management for children must include the needs and capacities of parents and other significant family members. None of the case management models describe how they interact with other formal service systems that have either an interest in the population or have primary responsibility for the population. When working with children and youth, the mental health authority may have less authority than the school system, the juvenile services system, or the social service system. Special attention should be paid to describing and shaping case management systems appropriate for children. (p. 9)

Brown (1989) described a single site, and Behar (1985) focused on a single model of case management for children in early research in this area. Efforts are underway to replicate programs such as the Alaska Youth Initiative (Dowrick, 1989), which utilized flexible fundings to care for children previously placed in residential treatment centers; and the Ventura County, California, program, which placed mental health professionals in usual care settings, such as schools or the juvenile justice system (Jordan & Hernandez, 1990). Efforts in Florida, New York, and North Carolina, among others in progress, are funded by the CASSP program of NIMH, the Robert Wood Johnson Foundation, the Civilian Health and Medical Program of the Uniform Services (CHAMPUS), and other special initiatives. Opportunities for research are unlimited, yet still much needed, in this important arena.

INITIAL RESEARCH ISSUES

Objectives

According to Intagliata (1982), the objectives of case management include the following: 1) enhancing the continuity of care (both *cross-sectionally*, so that at any time services provided are comprehensive and coordinated, and *longitudinally*, so that services continue over time and respond to an individual's changing needs); 2) accessibility; 3) accountability; and 4) efficiency. The CASSP view is that case management can ensure that multiple services will be delivered in a coordinated and therapeutic fashion, thus enabling youth with SED and their families to move through the service system in accordance with their changing needs (Fox & Wicks, 1991). For others, cost control is another objective—one that may or may not be obtained by case management.

Functions

According to the Joint Commission on the Accreditation of Hospitals (1979), the primary functions of case management are as follows: 1) assessment—determining an individual's current and potential strengths, weaknesses, and needs; 2) planning—developing a specific service plan for each customer, with provisions for day, evening, and night linkages to needed services; 3) linking—referring or transferring individuals to all required services in the formal and informal caregiving systems; 4) monitoring—continuous evaluation of consumer progress; and 5) advocacy—interceding on behalf of an individual to assure equity, both in the specific case and for any larger group or class to which the client might belong. To these functions, case identification and outreach for clients not using customary services, system-level advocacy in which new services are added or developed by the case manager, and crisis intervention may be added (Willenbring, Ridgely, Stinchfield, & Rose, 1990). Initial empirical data on functions from a New York study show the following breakout by time: administration (48%), monitoring (19%), travel (18%), linkage (9%), and planning (6%) (Evans, Armstrong, Huz, & Dollard, 1993).

To the preceding five primary functions of case management, supportive clinical services, such as counseling and psychotherapy, may also be added. Harris and Bergman (1988) argue that for persons with chronic mental illness, case management is *necessarily* a clinical process. Similar views have been reiterated around case management for children with chronic medical problems (Berkowitz et al., 1992; Kaufman, 1992).

Issues still needing attention include the following:

- What are the essential functions primarily performed by case managers for children and youth with SED?
- Are the critical functions the same for various child groups?
- Do therapeutic functions and case management brokering functions have to be separated for this population, given the needs for continuity of care and multiple services?
- Should the additional functions of case identification and outreach, crisis intervention, and system advocacy, described by Wil-

lenbring et al. (1990), be included among the designated case management functions for children and adolescents?

Models

In their review of case management knowledge and practice, Robinson and Toff-Bergman (1989) developed a typology of mental health case management models for adults. Four basic service models were derived: 1) *expanded broker*, in which the case manager assesses the client's needs and attempts to link him or her to the appropriate service; 2) *personal strengths*, in which the case manager identifies a client's strengths and attempts to create situations where these can be enhanced and where success can be achieved; 3) *rehabilitation*, the case manager identifies skill deficits, which act as barriers to achievement of personal goals, and teaches the needed skills; and 4) *full support*, in which the case management team combines the teaching of coping skills with clinical case management and the provision of whatever support is needed by clients (described previously as PACT). The expanded broker model stresses linkage to community resources, the personal strengths model works to improve patient quality of life and functioning based on existing strengths, the rehabilitation model aims to remedy deficits and overcome barriers, and the full support model attempts to reduce symptomatology and improve functioning. Clearly, there are overlapping functions; no hard and fast lines are drawn between models. These approaches differ chiefly in their underlying program philosophy.

Weil (1985) identifies seven case management models for human services programs (either for children or adults) as most promising. They may utilize professionals, paraprofessionals, and/or nonprofessionals. These models are as follows: the *generalist/service broker model*, the *primary therapist model*, the *interdisciplinary team model*, the *comprehensive service center model*, the *family as case manager model*, the *supportive care model*, and the *volunteer as case manager model*.

In the generalist/service broker model, the case manager is a professional such as a nurse, social worker, psychologist, rehabilitation counselor, or other specially trained individual who is responsible for service coordination for a client. In the *primary therapist* model, the case manager is usually a psychologist, psychiatrist, or social worker with a master's degree in social work whose relationship to the client is primarily therapeutic. Case management functions are undertaken as an extension of the therapeutic intervention. The *interdisciplinary team model* combines the activities of specialists to provide case management functions according to each person's area of expertise. In some of these models, one team member assumes primary responsibility for guiding the client through the service system. In the *comprehensive service center* model, full services are provided including social and emotional support, education and training, and residential facilities. The center typically provides basic services and linkage to the services of other agencies. The *family as case manager model* uses family members as case managers. In some models, the family is linked in a professional/parental relationship and given training in case management processes, including treatment planning and service coordination. Weil (1985) maintains that what is needed is service coordination and advocacy partnership among clients, families, and professional case managers. The *supportive care* model uses citizens in rural (and, occasionally, inner-city) areas to deliver mental health services and to provide linkage to community supports. Workers are paid to perform these services and are trained by local human services agencies, which retain legal and program obligations. Finally, in the *volunteer as case manager* model, volunteers assist clients under the supervision of those who are legally responsible after receiving professional training. Each model may be implemented in a range from minimal to full-scale comprehensive service systems.

Willenbring and colleagues (1990) discuss several other dimensions of case management that should be considered as important descriptors of service models. These dimensions are: intensity and duration of treatment, focus of services, availability (e.g., 24 hours per day), site (office vs. community-based), consumer direction, training, authority, and structure. It may be useful, for the purposes of clarifying the field and for research, to develop a schematic that describes models in terms of functions and dimensions. Progress in this area is now being reported in the adult case management research literature. The Weil (1985) approach to classifying models appears to be more useful for children than that of Robinson and Toff-Bergman (1989). Weil's approach is more comprehensive and flexible than that of Robinson and Toff-Bergmann, which is based on existing adult models. In addition, functions and dimensions specified by Willenbring and colleagues might be adapted to child-specific models based on Weil's approach.

The following research questions about child models are very much at a descriptive level, suggesting a need to survey and classify models currently in use:

• Can adult models of case management be adapted for children and youth, or will well-delineated child models emerge?

- How do case management models vary for different developmental stages and conditions?
- To what extent does the choice of model adopted depend on the context of the service system or systems in which it is embedded?

Organization and Service System Context

There is no single system of care for children with SED, either nationally or at a state level; rather there are a multiplicity of agencies, service providers, and patterns of service provision. Case management has been suggested as both a means to coordinate services and a means to create services when they are absent. Although it is clear that the characteristics of the service system will influence the organization of case management (Knitzer, 1982; Lourie & Isaacs, 1988; Weil, 1985), that issue is not addressed in this chapter.

Four questions identify the major research issues related to the organizational context of case management for children. They are as follows:

- *Auspices*—Which agency should be responsible for the provision of case management? The school system, social services, juvenile justice, mental health, and general health agencies are all potential candidates for the provision for case management services. Federal, state, and local agencies' mandates will influence the locus of responsibility for case management, and this is likely to vary by state.
- *Location*—Does the case management function belong within the service organization or outside of it? If it is placed within the service organization, there is the risk that advocacy needs will go unmet because of the potential of co-opting the case manager. If placed outside the organization, advocacy and brokerage needs can more easily be met, but the lack of proximity between the case manager and the service organization may weaken coordination of services.
- *Team or individual*—Is case management more effective when its functions are distributed among members of a team or when functions are unified and assumed by one individual? For example, in the Robert Wood Johnson Child Program in North Carolina, interagency teams of service providers are assuming responsibility for case management. Under one condition, a case manager is specifically designated; under the second condition, case management functions are assumed by the team members. Case management functions are being documented for all team

members to determine whether the presence or absence of a designated case manager influences the delivery of case management functions by other team members; client- and system-level outcomes are being assessed and compared.

• *Authority*—What is the status of case managers, and what authority do they have? What is the source of their authority? In some models, such as the Alaska Youth Initiative, case managers make decisions about spending flexible funds for individual clients. Are case managers expected to make treatment decisions? Do they control client placement? How much real "clout" do they have (Schwartz, Goldman, & Churgin, 1982)?

Implementation Practices

The number of clients per case manager (caseload size), the intensity of contact between client and case manager, and the duration of treatment are important parameters in the practice of case management. The client, the service provider, and the service system are affected by variation in implementation of these parameters. Being able to estimate these parameters is important for planning and setting standards necessary to ensure quality of care. An empirical base that links practice to outcomes is essential. The only preliminary data available on these parameters are from Louisiana, where child and adult case management services were compared. These findings indicate a need for a smaller number of clients per case manager, greater intensity, and longer duration for children than for adults (Lemoine et al., 1993).

Number of Clients   Case manager-to-client ratios may vary from 1:10 to 1:75, although the usual ratio is probably around 1:30; however, optimum numbers may be in the area of 1:15. The severity of client needs obviously effects the potential number of clients per case manager. This number will clearly influence the amount of out-of-office time available for outreach and coordination activities. The relationships among number of clients, intensity, severity, and functions require very careful examination.

Intensity   The frequency of contact between case managers and clients varies. It may range from very frequent contact (e.g., daily, with 24-hour availability during crises) to quarterly contact. In most situations, client plans require updating monthly; therefore, this becomes the minimum.

Duration   For adults with chronic mental illness, it is expected that case management services will extend throughout the lifetime of the client. Similarly, adults with developmental disabilities also may need lifetime support. For children and youth with SED, the necessary duration of case management services is not clear, but it is likely to be long term. Although the intensity of service needs may decrease over time, the importance of provider continuity mandates an ongoing relationship. Changing developmental needs of the client and his or her family may influence case management functions in the transitional process to adult status. Research needs to be directed toward these areas.

The following questions need to be addressed:

- Is there an optimum caseload size? Does it vary according to client, service provider, and system needs?
- How often should clients be seen and what factors influence this?
- How are the number of clients and intensity of contact related?
- Is there evidence to support more effective outcomes from more frequent contact?
- Over what time period will case management services be needed (e.g., only during high-risk episodes), or should the duration depend on the level of client functioning?

Qualifications of Case Managers

The level of training and skill required to carry out the case management role will influence the functions a case manager can handle and the degree of autonomy that can be assumed. Some persons argue that the case manager should be the most highly skilled member of the clinical team, preferably psychologists or psychiatrists (Lamb, 1980). More often, case managers are trained as nurses, social workers, and mental health aides; some are nonprofessionals, such as volunteers and consumers. For children with SED, family involvement in providing case management is strongly suggested by Friesen and Koroloff (1990). Educational backgrounds of case managers may vary from less than a high school diploma to a master's degree, M.D., or Ph.D. Often the case manager is a mental health counselor with a bachelor of arts degree who has developed a range of skills through experience. A Joint Commission on Accreditation of Healthcare Organizations (JCAHO)(Fisher & Weisman, 1989) volume on case management links diversity in professional background to specific clinical settings (e.g., master's-level social workers are most frequently found in private geriatric settings, but family members are utilized as case managers in a rehabilitation service setting for severe head injuries).

It is not clear what level of professional training is needed to handle case management functions or whether any professional or nonprofessional group is fully prepared to respond to the wide range of needs of children with mental disabilities. At one level an ability to communicate authority is required in order to negotiate successfully for resources. Alternatively, transportation and household assistance, sometimes identified as case management functions, require a different level of skill. Mental health professionals trained to value office-based long-term psychotherapy often find it difficult to reach out to children in their homes and the community and may view case management as a low-status role.

An alternative to trained professionals is the trained consumer or the parent of the child who acts as a *de facto* case manager when such services are not available. The parent/consumer has the advantage of knowing what needs to be done, but may not have the skills to negotiate with the service system. Bush (1988) suggests that service providers should train the client and his or her family in the knowledge and techniques necessary for evaluation and self-advocacy. The Rural Efforts to Assist Children at Home (REACH) project in north central Florida offered a curriculum on case management for family caregivers of children with chronic illnesses. Participants in the project learned the skills necessary to provide continuous technical and psychosocial care, becoming semi-independent case managers. In this program, professional case managers maintain ultimate responsibility for service plan management, but their role becomes one of consultant to the family caregiver (Pierce & Freedman, 1988). Ongoing training and education may be required at all levels, by advanced professionals and nonprofessionals, in order to meet both client and system needs.

These questions must be addressed:

- What level of professional training is needed to become a case manager?
- What skills are needed by nonprofessionals to perform case management functions?

Financing

Case management has been seen as a way to coordinate and deliver fragmented services in an efficient and cost-effective manner. Although a growing research base examines the economic benefits of case management for adults with chronic mental illness (Taube et al., 1990), no outcome studies of case management services for children have yet been reported. Since multiple agencies usually serve the needs of children with SED, it may be difficult to identify the costs of case management functions directly. Neither the federal nor state mental health data bases provide sufficient information (Knitzer, 1982).

In some instances, case managers are responsible for authorizing and arranging for mental health services under fee-for-service and prepaid capitated arrangements. For the growing number of children and adolescents who have SED and who have Medicaid coverage, the Medicaid program can be used to finance coordination of services (Fox & Wicks, 1991). Insurance coverage of case management for children with serious SED is not currently available under most commercial policies. Thus, it may be worthwhile to examine briefly how Medicaid coverage can be used for this population as commercial carriers might follow Medicaid policies in the future.

Since 1986, case management services have been covered by Medicaid. Broadly defined, the case management benefit may be used to assist eligible individuals to gain access to needed medical, social, educational, and other services. States may target these services to high-risk population groups, such as children in need of mental health treatment (e.g., children who have SED). Furthermore, states may, by specific exception, designate in their Medicaid plan amendment the particular types of service providers that will be permitted to become qualified (e.g., certain community mental health centers [CMHCs], state-operated agencies, schools, hospital outpatient departments). Health Care Financing Administration (HCFA) approval requires that the recipients' free choice among service providers not be restricted, that they cannot be forced to accept case management services, and that they may not be denied access to any other services available under the state Medicaid plan.

As of May 1991, nearly one half of the states (21) had established a targeted case management benefit to permit reimbursement for coordination of a wide range of services for children and youth with SEDs (Fox, Wicks, McManus, & Kelly, 1991). According to their survey, two thirds of the 21 states reimburse targeted case management services without a limit and more than one half have a reimbursement rate that falls between $25 and $50 an hour. Most states require that individual case managers have a minimum of a bachelor's degree and some relevant experience. A few states establish separate criteria for different case management functions (i.e., a master's degree is stipulated for assessing clients' needs and designing a care plan, but a bachelor's degree is adequate for arranging and monitoring service delivery).

Fox and Wicks (1991) estimate that approximately 450,000 children with SED were enrolled in Medicaid in 1989 and that numbers will increase substantially over the next 10 years as a result of the Omnibus Budget Reconciliation Act (OBRA) of 1990. The implementation of Medicaid's Early and Periodic Screening, Diagnosis, and Treatment (EPSDT) program can establish a model of an effective and rational financing approach for this population. Clearly, not all the children with SED in need of case management services are Medicaid eligible or are all nontherapeutic interventions (i.e., educational or vocational services) covered for those that are eligible. Multiple funding sources will continue to be needed. (See Fox & Wicks, 1991, and Fox et al., 1991, for a more complete description of Medicaid options available to the states.)

Questions to be examined include the following:

- What is the cost of treatment with and without case management or with different models of case management?
- How do costs of case management vary by diagnosis and developmental stage?
- How will Medicaid reimbursement policies influence the functions of case management (e.g., lack of coverage for direct assistance)?
- Under capitated approaches to financing services, to what extent can case managers assume expected functions such as advocacy?
- To what extent will case management of high-risk youth result in reduced expenditures for institutional care?

RESEARCH STRATEGIES

Although it appears that research on child case management services has a long way to go, it can move much faster than the adult research on case management as key events overshadow developments in the field. The definitional issues identified in the previous sections will be resolved by rapidly moving policy. Regulations relating to reimbursement with Medicaid coverage now under development will quickly determine the types of functions and service providers to be covered. Definitions of target populations and specifications for case management services are likely with the further implementation of PL 99-660 and other legislation. Research demonstrations of case management that are underway should begin to inform mental health service providers and researchers about current practices. Very active efforts to develop formal training programs (e.g., Weil's curriculum developed for the North Carolina Department of Mental Health, Substance Abuse, and Developmental Disabilities) will add an important qualitative dimension and begin to establish standards as well.

From a research perspective, keeping the research moving faster than policy developments is critical, so that research can in fact inform policy decisions. Extensive resources are going to be utilized in the absence of an empirical knowledge base because of faith in case management as an answer to the myriad of child service system problems. If case management does not succeed in solving these problems, the risk is that it will be discarded just as other approaches have been historically dismissed (e.g., the child guidance movement). A lack of treatment resources may be the issue that no amount of case management will resolve. Thus, well-considered research that carefully addresses the full spectrum of issues is essential. This may require employing the traditional evaluation paradigm of structure, process, and outcome.

Structure

From a structural perspective, objectives as specified in the adult literature do not appear to be controversial, but do need to be linked to concepts of a continuum of care for children and their families. The debate about functions is largely in the arena of whether to combine case management with other clinical functions and this, unfortunately, may be significantly influenced by reimbursement policies. Specification of models awaits, to some extent, clearer specification of functions and awaits gaining experience with multiple models and testing their effectiveness. The issues of organization and service system context bear examination but, independent of research findings, will be heavily influenced by local preference. However, more extensive information on issues, such as the benefits or problems with contracting for case management services, would be useful. Organizational issues, such as whether case management services are based in schools, in social services agencies, or mental health services agencies, will have important implications for which children are served and how services are paid for. Determining the qualifications of staff to provide case management is a structural issue that requires experimentation before decisions about reimbursement close the door on either well-trained graduate clinicians or family members and consumers. A survey research approach is appropriate to begin documenting the preceding parameters, exemplified in a state-level survey of case management by Jacobs (1992).

Process

Process issues relate to how services are provided and how they are paid for. The "how" of case management provision was labeled "implementation practices" earlier. Number of clients per case manager, intensity, and duration are highly interrelated and cannot be defined *a priori*. Experience with carefully defining each parameter and then comparing alternative definitions represents a first step toward understanding the relationship between number of clients and intensity of services. It will be essential to move beyond this to examine the influence of mixed clientele on related issues of case manager burnout and child and family satisfaction.

The financing of case management services carries a high priority for close scrutiny. As implied, financing policy cannot only *define* an intervention, but it also can bring services into, or put them out of, existence. Recent progress in obtaining reimbursement (under Medicaid) for case management merits significant attention to utilization patterns under such reimbursed services. Monitoring the quality of case management services constitutes an initial evaluation activity. As expenditures for case management increase, alternatives to fee-for-service reimbursement are needed and will be sought (i.e., the HCFA 1915[a] and [b] capitated demonstrations); therefore, preparing for research on this topic is urgent.

Outcome

The third stage of research, assessing outcomes, investigates the effectiveness of case management interventions at client and system levels. Assuming significant progress in specifying the structural and process aspects of case management and any of the preceding descriptors of case management (e.g., functions, models, qualifications of case managers) might appropriately be proposed for an assessment of impact on outcomes, as all are candidates for research. However, since the potential for research is wide open and the need for information is great, finding a prudent beginning place is relevant. The question is where to set the priorities in terms of potential payoff.

If the most encompassing concept to investigate was selected, it might be models of case management. In the same way that psychotherapy has been researched, types of psychotherapy (e.g., cognitive vs. interpersonal) are identified and contrasted, while carefully specifying the structural and process variables for each type of psychotherapy. Although clearly more complex than psychotherapy research because of the service system factors (e.g., effect of availability of other mental health services), the notion of models that can be "manualized" is appealing. This approach has been taken in one large-scale, randomized trial of three models of case management in New York State (Armstrong & Evans, 1992.) In this trial, intensive case management is compared with family-based treatment and with family-centered intensive case management. In another randomized trial within the Robert Wood Johnson Foundation Program for children in North Carolina, the use of an interagency team as case manager is compared with an interagency team that has a case manager added to it, and case management functions will be carefully identified in each condition (Behar, Morrissey, Burns, Angold, and Costello are the investigators). Extensive client- and system-level outcomes are being assessed in both studies.

Studies such as the two previously identified require significant resources and a very high level of cooperation. The minimum essentials include: 1) a large enough sample for sufficient power to detect differences; 2) a sufficient intervention and follow-up period for the intervention to have an effect; 3) adequate resources to implement the intervention; 4) a state-of-the-art comparison condition to avoid violating ethical considerations about withholding treatment; 5) standardized measures (including costs) for evaluating client (see Joyner, 1992, for a set of outcome indicators) and system outcomes; and 6) a services environment that is highly supportive of research and strong enough to handle the risks involved.

As case management research procedures become more sophisticated, additional considerations will emerge, such as examining the effects of a case management model for specific target populations or measuring cost shifting (Taube et al., 1990). Later stages of research can accomplish important tasks, such as examining cost effectiveness and taking models apart to determine which components are essential to improve client functioning.

CONCLUSION

Research on case management for children and adolescents and their families is timely and multifaceted. There are exciting opportunities for researchers who want to work with public sector agencies on issues that can influence the quality of life of children and their families. Research at multiple levels (e.g., structural, process, outcome) will be requested as accountability is demanded for this growing mental health intervention and as policy makers seek answers about reasonable and effective courses to take. Progress will be incremental initially as the basic parameters of case management within a continuum of care are spelled out. More descriptive studies are required initially to better define structural and process aspects of case management. Such studies can then be followed by clinical trials of case management models that assess client- and system-level outcomes. If research strategies are borrowed from the adult case management literature, breakthroughs for children could come quickly.

REFERENCES

Armstrong, M.I., & Evans, M.E. (1992). Three intensive community-based programs for children and youth with serious emotional disturbance and their families. *Journal of Child and Family Studies, 1,* 61–74.

Beachler, M. (1990). The mental health services program for youth. *Journal of Mental Health Administration, 17,* 115–121.

Behar, L. (1985). Changing patterns of state responsibility: A case study of North Carolina. *Journal of Clinical Child Psychology, 14,* 188–195.

Berkowitz, G., Halfon, N., & Klee, L. (1992). Improving access to health care: Case management for vulnerable children. *Social Work in Health Care, 17,* 101–123.

Bond, G.R., Miller, L.D., Krumwied, R.D., & Ward, R.S. (1988). Assertive case management in three CMHCs: A controlled study. *Hospital and Community Psychiatry, 39,* 411–418.

Brown, J. (1989). Case management and services for other at-risk children and youth. In *Children's mental health services and policy: Building a research base,* Second annual conference proceedings (pp. 138–141). Tampa: Research and Training Center for Children's Mental Health, Florida Mental Health Institute, University of South Florida.

Bush, G.W. (1988). A family member looks at catastrophic case management. In K. Fisher & E. Weisman (Eds.), *Case management: Guiding patients through the health care maze* (pp. 39–44). Chicago: Joint Commission on Accreditation of Healthcare Organizations.

Community Mental Health Services Act, PL 88-164. (October 31, 1963). Title 42, U.S.C. 2689 et seq: *U.S. Statutes at Large, 77,* 290–294.

Dowrick, P.W. (1989). Alaska Youth Initiative. In *Children's mental health services and policy: Building a research base,* Second annual conference proceedings. Tampa: Research and Training Center for Children's Mental Health, Florida Mental Health Institute, University of South Florida.

Education for All Handicapped Children Act of 1975, PL 94-142. (August 23, 1977). Title 20, U.S.C. 1401 et seq: *U.S. Statutes at Large, 89,* 773–796.

Education of the Handicapped Act Amendments of 1986, PL 99-457. (October 8, 1986). Title 20 U.S.C. 1400 et seq: *U.S. Statutes at Large, 100,* 1145–1177.

Evans, M.E., Armstrong, M.I., Huz, S., & Dollard, N. (1993, March 2). *Preliminary outcomes for children with serious emotional disturbance in two community-based service programs.* Presented at the sixth annual research conference of the Research and Training Center for Children's Mental Health, University of South Florida, Tampa.

Fisher, K., 7 Weisman, E. (Eds.). (1989). *Case management: Guiding patients through the health care maze.* Chicago: Joint Commission on Accreditation of Healthcare Organizations.

Fox, H.B., & Wicks, L.B. (1991, June). *Financing care coordination services for severely emotionally disturbed children and adolescents: How Medicaid can be used.* [Report prepared by Fox Health Policy Consultants, Inc., for the Research Foundation for Mental Hygiene, Inc., partly funded by the Child and Adolescent Service System Program of the National Institute of Mental Health].

Fox, H.B., Wicks, L.N., McManus, M.A., & Kelly, R.W. (1991). *Medicaid financing for mental health and substance abuse services for children and adoles-*

cents. [Technical Assistance Series No. 2, Financing Subseries, Volume I. PHS ADAMHA OTI]. Rockville, MD: U.S. Department of Health and Human Services. (DHHS Publication No. [ADM] 91-1743).

Franklin, J.L., Solovitz, B., Mason, M., Clemons, J.R., & Miller, G.E. (1987). An evaluation of case management. *American Journal of Public Health, 77,* 674–678.

Friesen, B.J., & Koroloff, N.M. (1990). Family-centered services: Implications for mental health administration and research. *Journal of Mental Health Administration, 17,* 13–15.

Goering, P.N., Wasylenki, D.A., Farkas, M., Lance, W.J., & Ballantyne, R. (1988). What difference does case management make? *Hospital and Community Psychiatry, 39,* 272–276.

Hargreaves, W.A., & Shumway, M. (1989). Effectiveness of services for the severely mentally ill. In C.A. Taube, D. Mechanic, & A. Hohmann (Eds.), *The future of mental health services research.* (DHHS Publication No. [ADM] 89-1600). Washington, DC: Superintendent of Documents, U.S. Government Printing Office.

Harris, M., & Bergman, H.C. (1988). Misconceptions about use of case management services by the chronic mentally ill: A utilization analysis. *Hospital and Community Psychiatry, 39,* 1276–1280.

Intagliata, J. (1982). Improving the quality of community care for the chronically mentally disabled: The role of case management. *Schizophrenia Bulletin, 8,* 655–674.

Jacobs, D.F. (1992). Children's case management state level survey. In *A system of care for children's mental health: Expanding the research base,* Fifth annual conference proceedings (pp. 315–322). Tampa: Research and Training Center for Children's Mental Health, Florida Mental Health Institute, University of South Florida.

Joint Commission on the Accreditation of Hospitals. (1979). *Principles for accreditation of community mental health service programs.* Chicago: Author.

Jordan, D.D., & Hernandez, M. (1990). The Ventura planning model: A proposal for mental health care reform. *The Journal of Mental Health Administration, 17,* 26–47.

Joyner, J.I. (1992). A method to assess client progress in a case management agency. In *A system of care for children's mental health: Expanding the research base,* Fifth annual conference proceedings (pp. 323–334. Tampa: Research and Training Center for Children's Mental Health, Florida Mental Health Institute, University of South Florida.

Kaufman, J. (1992). Case management services for children with special health care needs. *Journal of Case Management, 1,* 53–56.

Knitzer, J. (1982). *Unclaimed children.* Washington, DC: Children's Defense Fund.

Lamb, H.R. (1980). Therapist-case managers: More than brokers of service. *Hospital and Community Psychiatry, 31,* 762–764.

Lemoine, R.L., Speier, T., Ellzey, S., Balson, P., Dumas, T.D., & Shervington, W.W. (1993, March 2). *Case management services for children and adolescents with severe emotional disturbance: A state-wide analysis of service utilization patterns and outcomes.* Presented at the sixth annual research conference of the Research and Training center for Children's Mental Health, University of South Florida, Tampa.

Looney, J.G. (1988). The struggle for a strategy. In J.G. Looney (Ed.), *Chronic mental illness in children and adolescents* (pp. 237–260). Washington, DC: American Psychiatric Press.

Lourie, I.S., & Isaacs, M.R. (1988). Problems and solutions in the public sector. In J.G. Looney (Ed.), *Chronic mental illness in children and adolescents* (pp. 109–130). Washington, DC: American Psychiatric Press.

Omnibus Health Act, PL 99-660. (November 14, 1986). Title 42, U.S.C. 300x et seq: *U.S. Statutes at Large, 100,* 3794–3797.

Pierce, P.M., & Freedman, S.A. (1988). The REACH Project: Training in case management. In K. Fisher & E. Weisman (Eds.) *Case management: Guiding patients through the health care maze* (pp. 65–70). Chicago: Joint Commission on Accreditation of Healthcare Organizations.

Robinson, G.K., & Toff-Bergman, G. (1989). *Choices in case management: Current knowledge and practice for mental health programs.* [Prepared under Contract No. 278-87-0026, Institute of Mental Health, Department of Health and Human Services].

Rubin, A. (1992). Is case management effective for people with serious mental illness? A research review. *Health and Social Work, 17,* 138–150.

Schwartz, S.R., Goldman, H.H., & Churgin, S. (1982). Case management for the chronically mentally ill: Models and dimensions. *Hospital and Community Psychiatry, 33,* 1006–1009.

Singer, J., & Butler, J. (1987). The Education for All Handicapped Children Act: Schools as agents of social reform. *Harvard Educational Review, 57,* 125–152.

Stein, L.I., & Test, M.A. (1980). Alternative to mental hospital treatment: I. Conceptual model, treatment program, and clinical evaluation. *Archives of General Psychiatry, 37,* 392–397.

Stroul, B.A., & Friedman, R.M. (1986). *A system of care for severely emotionally disturbed children and youth.* Washington, DC: Georgetown University Child Development Center.

Stroul, B.A., & Friedman, R.M. (1988). Caring for severely emotionally disturbed children and youth. Principles for a system of care. *Children Today, 17,* 11–15.

Taube, C.A., Morlock, L., Burns, B.J., & Santos, A.B. (1990). New directions in research on assertive community treatment. *Hospital and Community Psychiatry, 41,* 642–647.

Weil, M. (1985). Key components in providing efficient and effective services. In M. Weil & J.M. Karls (Eds.), *Case management in human service practice: A systematic approach to mobilizing resources for clients* (pp. 29–71). San Francisco: Jossey-Bass.

Weil, M., & Karls, J.M. (1985). Historical origins and recent developments. In M. Weil & J.M. Karls (Eds.), *Case management in human service practice: A systematic approach to mobilizing resources for clients* (pp. 1-28). San Francisco: Jossey-Bass.

Weisbrod, B.A., Test, M.A., & Stein, L.I. (1980). Alternative to mental hospital treatment: II. Economic benefit-cost analysis. *Archives of General Psychiatry, 37,* 400–405.

Willenbring, M.L., Ridgely, M.S., Stinchfield, R., & Rose, M. (1990). *Application of case management in alcohol and drug dependence: Matching techniques and populations.* [Report submitted for NIAAA contract #89MF00933901D.]

States' Policy Response to the Need for Case Management

Deborah Franks Jacobs

Case management, or service coordination, for children and youth with serious emotional disorders and their families has been developing across the United States through the combined efforts of families, advocates, and legislative mandates, such as the State Mental Health Services Comprehensive Plan (in the Omnibus Health Act, PL 99-660), which requires all states to develop mental health plans that include case management services, and ADAMHA Reorganization Act (PL 102-321), which requires states to provide case management for persons using "substantial amounts of public resources." The Child and Adolescent Service System Program (CASSP) at the National Institute of Mental Health (NIMH) to advance child mental health services has also been a major contributor to the impetus for change. The CASSP program is now part of the newly created Substance Abuse Mental Health Services Administration (SAMHSA).

An increasing awareness of the need to span, or bridge, service arenas and treatment programs to ensure that youths do not fall between the cracks of a complex web of services as spawned a variety of demonstration, pilot, and model programs that show great promise. However, it is still clear that when it comes to viewing case management development from the national perspective "all is not well throughout the land." There appears to be an enormous variation in the quality, quantity, and availability of service coordination, in part because there is also still considerable controversy as to how

---

Although the term *coordination* has become the more acceptable term in this area, most states still refer to *case management* when discussing policy issues. For the purposes of this chapter, the two terms are used interchangeably.

The author wishes to acknowledge Trevor Hadley, Ph.D., and Martin McGurrin, Ph.D., of the University of Pennsylvania for the development of this study for the adult population and Dr. Hadley's contribution to the analysis of the child version of the study.

to define case management as a unique service differentiated from clinical or other treatment services. A result is that youths receiving case management in different cities may have access to very different types of assistance, despite their similar needs.

Given this state of affairs, a study was envisioned to explore, in detail, what the states were doing with regard to case management services. This study was undertaken while the author was on an NIMH postdoctoral research fellowship, sponsored by the National Association of State Mental Health Program Directors (NASMHPD) at the University of Pennsylvania, Department of Psychiatry, and the Commonwealth of Pennsylvania Children's Bureau of the Office of Mental Health. The study was an unfunded project that augmented an existing project that focused on the adult case management service system.

The purpose of this policy-level survey was to collect and analyze data on the nature of state-level implementation of case management services for children across the United States from a systems and organizational framework. The goal was not only to describe what is happening in the states on a policy level but also to evaluate any trends in development and the factors that may be influencing these trends. This information may assist in telling us the current stages of case management development, as well as where it is headed and how it may be guided to most effectively serve children with serious emotional disorders and their families.

THE SURVEY INSTRUMENT AND PROCESS

The survey focused on five major areas of the case management concept. They are as follows:

1. Concept/model issues regarding uniform definitions of case management, changes in definitions, eligibility requirements and referral processes, and organizational placement of case management in the larger service system
2. Staff issues including number of case manager positions required, funded, filled, and projected in the next fiscal year (i.e., what agencies employ the case managers, number of clients, productivity standards, and turnover rates)
3. Funding issues such as reimbursement/funding sources, methods of allocation, state budget for case management, costs per case manager, and changes in funding patterns
4. Human resources development issues, which included qualifications or classification system, salary range, and training packages

5. Collaboration issues regarding the nature and extent of cross-systems relationships with other public child-serving agencies

These questions focused on state-level policies and practices that facilitated integration and coordination across child-serving systems.

The major source of information for this survey was a telephone interview with a senior state-level policy staffperson whose primary responsibility was child and adolescent service development. In larger states, this tended to be a person in the children's division of the mental health authority who specialized in case management or CASSP activities in general. In smaller states, it was frequently a child specialist or, occasionally, a case management specialist who was responsible for both adult and child services. A secondary source of data for this study was the PL 99-660 plans submitted by the states to NIMH as required by federal law. These state mental health plans are supposed to have specific defining and describing case management services, with, as of 1991, a distinct section for children and adolescents.

Data were collected from 35 states in the survey. Initial efforts were made to contact all 50 states, but the time and funds available for the study and difficulty accessing key informants precluded collection of adequate information from all states. The 35 states for which complete data were obtained represent all geographic regions of the continental United States.

Three of the states in the survey were described by the state informant as having consolidated or integrated systems in which children's mental health services had been placed under an umbrella family and children's agency, including child welfare and various other child and family services depending on the state. These states tended to have difficulty responding to the survey when the questions were directed specifically at the mental health system of services and, thus, were removed from the analysis for the systems analysis. They were included in the systems coordination analysis since the cross-systems coordination issues appeared to be more salient to states that had implemented sweeping structural changes in the ways that they served children and their families.

FINDINGS OF CASE MANAGEMENT SYSTEMS

Definitions and Structure

The elements in this section of the study focused on definitions of case management, specific eligibility requirements, target populations, and forms of case management. The large majority of the 35 states did report uniform definitions of case management that were generally accepted throughout the state's mental health system. However, many states did not have general agreement on the concepts of other child-serving systems, such as child welfare or juvenile justice. This appears to be an issue for future development.

More than one half of the states had more than one kind of case management for various target populations. A common example of the variation might be the following: Children and youth who have serious emotional disorders could receive an intensive form of service that involves a full range of case management services on a frequent basis, including such activities as advocacy, crisis intervention, brokering, assessment, and service planning. Other children from lower priority groups within the mental health system received less comprehensive or intensive forms of service coordination that primarily offer monitoring and annual service plan updates.

Eligibility requirements for services were in place in more than three fourths of the states in the study; however, the level of specificity and restrictiveness varied considerably across states. Some states have very refined definitions of serious emotional disorders that drive eligibility for case management, while other states have not yet adopted any policy-level definition of this target population. Some states include out-of-home placement, psychiatric hospitalization, or imminent risk of placement or hospitalization as eligibility criteria for specific types of case management services. To qualify for intensive forms of case management, the child or youth in most states must be involved with at least two child-serving agencies and have a *DSM-IV* (American Psychiatric Association, 1994) diagnosis. Unlike many adult programs that specify diagnostic categories in the eligibility standards, the majority of children's policymakers seemed to be aware of the variability in childhood diagnoses and the need to be inclusive rather than exclusive on this criteria. Table 20.1 shows the percentage of states reporting various structural elements of their case management policy.

Funding of Services

Funding for case management/service coordination services was reported as coming from two primary sources: federal Medicaid dollars and state mental health dollars. Eighty-three percent of the states had some form of Medicaid reimbursement for case management services. Fox and Wicks (1991) have detailed these financing options on a state-by-state basis. The most frequent form of Medicaid funding is through the targeted case management program that permits a state to provide Medicaid-reimbursable case management services to a specific group of Medicaid recipients as defined in a

Table 20.1. Structural elements of state case management systems ($n = 35$)

Element	Yes (%)	No (%)	Unknown/other (%)
Uniform definition	74	20[a]	6
Different types/target groups	57	43	0
Eligibility requirements/prior-ity groups	77	14	9
Use state funds	63	20	17
Medicaid funded	83	17	0
State employees	29	—	—
Private agency employees	66	—	—
County employees	26	—	—

[a]Three of the seven states have consolidated mental health with other child-serving agencies.

state Medicaid plan amendment. In the case of many states, the first group targeted was a group of adults with serious and persistent mental illness; children's services were implemented more slowly and often, apparently, as an afterthought. This left the service inappropriately defined for the younger target population. Approximately 20% of the states still include case management in the "bundled" package of services required to be offered by the community mental health centers to clients. This method makes it impossible to accurately track case management services or Medicaid spending on case management as a separate service.

Slightly fewer than two thirds of the states provided state dollars to fund services for clients who were not Medicaid eligible. At the time of data collection, in 1991, three particularly resource-poor states were reported as eager to utilize Medicaid funding for targeted case management but were not able to apply for a Medicaid plan amendment because they did not have state dollars available to provide matching funds (i.e., the state share of Medicaid payments). This left non-Medicaid clients in those states without access to case management services unless the family could pay the full cost of the service.

Service Providers

Case management services were reported as provided by three main types of employment: state employees, private agency employees, or county employees. Private agency staff, under contract to a governmental body, was the most frequent type of arrangement reported. Some states had more than one type of arrangement for staff employment depending on geographic location or whether the programs were pilots or demonstrations. States with traditionally strong county-run mental health systems were likely to have county employees serving as case managers. Some western states, which frequently have state-operated community and institutional systems, were likely to have state employees as a predominant staffing arrangement.

The organizational entity in which case managers were employed took on various forms both within and across states. As can be seen in Table 20.2, the single most common placement of case management services was in community mental health centers that were usually organized as private nonprofit entities. The second most frequent arrangement, or location of case managers, was a combination of several options including other private agencies, community mental health centers (CMHCs), and county mental health programs (states could report more than one arrangement). This option appears to allow flexibility to local authorities in their implementation of case management services. Five states have dedicated case management units within another organizational structure.

Number of Clients and Staff

A major issue in understanding the extent to which case management is implemented focused on the number of case managers serving children and youth within each state. Only 40%, or 14, of the states surveyed could report a specific number of case managers for this population of children and youth with serious emotional disorders. The unavailability of data may be significant in itself. The states that were unable to provide specific numbers of staff had service providers with both adults and children as clients who had mental disabilities and/or mental retardation, or had locally run ser-

Table 20.2. Organizational placement of case management

Location of case managers	Number of states
Community mental health centers	9
County mental health programs	5
Dedicated case management units	5
Other (non-CMHC) private agencies	5
CASSP project staff	2
Area mental health staff	1
Combination of above	8

CASSP, Child and Adolescent Service System Program; CMHC, community mental health center.

vices that were not required to report such specific information to the state mental health authority. The average number of children's case managers was 47 for states that could provide this information. The range of case managers reported from 15 to 150 did not appear to be directly associated with the population of the state (i.e., large states were not necessarily the states with high numbers of children's case managers), but more likely reflect the developmental level of the system. These data are reported in Table 20.3.

The number of clients is another important factor in understanding the implementation of case management or service coordination services. Less clients obviously permit service providers to spend more time per case, but may also require the service provider to perform a larger range of services. Case management services were grouped into the category of general (regular) or intensive (specialized) for the purpose of this analysis, although states used a variety of names for these generic types. General case management tended to include little more than assessment, monitoring, annual service plan updates, and some brokering. Intensive services included a full range of functions including support for families and other assistance with life needs such as transportation and support for involvement with community activities. The number of clients was much higher with a mean of 29 and a range of up to 80 children and families per service provider. Intensive services had a significantly lower mean of 15, with some extremely specialized services having only two families as clients at any one time. These latter services tended to be demonstration or pilot programs that went well beyond the brokering functions of case management and entailed clinical treatment services of an intensive nature. In these services, the service coordination functions could not clearly be differentiated from the treatment services.

Table 20.3. Characteristics of case management systems

Case managers per state
  Mean 47
  Range 15–150
Number of clients per case manager
  Regular
    Mean 29
    Range 10–80
  Specialized
    Mean 15
    Range 2–40

Creating a Schema of Case Management Development

Using the previously discussed data, a schema for rating states in their development of case management systems was created. Six characteristics of the case management systems were identified that reflected information provided by the state-level policy informants. These characteristics included: 1) statewideness—case management was universally available throughout the state; 2) target group and service definitions—the service itself and the group of eligible children and their families had been formally and specifically defined; 3) state funding—the state contributed mental health dollars to provide case management to nonmedical children; 4) capacity—the state was expanding as compared to contracting or remaining static in the number of children who could be served and the number of service providers available; 5) training—the existence of a formal training program specific to case management (programs specific to child case management were too few to consider in this analysis); and 6) pilots or demonstration projects that were testing methods of case management through the use of funds from the federal government or private foundations, in addition to state funds. Each characteristic was rated on a scale from 0 to 5, with 0 indicating no development and 5 indicating extensive development. Figure 20.1 indicates that 26% ($n = 9$) of states surveyed were assessed to have considerable or extensive development of case management systems based on the previously listed characteristics. The remaining states were in a much lower stage of development.

FINDINGS OF SYSTEMS INTEGRATION DEVELOPMENT

The integration section of the survey focused on the mechanisms and methods for coordinating and/or integrating services across child-serving systems that have been or are being developed in the states. Analysis of the data indicated that six kinds of activities were part of this process. They are as follows: 1) formal interagency agreements on local, regional, and state levels; 2) interagency committees focusing on specific issues of coordination and service enhancement; 3) court orders or legislative mandates that require a state or county government to improve coordination and/or provision of services to children; 4) formalized mechanisms for joint funding of services or "blended funding" (i.e., mental health, child welfare, education); 5) demonstration or pilot programs that incorporate cross-systems service coordination; and 6) the existence of an organizational structure that connects the various child-serving agencies in some kind of formal relationship.

Ratings for the states on each of these characteristics ranged from 0 for no development in this area to 5 for extensive development. The summative ratings indicated that 29% of the 35 states ($n = 10$) surveyed had considerable or extensive development in the area of systems integration or coordination (see Figure 20.1). The remaining 25 states did not demonstrate systems coordination across the range of activities previously described.

Case Management and Systems Integration

After states were rated on each of the individual attributes of case management systems and systems integration, they were assessed to determine the percentage of states that were simultaneously successful at developing case management services and creating mechanisms for integrating child-serving systems. States that were rated high (4–5) on both scales were grouped together. States that were not rated above a 3 (some development) on either scale were grouped together. The bars labeled "neither" and "both" in Figure 20.1 represent these findings. Thirty-four percent ($n = 12$) of states have less than considerable development in both areas. This group represented the largest percentage of the states surveyed as can be seen graphically in Figure 20.1. Only 4 of the 35 states (11%) were

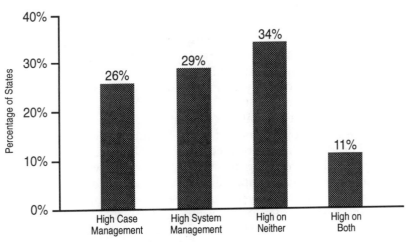

Figure 20.1. States' levels of development.

found to have considerable development on both case management systems and cross-systems integration.

Identification of Factors Influencing States' System Development

Given the varying political and economic climates of the states, it is clear that a wide variety of factors may be contributing to the rate of development of case management services and cross-systems integration or coordination within the states surveyed. State fiscal rises during a national recessionary period may affect start-up increase, as well as system capacity increase. "Turf" issues in state or local bureaucracies may thwart efforts at cross-agency coordination. Political forces may have a strong institutional lobby that slows the process of community services development within the mental health field. Some states have strong family advocacy groups that have an impact on system development. In addition, the "vision" to create a broad-based service continuum may not exist where statewide decisions for system design are made. Many of these issues were mentioned in the phone interviews, but they were not systematically measured in this study.

Two potentially influential factors that could be measured and may be considered proxies for some of these issues were identified. When and if a state had obtained Medicaid reimbursement for case management as a distinct service was the first of these factors. The year that a state received Medicaid approval for case management services was determined from survey information and data from the Fox and Wicks (1991) report. The range in years was from 1986 (the year it was first possible to request a state plan amendment to include case management) to 1992 (the year of the survey). The states were rated on a scale of 0 to 3 with 0 representing no approval requested or received and 1, 2, or 3 representing approval requested or received (early 1986–1988 = 3, mid-1989–1990 = 2, or late 1991–1992 = 1) in terms of the year federal dollars were obtained to pay for case management services.

The year that each state received its first CASSP grant was also used as a proxy for factors that could be influencing state development. These data were obtained from the NIMH CASSP program. States receiving CASSP grants in the beginning years of awards were assumed to have initiated the process of systems change and coordination early. The years of these awards ranged from 1983, when the first awards were granted, to 1990, the last year that 3-year systems development grants were awarded. The states were then grouped in the same fashion as the Medicaid year of implementation. A scale was constructed: 0 for states that had never received a CASSP grant; 1 for late grantees, 1989–1990; 2 for mid-range grantees, 1986–1988; and 3 for states that had been awarded a grant between 1983 and 1985, the first years of the grant awards.

The mean rating (0–5) on the case management and systems integration scales were then analyzed using early and late CASSP and Medicaid states as the groupings and comparing these scores to the mean values for the total sample of 35 states. Table 20.4 indicates the results of this analysis. As can be seen, states that received Medicaid approval earliest (1986–1988) had higher ratings on their case management systems development than did the states as a whole or the later and non-Medicaid states. This would suggest that the infusion of new Medicaid dollars into the system permitted it to expand its service capacity. This form of funding would also increase the extent to which the system is statewide since Medicaid coverage must pertain to the entire state even if a specific population was defined, as in targeted case management.

These states with early Medicaid approval did not, however, have higher scores on systems integration. In fact, their mean scores were the lowest of all the groups. One interpretation of this finding may be that the rigidity of Medicaid rules, which often presume a "medical model," made the cross-systems coordination more complicated to pursue. However, existing data do not permit a definitive explanation for this finding. The states rated highest on the systems integration factor were those that received CASSP grants during the last cycle of funding. Although this finding is counterintuitive given the purpose of CASSP to encourage such action, it may be that those states that were last on the "bandwagon" had benefitted from the experience of the early states' struggles and were able to achieve movement more quickly.

Table 20.4. The effects of Medicaid and CASSP on case management and systems integration development

| | Mean scale values | |
	Case management	Systems integration
Total of all states	**2.7**	**3.7**
Early CASSP	2.9	3.6
Late CASSP	2.3	4.2
Early Medicaid	3.3	3.3
Late Medicaid	2.1	3.9

CASSP, Child and Adolescent Service System Program.

CONCLUSION

This policy-level state survey indicates that action to develop case management systems and cross-systems coordination is occurring in almost every state. It is also quite clear that development is at varying levels of intensity and achievement. These variations result in differential treatment of youths and their families despite commonality of needs. Although it is important for each state to customize services to their community needs, it seems that the lack of consistency represented must not comfort youths and their families who reside in less extensively developed states.

The 1980s was a time of decreased federal involvement in both dollars and influence in regard to the development of state mental health services. Perhaps in the future there will be the recognition of the needs of youths and their families. Increased standardization of service development may require more national-level involvement to ensure that some standard of service accessibility and adequacy, both withing mental health and across child-serving systems, is available to children and youths with serious emotional disorders and their families.

While much remains to be done, several points should be kept in mind as we look to the states and their systems development. First, 10 years ago there was little in the way of public-community-based mental health services for children. Knitzer's *Unclaimed Children* (1982), which documented the abominable condition of children's mental health services, had just been released. Today, the state mental health authorities are recognizing children as a population they are designated and responsible for serving. This in itself is a significant step. Second, mental health authorities are now acknowledging that there are many children in other child-serving agencies who need, but have not been receiving, mental health services. This is particularly true about children in the child welfare system whose parents have given up custody so that their children can receive care, but it is also true of other levels of need. Third, we now have some understanding of the states' response to internal and external pressures as part of systems development. Pressures include legislative push, court cases, CASSP projects, family advocacy efforts, and requirements of federal funding sources. Knowledge of these factors can give guidance about how to push the system development farther and faster. Fourth, blended funding has not yet become commonplace, but respondents were aware of its feasibility and desirability; an increasing number of states have mechanisms to designate the responsible authorities and assign fiscal accountability. Fifth, in many states, certain target populations are not only defined, but subgroups are prioritized. Many priority groups put emphasis on youths with serious emotional disorders who reside in out-of-home placements, which may be appropriate. However, these choices need to be assessed in light of the fact that they may penalize families who have struggled under enormous odds to keep their children at home. Sixth, almost all states are doing some kind of interagency coordination, but some states are doing it only informally, and few can say how well it is working in terms of individual case outcomes.

As federal mandates combine with other motivating factors, we should expect to see the states advancing in their development of vital service coordination within mental health and across child-serving systems. Hopefully, any follow-up survey will find a new level of achievement in response to the need expressed throughout the country by youths with serious emotional disorders and the families who care for them.

REFERENCES

ADAMHA Reorganization Act, PL 102-321. (July 10, 1992). Title 42, U.S.C. 201 et seq: *U.S. Statutes at Large, 106,* 349–358.
American Psychiatric Association. (1994). *Diagnostic and statistical manual of mental disorders* (4th ed.). Washington, DC: Author.
Fox, H.B, & Wicks, L. B. (1991). *Using Medicaid to finance care coordination services for children and adolescents with severe emotional disorders.* Washington, DC: Fox Health Policy Consultants, Research Foundation for Mental Hygiene.
Knitzer, J. (1982). *Unclaimed children: The failure of public responsibility to children and adolescents in need of mental health services.* Washington, DC: Children's Defense Fund.
Omnibus Health Act, PL 99-660. (November 14, 1986). Title 42, U.S.C. 300x et seq: *U.S. Statutes at Large, 100,* 3794–3797.

Service Coordination in Children's Mental Health
A Vision for the Future

John Poertner and Barbara J. Friesen

This book addresses the rapidly developing field of children's mental health and a central concept within this field, described by the terms *case management* and *service coordination*. Many issues addressed in this book will continue to require attention at least until the beginning of the 21st century. For example, questions of definition and terminology, including the central goals and purposes of case management or service coordination, are recurring concerns. Another concern centers on how case management can be most effectively structured and supported. This area includes making decisions on the issue of using the proper balance of informal and formal services and determining who should carry out service coordination functions. Also involved is the provision of appropriate training, supervision, and support for service coordinators. Implementation and effectiveness questions address ways of tracking child- and family-level needs as well as service coordination activities. Finally, crossing each area is the need for systematic evaluation and research to ensure that practice is based on knowledge about the most effective service coordination strategies, structures, and administrative processes.

DEFINING CASE MANAGEMENT OR SERVICE COORDINATION—A CONTINUING CHALLENGE

Nearly half of the chapters in this book identify perspectives on what case management is or ought to be. The definitions and approaches may at first seem to produce as much confusion as clarity. For example, when the reader encounters the six state-of-the-art program models, it may be difficult to compare them or even to identify practices unique to a particular program. The family-centered intensive case management program (see Chapter 13), the strengths program (see Chapter 14), and the Vermont model (see Chapter 15) share similar values, thus, unique features of each are difficult to identify. The transition program (see Chapter 16) appears different in terms of target population (having a focus on older youth preparing to leave the child-serving system), but little else. This assessment is not a criticism of any of these programs, but is merely an evaluative statement of where we are in the service coordination field. It serves as a central challenge to the field of children's mental health. For instance, a common language and better tools to compare case management practice across settings are needed (Graham & Birchmore-Timney, 1989). This new level of precision is necessary so that caregivers can judge a particular program against their expectations, so that individuals who want to be involved in case management know what to do, and so that researchers can specify interventions clearly enough to test their implementation and efficacy. As the field of children's mental health continues its rapid development, the process of definition and clarification will certainly continue to be of concern.

It is important to remember that the role that we term *service coordinator* or *case manager* in children's mental health emerged both as a response to the complex needs of children and their families and as a way to address the limitations of the fragmented service delivery system. As the needs of children and their families change and as the service delivery system develops (e.g., in response to service integration initiatives or health care reform), the definition, scope, central goals, and purposes of case management or service coordination will also evolve. Coupled with an approach to children's mental health services that emphasizes responsiveness and flexibility, these changes will continue to promote definitions that are abstract and process-oriented and that mitigate against the development of clear, behaviorally specific definitions.

Pressure to achieve clarity about the goals, purposes, and functions of case management will continue to mount as states move forward to carry out mandated case management services for children and youth. Also, as service coordination activities are increasingly included in funding mechanisms (e.g., Medicaid) and in strategies associated with health care reform, the drive toward commonly agreed-upon definitions and standards of practice will escalate.

These demands will undoubtedly highlight the potential conflict between a desire for standardization, predictability, and routinization and the principles of individualization, flexibility, and responsiveness. As these competing themes are enacted we must be careful to not lose the progress that we have made in increasing the appropriateness and responsiveness of services for children and their families. In the midst of health care reform, for example, much progress could be undone if the definition of service categories, including case management, is developed by individuals who are not familiar with or invested in the principles emphasized by the Child and Adolescent Service System Program (CASSP) (Stroul & Friedman, 1988) and in this book. Service providers, policy analysts, researchers, and advocates alike must be aware of the importance of this definitional issue. We need ways to characterize service coordination functions and activities so that they are understood and accepted by multiple constituencies. The authors of this chapter believe that the first step is to attend to the opinions and preferences of the children and families who use service coordination.

It is useful to begin the process of clarifying the goals and functions of service coordination by examining the desired outcomes for children and their families. What should be the results of children's and family caregivers' contacts with mental health service providers? Generally, there is agreement that children with emotional disorders should be part of the community, be cared for within a family, engage in normal activities with their peers, and learn the skills needed to become an adult member of the community. Family caregivers should not become casualties in this process but instead should receive the assistance and support needed to provide for the special needs of their child in ways that allow all family members to live balanced, healthy lives.

Families expect assistance with negotiating the service system. In many states and communities, rapidly expanding children's mental health services are relatively new to a child-serving system that includes education, health, child welfare, and juvenile justice. Each of these arenas includes multiple programs, policies, procedures, and professionals. It is not easy to describe this system to anyone, and it is this complexity that underscores the need for competent service coordination.

The caregiver expectation of help with the service system contributes to the desire on some people's part to change the label from "case management" to "service coordination," and indeed this change has largely been accomplished in the early intervention field. This change has been made mostly so that children, mothers, fathers, aunts, grandparents, and foster parents are viewed as people, not as "cases." In addition, the service system is complex, requiring a service provider to coordinate the parts to obtain the desired results. It is important, however, to guard against a literal interpretation of this new language, which could work against another important caregiver expectation. If service coordination is interpreted as merely bringing services together to help children and their families, the development of a "supportive network of informal resources" may be lost.

Family caregivers understand that if their children are to be included in the community, inclusion in regular school, recreational, and community environments is required. If the child with an emotional disorder is to become a productive adult member of the community, this is most likely accomplished through the principle of inclusion, which necessarily involves a rich array of formal and informal resources. If service providers view their role narrowly in terms of service coordination, it is likely that they will rely on formal and non-normal services that focus on exclusion rather than inclusion.

Another category of caregiver expectations involves organizational policies or practices that allow service providers to meet expectations. These are primarily policies and supports that allow service providers to be creative and spend sufficient time with caregivers, who know the time required to respond to the needs of their children, whether the needs are due to the special demands of the child or to the complex service system. When the child is growing, developing, and changing, this is reflected in sometimes increasing and sometimes decreasing caregiving demands. Responsive services must be flexible, creative, and sometimes immediate.

Chapter 2 of this book presents the perspectives of a group of family caregivers on their desired results and their expectations for case management. These perspectives are critical to the development of case management or service coordination. Parental caregivers emphasize the necessity for service providers to develop a collaborative relationship with both family members and youth, with this relationship embodying positive attitudes of hope and respect. Service providers may view this expectation as natural, currently being fulfilled, and therefore not needing articulation. However, parental caregivers are clear that collaboration has not characterized service provision in the past. It is hoped that we are approaching a time when no group of parents would raise this as an expectation because it has become a normal part of all service provision.

Family expectations will and should change as the field of children's mental health continues to evolve. These expectations need to be included in the dialogue about the future of service coordination. The inclusion of parental caregivers in examining what is needed to obtain the outcomes identified for children and their families will keep developments in the field grounded in reality.

ORGANIZING AND SUPPORTING
CASE MANAGEMENT SERVICES

Family expectations that directly affect the practice of service coordination have been examined previously. Beyond these immediate issues are several important questions related to the administrative and fiscal support needed to sustain effective practice. In this section, we address a number of pertinent questions: 1) Who should be involved in case management or service coordination? 2) How should services be structured? 3) What agency and community supports will be needed? 4) How can we pay for service coordination activities? and 5) How do we promote high-quality, effective services? Addressing each question poses specific challenges for the future.

Who Should Be Involved in
Case Management or Service Coordination?

In other words, to what extent should service coordination and other activities be performed by family members or require assistance by a representative of the formal service system? This issue is not often addressed in the case management literature. In practice, however, this choice is made every day (although not always consciously) as scarce services are distributed to children and their families. In this triage process, some children with emotional and behavioral disorders and their families have the opportunity to receive formal service coordination assistance, while others (the majority) do not. When families do not have access to formal assistance, parents or other caregivers must attempt to obtain and coordinate appropriate services for their children (i.e., serve as their own case managers).

The idea of parents as case managers is not new to family members who have been struggling with providing care to a child with an emotional disorder. One of the authors of this chapter listened to one parent's year-by-year summary of the difficulties of providing care to a child during a 12-year period after she assumed responsibility for the child when the the child was 4 years of age. Never once in these 12 years was there a case manager other than herself. Each year was filled with challenges presented by the child, his disorder, and various service systems and their problems. This mother was the consummate case manager; she performed this duty without supervisor, policy or agency support.

Community members, policy makers, and taxpayers should all be thankful for this mother's efforts because she kept her child in the community, worked to secure appropriate services, and did not demand or receive public financial support. Her efforts raise questions about how society ought to support this mother from a service coordination point of view. The Illinois Family Assistance Program (see Chapter 18) suggests one possibility. If the mother in the authors' account had a monthly check that she could use to purchase the assistance needed to care for her son, everyone would be better off. Considering that it may cost several hundred dollars per day to care for this child in a hospital setting, several hundred dollars per month seems like a worthwhile investment. Yet, the Illinois account in Chapter 18 raises important issues about widespread application of this idea, beginning with determining who should be eligible for such benefits. Although we might argue that any parent having difficulty with providing care for a child should be eligible for this benefit, fiscal and political considerations indicate that this is unlikely to be an acceptable response. In Illinois, it is clearly indicated that maintaining a $400-per-month stipend for even 284 families is politically and fiscally difficult.

Yet the idea that family members may be hired as service providers within the formal system is still gaining popularity throughout the United States. It is a feature of innovative programs, including the state service initiative programs funded by the federal government beginning in 1993 (see Chapter 1). This developing practice of hiring family members as case managers seeks to capitalize on their direct experience with trying to locate, access, and use services. These programs provide training, supervision, and financial support to parents and other caregivers who choose to undertake formal service provision roles. The authors are aware of "parents as case managers" programs in children's mental health in Kansas, New Mexico, New York, Rhode Island, Washington, and Wisconsin, among others. Most of these programs involve paid positions for family members who are involved in a variety of roles. The program in the state of Washington involves a cooperative approach by which family members receive case management training in exchange for their provision of service to another family. These new programs will need careful evaluation to help improve and refine their operations and track service outcomes.

Chapter 17 presents several options for parents as case managers. Their chapter contains several examples of roles including parents as mentors, collaborators, case managers, and in-home staff. One of the authors was involved in a protection and advocacy agency for persons with developmental abilities. The advocates employed by this agency were primarily mothers who had raised a child with a severe developmental disability. All indications were that these mothers were extremely effective. They knew the formal system and the law. From their own caregiving experience, they knew the struggles that were undergone by people with disabilities. Few if any of these parents were Medicaid reimbursable according to many state regulations. These parents had great experience and knowledge but lacked the formal education that many systems require. They often were caring for their child while other people were obtaining professional degrees. The field of mental health, similar to the broader health arena, is heavily professionalized. To realize the potential of parents as employees, the professionalization issue needs to be addressed.

How Should Services Be Structured?

Chapter 4 discusses the implications of various ways of organizing service coordination activities and suggest a set of advantages and disadvantages for each approach. Their work, however, is just a beginning step, a heuristic device for organizing observations about the current system. Much additional research will be needed to learn about the impact of structure on the quality and effectiveness of service coordination.

However, intuitively, most people agree that structure does make a difference. If the service coordinator is in a structure requiring attention to "billable" hours at a level that requires agency-based practice, it is unlikely that the service coordinator can realize parental caregiver expectations for flexible, timely services. In this structure, phone calls typically are returned between appointments, and family caregivers and children are seen only in the office. Although the field is moving away from these structural constraints, more study is needed to identify structural approaches that support flexibility and creativity on the part of case managers.

Service coordination in children's mental health is relatively new but was not created in a vacuum. Mental health service coordination entered a child- and family-serving system that included public child welfare, juvenile justice, health programs, and education, including special education. Will service coordination be most effective as a part of the mental health system, located in one of the other systems, or an entirely separate entity? The protection and advocacy agencies established through federal legislation are required to be separate from the service provision agencies in the states. Presumably this is due to the belief that to be effective, advocates must have a certain degree of independence from those who are creating service provision policies. Perhaps this suggests that service coordination must be a separate entity to be effective if it includes advocacy. Or perhaps it suggests that service coordination is another service that exists somewhere in the existing maze of service providers. It is just not possible at this time to determine where the "best" location would be.

What Agency and Community Supports Will Be Needed?

While the field is learning about where to locate service coordination, service coordinators will be operating in a variety of locations. For these service coordinators to achieve the desired goals for children and their families, they need a supportive, nurturing environment. Section IV of this book, which focuses on training and supervision, identifies some of the ways that service coordinators need to be supported. Chapter 12 specifically addresses supervision. If the premise of this chapter (that the starting point is the stated outcomes for children and their families and that the ends need to be achieved through parental collaboration that fulfills all expectations) is accepted, then the supervisor's job is easy to define. He or she must help the service coordinator to achieve the desired ends. Although this is easily said, it is difficult to achieve. The desired outcomes and caregiver expectations must be pursued in an agency that may or may not understand and support the same ends. The agency may not have policy supports, such as flexible funds, readily available, meaning that the supervisor's job includes an entire set of tasks that focus on influencing the larger agency, as well as providing guidance for direct practice.

Service coordination also exists in a community environment that may not have the same goals. Schools struggling with educating large numbers of children who have disabilities and people who are fearful of behavior that they do not understand can serve as powerful advocates for goals of exclusion. Promoting inclusion, not exclusion, requires considerable effort on the part of parental caregivers, service coordinators, and supervisors. They must educate communities to the possibilities and the potentials of children with emotional disorders. The community is clearly an important context for service coordination about which knowledge and practice strategies need to be developed.

How Can We Pay for Service Coordination Activities?

Funding of service coordination is equally complex and requires ongoing work. Current funding is fragmented and categorical. On a positive note, however, there are a variety of ways in which service coordination can be funded. Unfortunately, this variety is related to the tendency of policy makers at the federal and state levels to create categorical programs as a way to control costs, which has resulted in a badly fragmented system. This book was written at a time when the United States had health care reform on its agenda with uncertain progress and results, exacerbating a service coordination funding and policy morass. Clearly, much work needs to be done in this area.

Chapter 6 discusses case management within the insurance industry, which proves extremely timely in this period of health care reform. Broskowski's illustration of how appropriate services can also be cost effective is exactly the kind of information needed by families, service providers, and advocates, regardless of how the debate over national health care reform is concluded. With or without national legislation, very important changes in the U.S. health care financing and delivery system are occurring. Examples that blend the values of community-based services and least restrictive care with concerns about health care cost containment are needed to promote responsible reform. Medicaid benefits, including case management options such as those described by Fox and Wicks (Chapter 5), also will likely undergo fundamental change as we enter the 21st century. Ongoing evaluation of these system changes efforts is needed to ultimately answer complex questions about cost effectiveness and service appropriateness.

Another consideration related to funding has to do with fiscal incentives. State legislatures in particular would be well served to make fiscal incentives as important a consideration as any other funding issue. Incentives inherent in a public fiscal policy ought to further the desired outcomes of the system. For example, the mother who cared for a child with an emotional disorder for 12 years experienced many difficulties in providing care, including financial burdens. At the time there was no financial assistance for the mother; however, when she could no longer provide care to the child and relinquished custody of him to the state, the fiscal burden was transferred to the state at a much higher cost because the child was placed in a hospital. Therefore, the fiscal incentive in this case was to place the child outside the family home. With funding involving so many systems, it is easy to inadvertently create a system with incentives that work *against* desired outcomes. Careful examination of fiscal incentives in light of outcomes is a critical area for future work.

A further fiscal policy complication is that many states are strengthening parental responsibility policies. That is, parental caregivers may receive a bill for hospital care that the family will be unable to pay, forcing the family into bankruptcy and consequently making them unavailable as caregivers. Fiscal policies of this kind place the burden or blame for hospitalization on the family caregiver. Yet, it seems that the community is equally responsible for the child's hospitalization because of its lack of alternative services and supports for the family.

Parental responsibility policies arise out of a concern for accountability. Well-intentioned state legislators want parents to be accountable. However, the issue of accountability in children's mental health is much broader than parental responsibility, and is complex. (Section III of this book addresses some accountability concerns.) To many people, the term *accountability* is synonymous with responsibility. However, Taber (1988) has suggested that in the social services accountability might be more appropriately defined as all persons involved in the service transaction having the information that they need to play their roles. Using this definition, it is necessary to include all of the decision makers who are needed to achieve the desired outcomes for children and their families in thinking about accountability. Of course children and their families head this list and service coordinators, the agency, and the community in which they operate have been discussed in brief. Future conceptual and empirical attention should also be directed to state-level administrators and policy makers, including legislators, who are critical decision makers.

How Do We Promote High-Quality and Effective Services?

Chapter 7, which focuses on a state-level perspective for implementing and monitoring case management, is an important contribution to this book. Clearly, state agencies must take the lead in constructing the policies and structures must achieve the inclusionary outcomes for children with emotional disabilities and their families. As Taber's (1988) definition of accountability suggests, state agencies need certain types of information to play their role. Chapters 8 and 9 begin to address these information concerns. In the authors' experiences, this area needs considerable development. Few states have the information they need to play their role, and many states lack the mechanisms to collect and analyze even the most rudimentary data.

State legislators are also key decision makers. In an ideal world, one might expect state agencies, together with parents and community leaders, to provide the information legislators need to make decisions consistent with desired outcomes. Unfortunately, most states do not have the needed legislative supports in place, and in spite of the public outcry for term limits, most legislatures do not have a good memory and must be constantly reeducated. Children's issues at the state level are so complex that few legislators understand them and their multiple interactions. Parental responsibility sounds good politically until legislators are educated, and it is redefined. The state legislature level of accountability is not addressed in this book and clearly needs much development on the part of parental caregivers and children's advocates.

KNOWLEDGE FOR THE FUTURE

Chapter 19 provides a comprehensive overview of the research challenges associated with case management in children's mental health. Throughout this chapter the authors also suggest specific areas in which program evaluation and research is needed. The authors think it is important to flag three other research-related considerations: the need for new research methods, the importance of expanding case management outcomes, and the importance of tracking unintended consequences associated with service coordination efforts.

The emphasis on individualized, flexible services in the children's mental health field has not been matched by the development of research approaches that can capture and describe the dynamic nature of the service delivery process. Although the development of advanced statistical methods allows for complex multivariate studies, much basic work remains before we can fully use these research approaches. Much conceptual and descriptive empirical work, especially in the areas of model development and measurement, remains to be accomplished. An ongoing challenge is likely to be finding ways to measure and analyze complex, dynamic phenomena without unduly interfering with service delivery or imposing unreasonable data collection burdens on service providers, families, and children.

The list of legitimate service outcomes should be expanded to fully reflect the perspectives of all persons who have a stake in children's mental health services. This means, first, increased attention to the needs, goals, and preferences of children and their families. The perspectives of the children who have emotional disorders must be added to the debate about the goals and results of services. Additional work is also needed to more closely and immediately tie research findings about service outcomes to the policy and program development processes. Accelerated research efforts are needed to respond to the injunction of Burns et al. (Chapter 19) to ensure that the research process leads and influences developments in the field.

The last area the authors want to emphasize is the importance of tracking unintended consequences. For example, it is possible that the availability of a formal service coordinator could result in parents or other caregivers relinquishing responsibilities and functions that they are prepared and willing to discharge. This may be a positive consequence. However, the line between providing appropriate support and encroaching on family caregiving functions may be thin for some families. It is also possible to disrupt the distribution of tasks within families. For example, Seltzer, Ivry, and Litchfield (1987) found that training family caregivers of elderly relatives to act in case management roles appeared to decrease the extent that the elderly persons performed such functions for themselves. In this case, a negative consequence prevails as the elderly relative becomes more dependent, rather than less so.

Programs for new service coordination roles involving family caregivers also must be carefully monitored to ensure that the principle of "family choice" is not neglected. Innovative "parents as case managers" programs may initially respect parents' and other family caregivers' preferences about the extent to which they assume service coordination responsibilities for their own or other children. Yet, as these programs evolve or are replicated, there is the risk that caregiver preferences will be engulfed by enthusiasm for cost savings or other system-centered issues. Information from ongoing research and evaluation efforts is crucial in ensuring that future service innovations are *truly* family centered.

CONCLUSION

In many ways this book lays out the beginning of a long journey. Unfortunately, service coordination in children's mental health is at an early milestone. Close examination of the many aspects covered in this book demonstrates that the road to a system that provides children and families what they need to grow and develop within communities is a long and arduous one.

Chapter 3 provides an overview of current practices at a conceptual level. This is not an identification of what is possible or what ought to be, but rather a summary of what exists. The authors describe four current case management approaches. Examining these approaches in the light of outcome research provides little insight, because currently there is little empirical knowledge about the efficacy of any approach. Furthermore, examining these approaches in light of family member expectations presents a rather bleak picture. There seems to be a considerable lack of "goodness of fit" between parental expectations and current approaches. Although the strengths approach may be the closest to meeting caregiver expectations, some professionals respond that this is more of a philosophy than a specific service coordination approach. Clearly defining and operationalizing service coordination is a challenge.

Organizing and supporting service coordination does not fare much better. There is a long list of system features that need to be determined. Families need case managers that can get the job done. They need skills that enhance their work. We need personnel systems that select people based upon skills and interests rather than arbitrarily excluding people based upon lack of a specific degree. Finding a place within the community that operates from the "whatever it takes philosophy" is not easily accomplished. There do not appear to be a large number of these places within most communities.

Funding the type of service coordination that the authors have been envisioning is a continuing struggle. The funding options currently available provide insufficient resources and lack of flexibility. Legislators may be more likely to support increased funding as they understand service coordination and its benefits. This is the central idea behind accountability. Service coordination in children's mental health involves a large number of "key actors." Each of these individuals needs certain information to play his or her role within the overall system that is oriented toward assuring that children and families get what they need to be successful in the community. Currently, this basic information for each person is not available.

Linking accountability to information ties into the final topic considered in this book. There is a huge gulf between what we know and what we need to know. It is hoped that this book will add to what we know as well as further encourage readers to seek the knowledge needed to make service coordination effective for children with emotional disorders and their families.

REFERENCES

Graham, K., & Birchmore-Timney, C. (1989). The problem of replicability in program evaluation. *Evaluation and Program Planning, 12,* 179–187.
Seltzer, M.M., Ivry, J., & Litchfield, L.C. (1987). Family members as case managers: Partnership between the formal and informal support networks. *The Gerontologist, 27*(6), 722–728.
Stroul, B.A., & Friedman, R. (1988). Principles for a system of care. *Children Today, 17*(4), 11–15.
Taber, M.A. (1988). A theory of accountability for the human services and the implications for program design. *Administration in Social Work, 11*(3/4), 115–126.

Index

Page numbers followed by a "t" or "f" indicate tables or figures, respectively.

CareTrack—*continued*
  events, 199–200, 199*f*
  language of local system of
    care, 200
  people, 199
  plan of care, 200
  case process using, 200–205,
    201*f*
  case preparation, 202, 203*f*
  monitoring clinical progress
    and financial expendi-
    tures, 205
  monitoring system perfor-
    mance, 205
  referral information, 200–201
  structure of plan of care,
    202–205
  computer requirements for,
    197
  confidentiality and, 198
  design of, 197
  development of, 189–190
  interaction with other computer
    systems, 198
Case management, 8–23
  comprehensiveness of, 68
  conceptual foundation of, 225
  criteria for termination of ser-
    vices, 263
  definition of, 10, 38–39, 67–68,
    139, 211, 328, 353–354,
    375–376
  developmental model for,
    328–329
  escalating need for, 213–214
  evaluation of, 14, 52–53,
    163–164
  financing of, 95–148, 160–162,
    258–259
    under Medicaid, 95–129,
      160–161
    in private sector, 133–148,
      161–162
  functions of, 13–15, 38, 44*t*–45*t*,
    206–207, 211–212, 212*f*,
    257, 358–359
  goals of, 38–39, 67, 212, 357–358
  history of, 10–12, 353
  impact on how services are of-
    fered, 327–328
  implementation of, 14, 151–162

differences specific to chil-
    dren, 328, 355–356
  questions about effectiveness,
    354–355
  research questions about,
    362–363
  literature on, 39–42
  monitoring of, 14, 45*t*, 162–163,
    169–187
  outcome data on, 40, 171–173,
    354–355, 368–369,
    397–398
  rationale for, 213
  research questions on, 353–369
  terminology for, 9, 38, 212
  therapeutic, 301–315
  tracking unintended conse-
    quences of, 398
  transitional, 317–326
  variables in, 15–23, 360
    authority, 22–23, 72–73,
      263–265
    caseload size, 18, 261–263, 362
    clinical services, 15, 16
    duration, 362–363
    financial management, 15–17
    intensity, 17–18, 362
    organization and structure,
      22, 63–91
    philosophy, 18–19
    specialization, 19–20
    staff qualifications, 20–21, 56,
      216, 258, 260–261
    use of teams, 21–22, 44*t*–45*t*,
      48–50, 359–360
  vision for future of, 387–399
Case management approaches,
    42–45*t*, 359–361
  brokerage, 47–48, 359
  comparing practice with caregiv-
    ers' desires, 53–55
    broker/case manager, 54
    strength-based approach, 55
    team approach, 54
    therapist/case manager, 53–54
  comprehensive service center
    model, 360
  evaluation of, 52–53
  family as case manager model,
    20–21, 75–78, 75*f*,
    327–336, 360, 393–393

implications for service development, 55–57
interdisciplinary or interagency
team, 44t–45t, 48–50,
359–360
obtaining parents' views on,
27–36, 52–53
research on, 360–361, 368–369
strengths-based, 50–52
supportive care model, 360
therapy/case management,
43–47, 301–315, 359
volunteer as case manager
model, 360
Case Management for Children's
Mental Health: A Train-
ing Curriculum for Child-
Serving Agencies,
214–235
see also Training for case management
Case managers
competencies of, 222–230
knowledge, 227–228
skills, 228–230
values, 224–227
creating and maintaining support and structure for,
257–274,
see also Supervision of case
management
for Family-Centered Intensive
Case Management Pro-
gram (New York),
283–284
organizational variables that are
supportive of, 33–34
parents as, 20–21, 75–78, 75f,
327–336, 360, 391–393
advantages of, 76–78
effect on family roles, 398
lack of recognition of, 327
limitations of, 76–78
new roles for family mem-
bers, 329–331
payment for, 331–335, 392
training of, 334, 364, 392
unintended consequences of,
398
parents' expectations of, 27–36,
52–53, 389–391, 399

assistance with service system, 32, 389
attitudes, 29–30, 260t
commitment to establishing relationship with families,
30–32, 259, 264, 331
process for determining,
28–29
supportive network of informal resources, 32–33
providing transitional case management, 325
qualifications of, 20–21, 56, 216,
258, 260–261
research questions about,
363–364
role in private insurance sector,
140
role in system of care, 193
roles of family advocate,
297–299
training of, 20–21, 56, 158–160,
211–237
tripartite focus of, 223–224, 224f
variations in state policies on,
377–378t
vision for future, 391–393
volunteers as, 360
Caseload size, 18, 261–263, 362
for therapeutic case management (Vermont), 314
variations in state policies on,
378–379t
CASSP, *see* Child and Adolescent
Service System Programs
Center for Mental Health Services
(CMHS), 4, 12
CHAMPUS, *see* Civilian Health
and Medical Programs of
the Uniformed Services
Child abuse, 211
Child and Adolescent Service System Program (CASSP), 4,
151, 161, 191, 217, 226,
239, 353, 357, 373,
382–383t
in Pennsylvania, 239–253
Child Mental Health Services Initiative, 12
Child welfare system, 356, 389
Children's Defense Fund, 3